BLADE
OF THE IMMORTAL

Trickster

publisher
Mike Richardson

series editor
Philip Simon

collection editor
Chris Warner

collection designer
Debra Bailey

art director
Lia Ribacchi

BLADE OF THE IMMORTAL VOL. 15: TRICKSTER
Blade of the Immortal © 2005, 2006 by Hiroaki Samura. All rights
reserved. First published in Japan in 2002, 2003 by Kodansha Ltd.,
Tokyo. English translation rights arranged through Kodansha Ltd.
This English-language edition © 2005, 2006 by Dark Horse Comics,
Inc. All other material © 2006 by Dark Horse Comics, Inc. All rights
reserved. No portion of this publication may be reproduced, in any
form or by any means, without the express written permission of
the copyright holders. Names, characters, places, and incidents
featured in this publication either are the product of the author's
imagination or are used fictitiously. Any resemblance to actual per-
sons (living or dead), events, institutions, or locales, without satiric
intent, is coincidental. Dark Horse Manga™ is a trademark of Dark
Horse Comics, Inc. Dark Horse Comics® and the Dark Horse logo
are trademarks of Dark Horse Comics, Inc., registered in various
categories and countries. All rights reserved.

This volume collects issues ninety-nine through
one hundred and five of the Dark Horse comic-book series
Blade of the Immortal.

Published by
Dark Horse Manga
A division of Dark Horse Comics, Inc.
10956 SE Main Street
Milwaukie, OR 97222

darkhorse.com

To find a comics shop in your area, call the
Comic Shop Locator Service toll-free at 1-888-266-4226

First edition: February 2006
ISBN: 1-59307-468-9

1 3 5 7 9 10 8 6 4 2

Printed in U.S.A.

BLADE
OF THE IMMORTAL

art and story
HIROAKI SAMURA

translation
Dana Lewis

lettering and retouch
Tomoko Saito

Trickster

DARK HORSE MANGA™

ABOUT THE TRANSLATION

The Swastika

The main character in *Blade of the Immortal*, Manji, has taken the "crux gammata" as both his name and his personal symbol. This symbol is also known as the *swastika*, a name derived from the Sanskrit *svastika* (meaning "welfare," from *su* — "well" + *asti* "he is"). As a symbol of prosperity and good fortune, the swastika was widely used throughout the ancient world (for example, appearing often on Mesopotamian coinage), including North and South America and has been used in Japan as a symbol of Buddhism since ancient times. To be precise, the symbol generally used by Japanese Buddhists is the *sauvastika*, which moves in a counterclockwise direction and is called the *manji* in Japanese. The arms of the *swastika*, which point in a clockwise direction, are generally considered a solar symbol. It was this version (the *hakenkreuz*) that was perverted by the Nazis. The *sauvastika* generally stands for night, and often for magical practices. It is important that readers understand that the swastika has ancient and honorable origins, and it is those that apply to this story, which takes place in the 18th century [ca. 1782–3]. *There is no anti-Semitic or pro-Nazi meaning behind the* use of the symbol in this story. Those meanings did not exist until after 1910.

The Artwork

The creator of *Blade of the Immortal* requested that we make an effort to avoid mirror-imaging his artwork. Normally, Westernized manga are first copied in a mirror-image in order to facilitate the left-to-right reading of the pages. However, Mr. Samura decided that he would rather see his pages reversed via the technique of cutting up the panels and re-pasting them in reverse order. While we feel that this often leads to problems in panel-to-panel continuity, we place primary importance on the wishes of the creator. Therefore, most of *Blade of the Immortal* has been produced using the "cut and paste" technique. There are, of course, some sequences where it was impossible to do this, and mirror-imaged panels or pages were used.

The Sound Effects & Dialogue

Since some of Mr. Samura's sound effects are integral parts of the illustrations, we decided to leave those in their original Japanese. We hope readers will view the unretouched sound effects as essential portions of Mr. Samura's extraordinary artwork. In addition, Mr. Samura's treatment of dialogue is quite different from that featured in typical samurai manga and is considered to be one of the features that has made *Blade* such a hit in Japan. Mr. Samura has mixed a variety of linguistic styles in this fantasy story, with some characters speaking in the mannered style of old Japan while others speak as if they were street-corner punks from a bad area of modern-day Tokyo. The anachronistic slang used by some of the characters in the English translation reflects the unusual mix of speech patterns from the original Japanese text.

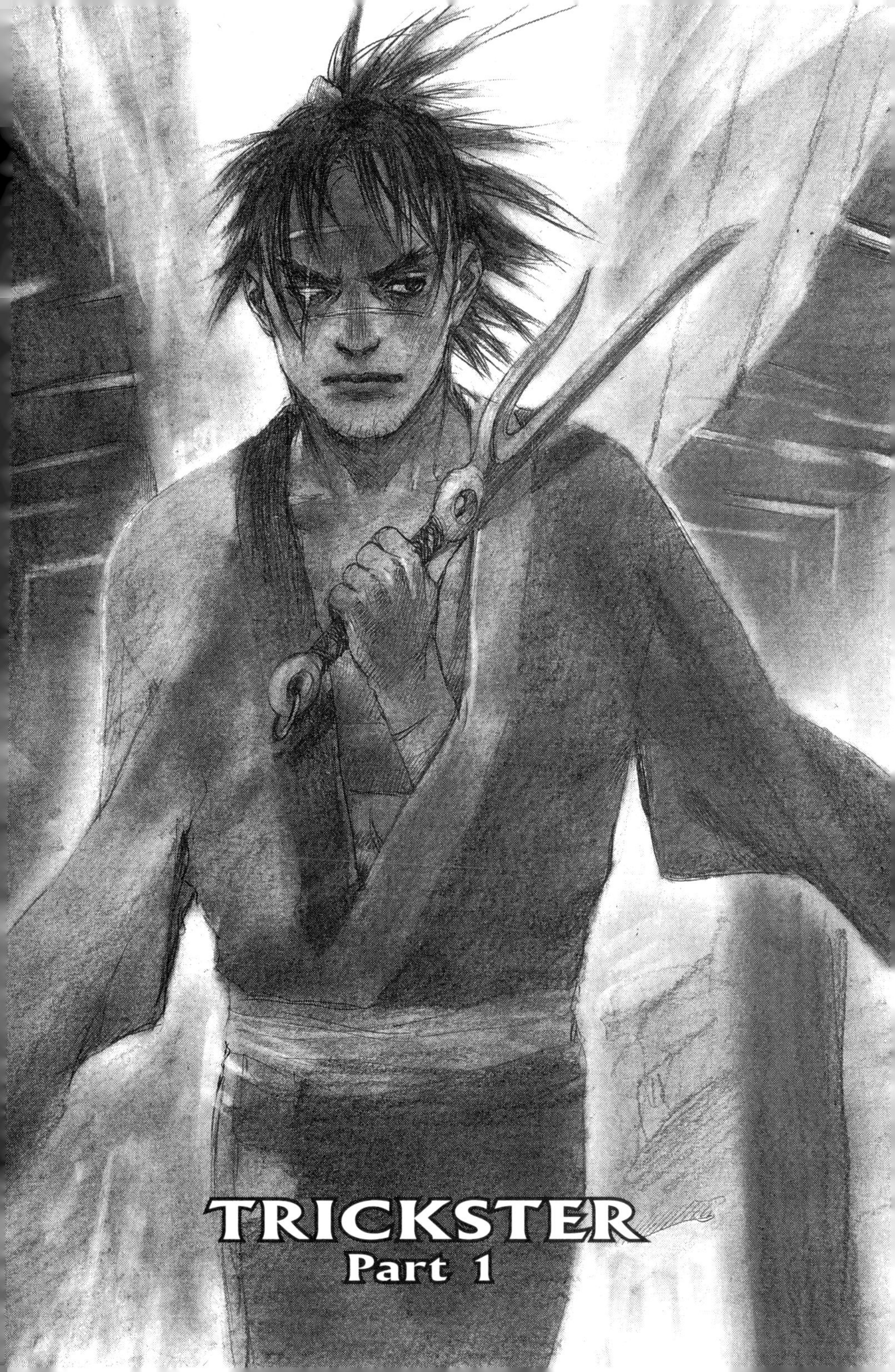

TRICKSTER
Part 1

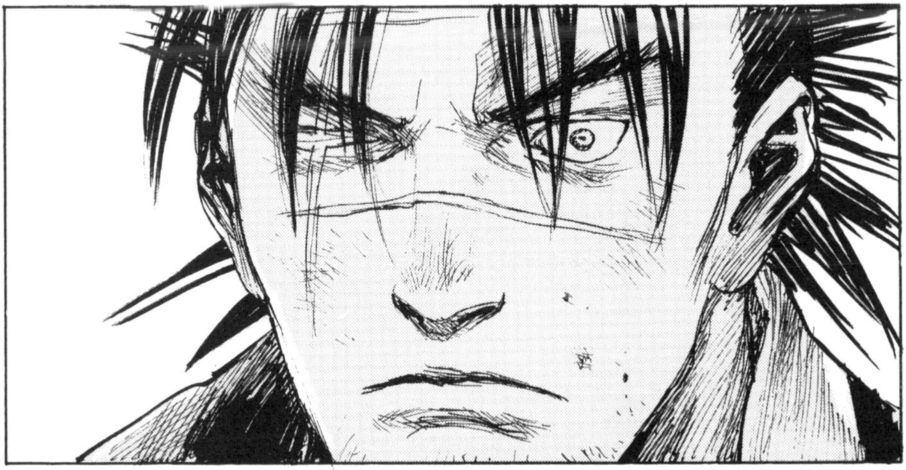

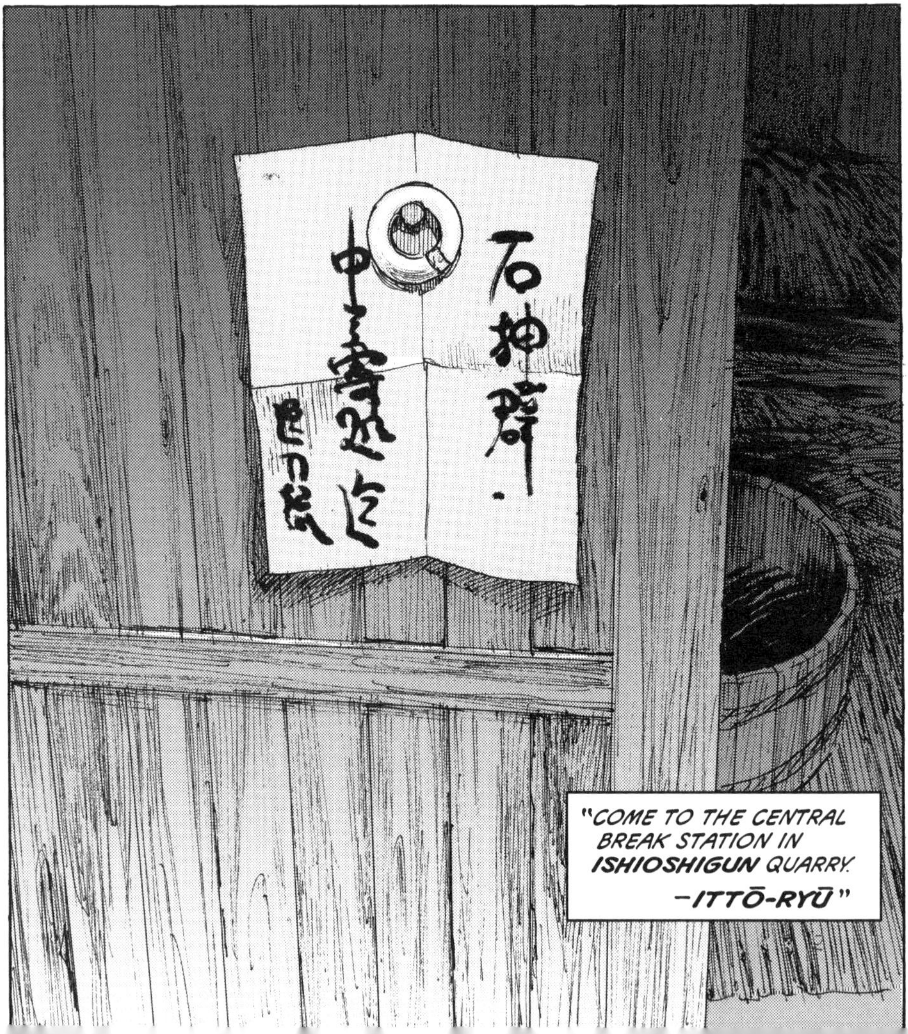
"COME TO THE CENTRAL BREAK STATION IN ISHIOSHIGUN QUARRY.
–ITTŌ-RYŪ"

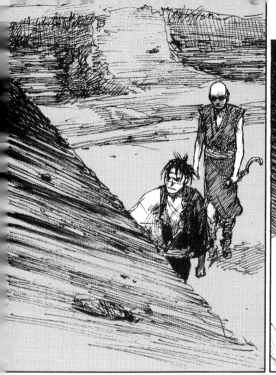

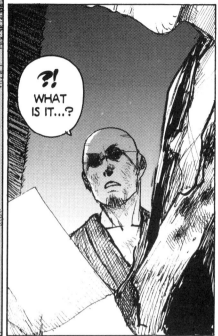

?!
WHAT IS IT...?
GIICHI. SORRY, MAN.
I GOT SOME WORK TO DO BEFORE WE HEAD OUT.
...SO BE IT.
I'LL JOIN YOU.

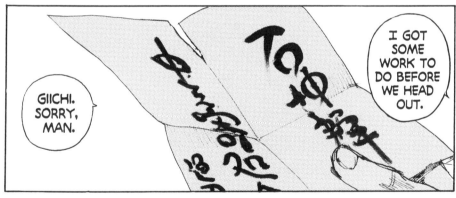

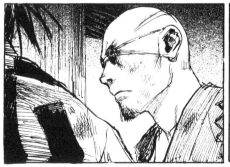

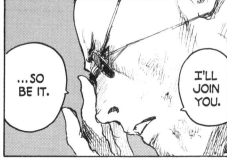

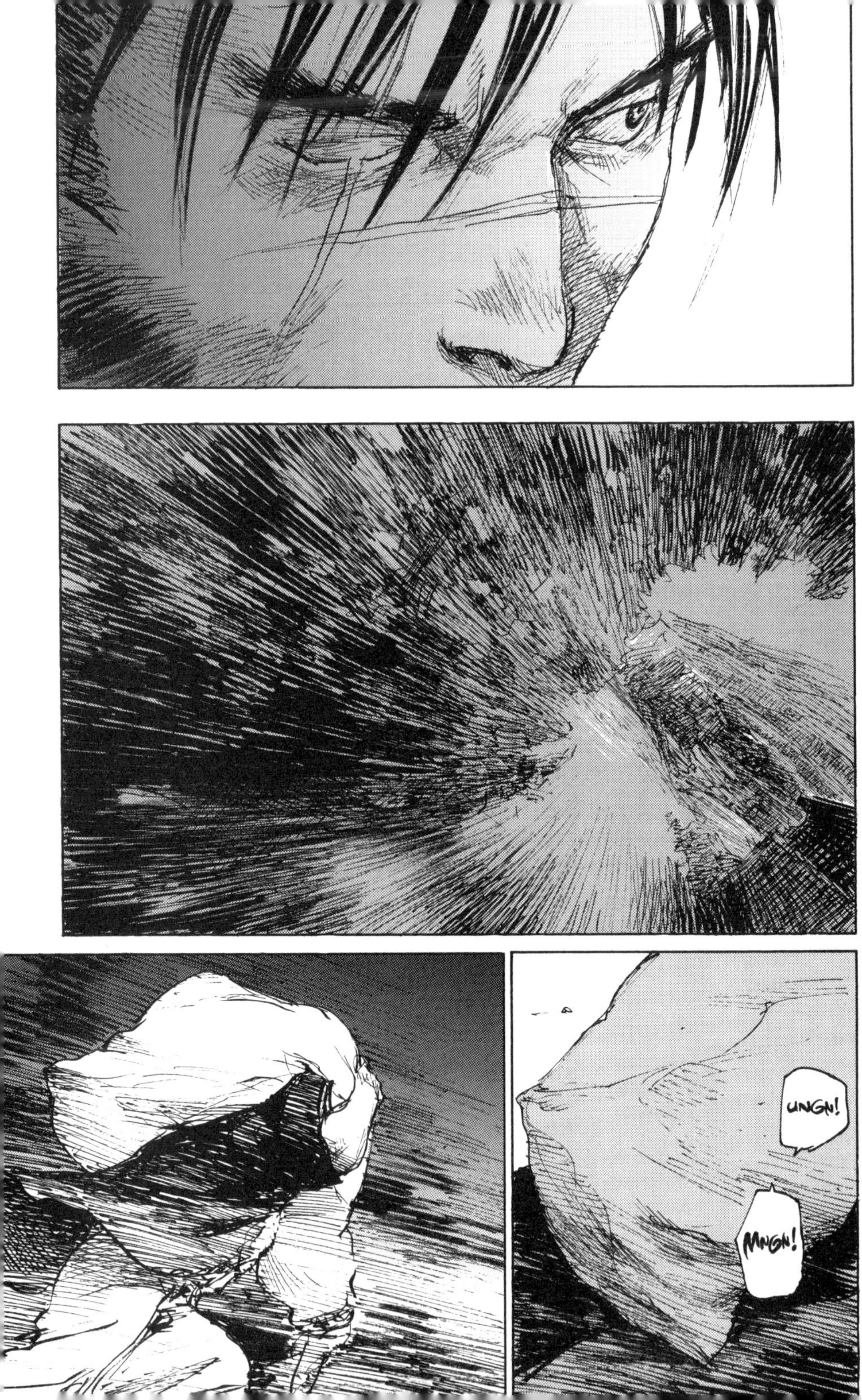
UNGN!
MNGN!

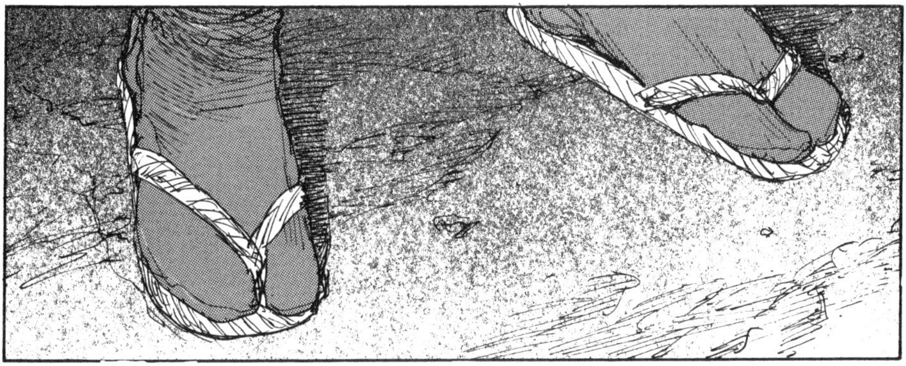

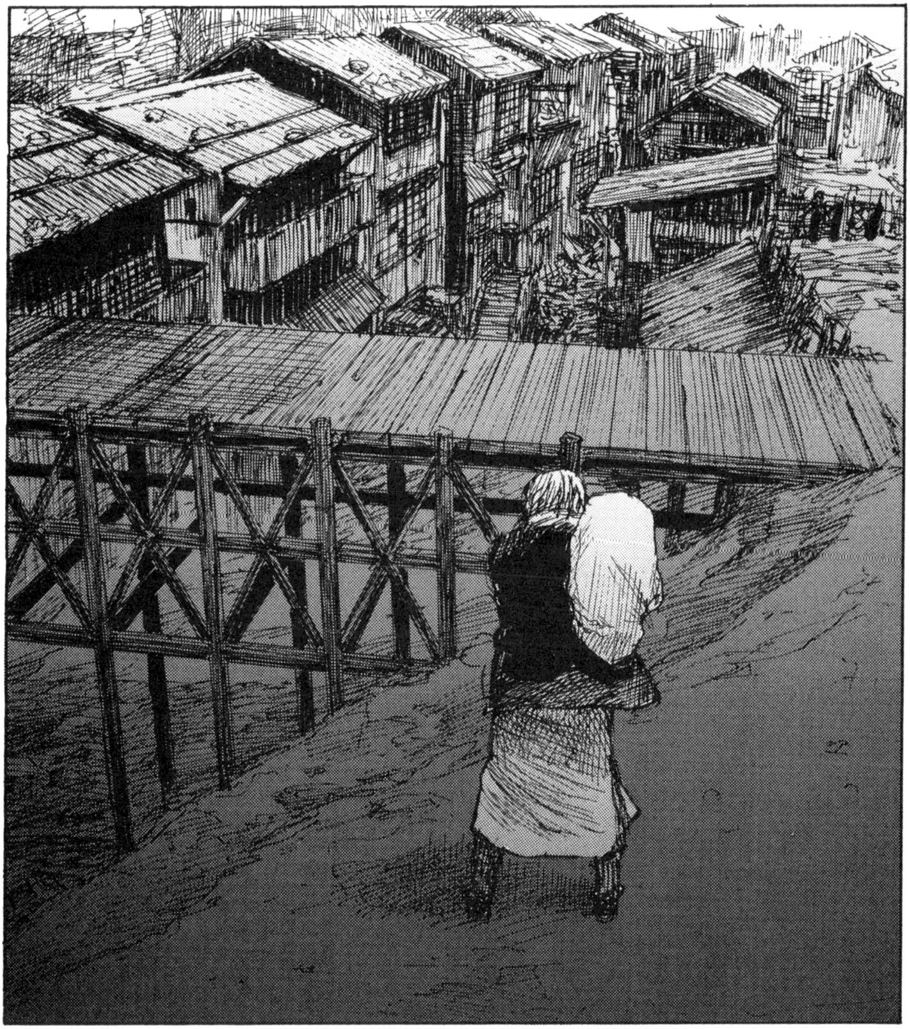

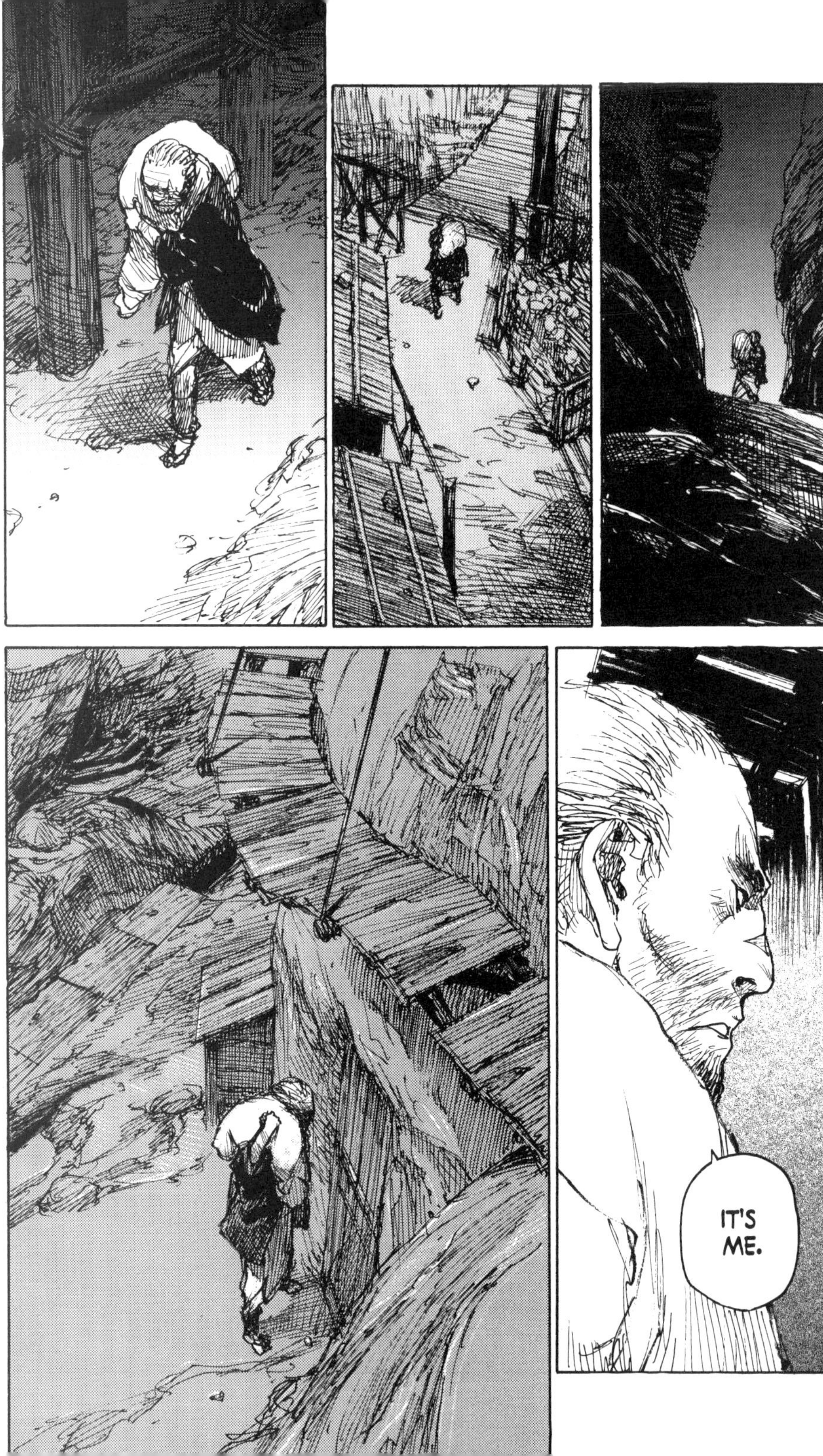
IT'S ME.

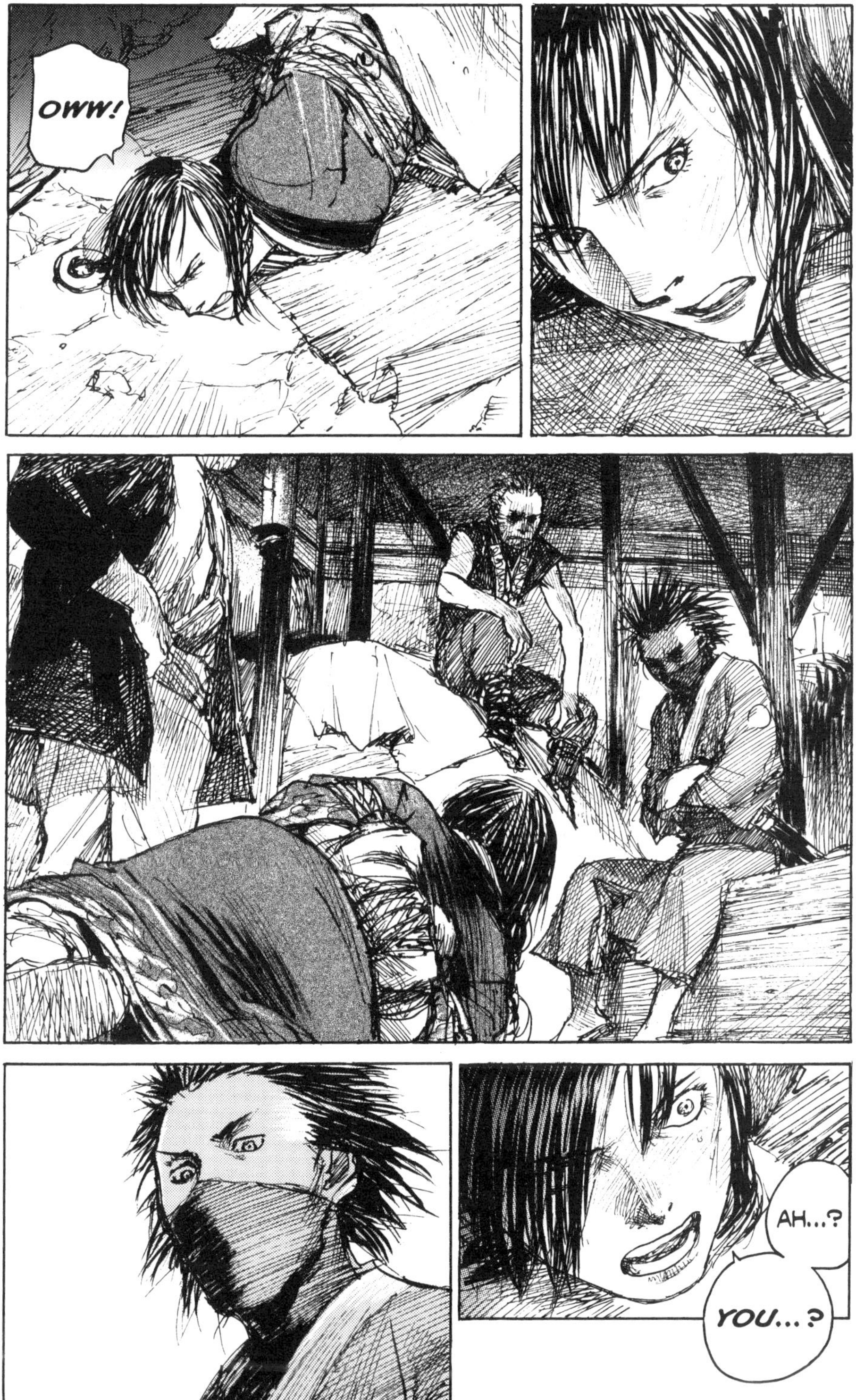
OWW!
AH...?
YOU...?

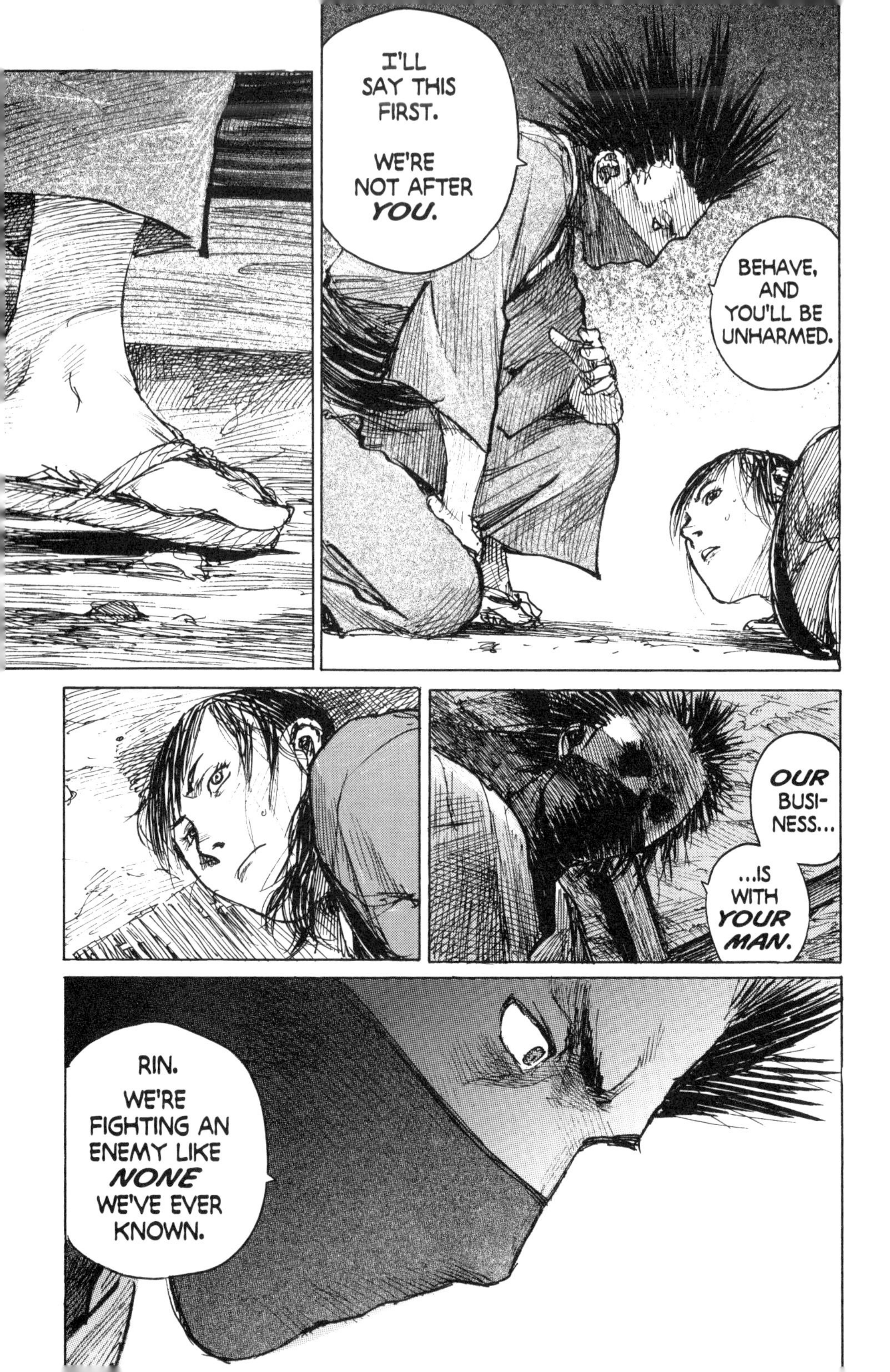
I'LL SAY THIS FIRST.
WE'RE NOT AFTER *YOU.*
BEHAVE, AND YOU'LL BE UNHARMED.
OUR BUSI-NESS...
...IS WITH *YOUR MAN.*
RIN. WE'RE FIGHTING AN ENEMY LIKE *NONE* WE'VE EVER KNOWN.

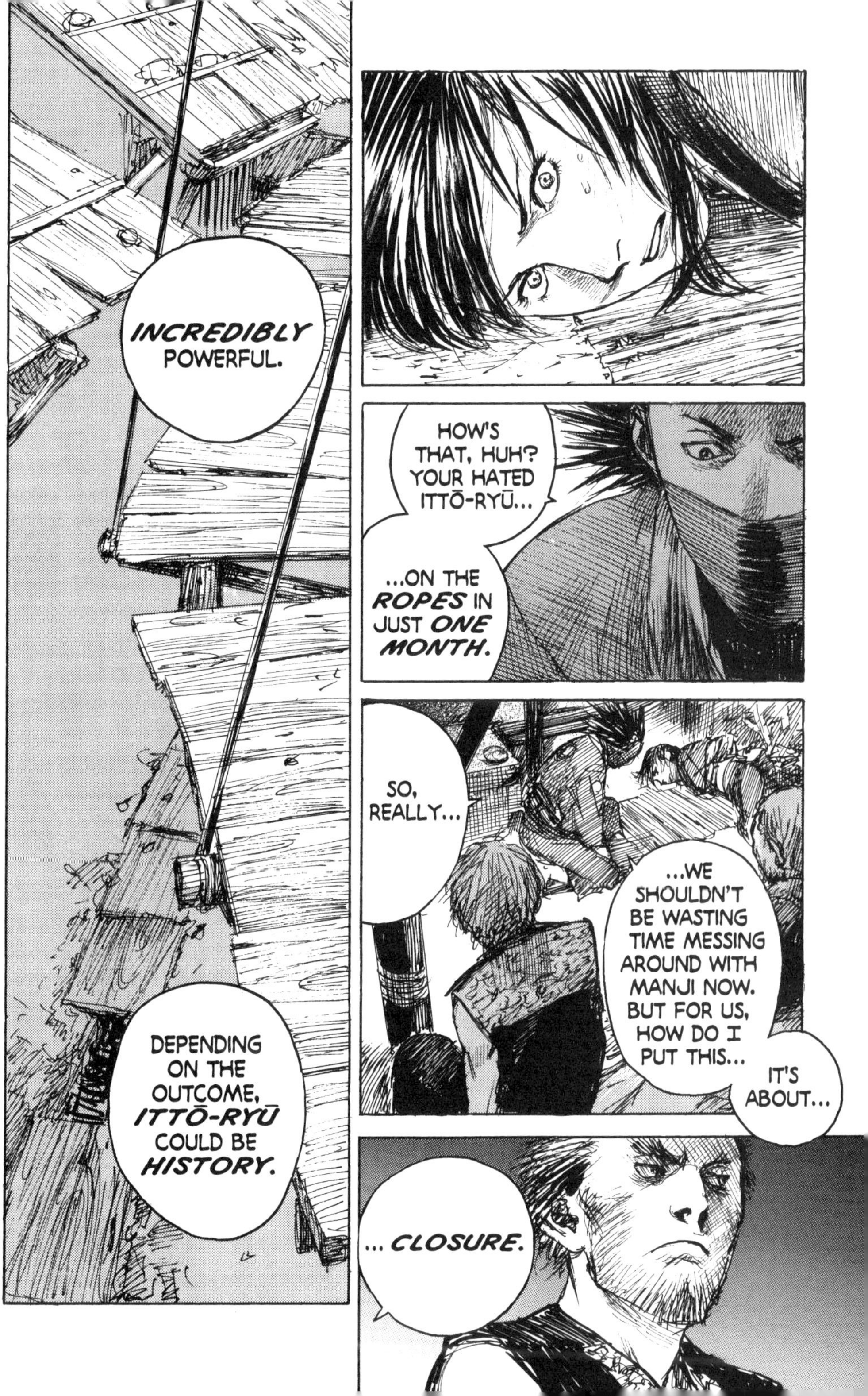
INCREDIBLY POWERFUL.
DEPENDING ON THE OUTCOME, ITTŌ-RYŪ COULD BE HISTORY.
HOW'S THAT, HUH? YOUR HATED ITTŌ-RYŪ...
...ON THE ROPES IN JUST ONE MONTH.
SO, REALLY...
...WE SHOULDN'T BE WASTING TIME MESSING AROUND WITH MANJI NOW. BUT FOR US, HOW DO I PUT THIS...
IT'S ABOUT...
... CLOSURE.

WITH *HIM* FOR A BODYGUARD, YOU'VE KILLED *TWENTY* OF OUR GUYS.

I'M NOT GOING THERE, NOT NOW. I *REMEMBER* WHAT WE DID TO YOU TWO YEARS AGO...

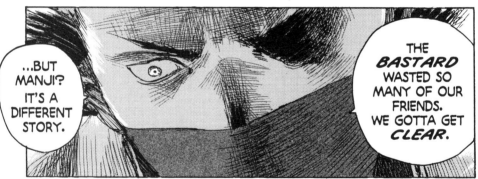

...BUT MANJI? IT'S A DIFFERENT STORY.

THE *BASTARD* WASTED SO MANY OF OUR FRIENDS. WE GOTTA GET *CLEAR*.

OR SO SAY...

...THE TWO GENTS OVER THERE.

KNOW WHAT THIS SUCKER IS?

...?

THIS LITTLE *TOY*?

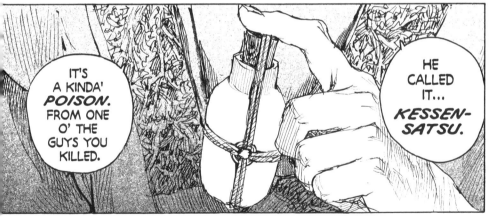

IT'S A KINDA' *POISON.* FROM ONE O' THE GUYS YOU KILLED.

HE CALLED IT... *KESSEN-SATSU.*

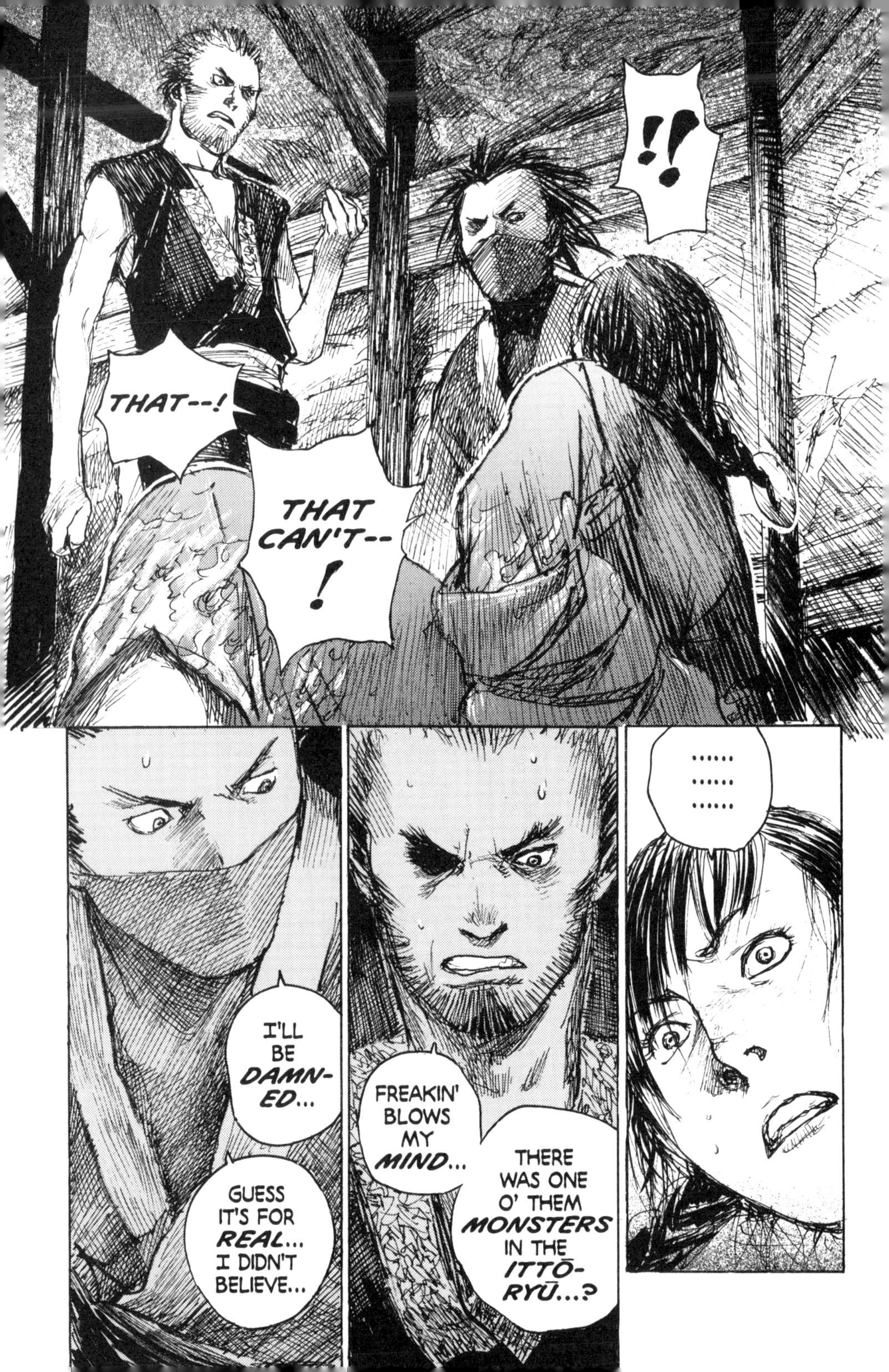
!!
THAT--!
THAT CAN'T-- !
I'LL BE DAMNED...
GUESS IT'S FOR REAL... I DIDN'T BELIEVE...
FREAKIN' BLOWS MY MIND...
THERE WAS ONE O' THEM MONSTERS IN THE ITTŌ-RYŪ...?
......
......
......

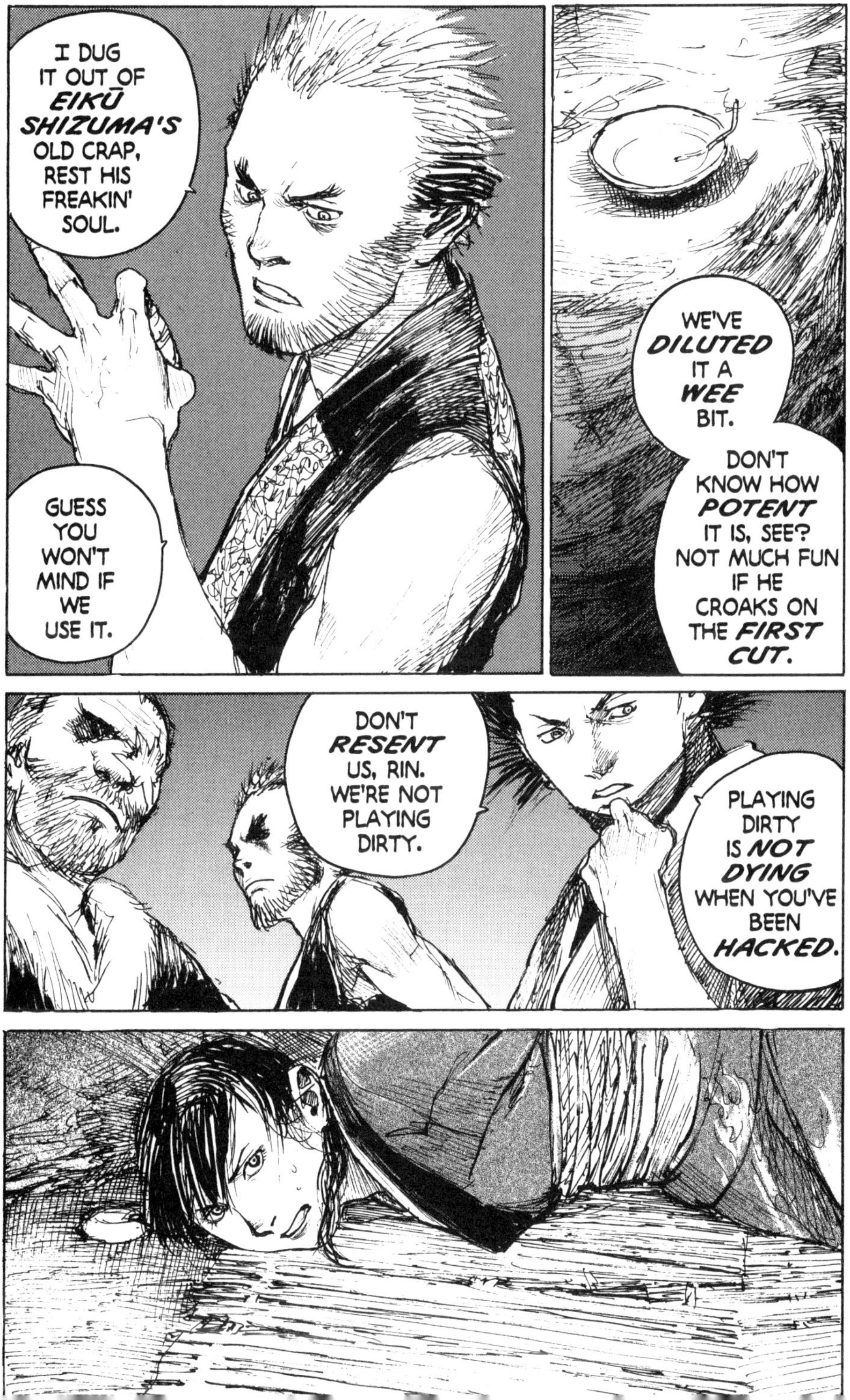
I DUG IT OUT OF *EIKŪ SHIZUMA'S* OLD CRAP, REST HIS FREAKIN' SOUL.
GUESS YOU WON'T MIND IF WE USE IT.
WE'VE *DILUTED* IT A *WEE* BIT.
DON'T KNOW HOW *POTENT* IT IS, SEE? NOT MUCH FUN IF HE CROAKS ON THE *FIRST CUT*.
DON'T *RESENT* US, RIN. WE'RE NOT PLAYING DIRTY.
PLAYING DIRTY IS *NOT DYING* WHEN YOU'VE BEEN *HACKED*.

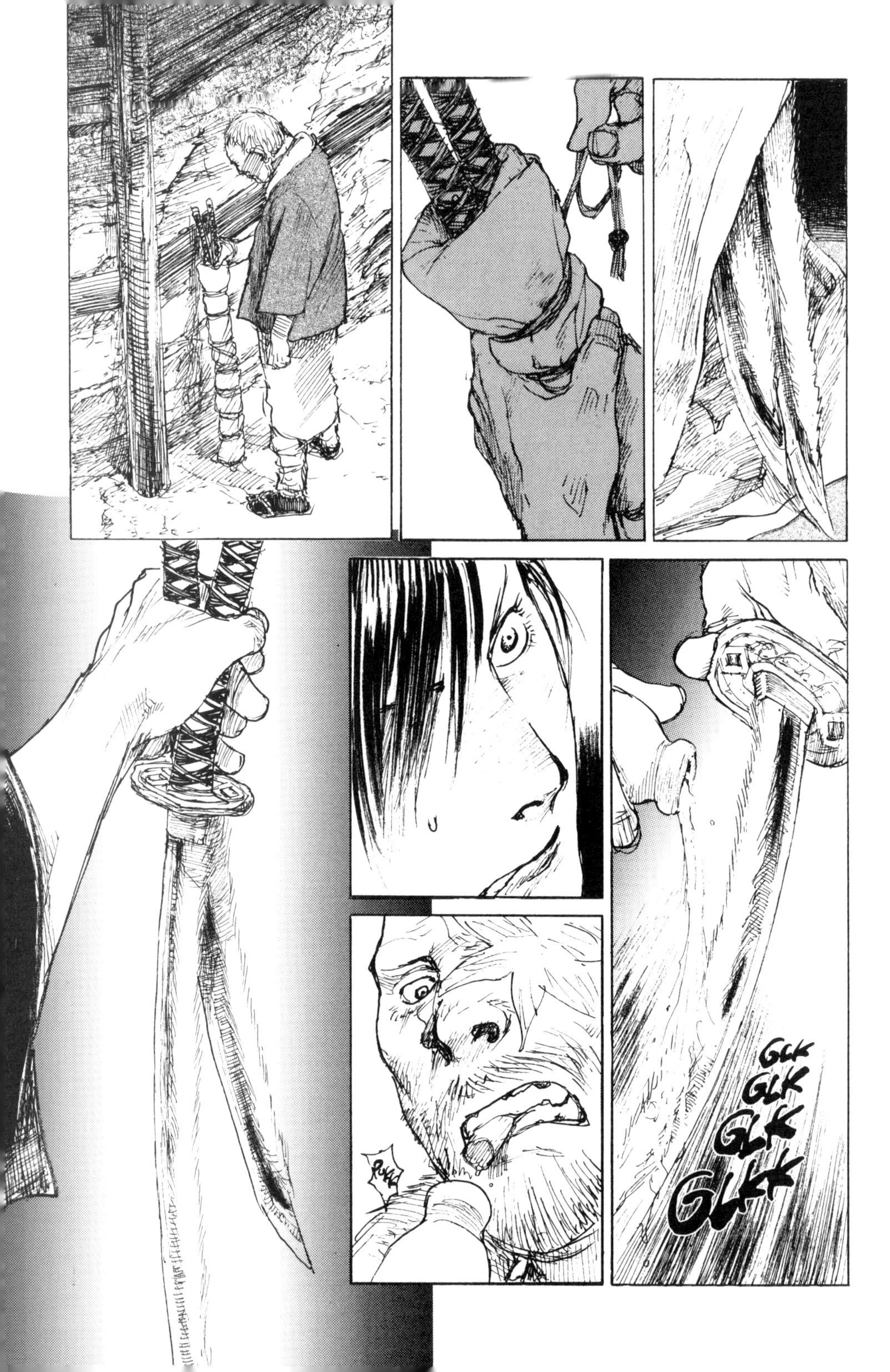
PUKK
GLK
GLK
GLK
GLK

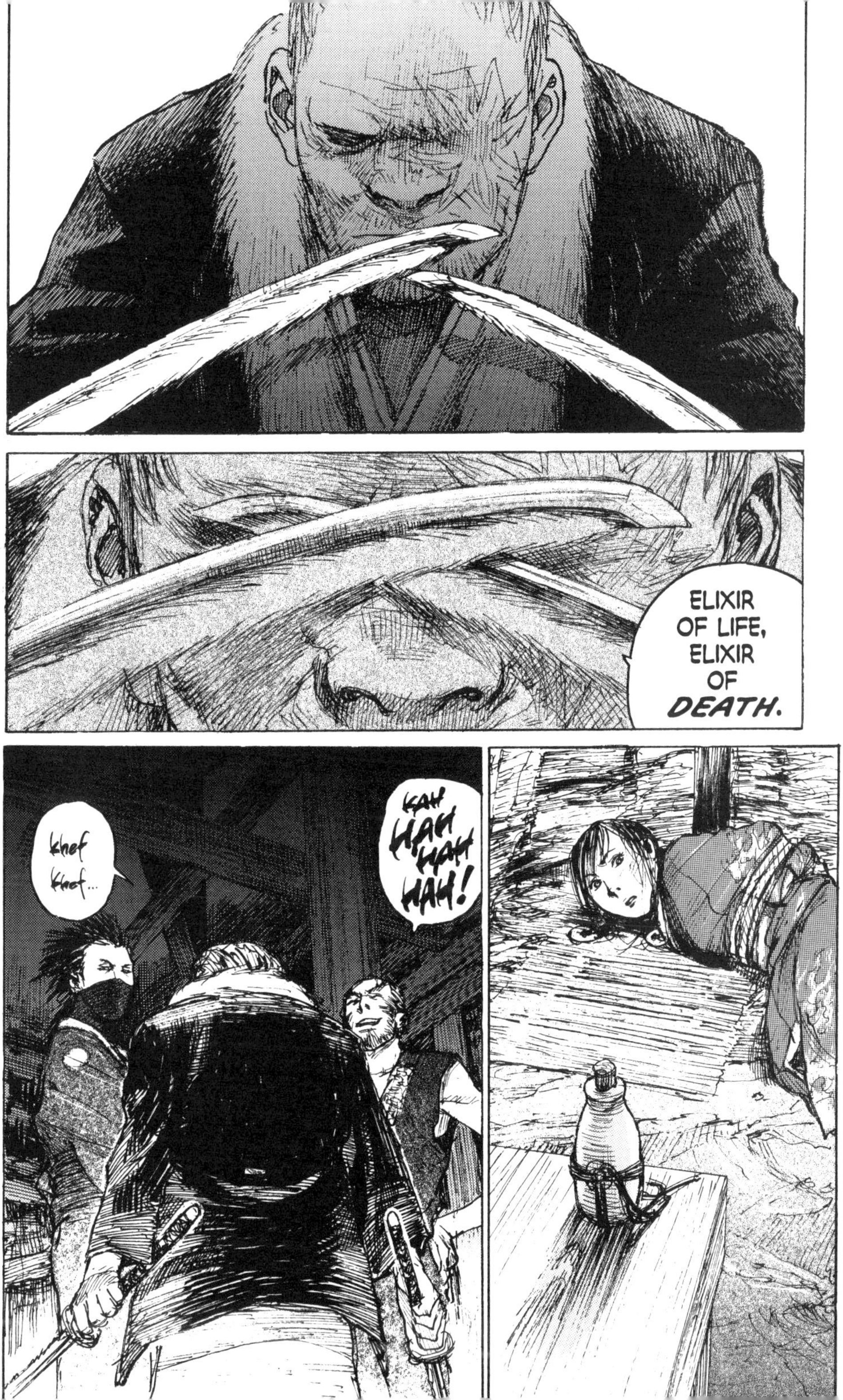
ELIXIR OF LIFE, ELIXIR OF DEATH.
khef khef...
KAH HAH HAH HAH!

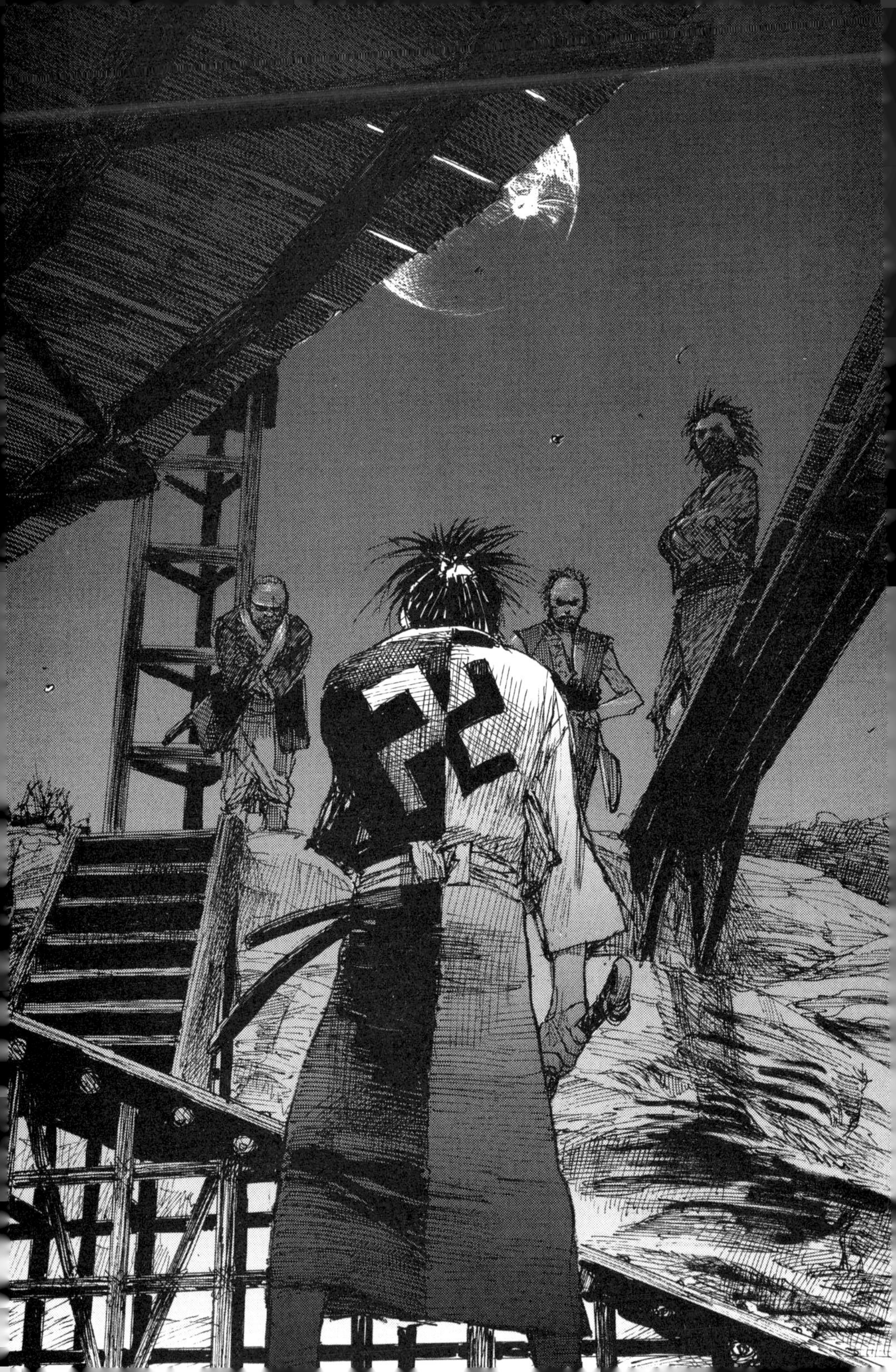

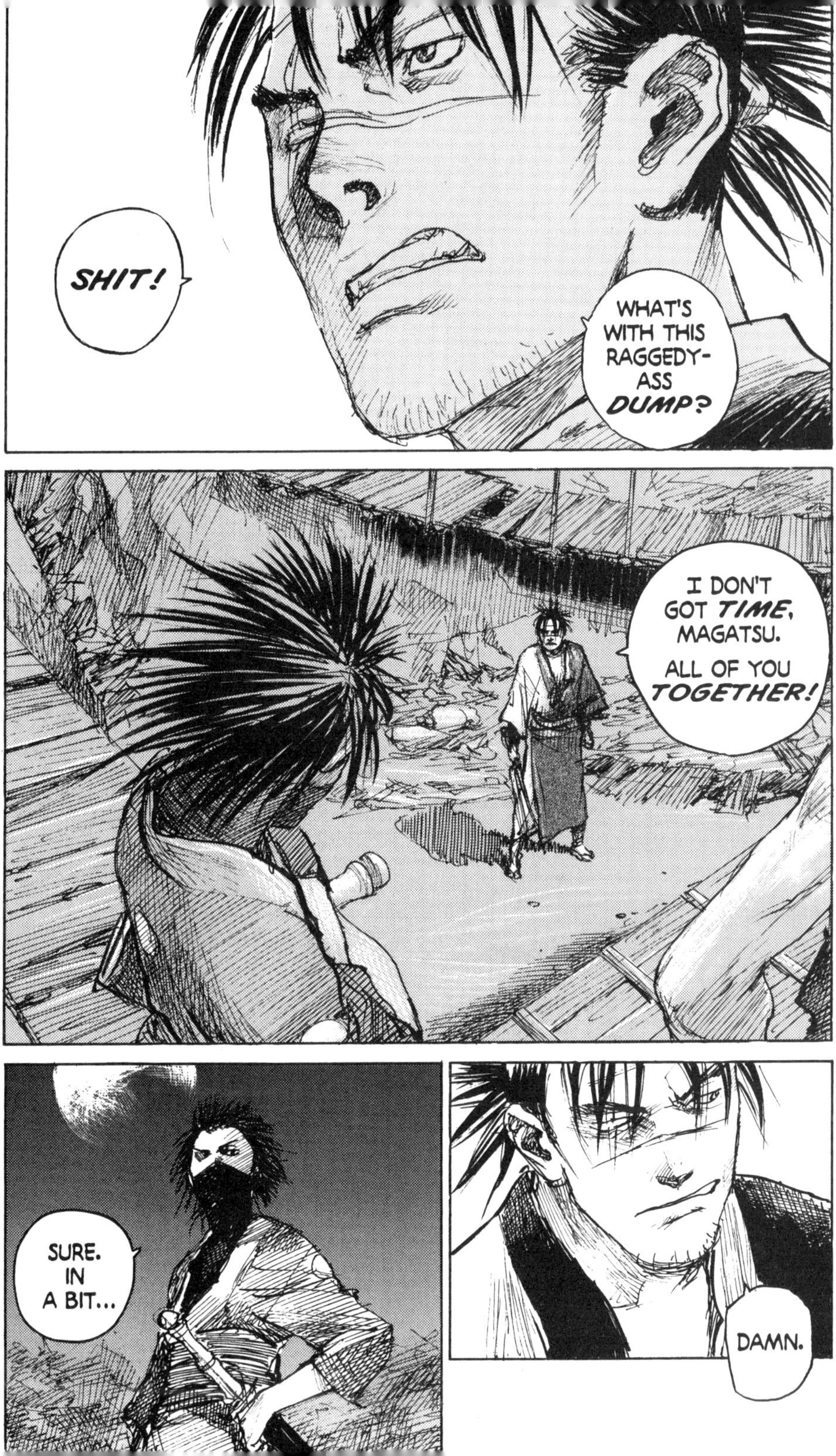
SHIT!
WHAT'S WITH THIS RAGGEDY-ASS DUMP?
I DON'T GOT TIME, MAGATSU.
ALL OF YOU TOGETHER!
SURE. IN A BIT...
DAMN.

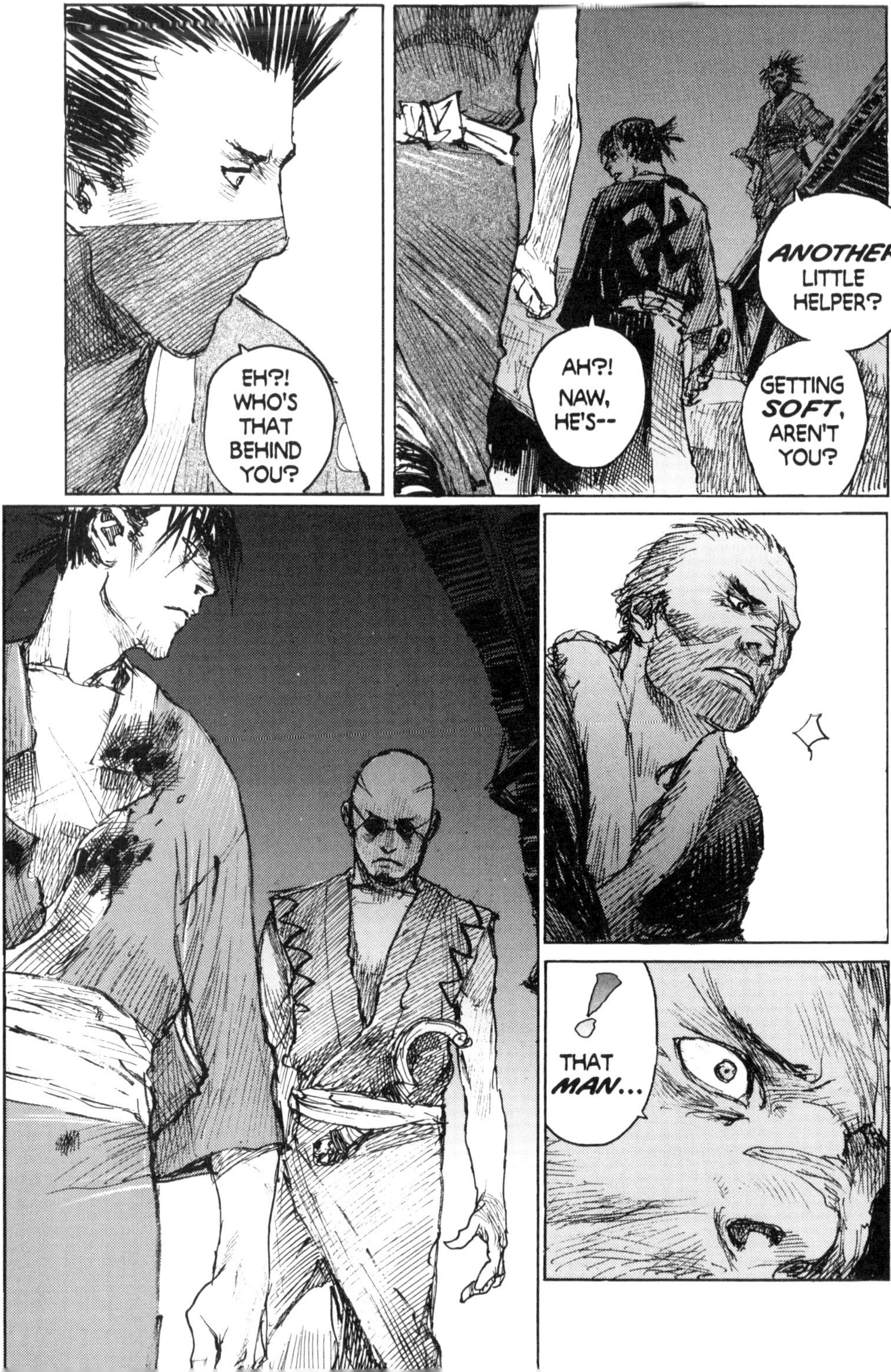
EH?! WHO'S THAT BEHIND YOU?
AH?! NAW, HE'S--
ANOTHER LITTLE HELPER?
GETTING SOFT, AREN'T YOU?
!
THAT MAN...

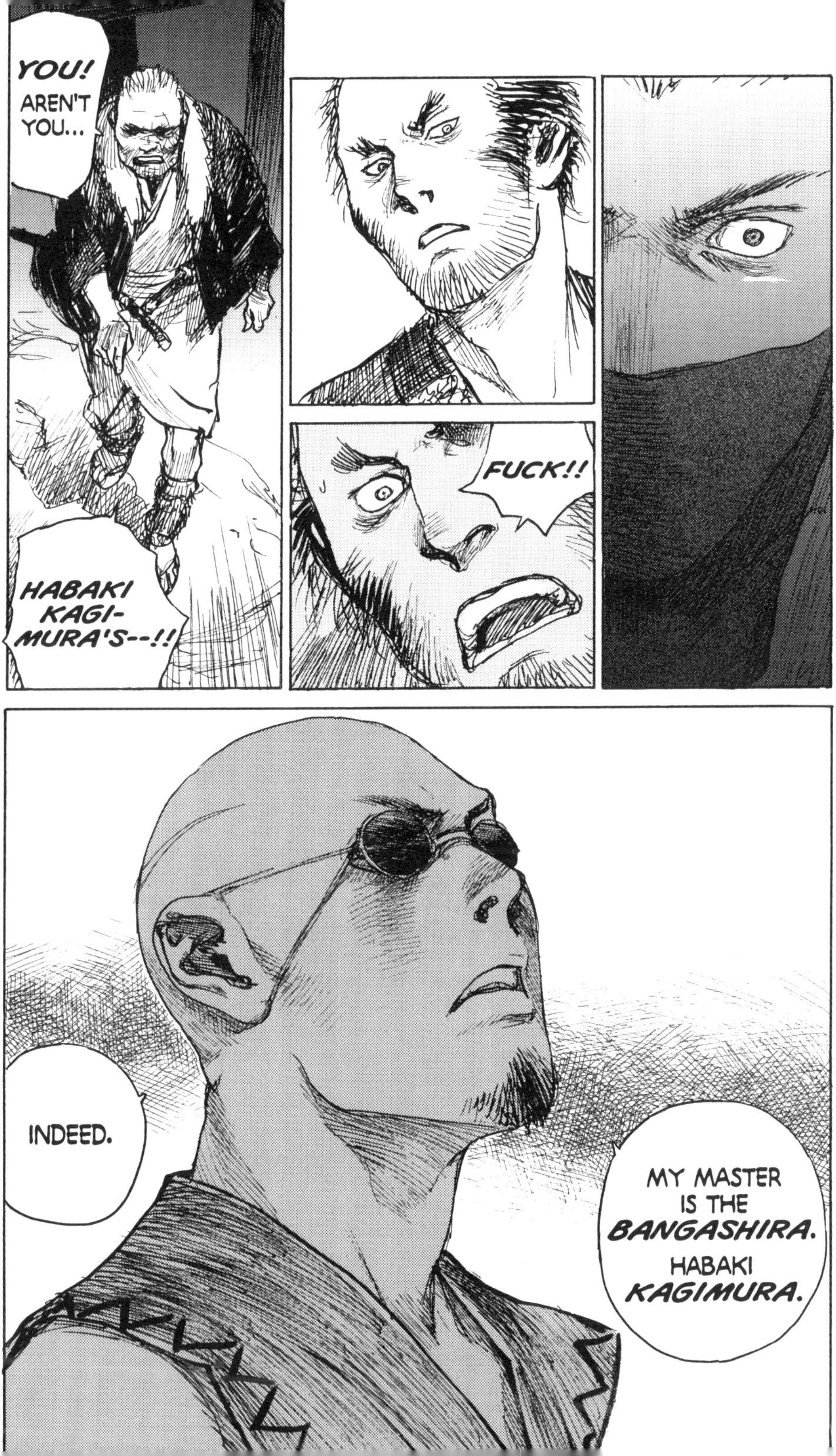
YOU! AREN'T YOU...
HABAKI KAGI-MURA'S--!!
FUCK!!
INDEED.
MY MASTER IS THE BANGASHIRA. HABAKI KAGIMURA.

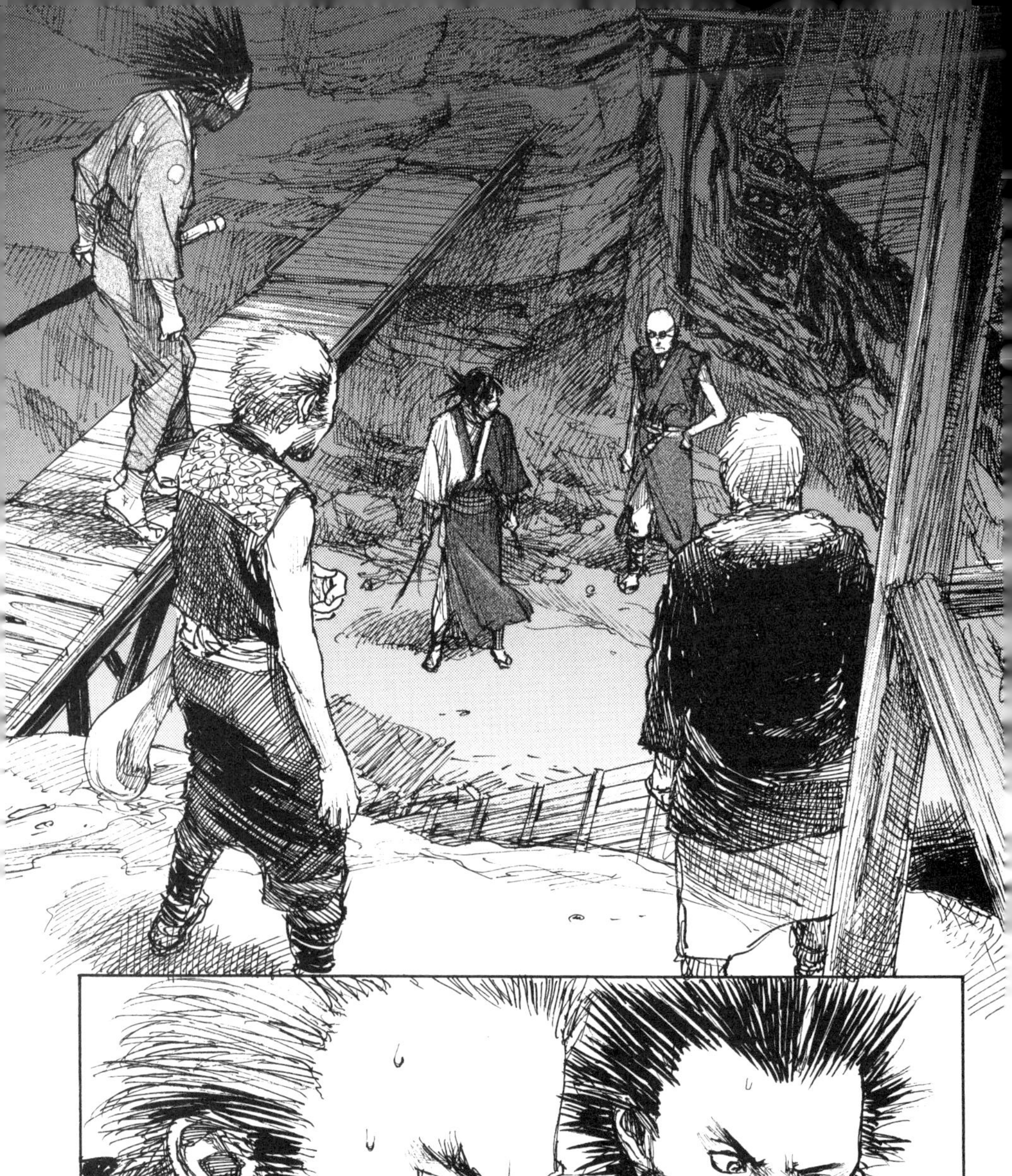

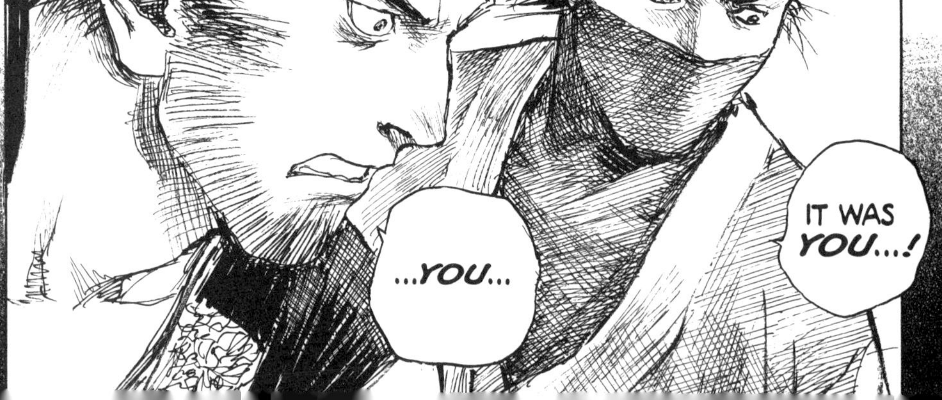
...YOU...
IT WAS YOU...!

GREAT.

I DRAGGED ALONG A *RIPE ONE.*

I'M NOT A HELPER.

YOU INTER- RUPTED OUR TALK.

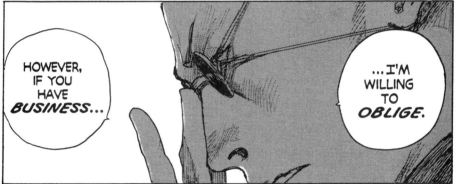

HOWEVER, IF YOU HAVE *BUSINESS*...

...I'M WILLING TO *OBLIGE.*

....

KRRK

UHF...

NGN...

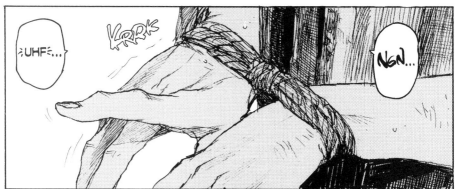

RIN!
LISTEN...
IF I
DIE...
DON'T...

...DON'T
GO AFTER
ANOTSU
ALONE!
FIND
ANOTHER--

*SHUT
UP!*

I DON'T
WANT TO
HEAR IT!
I
WON'T!

MANJI--
TAKE
THESE.

UNGG...

=shaff=

HNFF...

IT'S AN
ANTI-DOTE
I LEARNED
ABOUT
FROM MY
MOTHER.

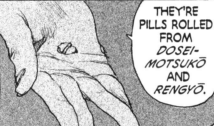

THEY'RE
PILLS ROLLED
FROM
DOSEI-MOTSUKŌ
AND
RENGYŌ.

...HNG...

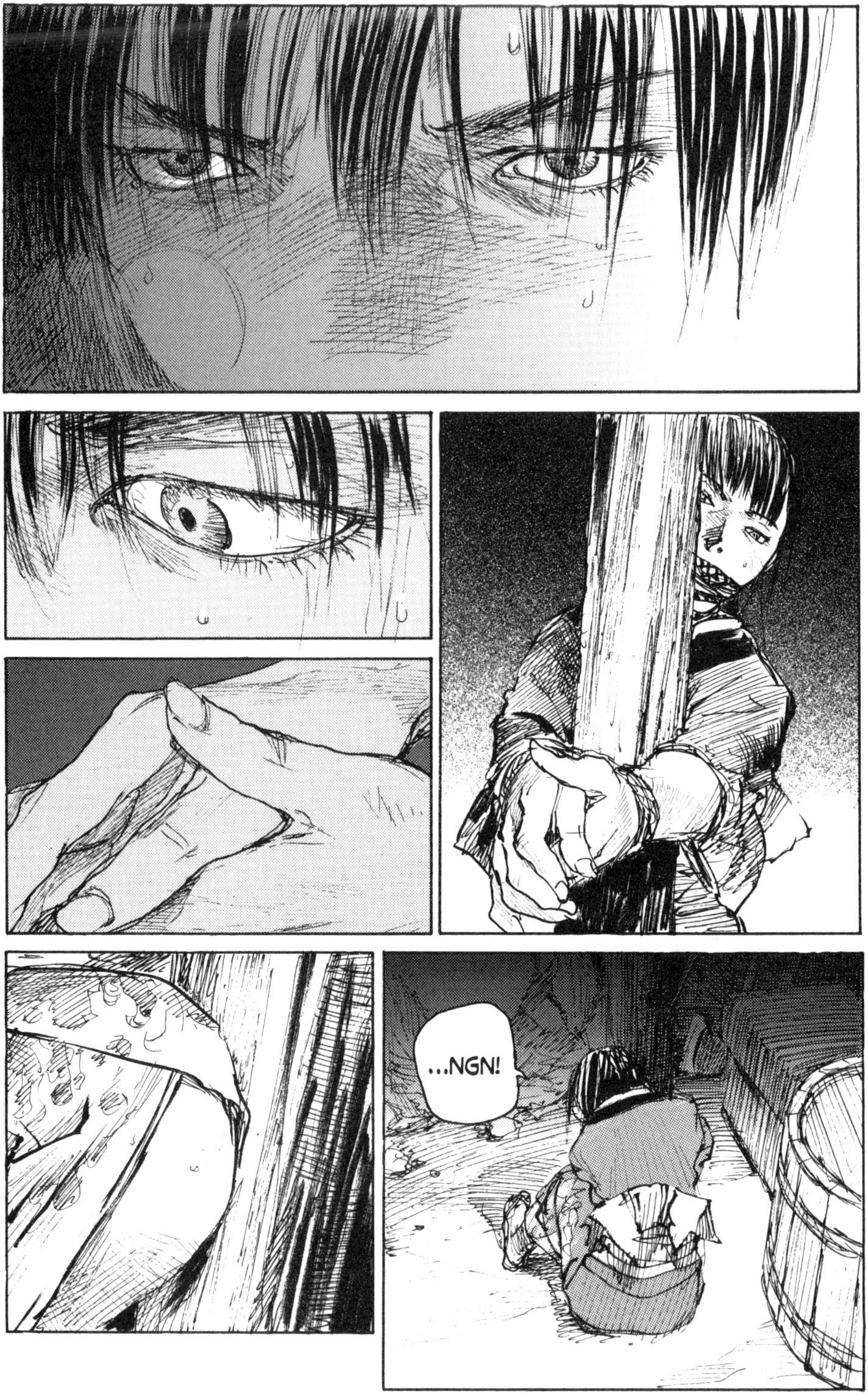
...NGN!

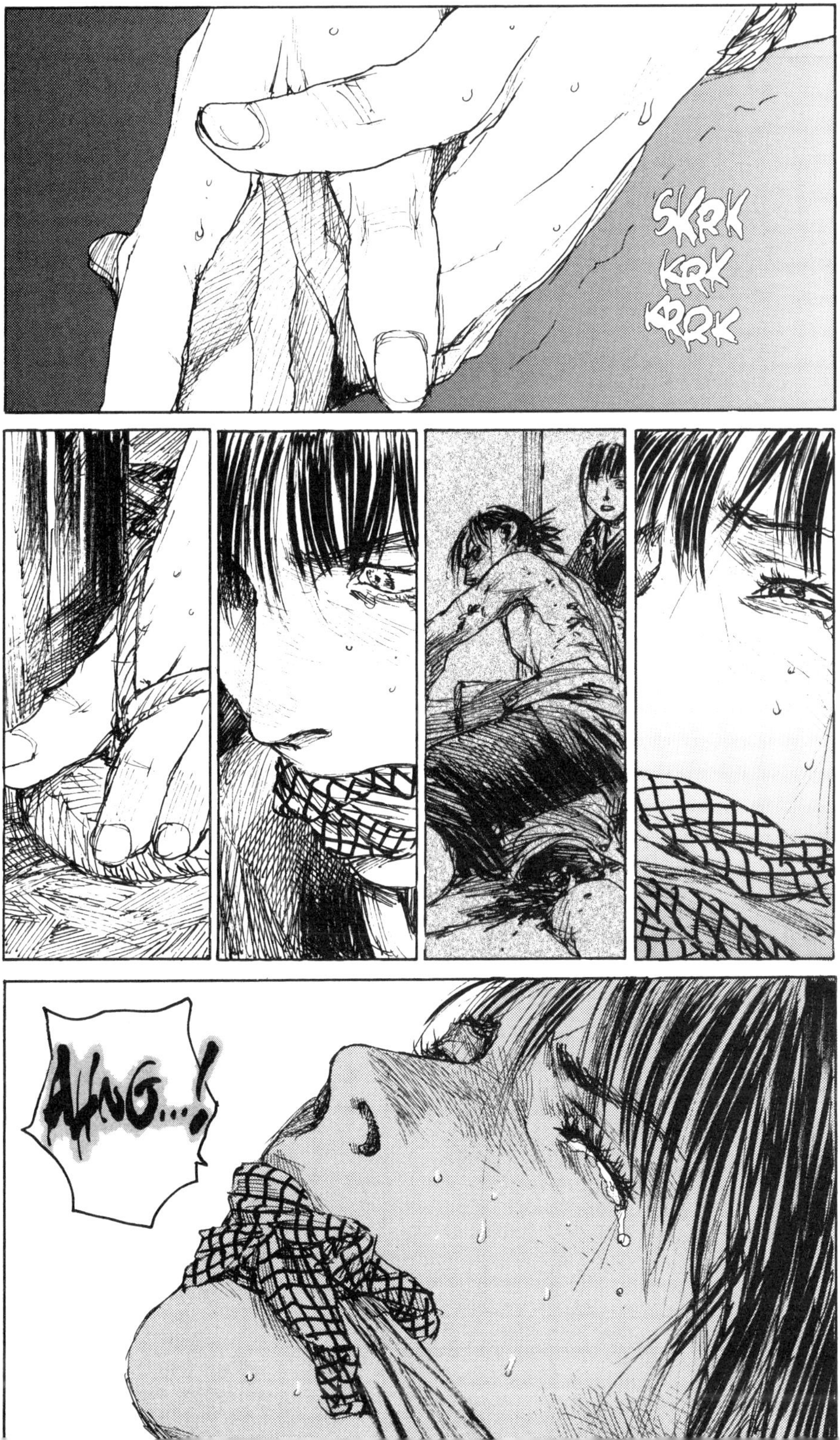
SKRK
KRK
KRK
AUNG...!

MANJI, I'LL SAY IT *ONCE.*

HAHN?

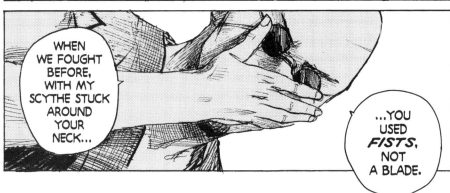

WHEN WE FOUGHT BEFORE, WITH MY SCYTHE STUCK AROUND YOUR NECK...

...YOU USED *FISTS*, NOT A BLADE.

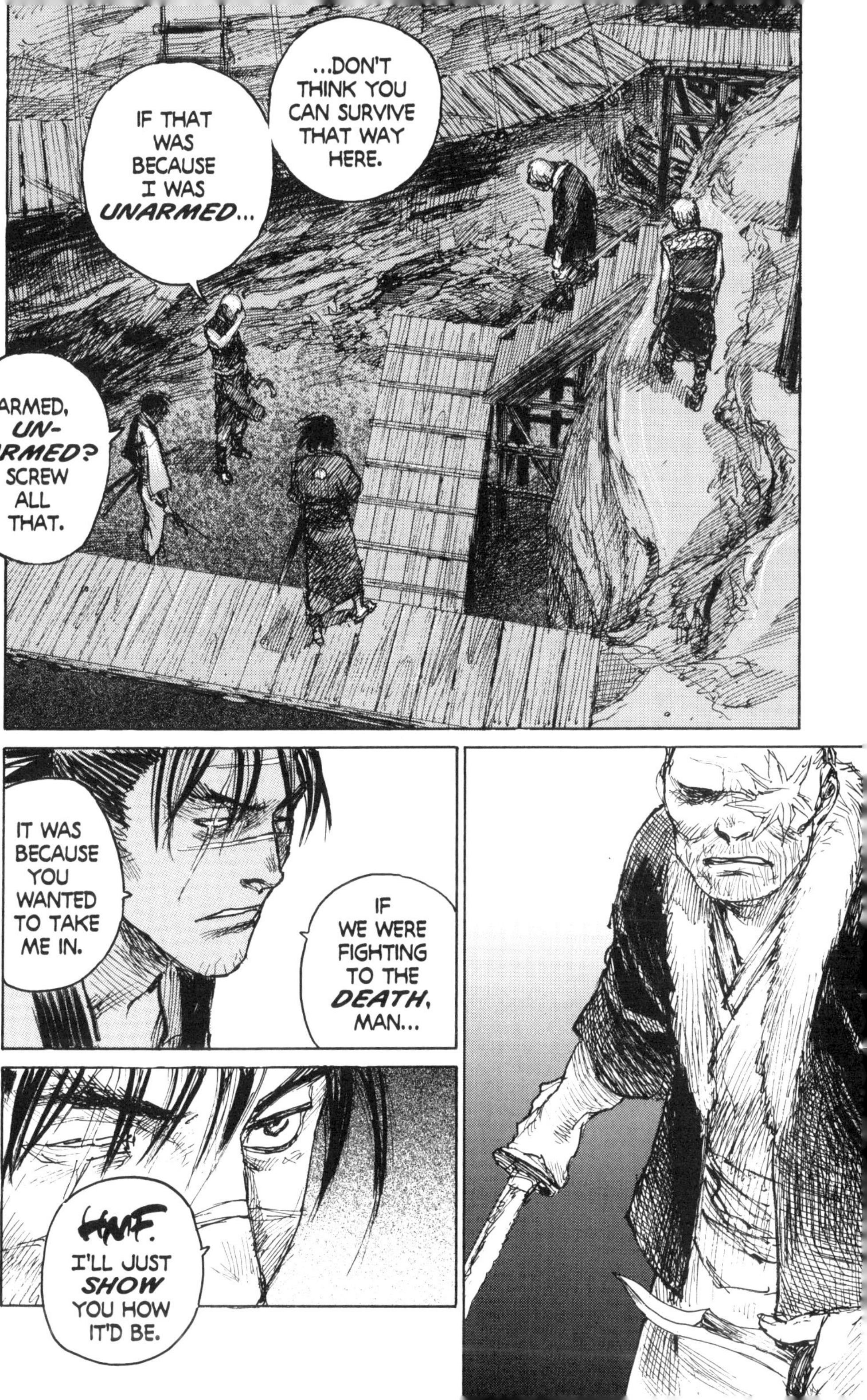
IF THAT WAS BECAUSE I WAS UNARMED...
...DON'T THINK YOU CAN SURVIVE THAT WAY HERE.
ARMED, UN-ARMED? SCREW ALL THAT.
IT WAS BECAUSE YOU WANTED TO TAKE ME IN.
IF WE WERE FIGHTING TO THE DEATH, MAN...
HMF.
I'LL JUST SHOW YOU HOW IT'D BE.

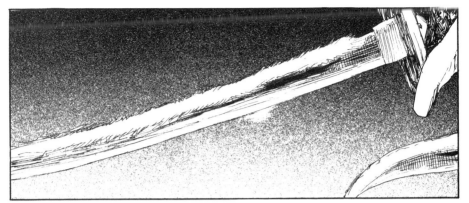

?!

THAT *SWORD*...

WAYAN KURISHIGE. *ITTŌ-RYŪ.* I WILL *FIGHT* YOU...

...THE *"ONE-HUNDRED-MAN MURDERER."*

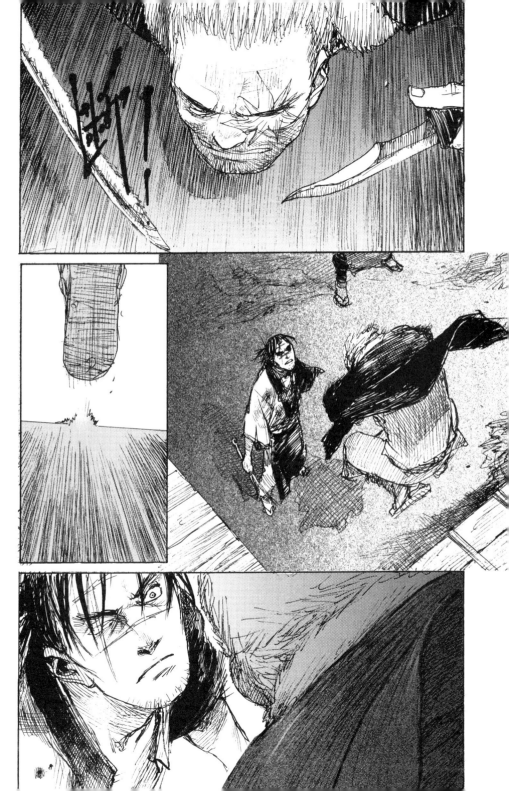

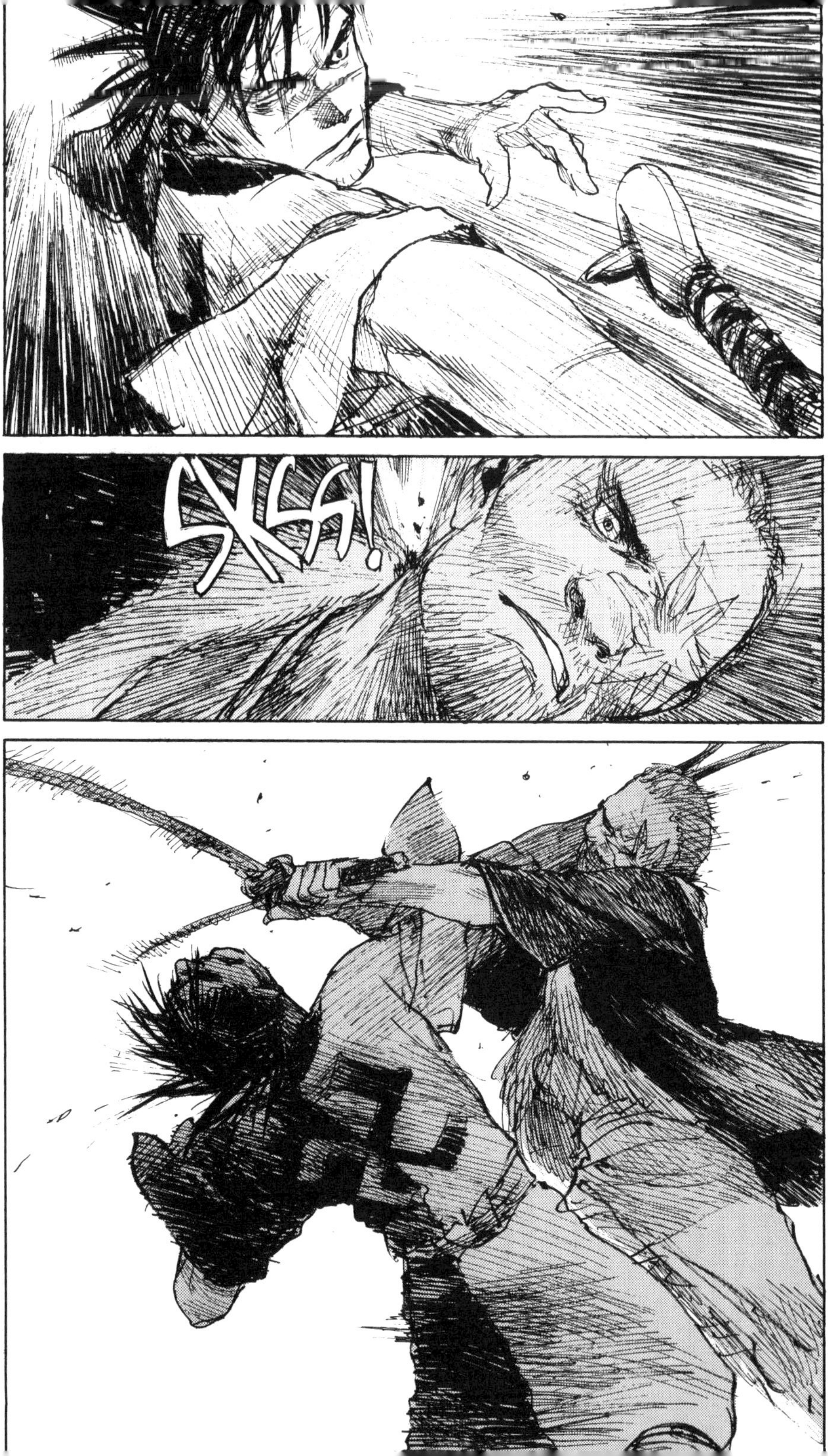
SKSS!

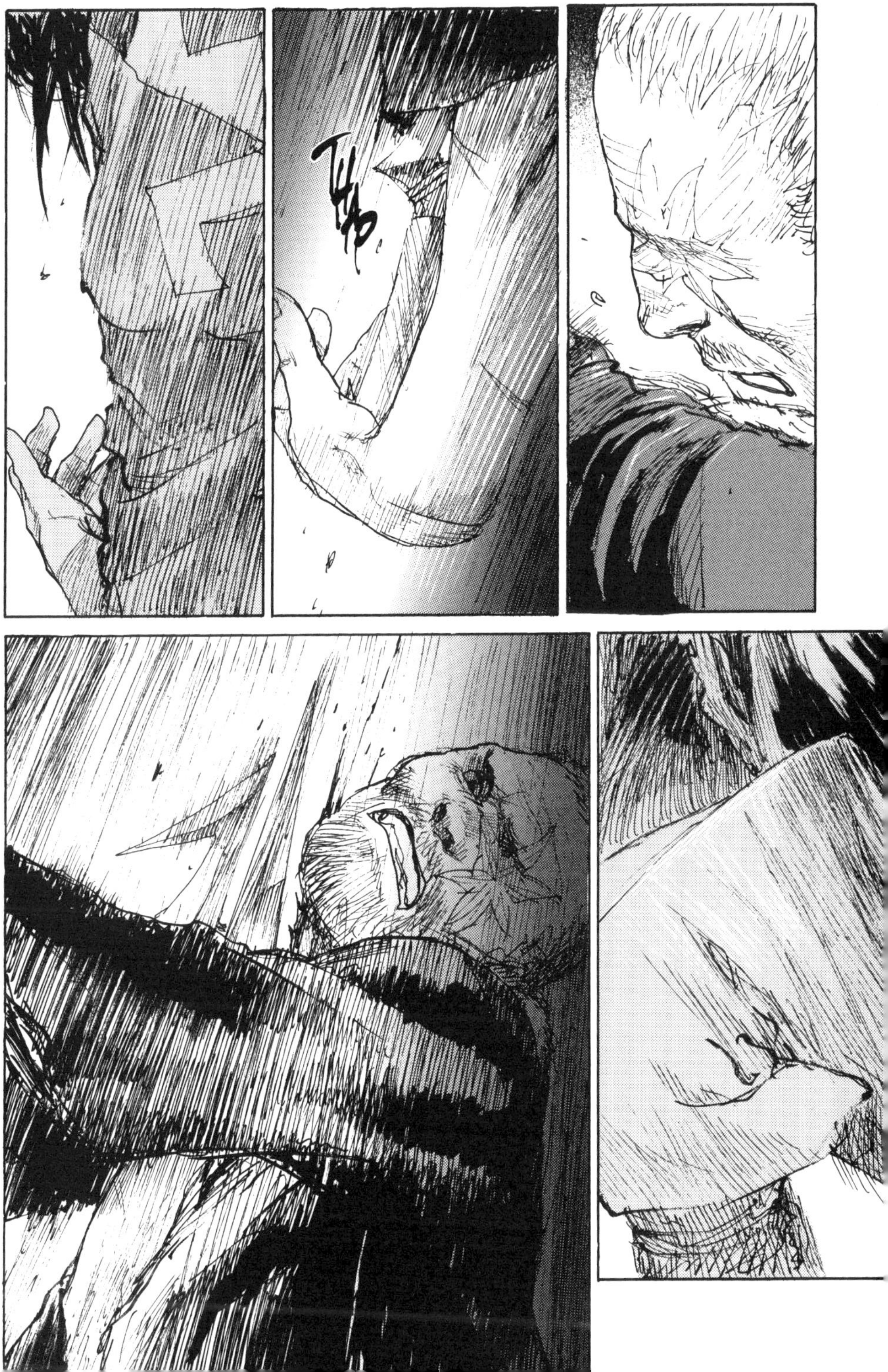
THAP

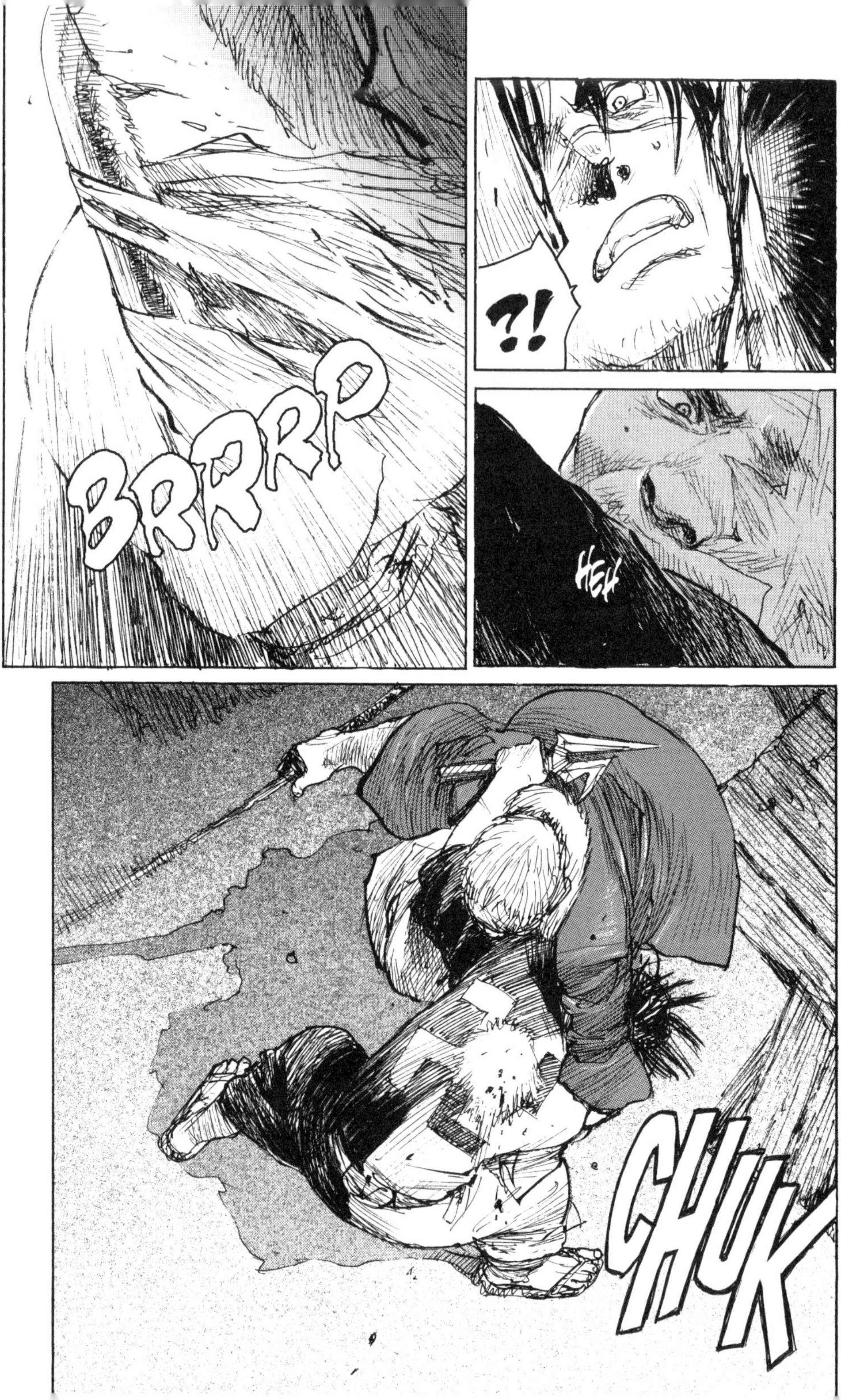
BRRRP
?!
HEH
CHUK

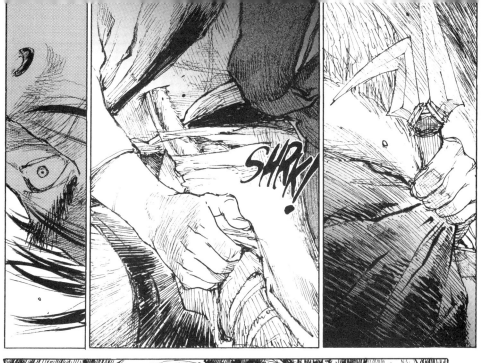

SHRK!

GRR YAAHH!

TH NNK!

HHRR...

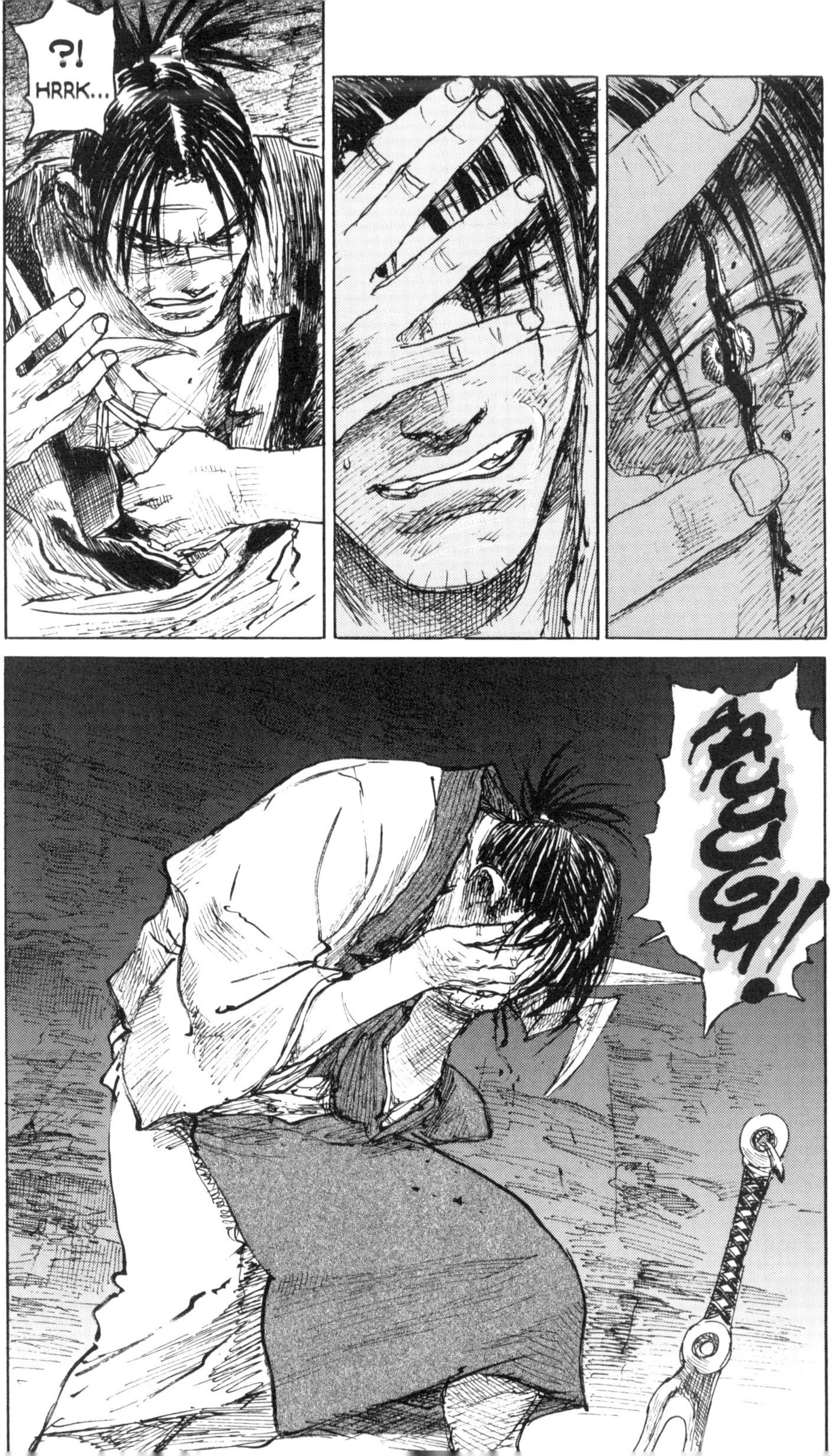
?!
HRRK...
AUUGH!!

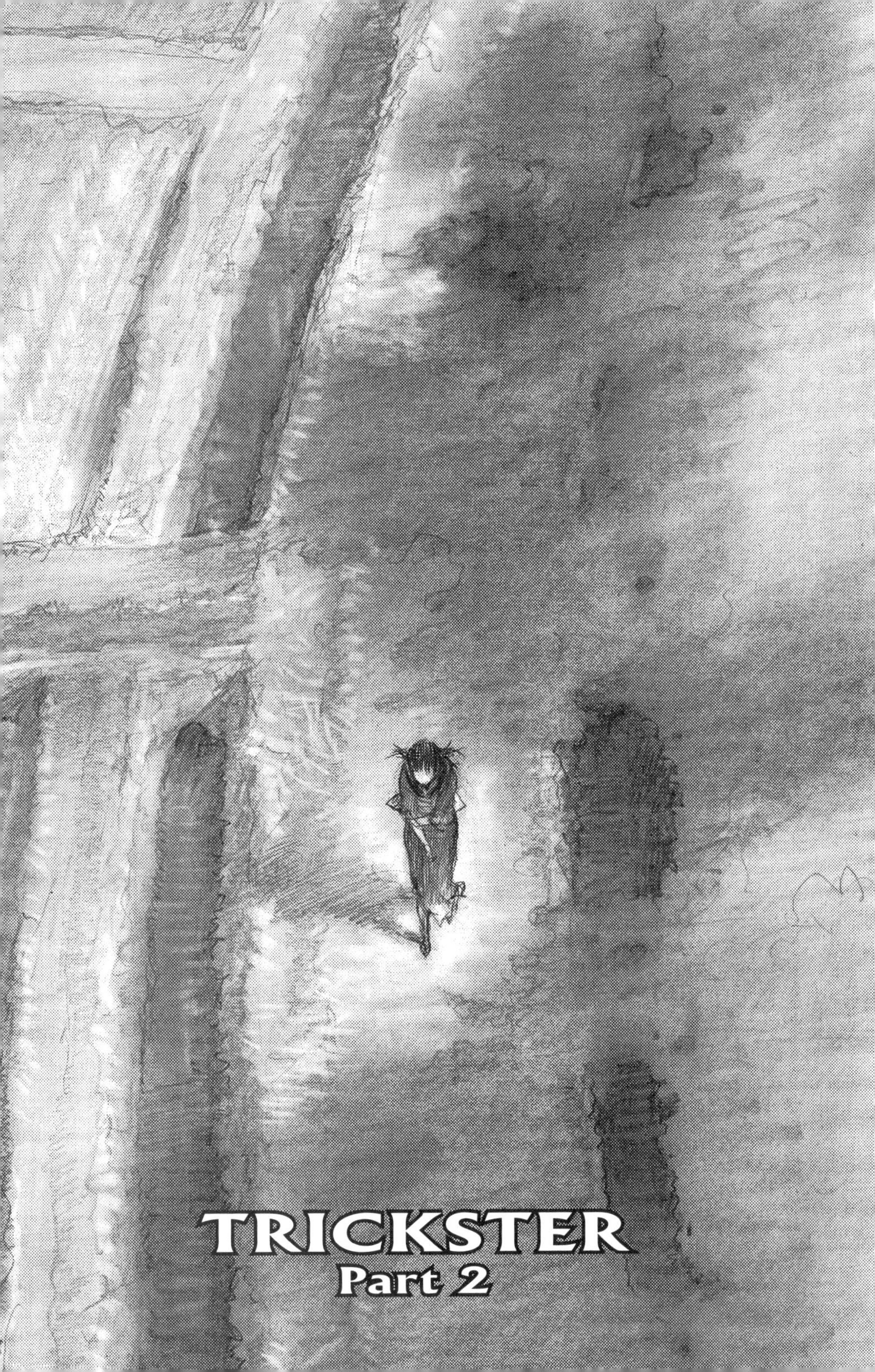

TRICKSTER
Part 2

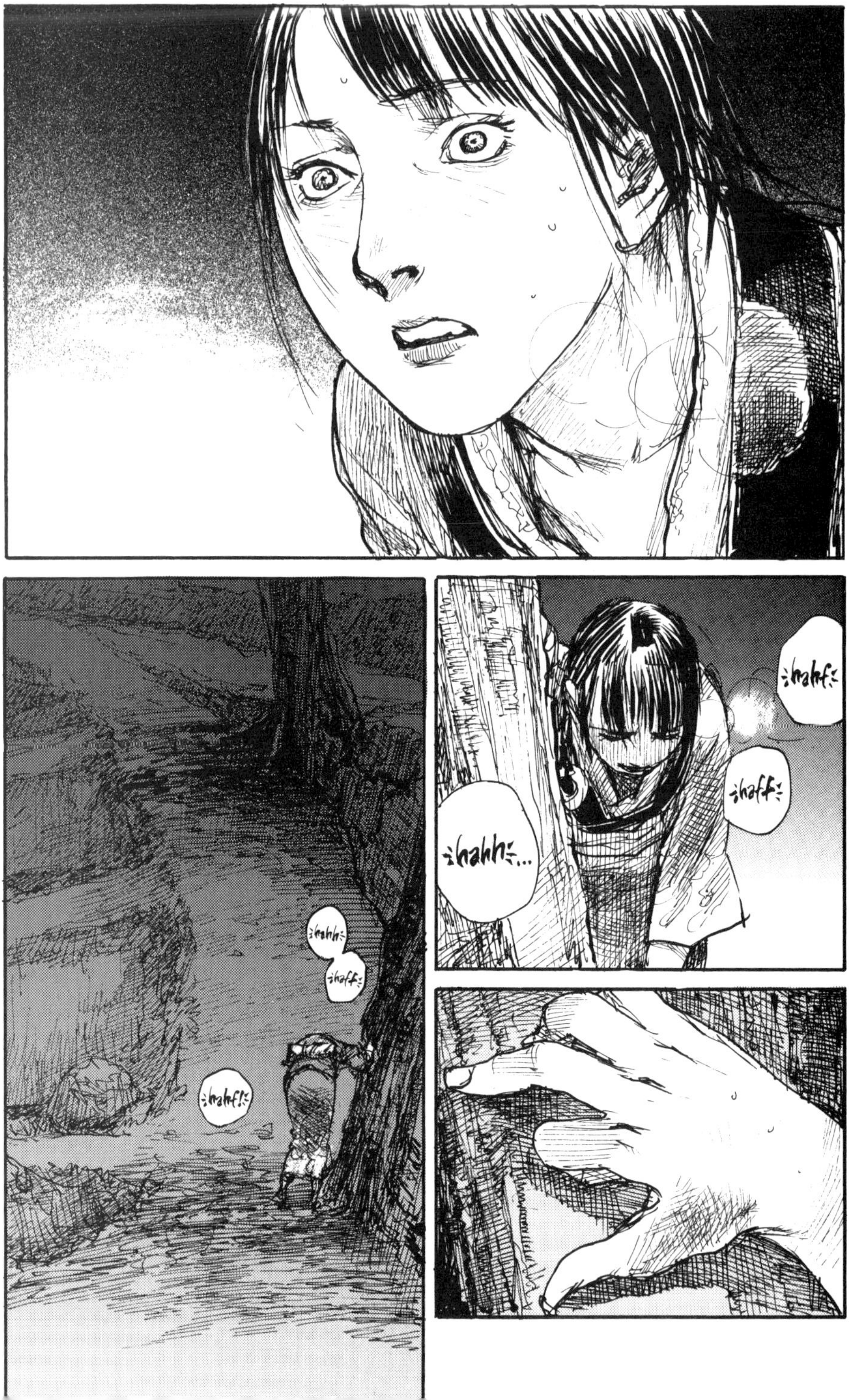
hahh
haff
hahf!
hahf
haff
hahh...

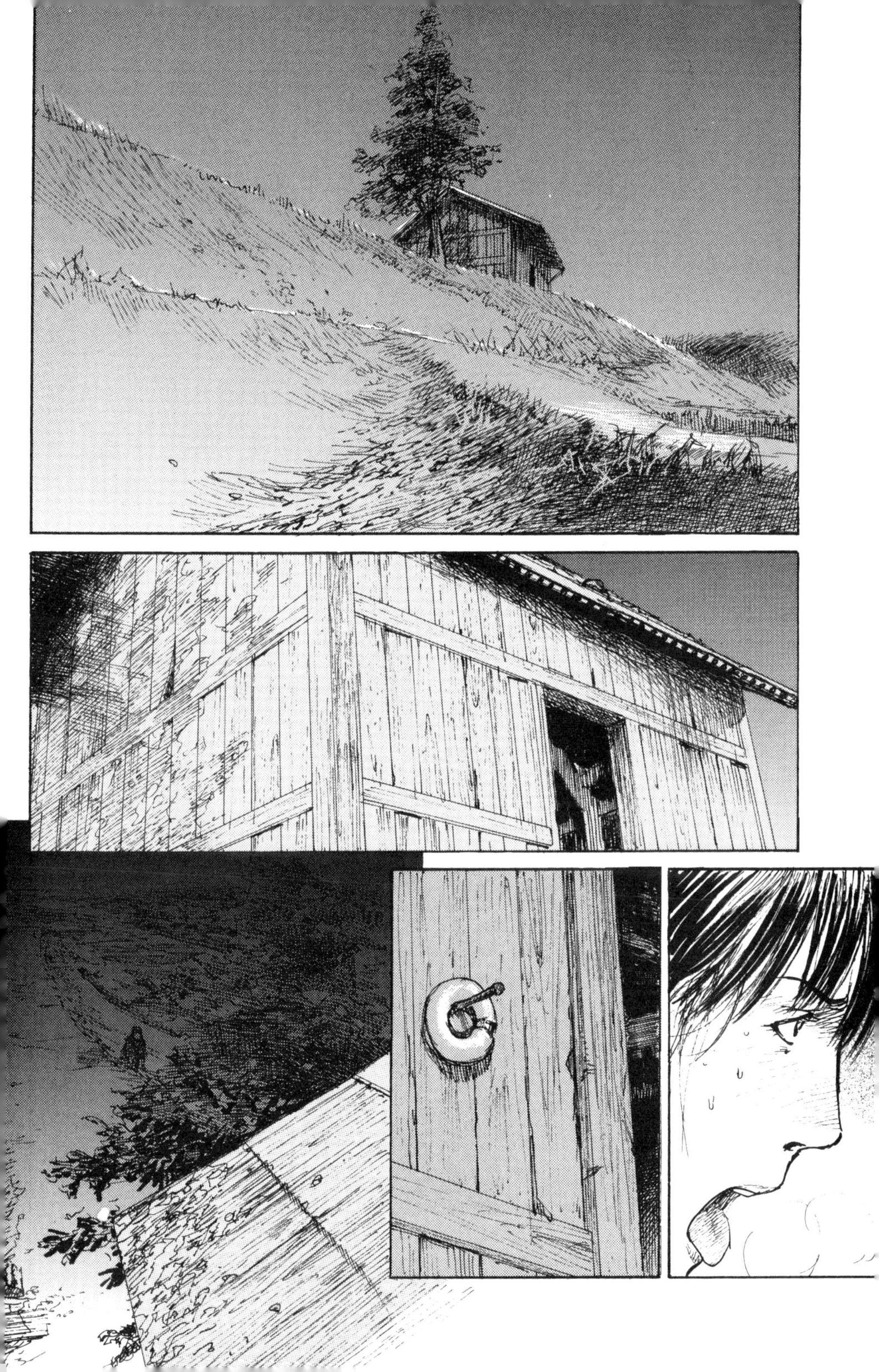

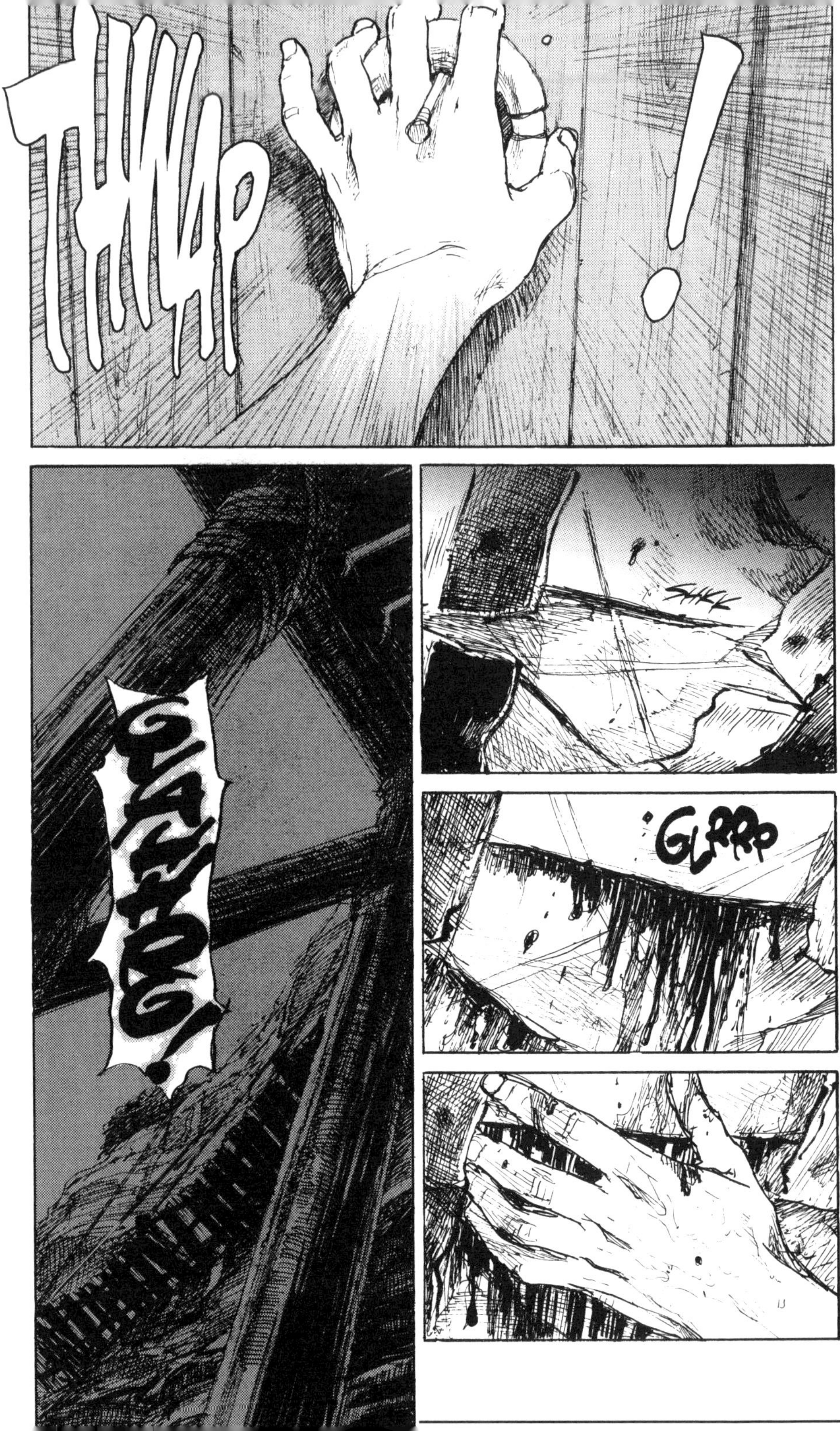
THWAP!
SHKK
GLRRP

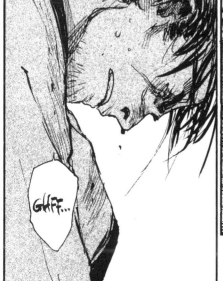

GHFF...

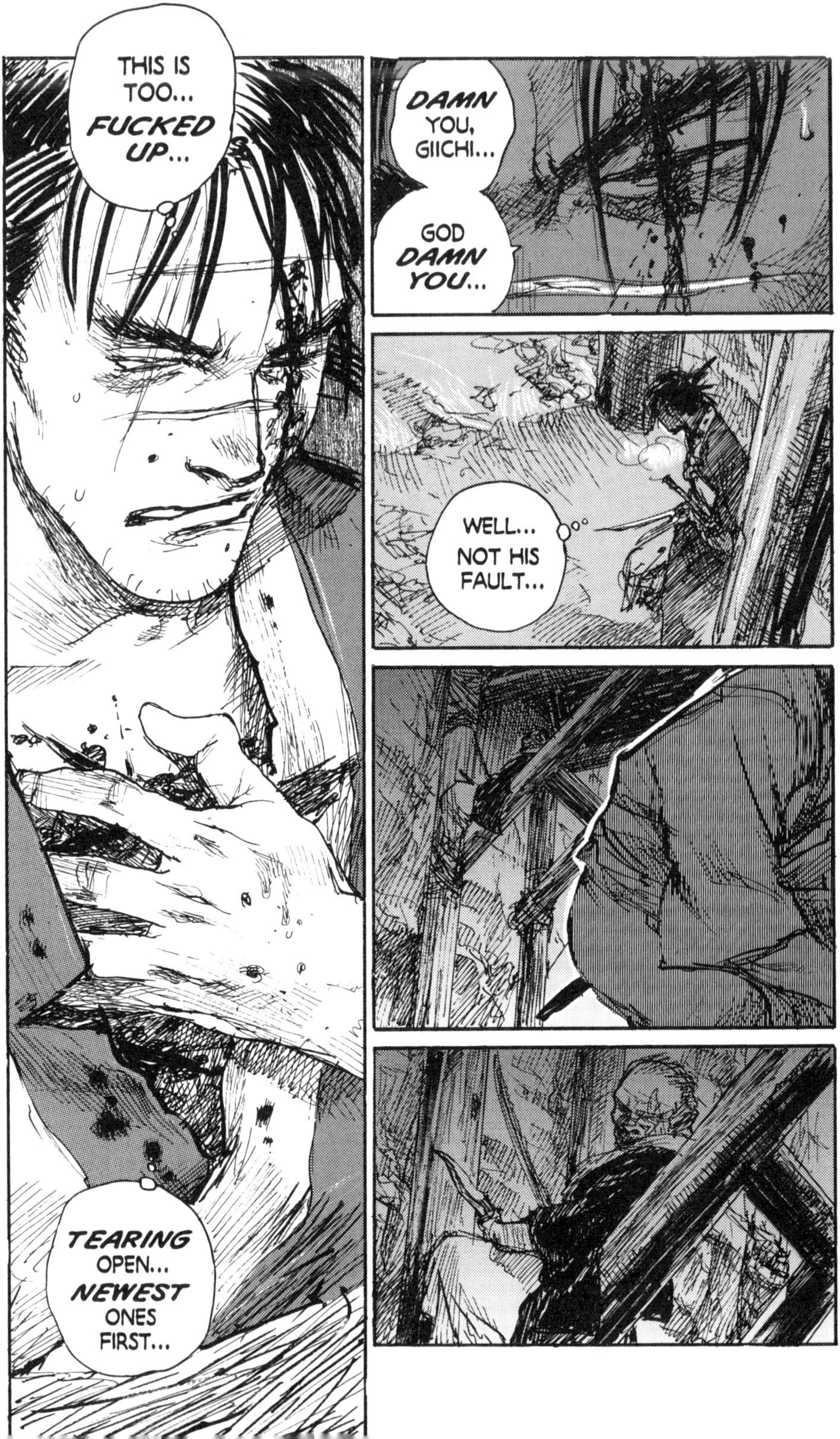
THIS IS TOO... FUCKED UP...
TEARING OPEN... NEWEST ONES FIRST...
DAMN YOU, GIICHI...
GOD DAMN YOU...
WELL... NOT HIS FAULT...

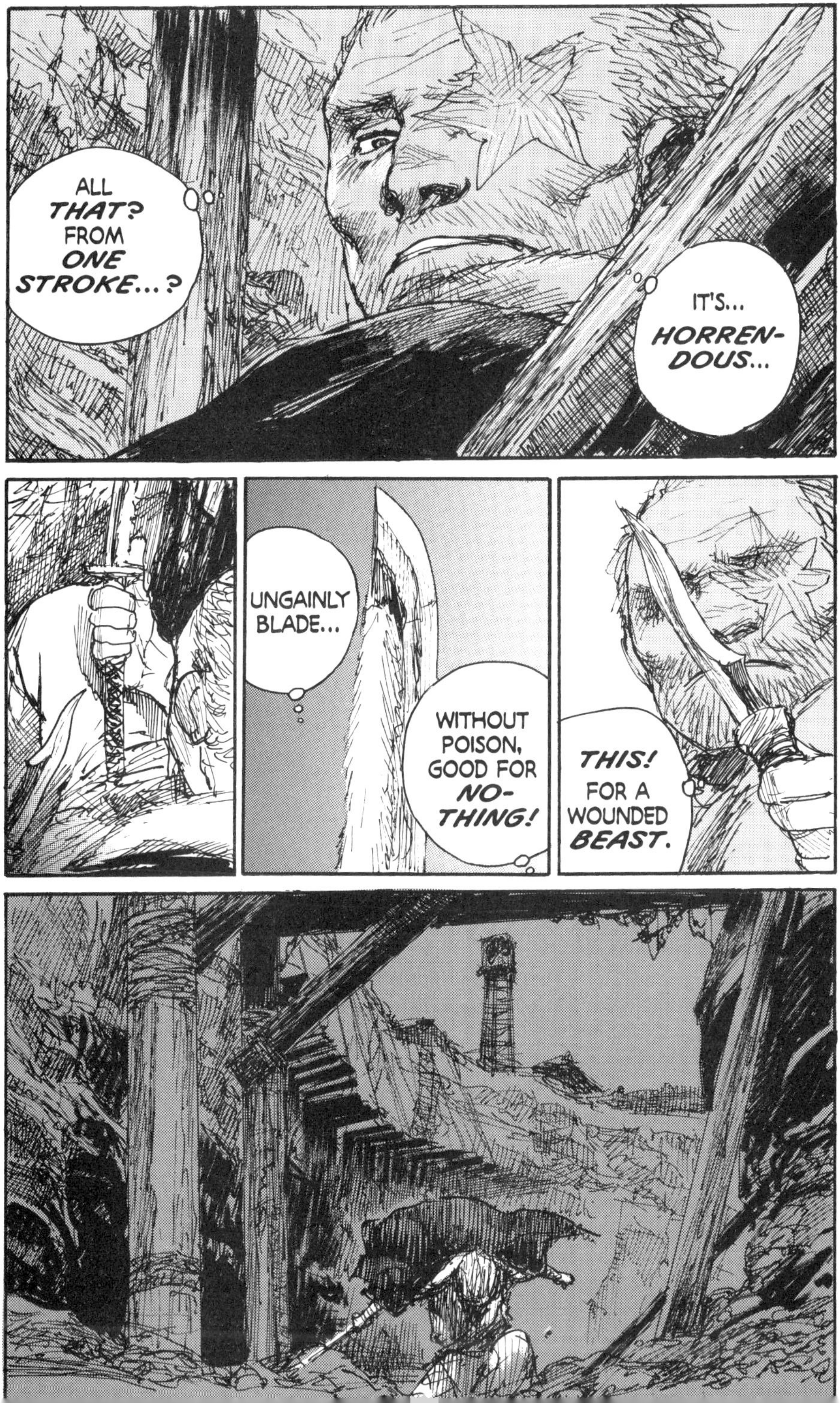
ALL THAT? FROM ONE STROKE...?
IT'S... HORREN-DOUS...
UNGAINLY BLADE...
WITHOUT POISON, GOOD FOR NO-THING!
THIS! FOR A WOUNDED BEAST.

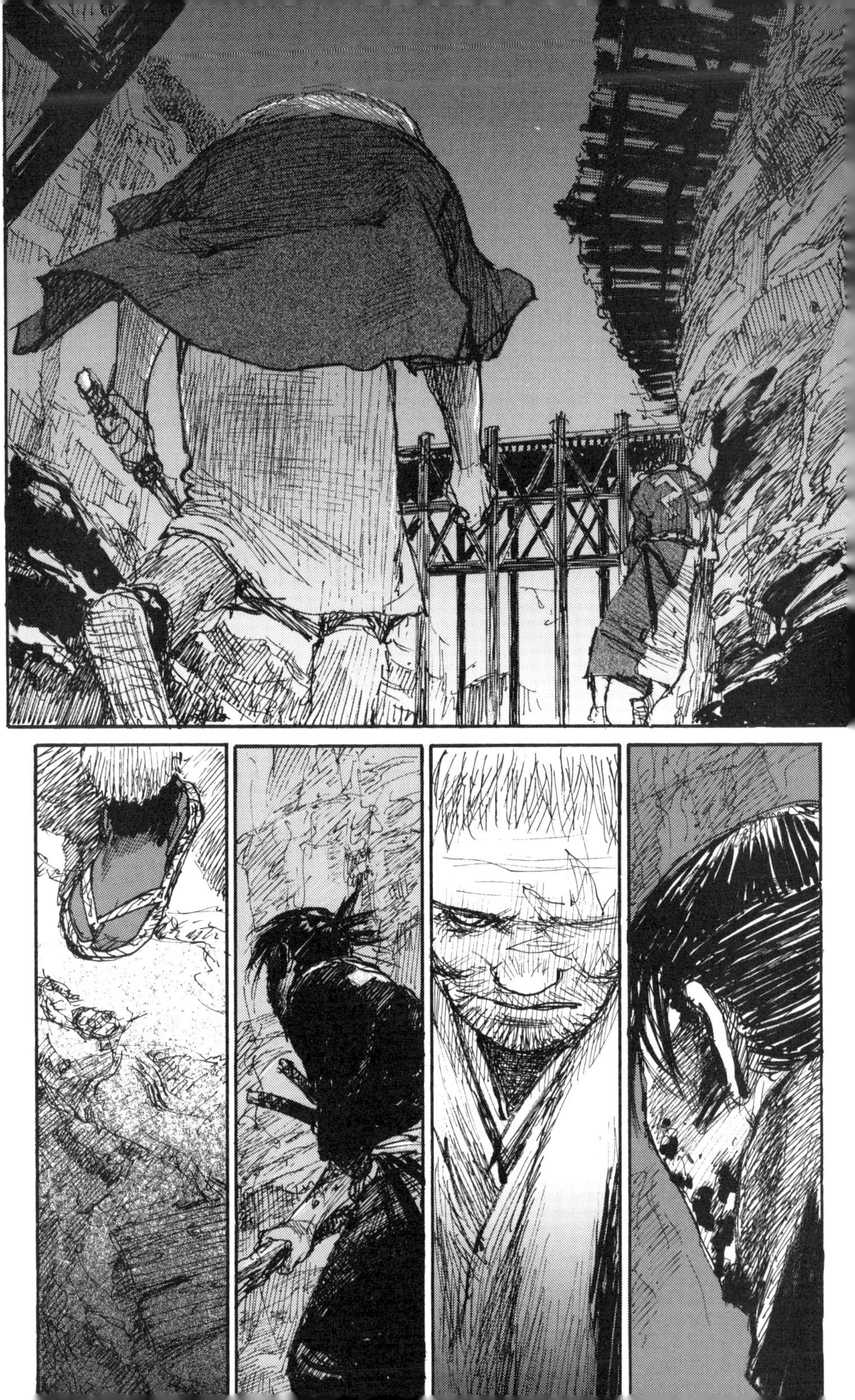

SSST!

!

URNG...?

KRK

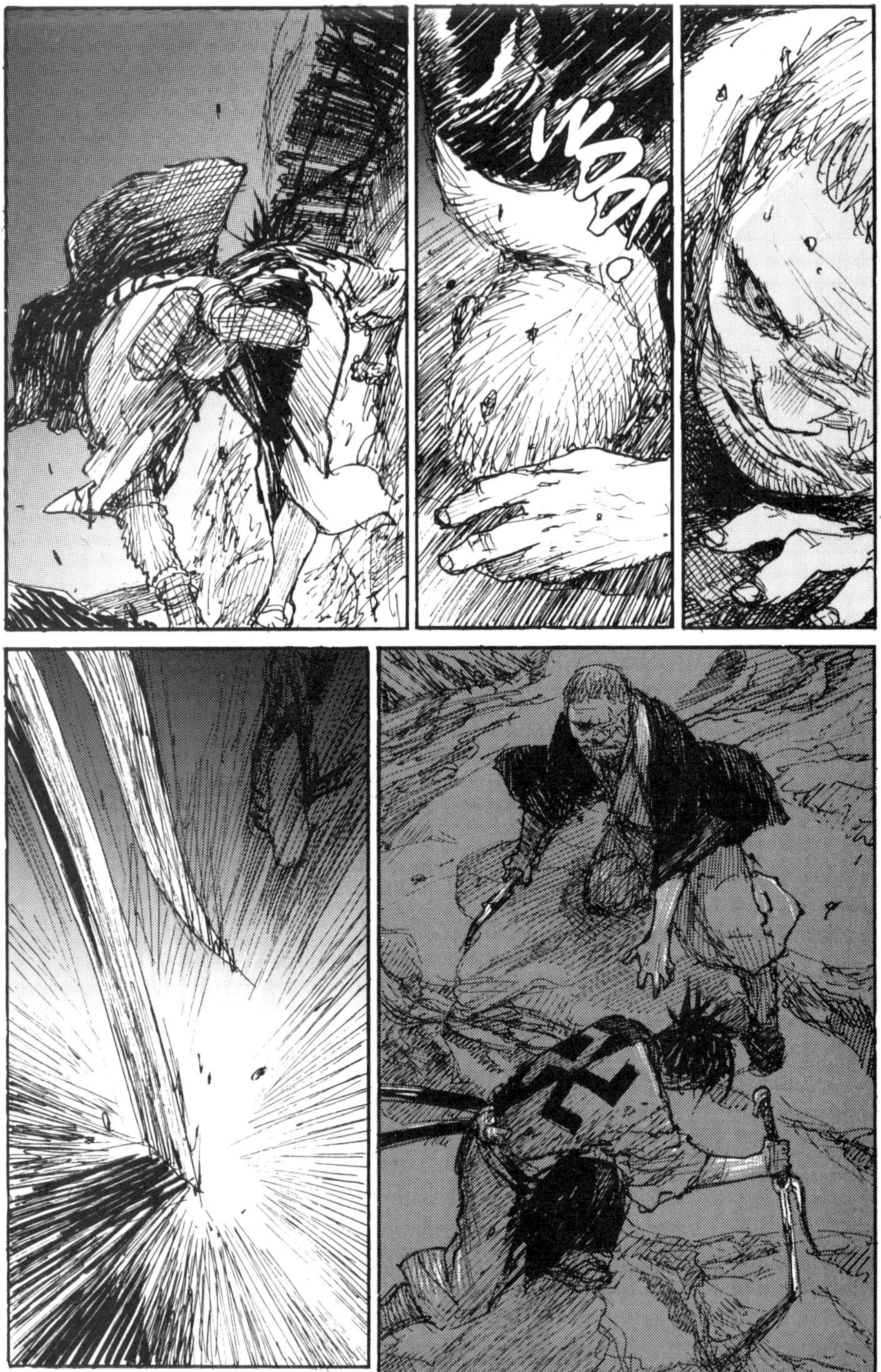

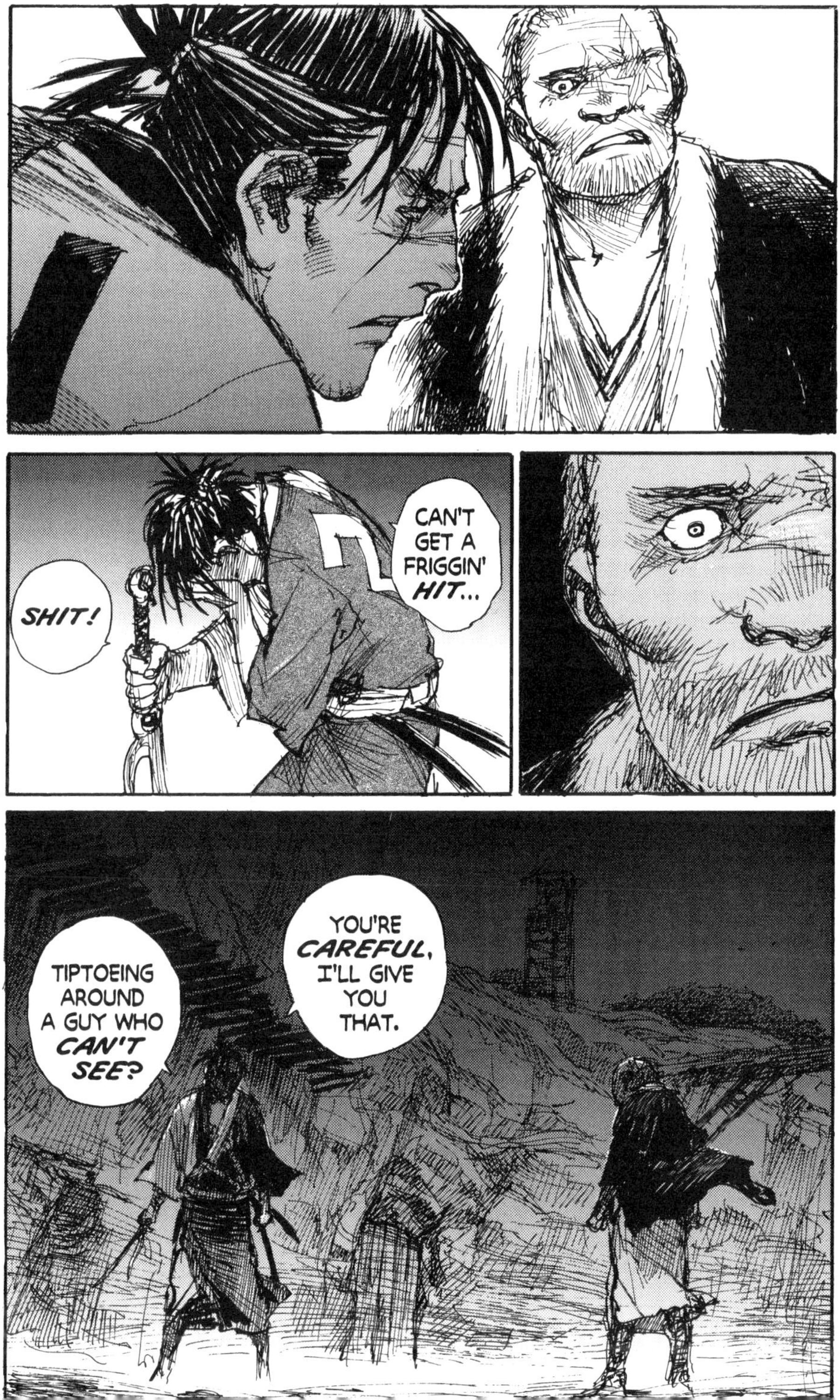
CAN'T GET A FRIGGIN' HIT...
SHIT!
TIPTOEING AROUND A GUY WHO CAN'T SEE?
YOU'RE CAREFUL, I'LL GIVE YOU THAT.

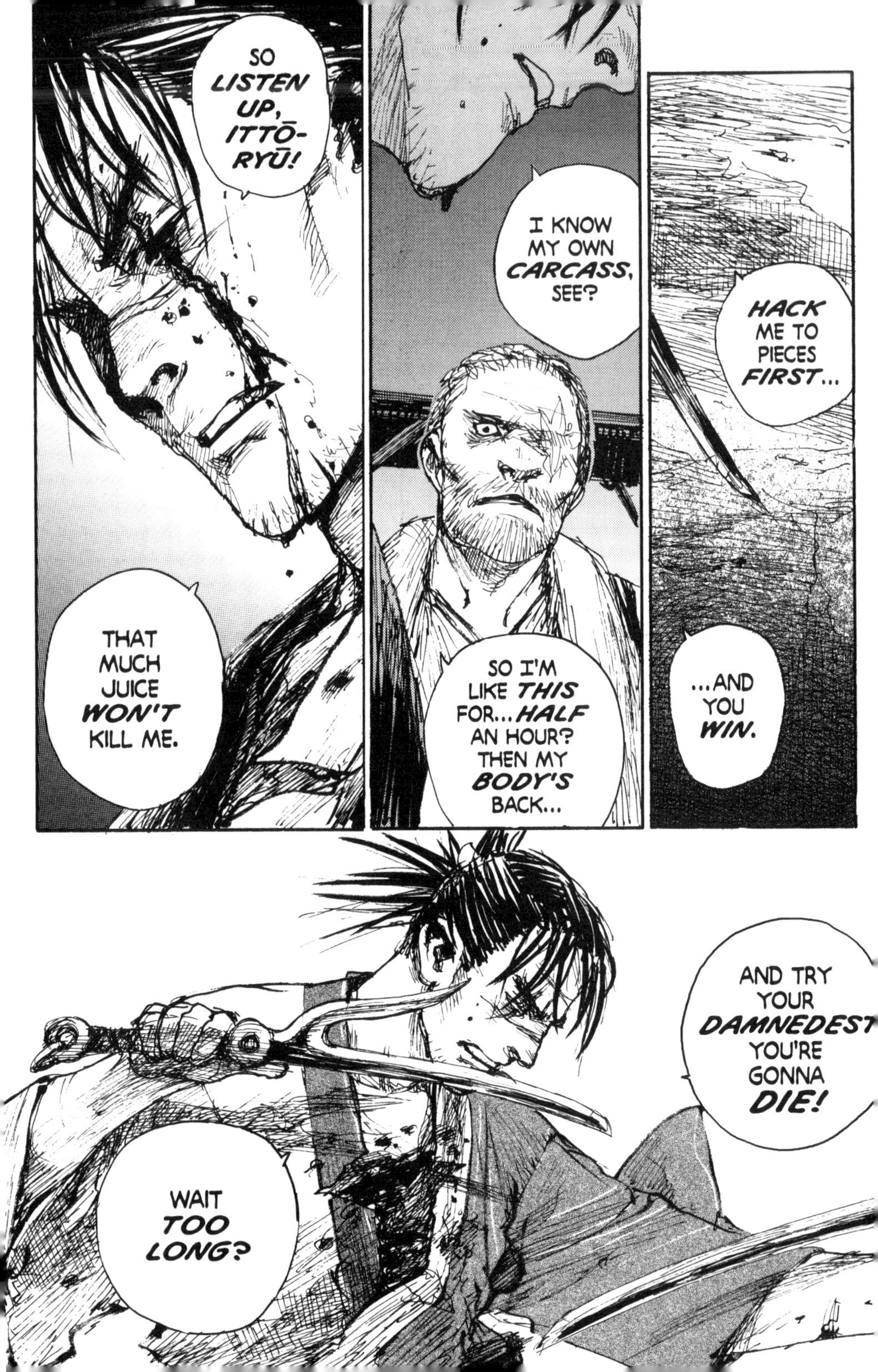
SO LISTEN UP, ITTŌ-RYŪ!
THAT MUCH JUICE WON'T KILL ME.
I KNOW MY OWN CARCASS, SEE?
SO I'M LIKE THIS FOR... HALF AN HOUR? THEN MY BODY'S BACK...
HACK ME TO PIECES FIRST...
...AND YOU WIN.
WAIT TOO LONG?
AND TRY YOUR DAMNEDEST YOU'RE GONNA DIE!

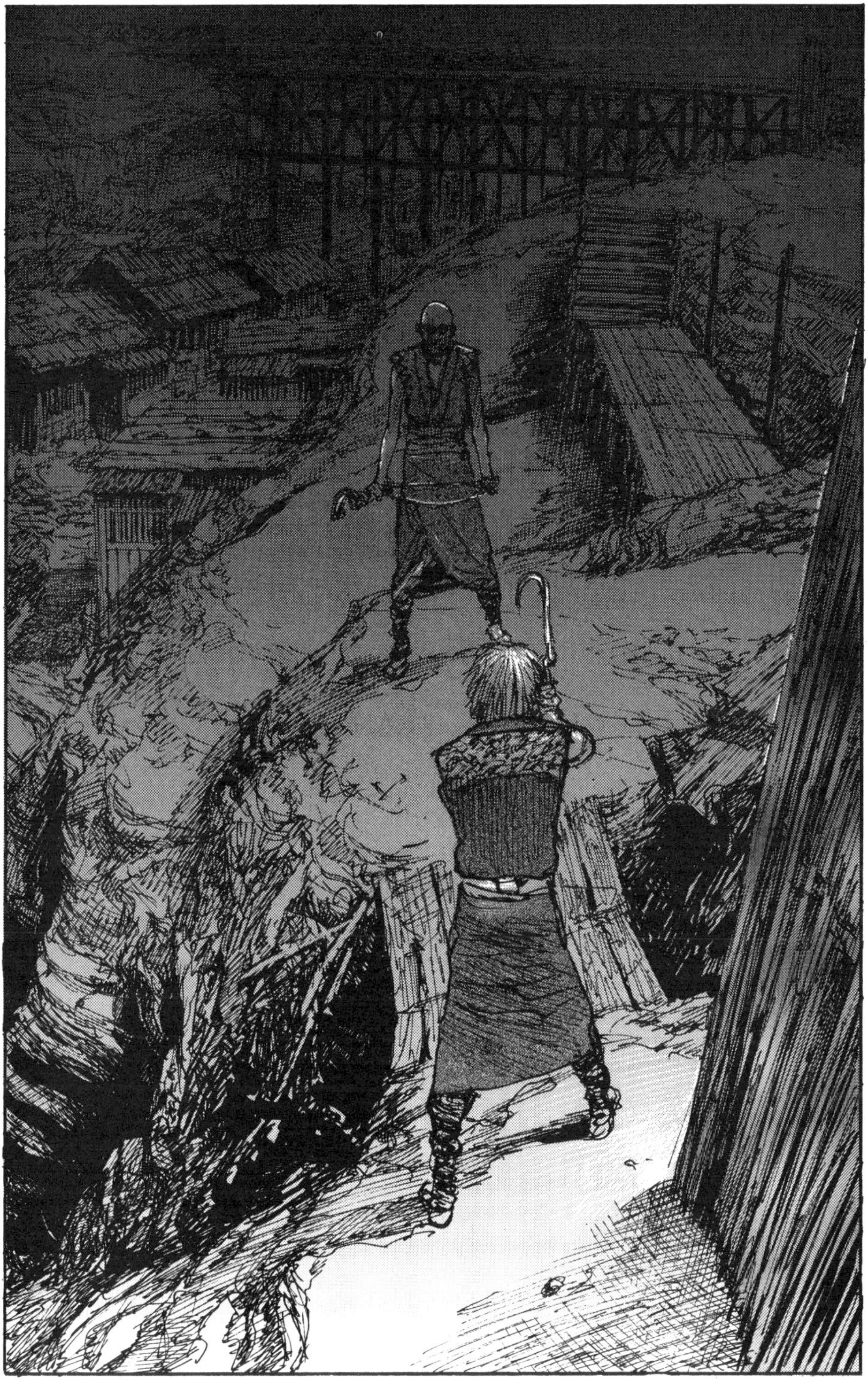

OF THE *ITTŌ-RYŪ* WHO SAW YOUR FACE...

...*TWO* CAME BACK ALIVE.

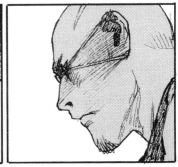

YOU SOME SORTA *RE-TARD...*?

OR JUST FUCKIN' *CON-FIDENT*?

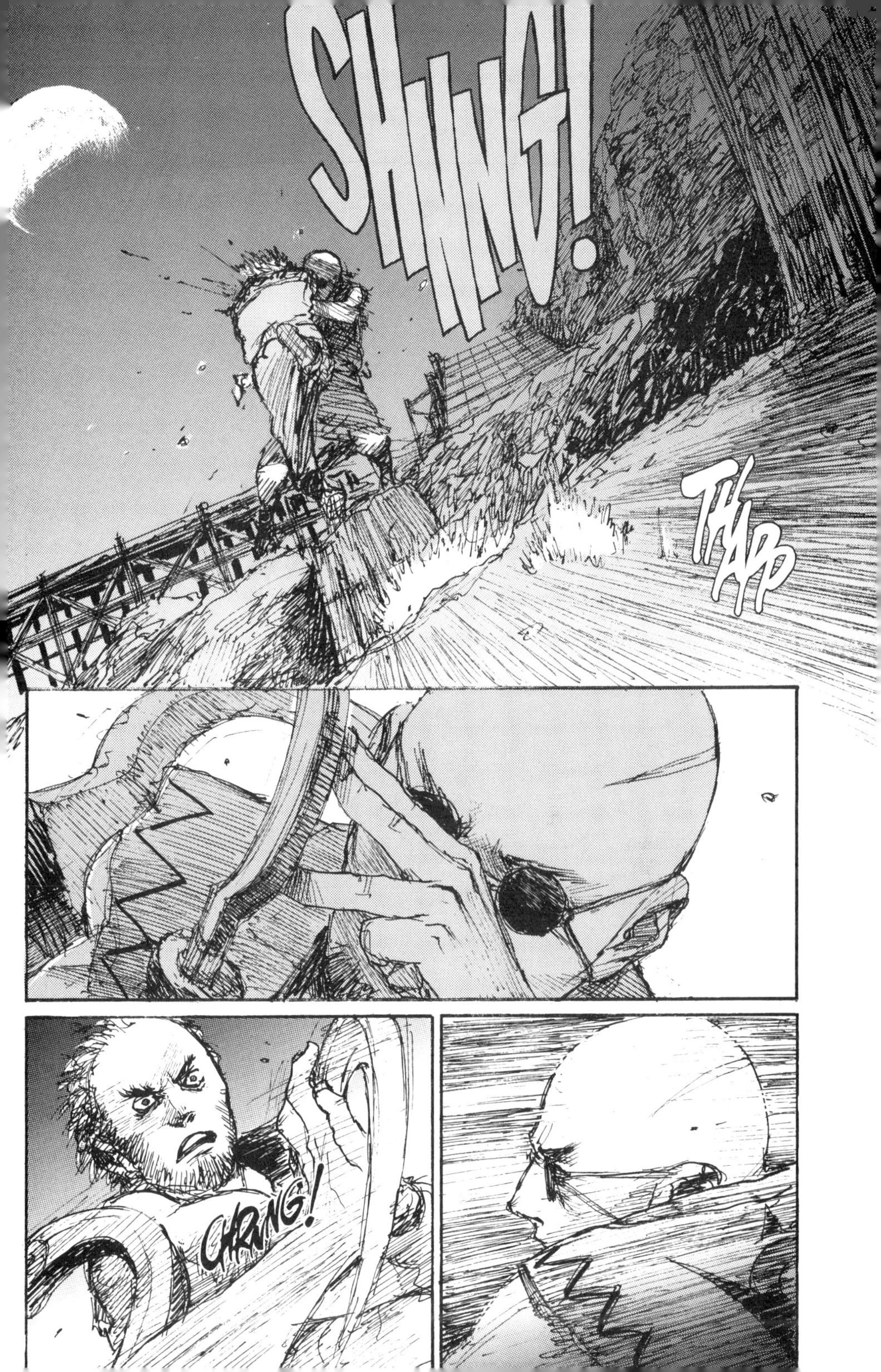
SHING!
TH'APP
CHRNG!

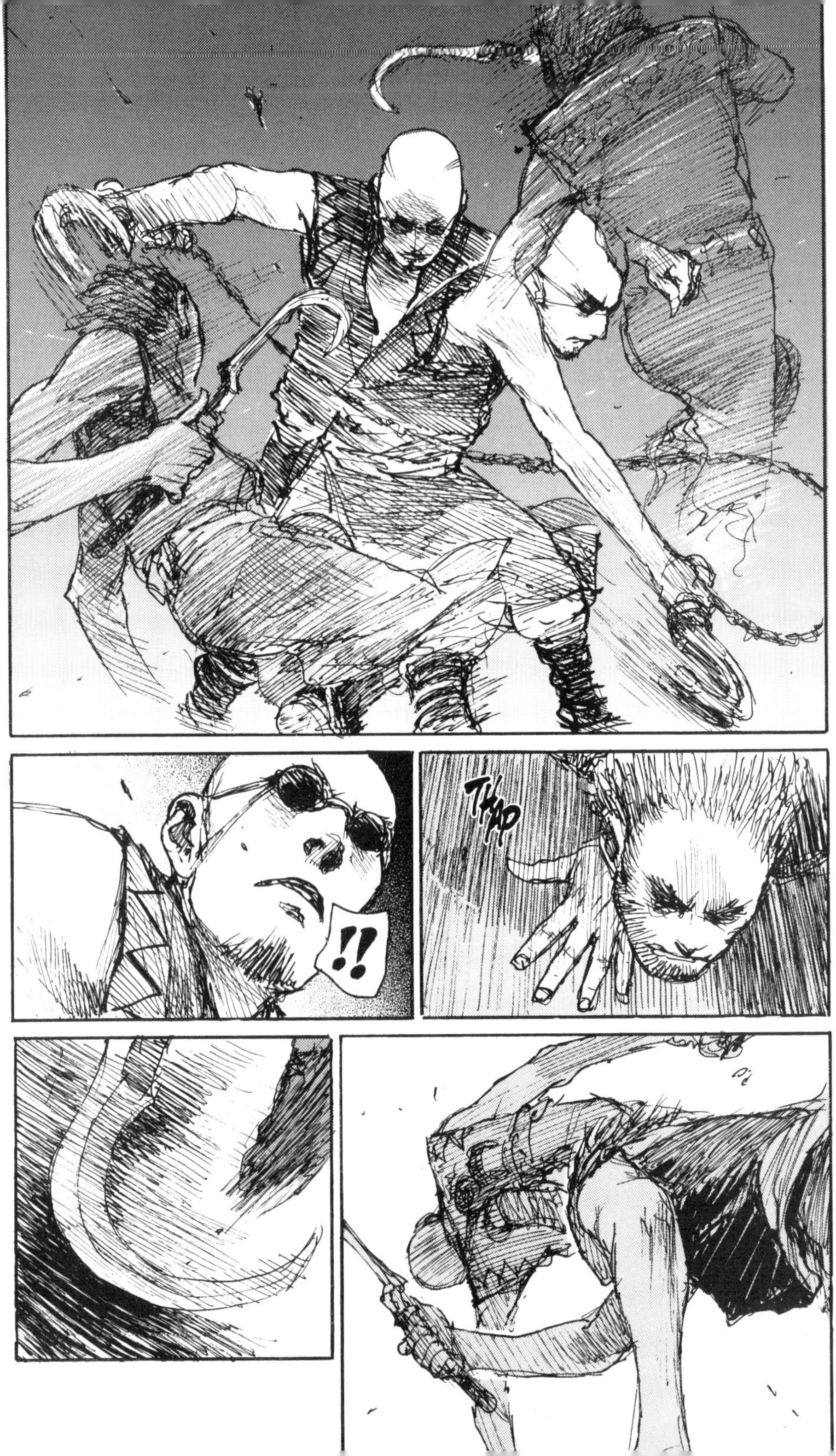
!!
THAP

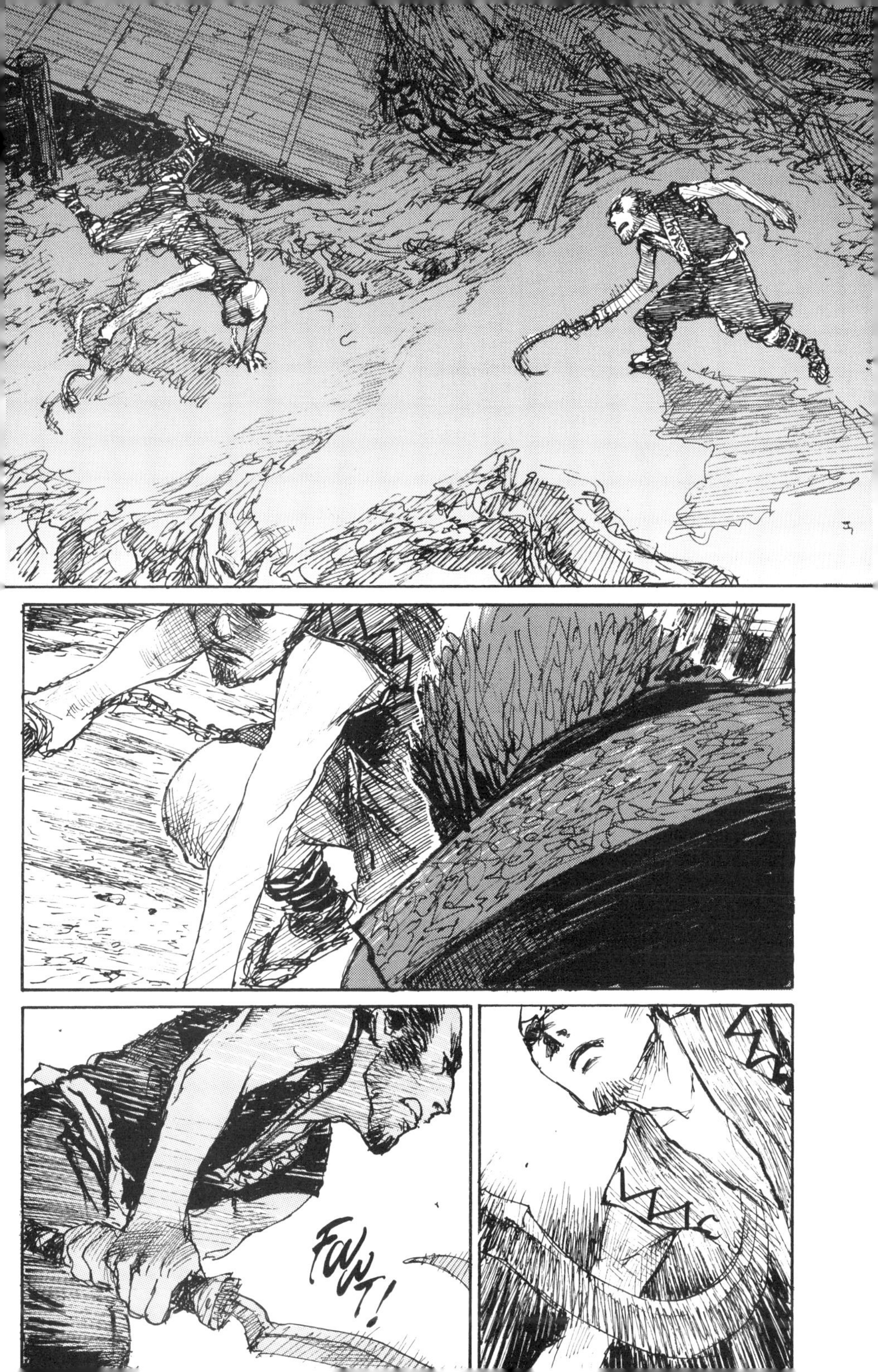
FWNT!

SHAK
!

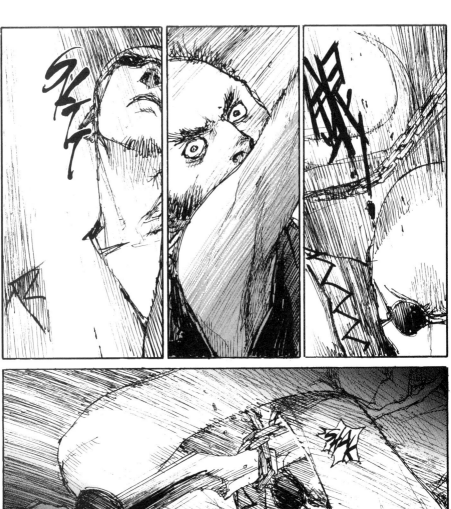

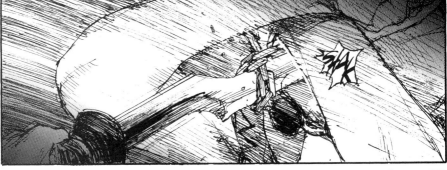

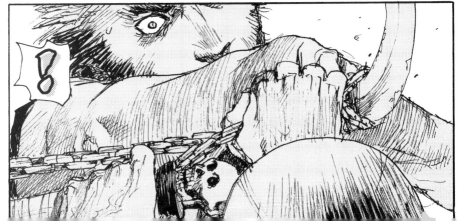

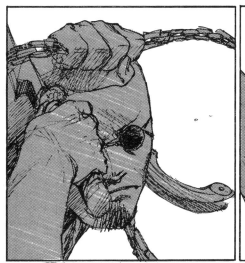

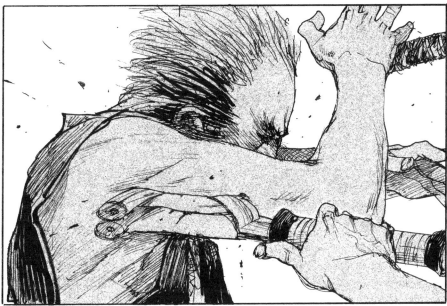

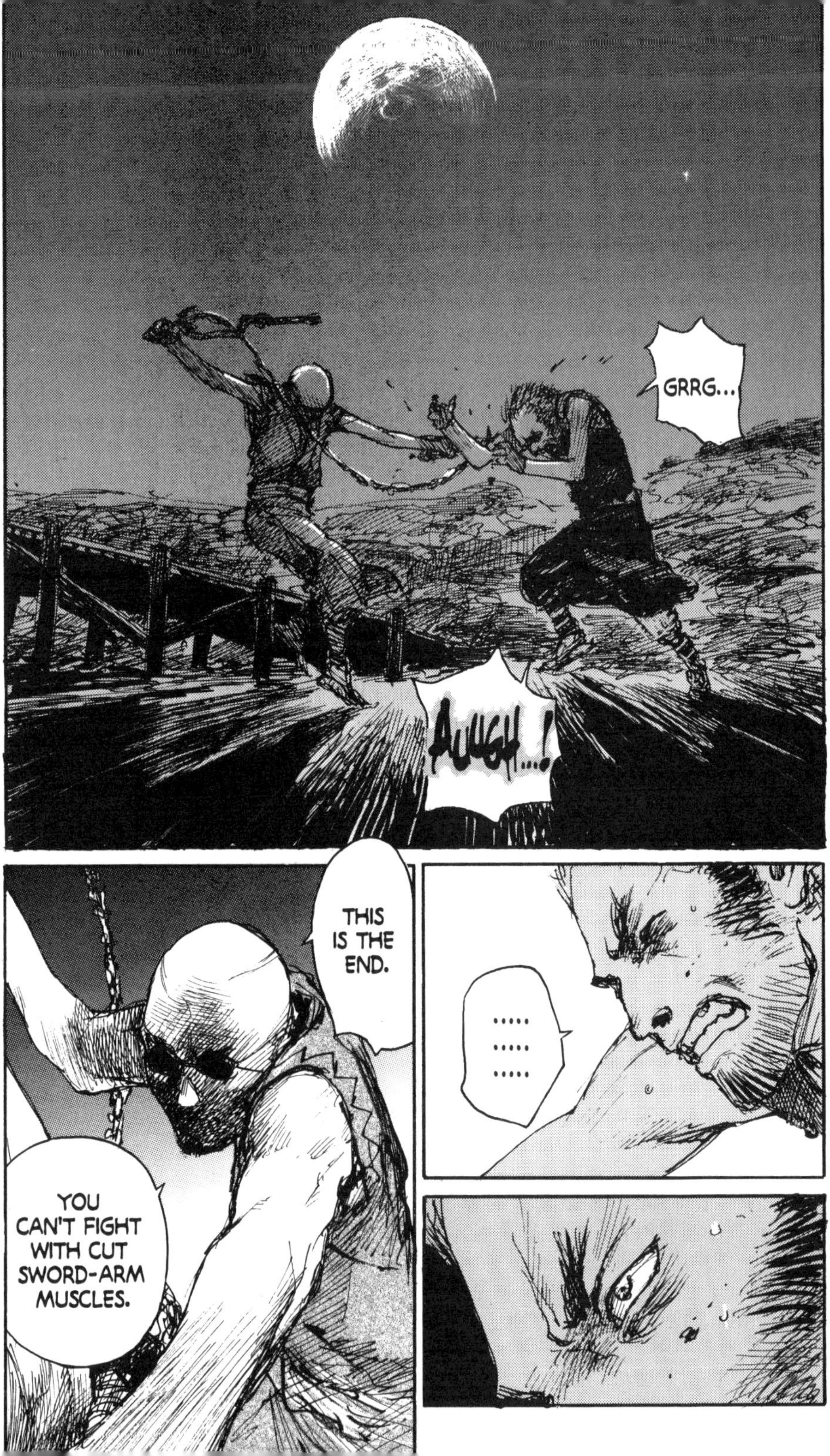
GRRG...
AUUGH...!
THIS IS THE END.
YOU CAN'T FIGHT WITH CUT SWORD-ARM MUSCLES.
.....
.....
.....

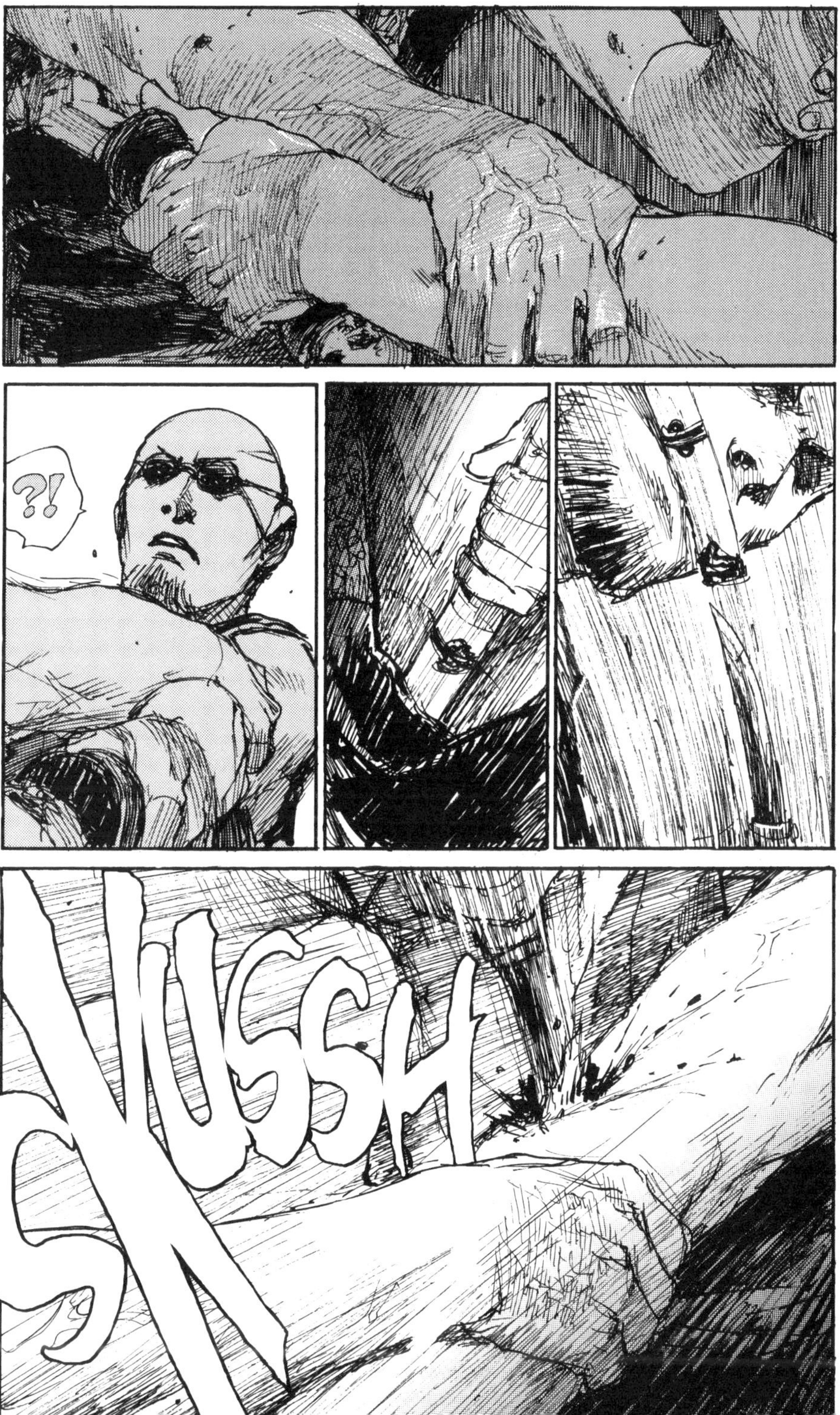
?!
SKUSSH

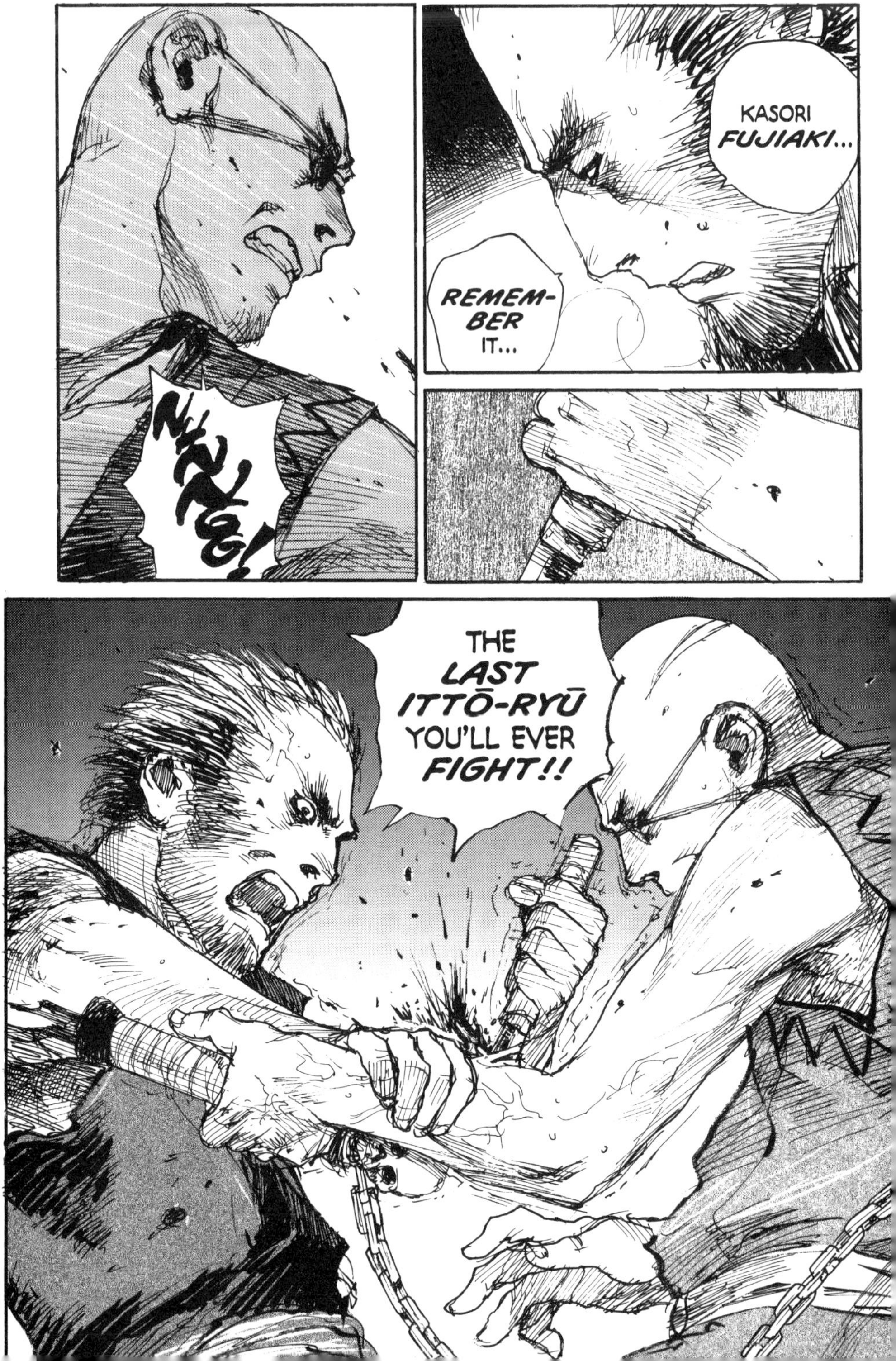
NNNGG!
KASORI FUJIAKI...
REMEMBER IT...
THE LAST ITTŌ-RYŪ YOU'LL EVER FIGHT!!

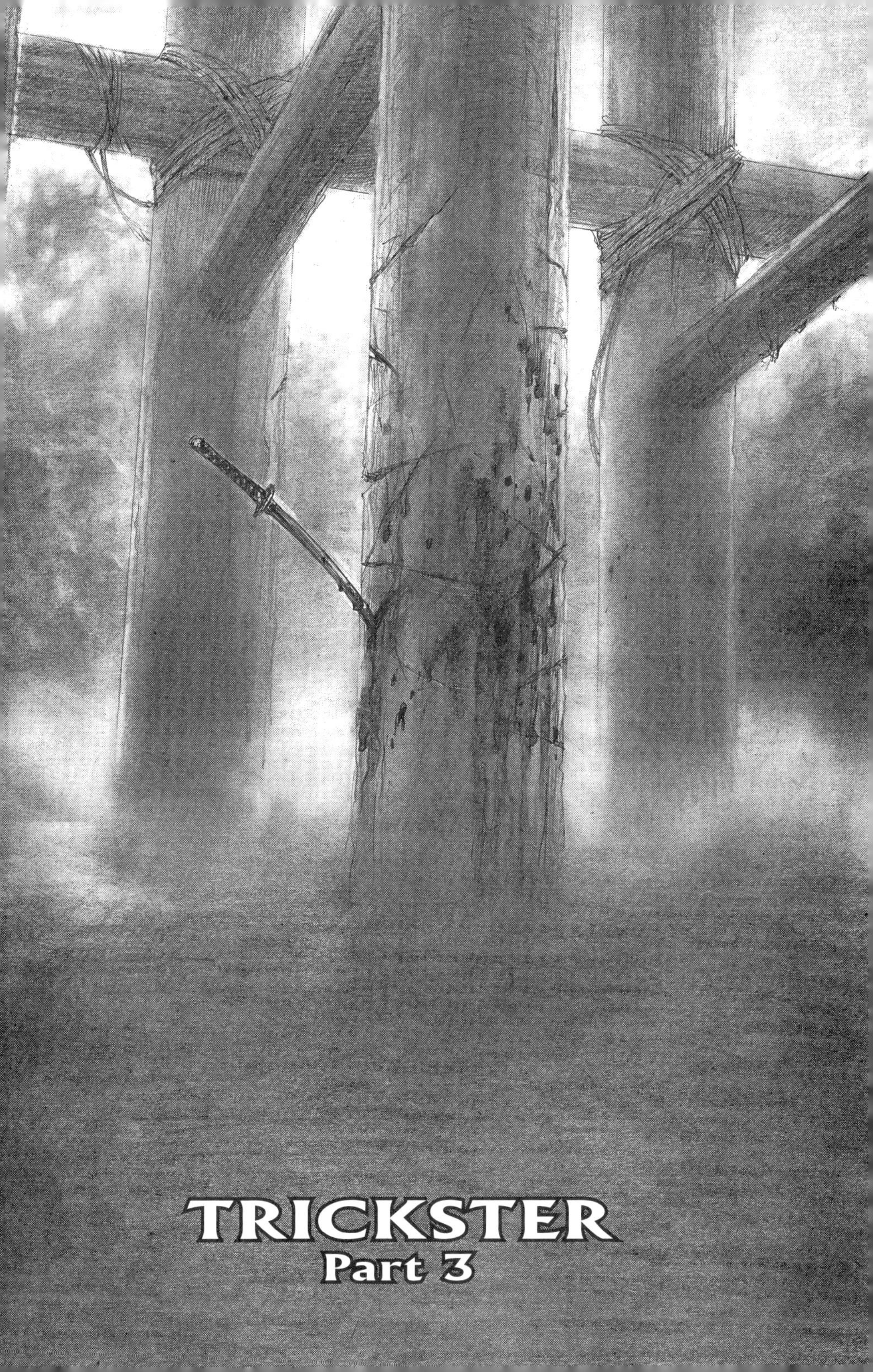
TRICKSTER
Part 3

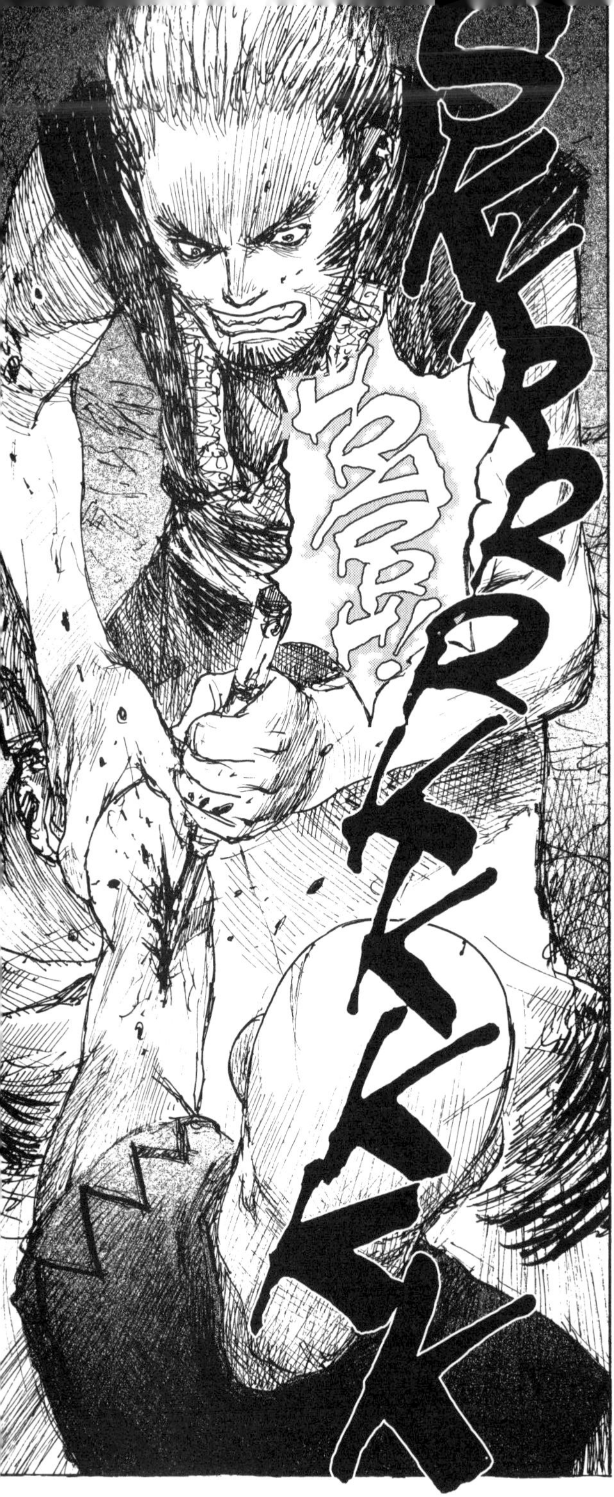

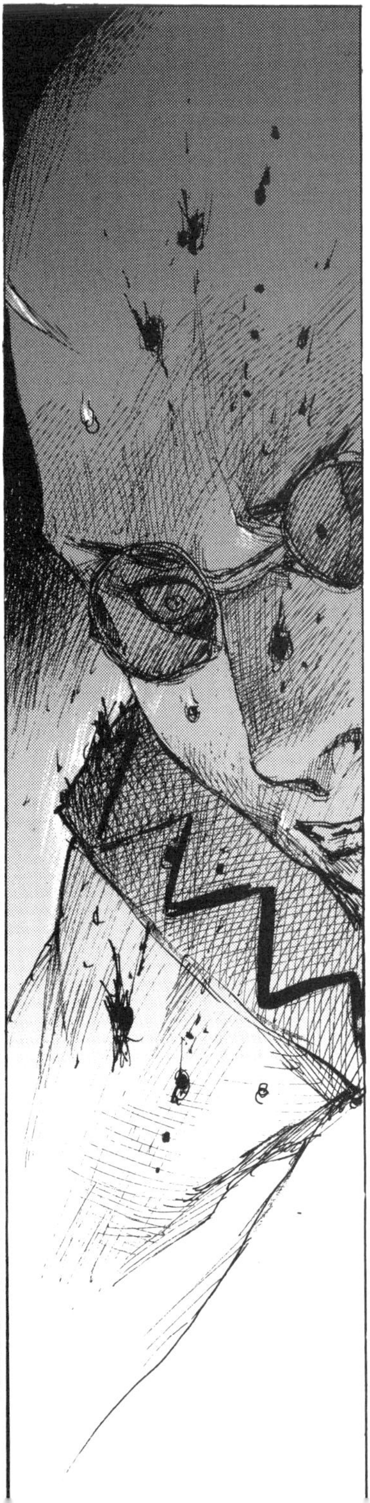

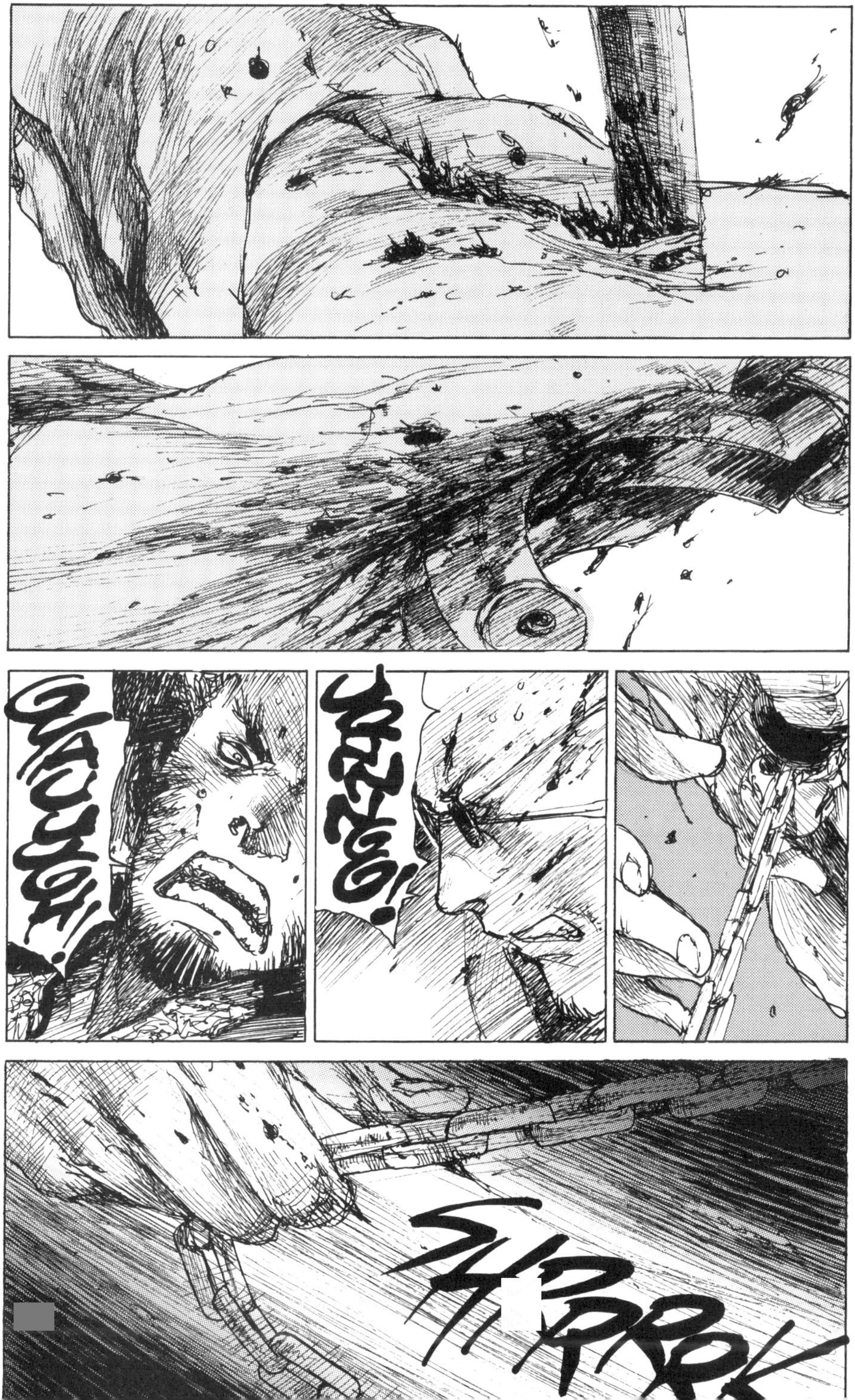
SHRRRK

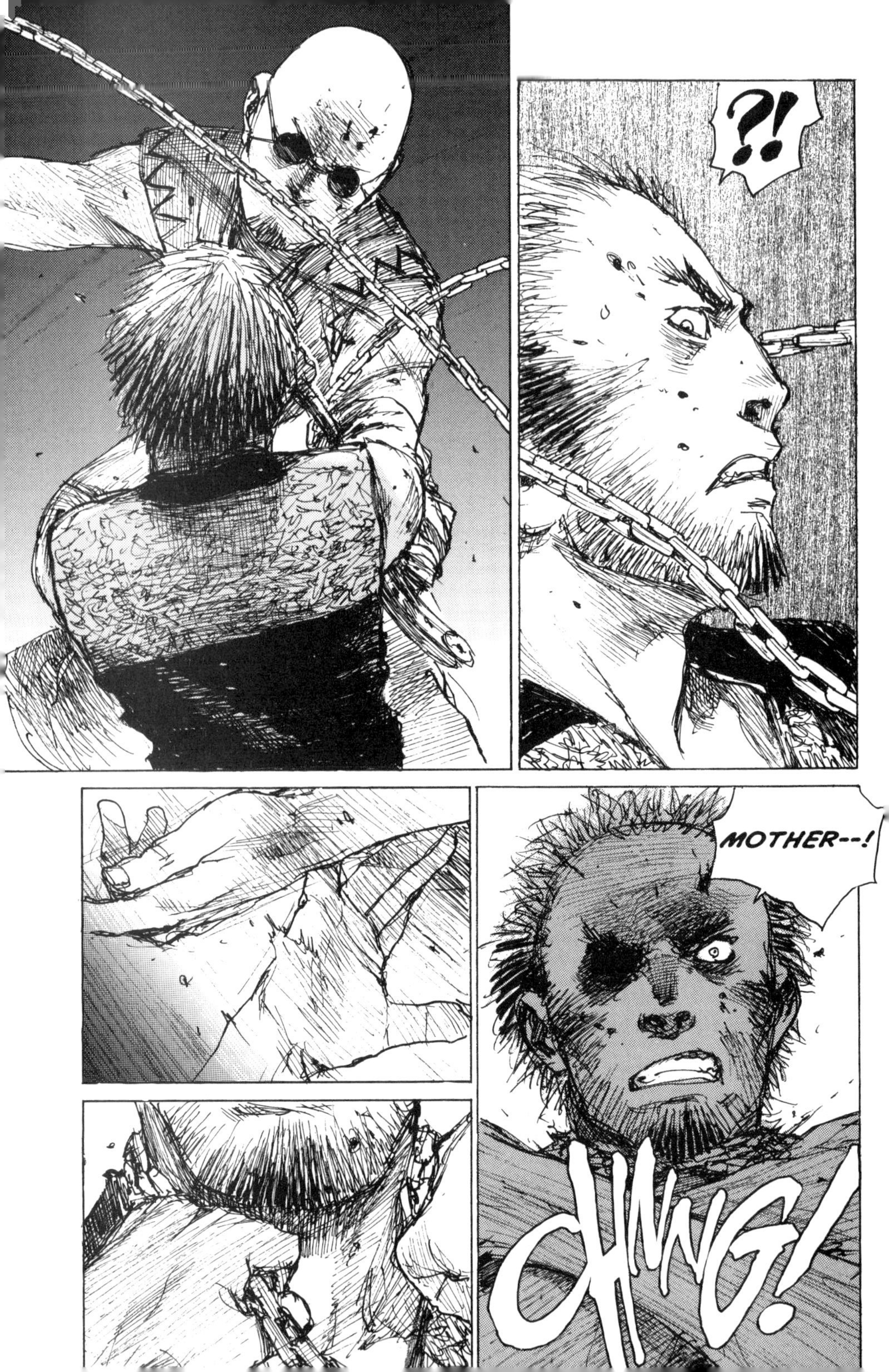
?!
MOTHER--!
CHANG!

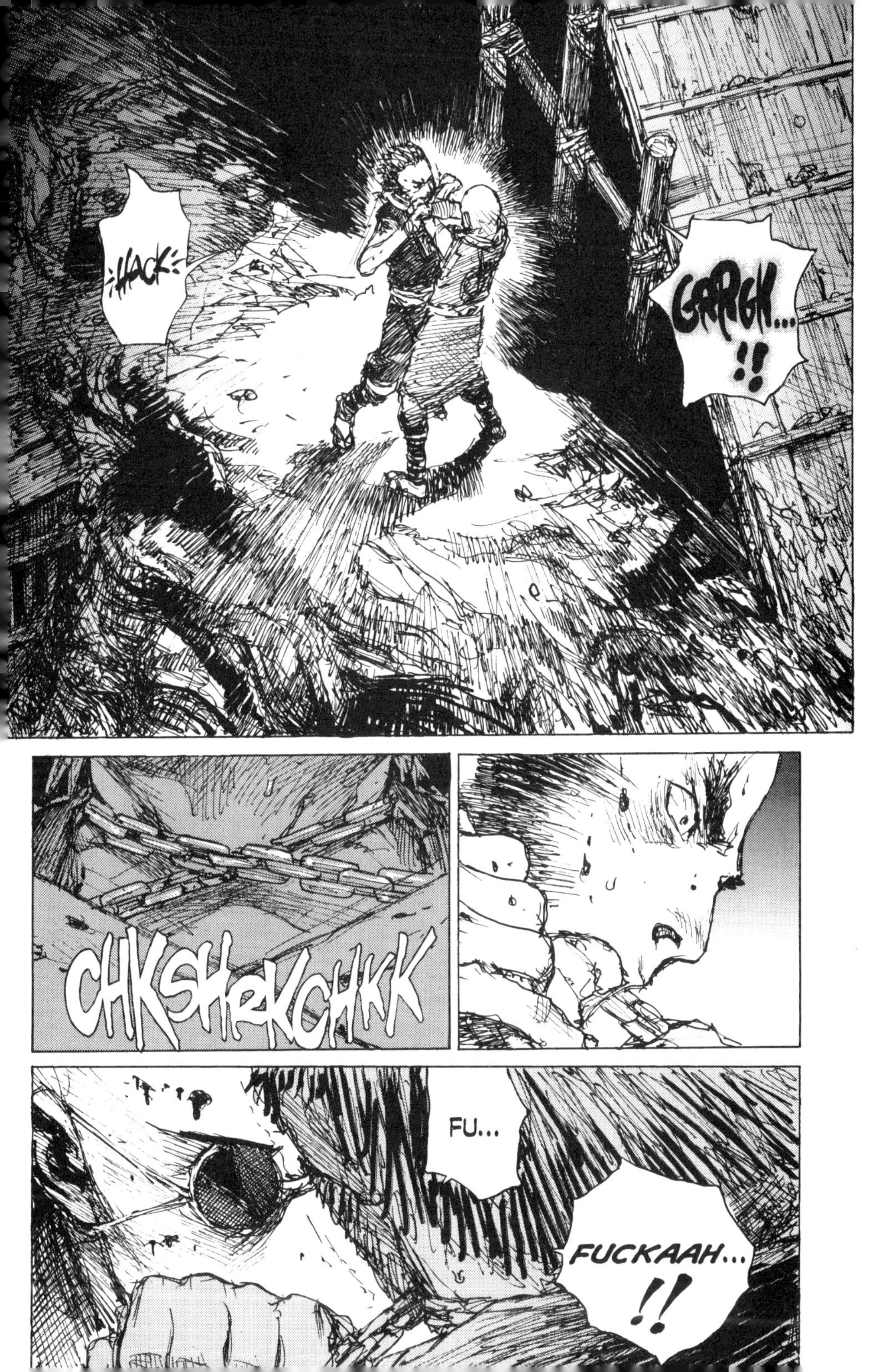
HACK
GRRGH...!!
CHKSHRKCHKK
FU...
FUCKAAH...!!

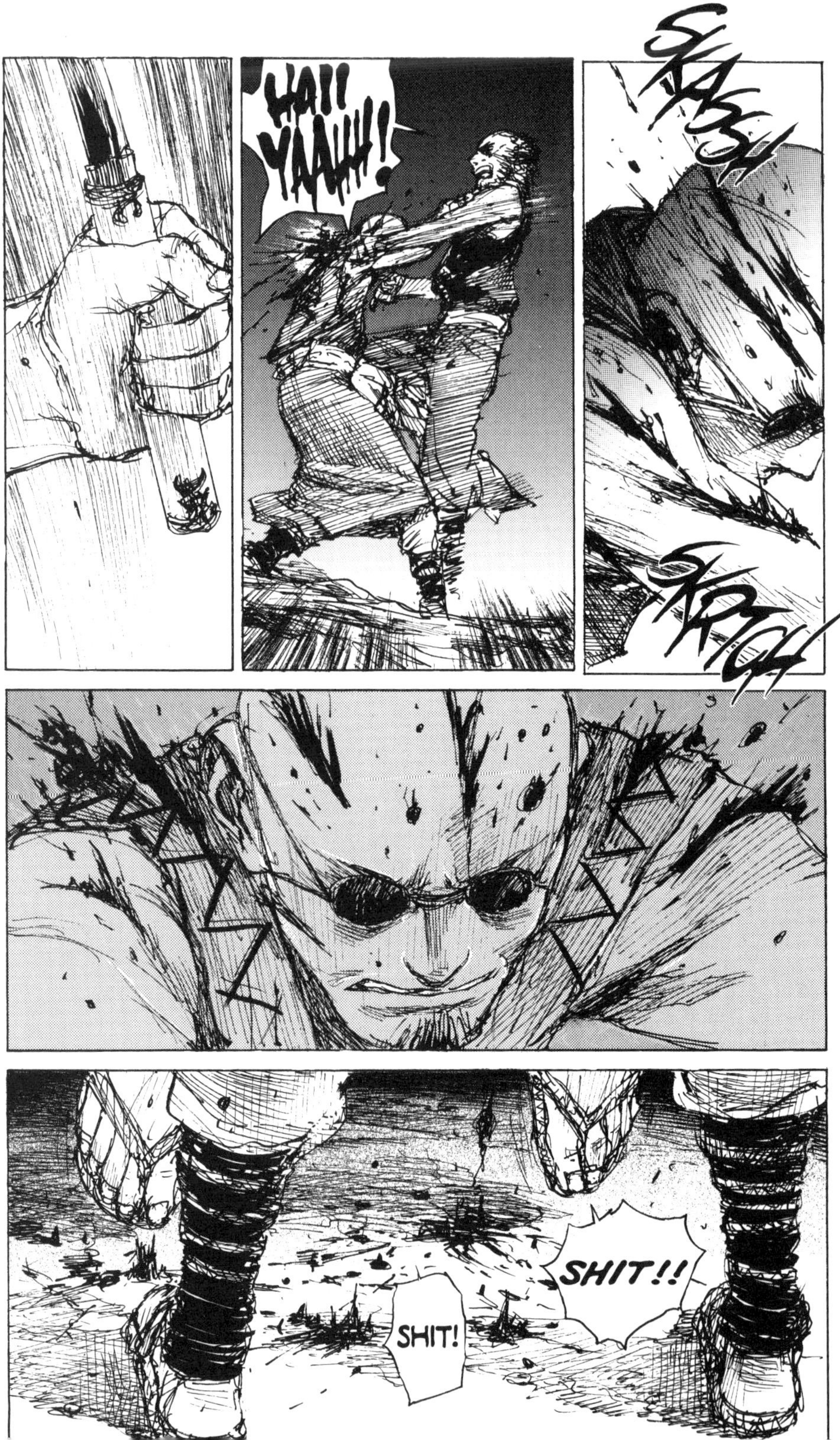
HAI! YAAH!
SKASH
SKRITCH
SHIT!
SHIT!!

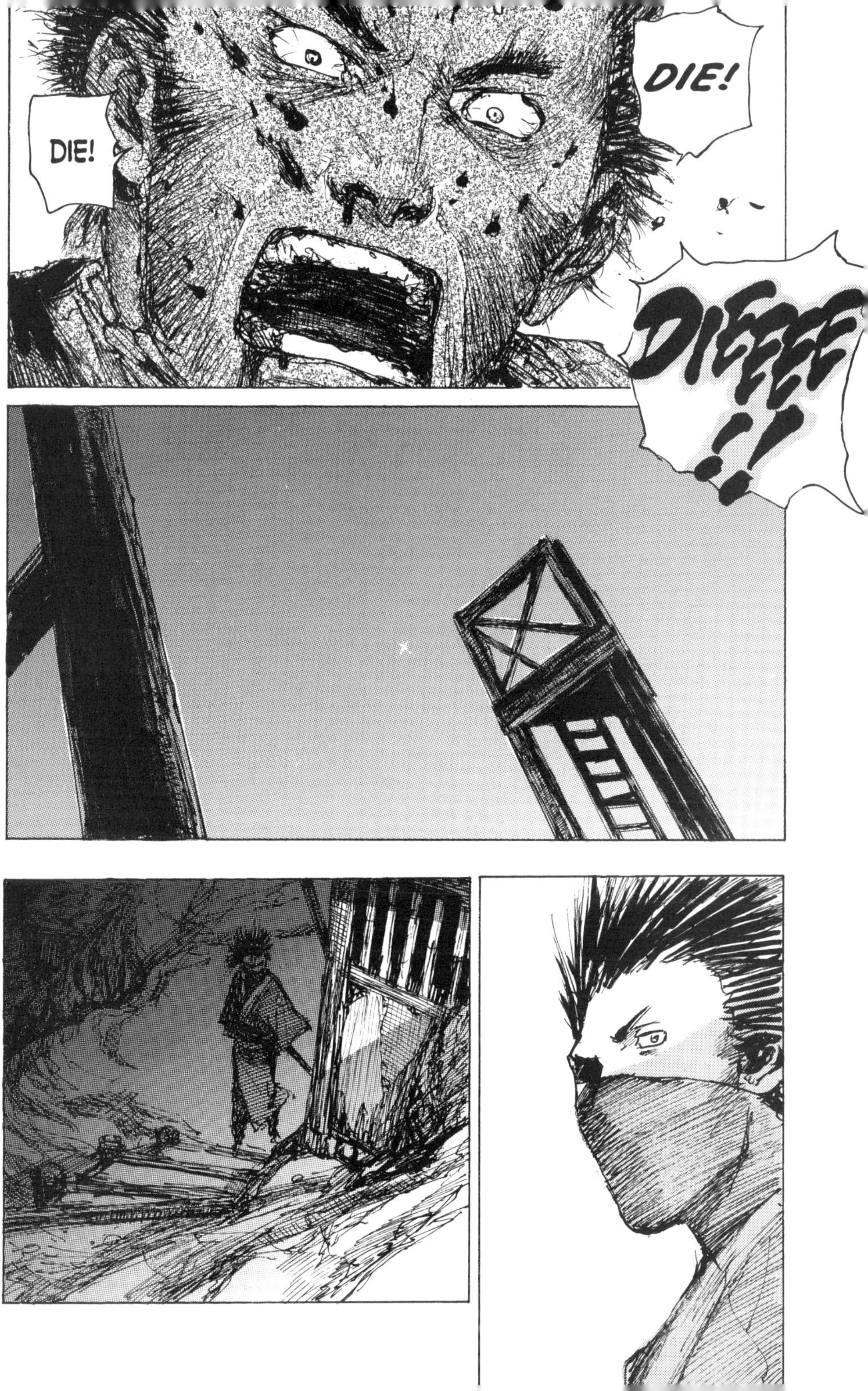
DIE!
DIE!
DIEEEE!!

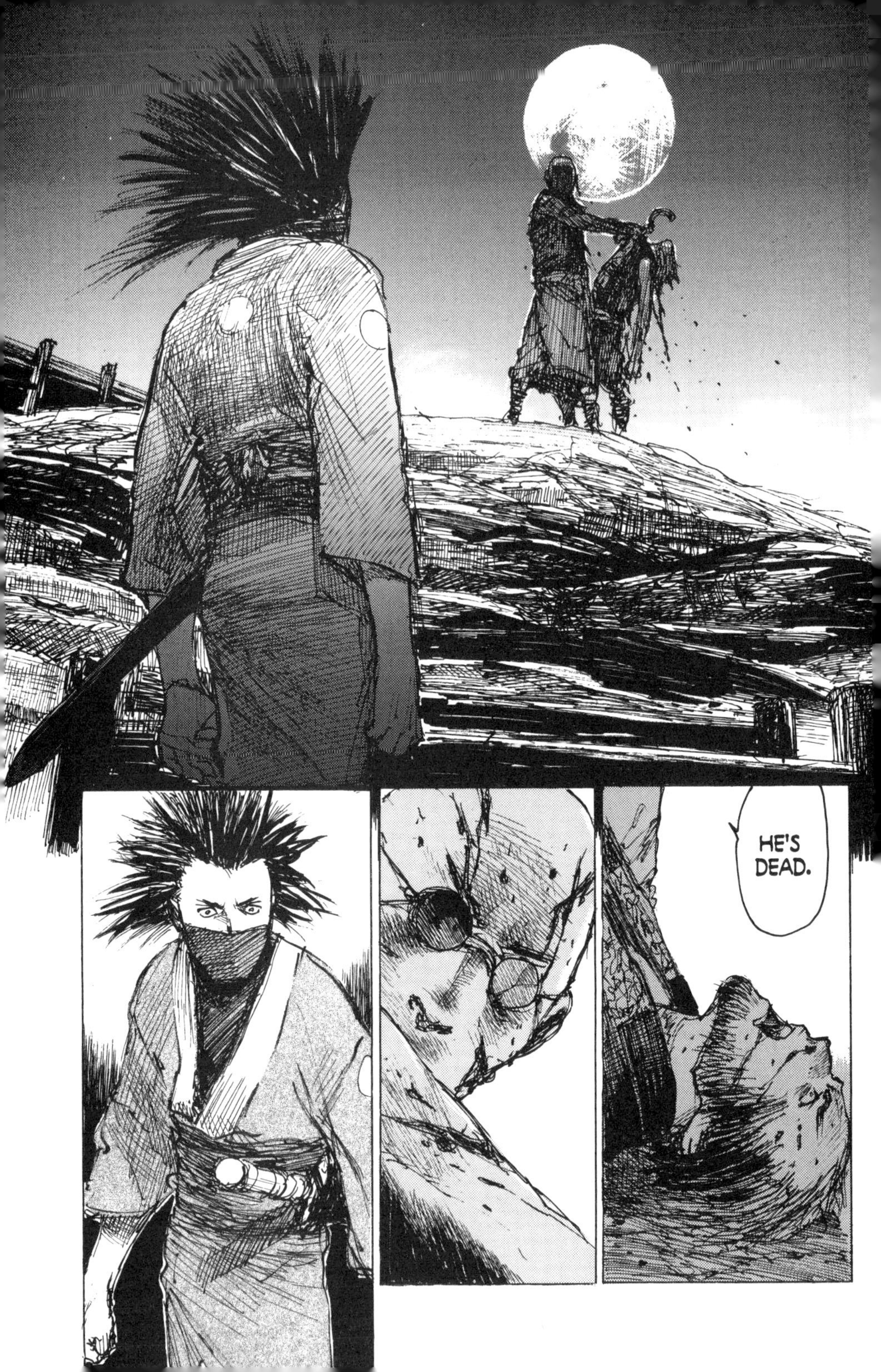
HE'S DEAD.

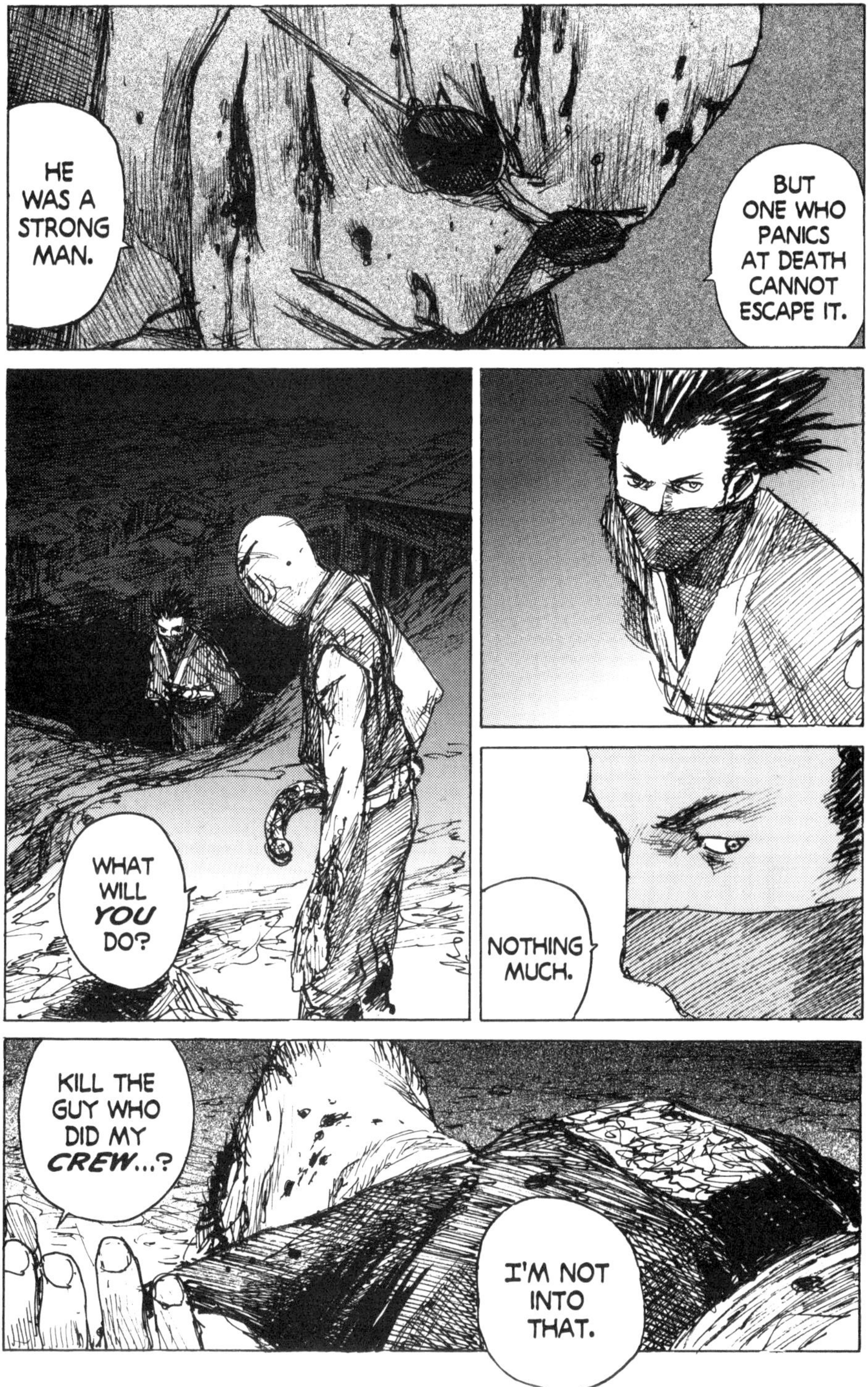
HE WAS A STRONG MAN.
BUT ONE WHO PANICS AT DEATH CANNOT ESCAPE IT.
WHAT WILL *YOU* DO?
NOTHING MUCH.
KILL THE GUY WHO DID MY *CREW*...?
I'M NOT INTO THAT.

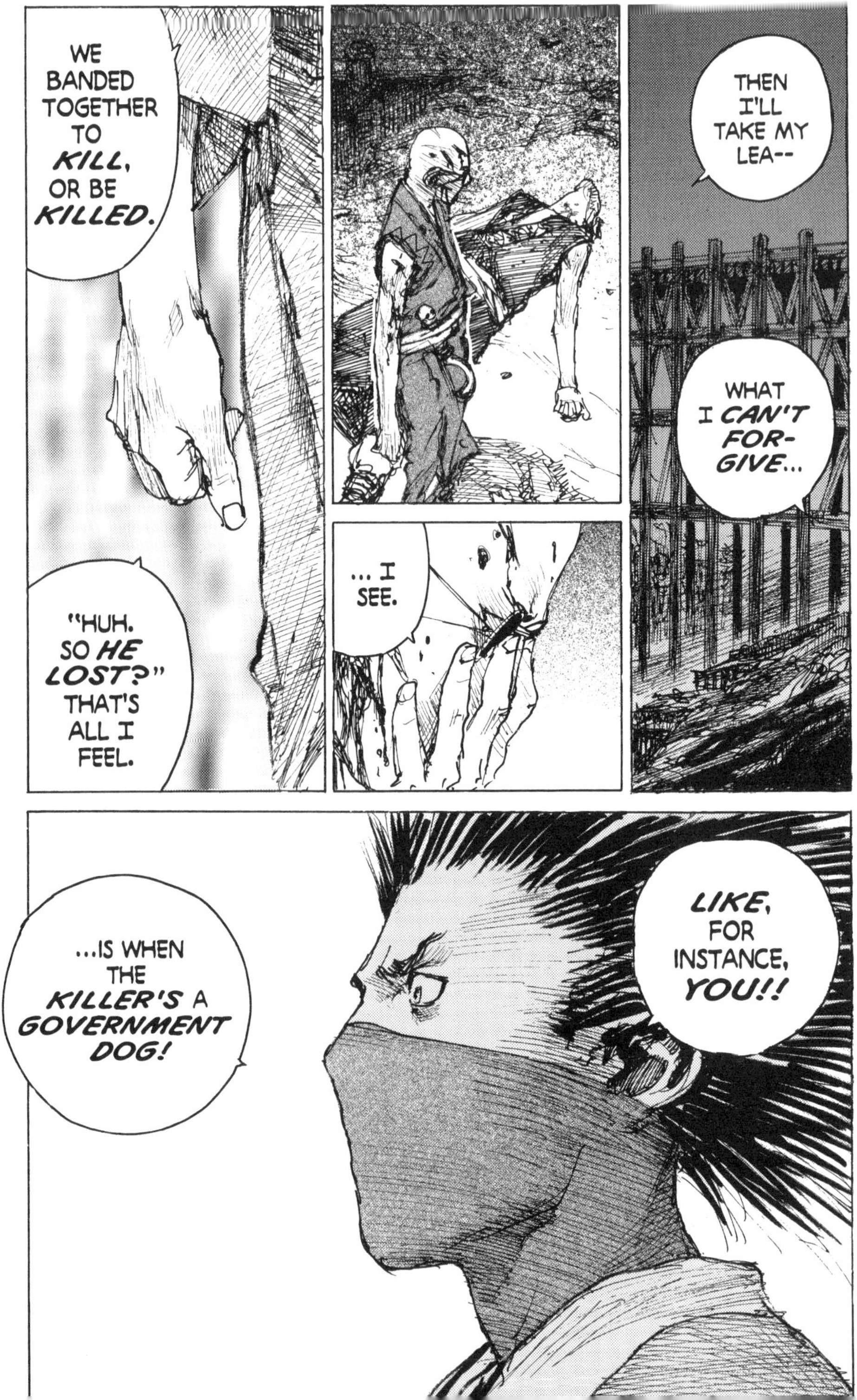
WE BANDED TOGETHER TO KILL, OR BE KILLED.
"HUH. SO HE LOST?" THAT'S ALL I FEEL.
... I SEE.
THEN I'LL TAKE MY LEA--
WHAT I CAN'T FOR-GIVE...
...IS WHEN THE KILLER'S A GOVERNMENT DOG!
LIKE, FOR INSTANCE, YOU!!

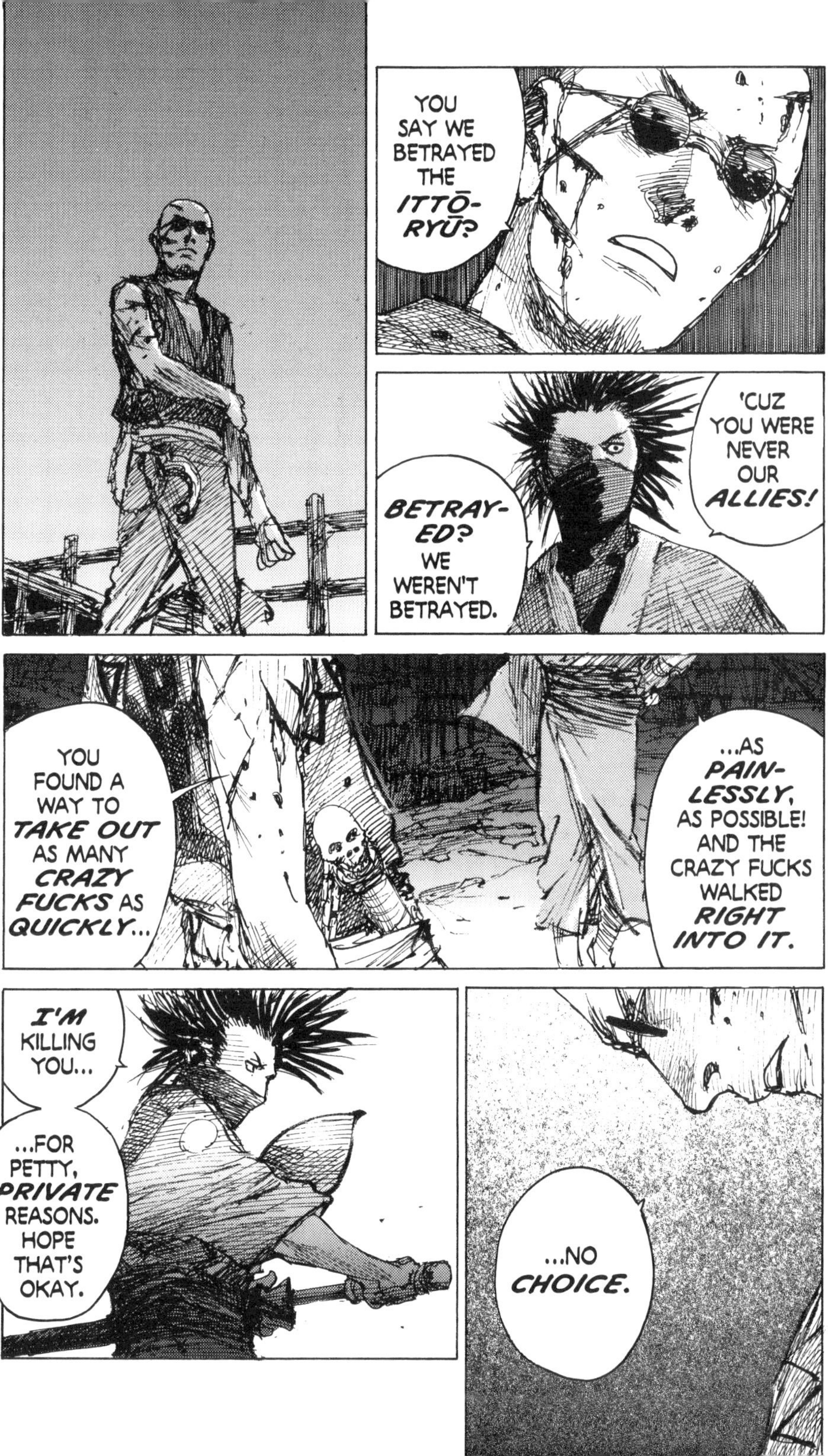
YOU SAY WE BETRAYED THE ITTŌ-RYŪ?
BETRAYED? WE WEREN'T BETRAYED.
'CUZ YOU WERE NEVER OUR ALLIES!
YOU FOUND A WAY TO TAKE OUT AS MANY CRAZY FUCKS AS QUICKLY...
...AS PAINLESSLY, AS POSSIBLE! AND THE CRAZY FUCKS WALKED RIGHT INTO IT.
I'M KILLING YOU...
...FOR PETTY, PRIVATE REASONS. HOPE THAT'S OKAY.
...NO CHOICE.

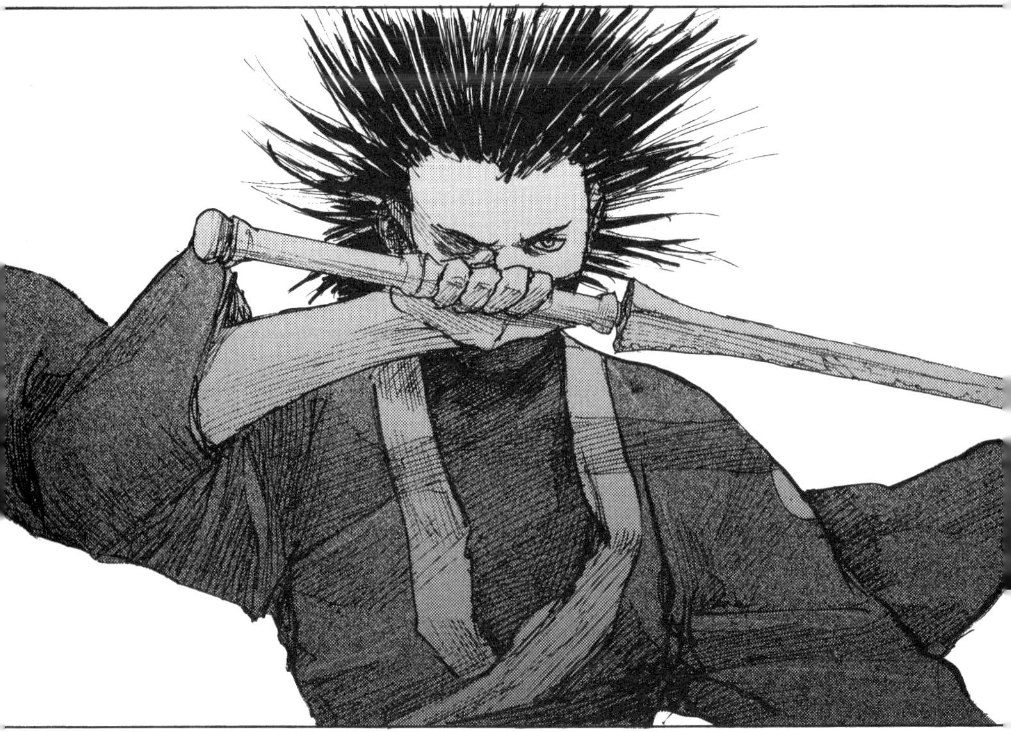

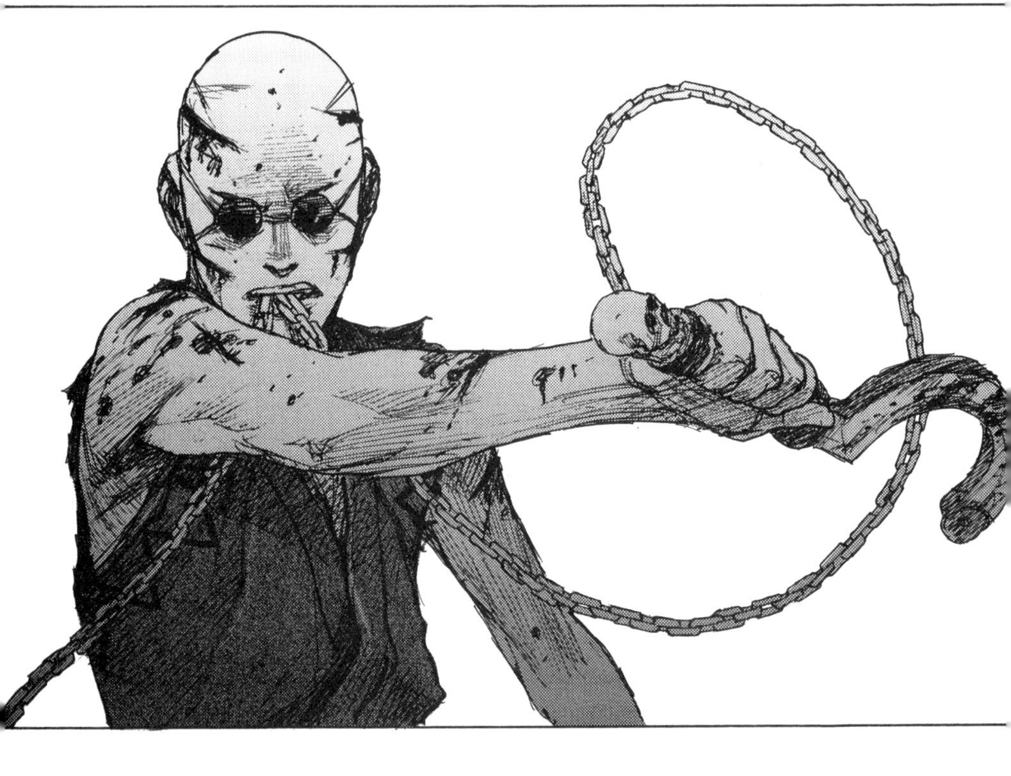

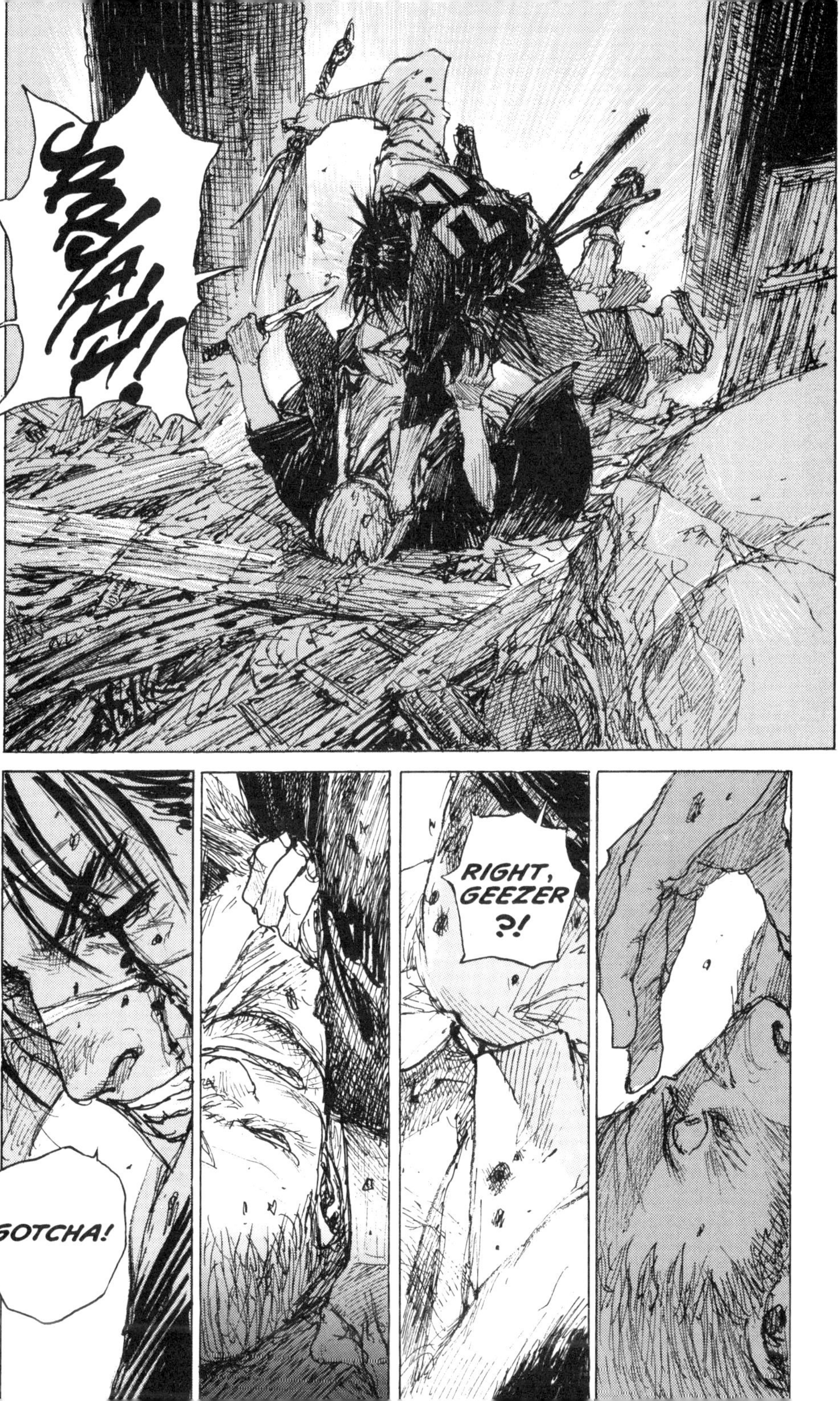
GOTCHA!
RIGHT, GEEZER ?!

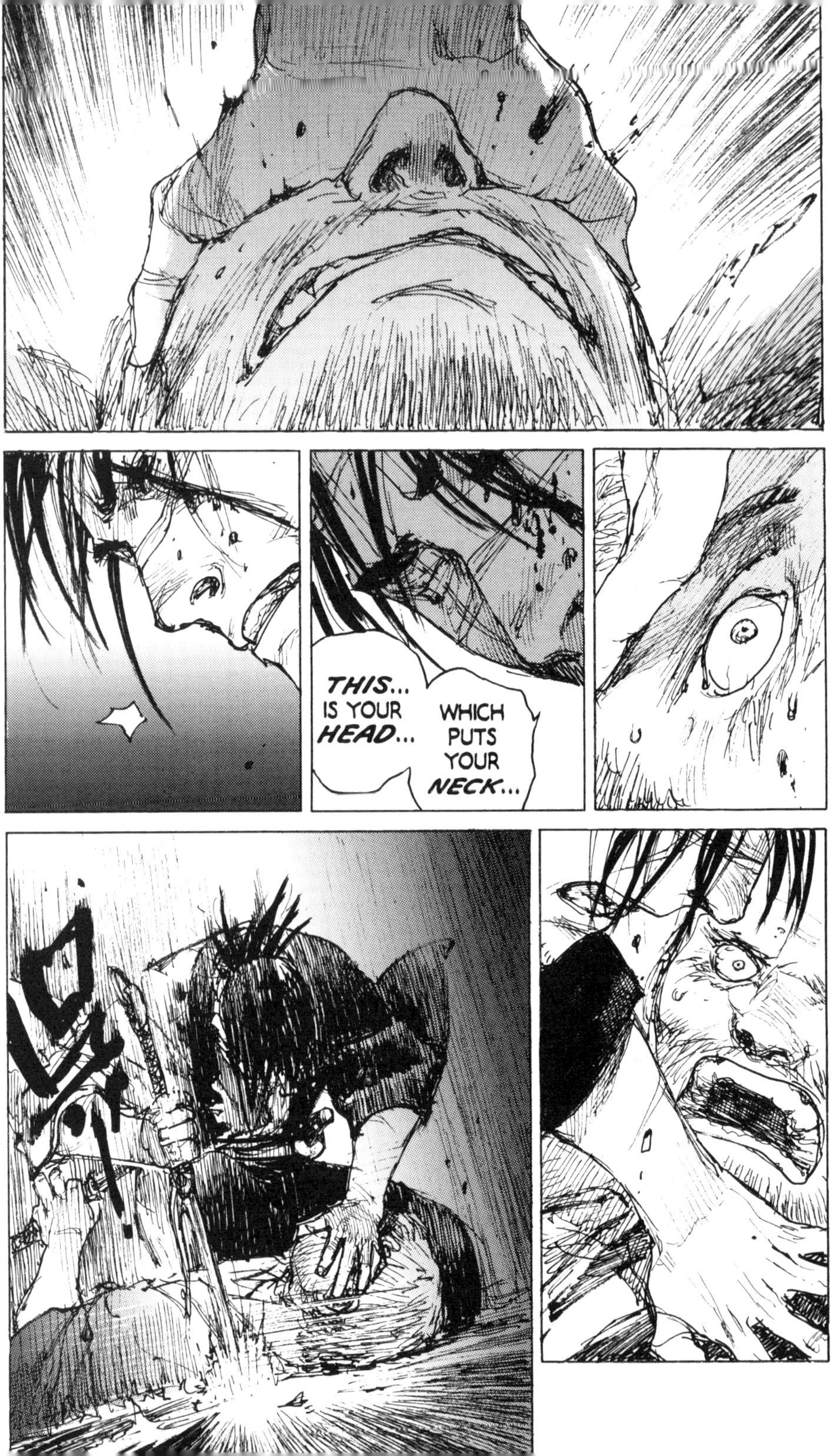
THIS... IS YOUR HEAD...
WHICH PUTS YOUR NECK...

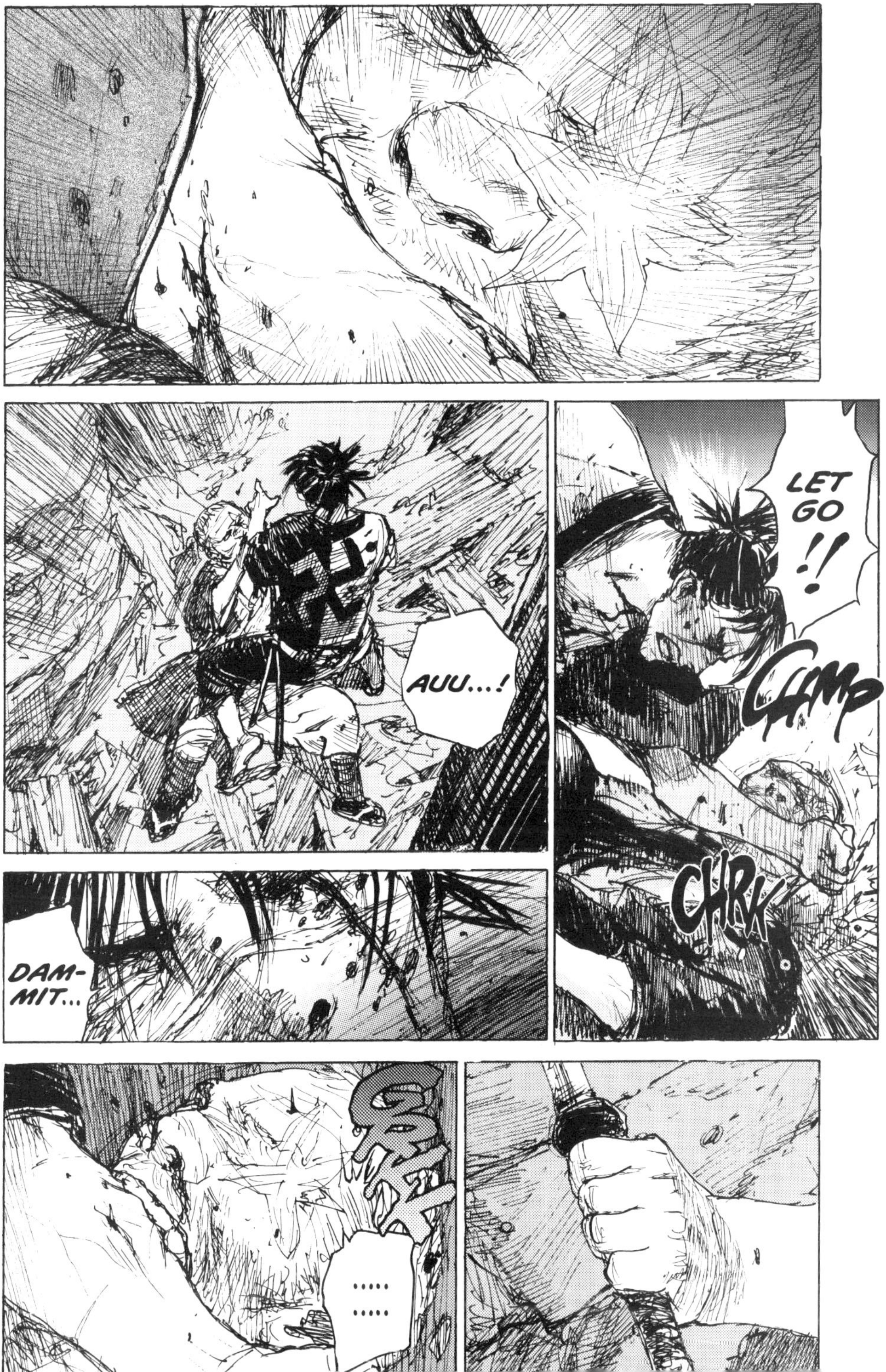
AUU...!
DAM-MIT...
LET GO!!
CLAMP
CHRK
......
......

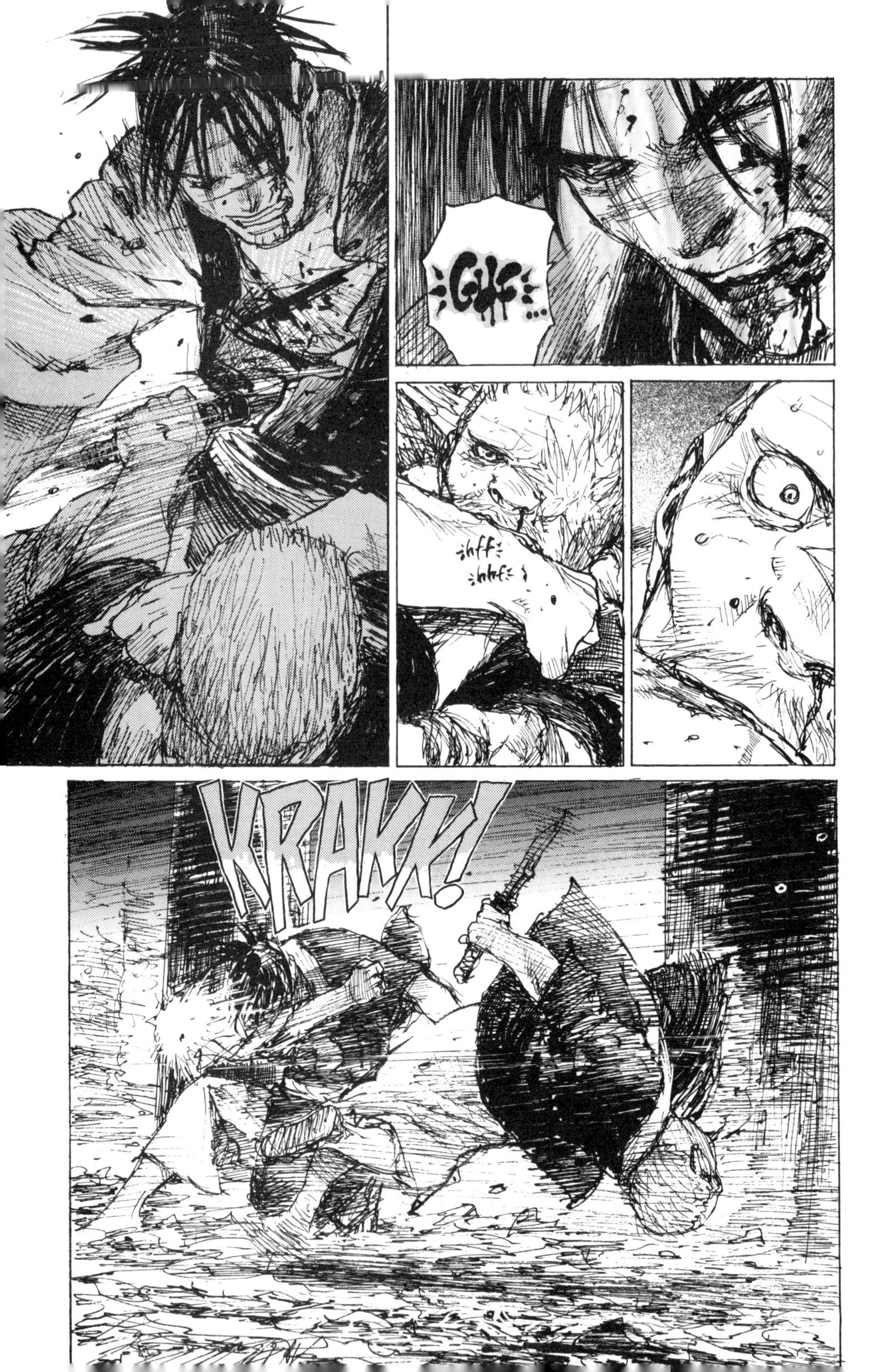
GHF...
hff
hhf
KRAKK!

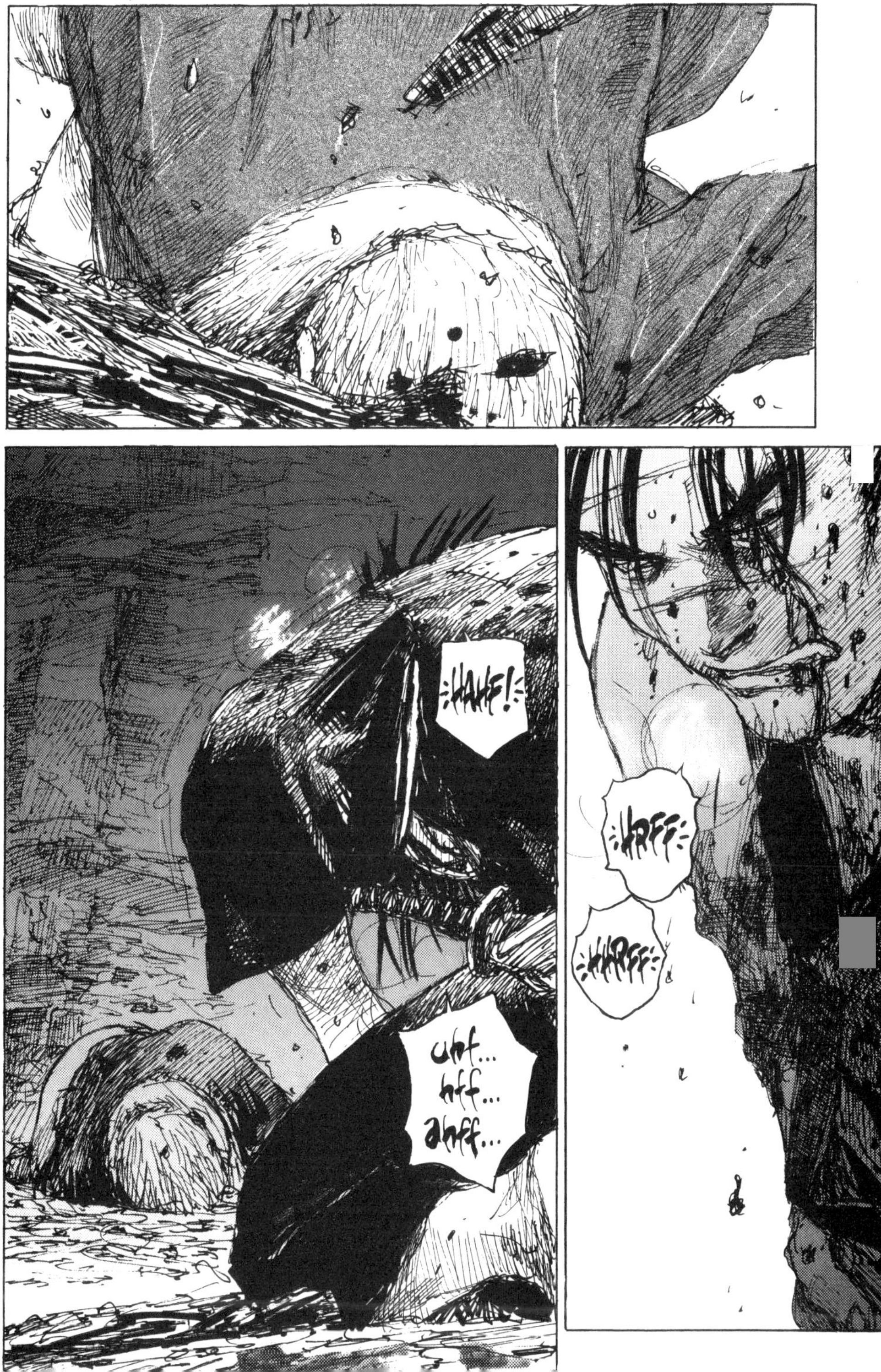
HAHF!
uhf... hff... ahff...
HAFF
HHAFF

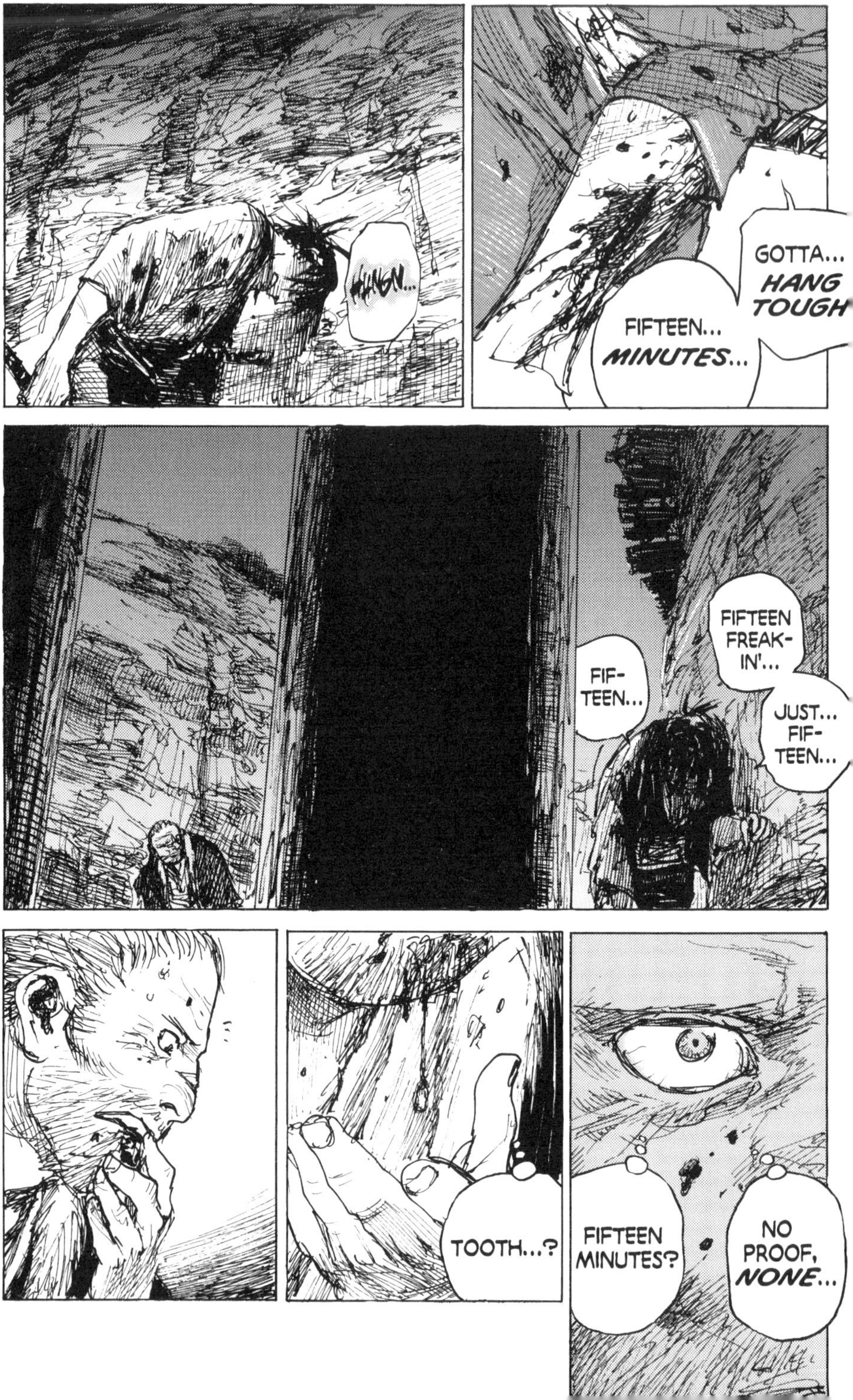
HNGN...
FIFTEEN... MINUTES...
GOTTA... HANG TOUGH
FIF-TEEN...
FIFTEEN FREAK-IN'...
JUST... FIF-TEEN...
TOOTH...?
FIFTEEN MINUTES?
NO PROOF, NONE...

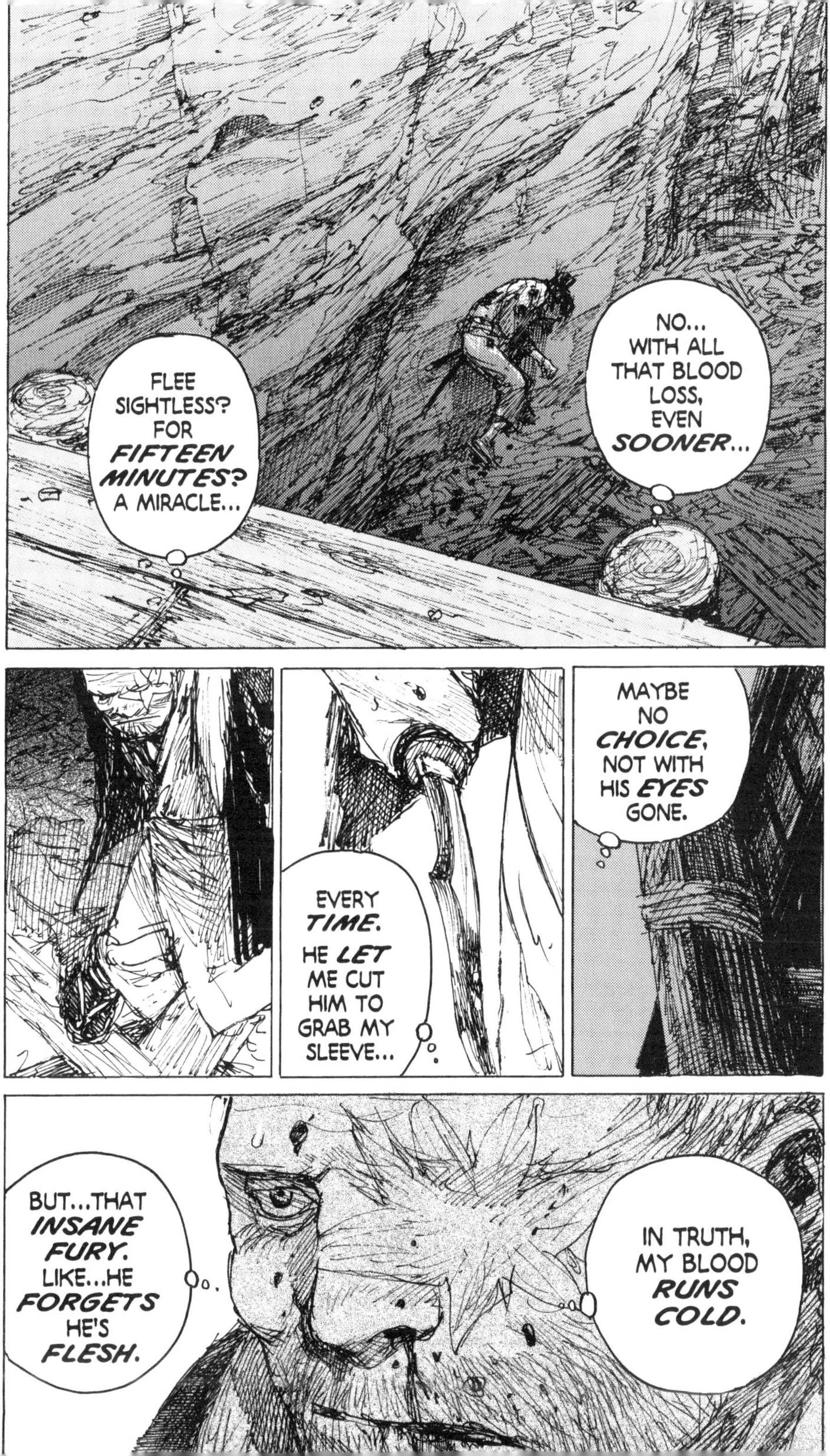
FLEE SIGHTLESS? FOR *FIFTEEN MINUTES?* A MIRACLE...
NO... WITH ALL THAT BLOOD LOSS, EVEN *SOONER*...
EVERY *TIME*.
HE *LET* ME CUT HIM TO GRAB MY SLEEVE...
MAYBE NO *CHOICE*, NOT WITH HIS *EYES* GONE.
BUT...THAT *INSANE FURY*. LIKE...HE *FORGETS* HE'S *FLESH*.
IN TRUTH, MY BLOOD *RUNS COLD*.

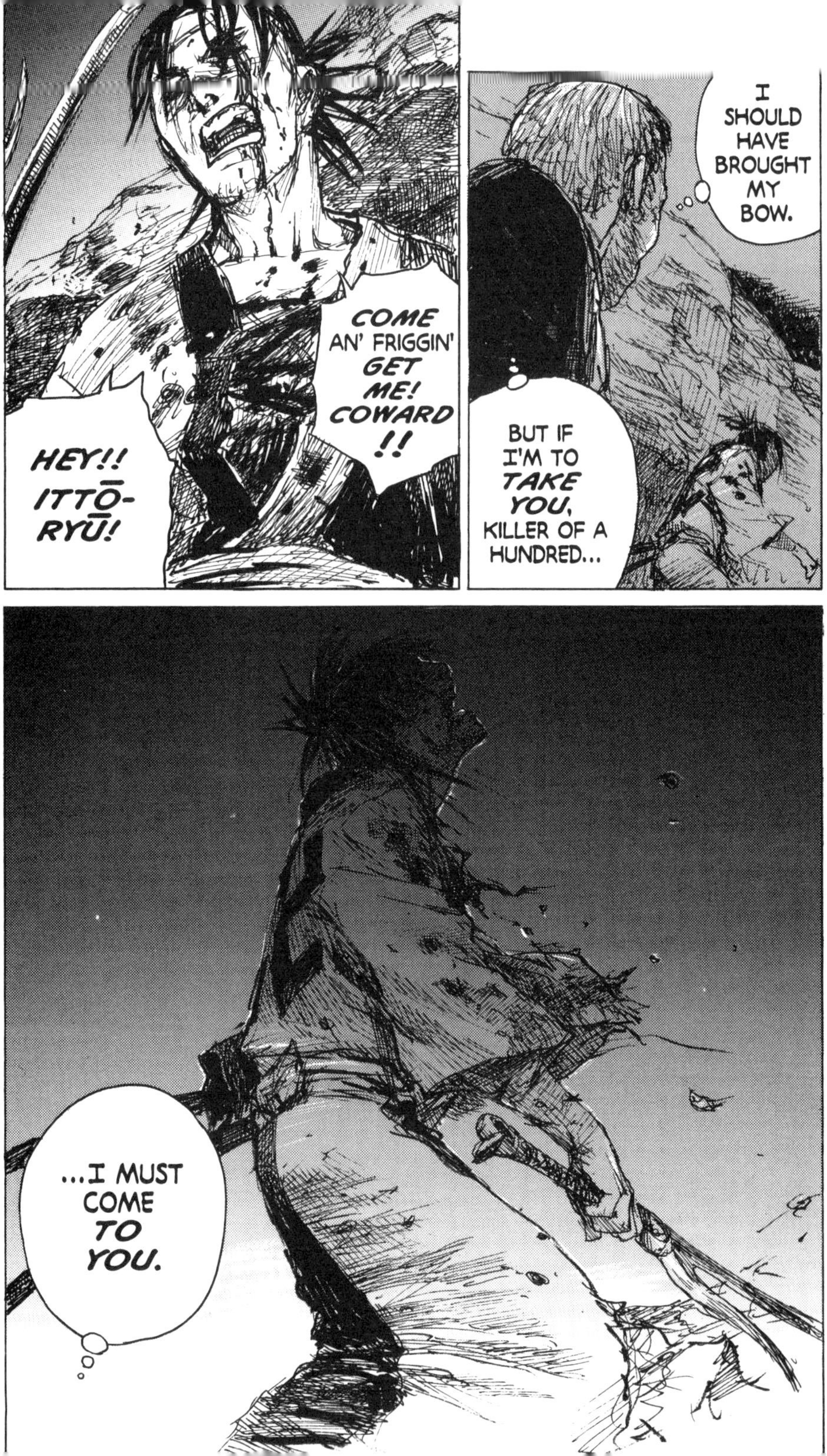
HEY!! ITTŌ-RYŪ!
COME AN' FRIGGIN' GET ME! COWARD!!
I SHOULD HAVE BROUGHT MY BOW.
BUT IF I'M TO TAKE YOU, KILLER OF A HUNDRED...
...I MUST COME TO YOU.

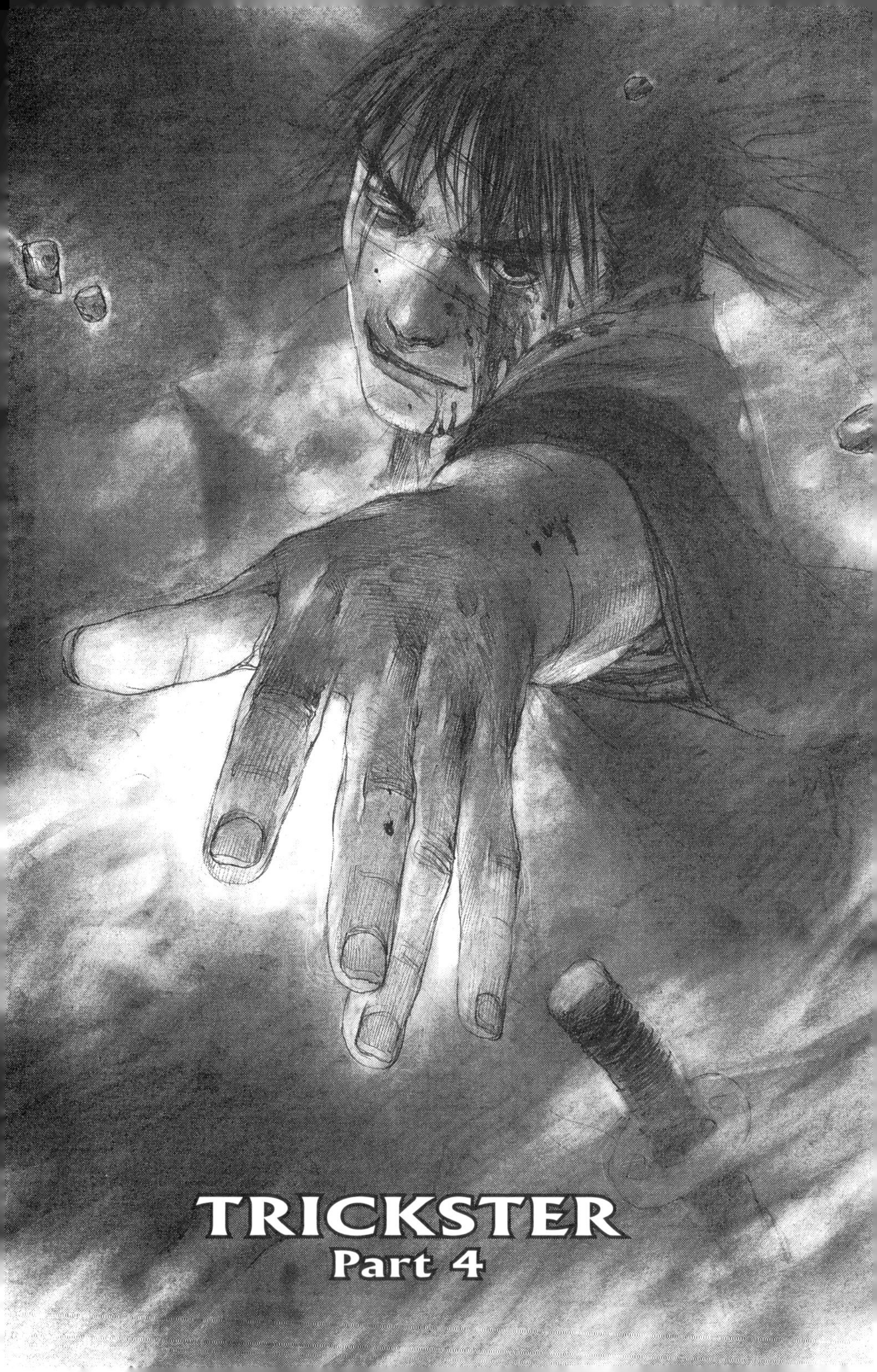
TRICKSTER
Part 4

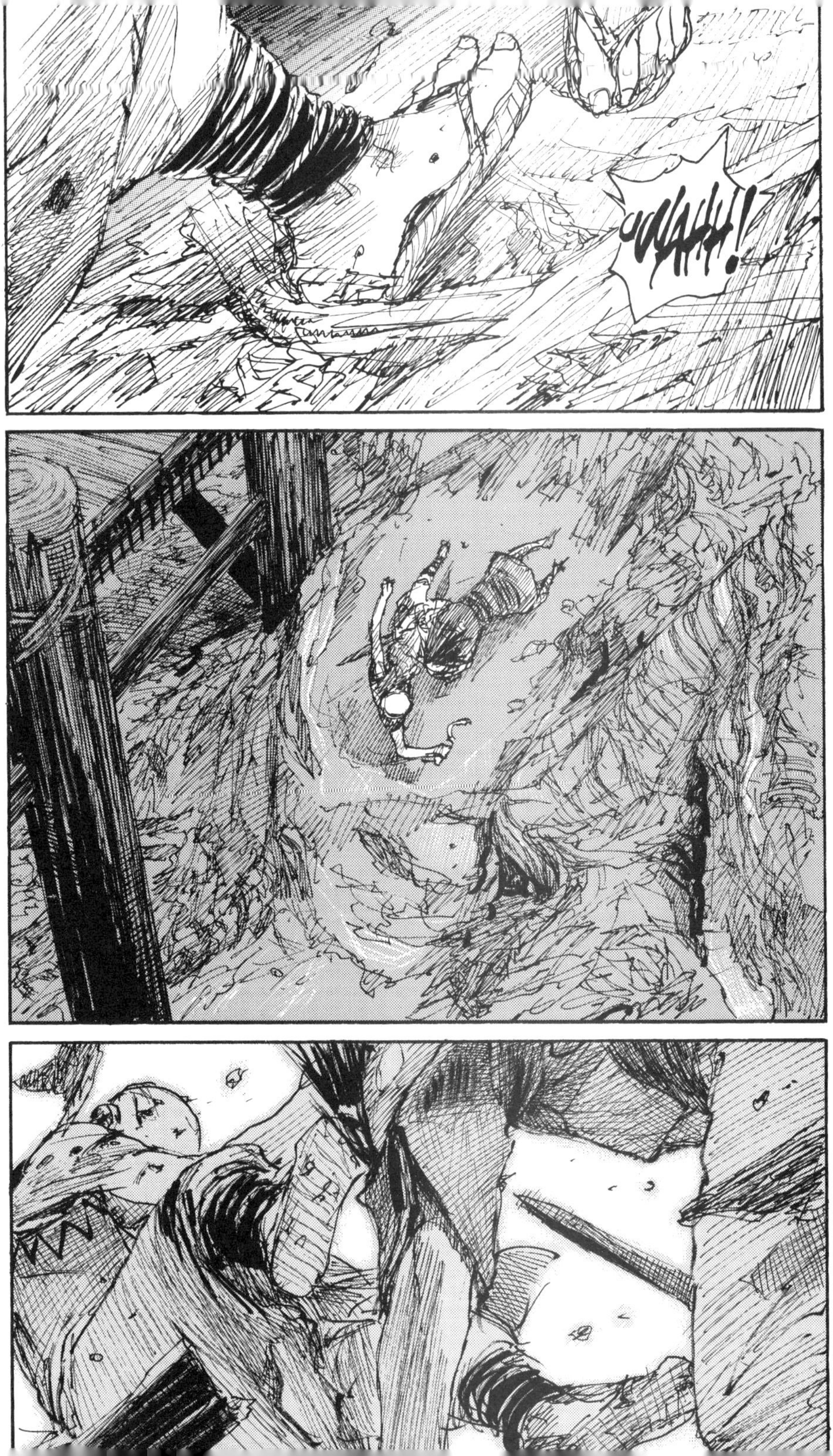
UWAHH!

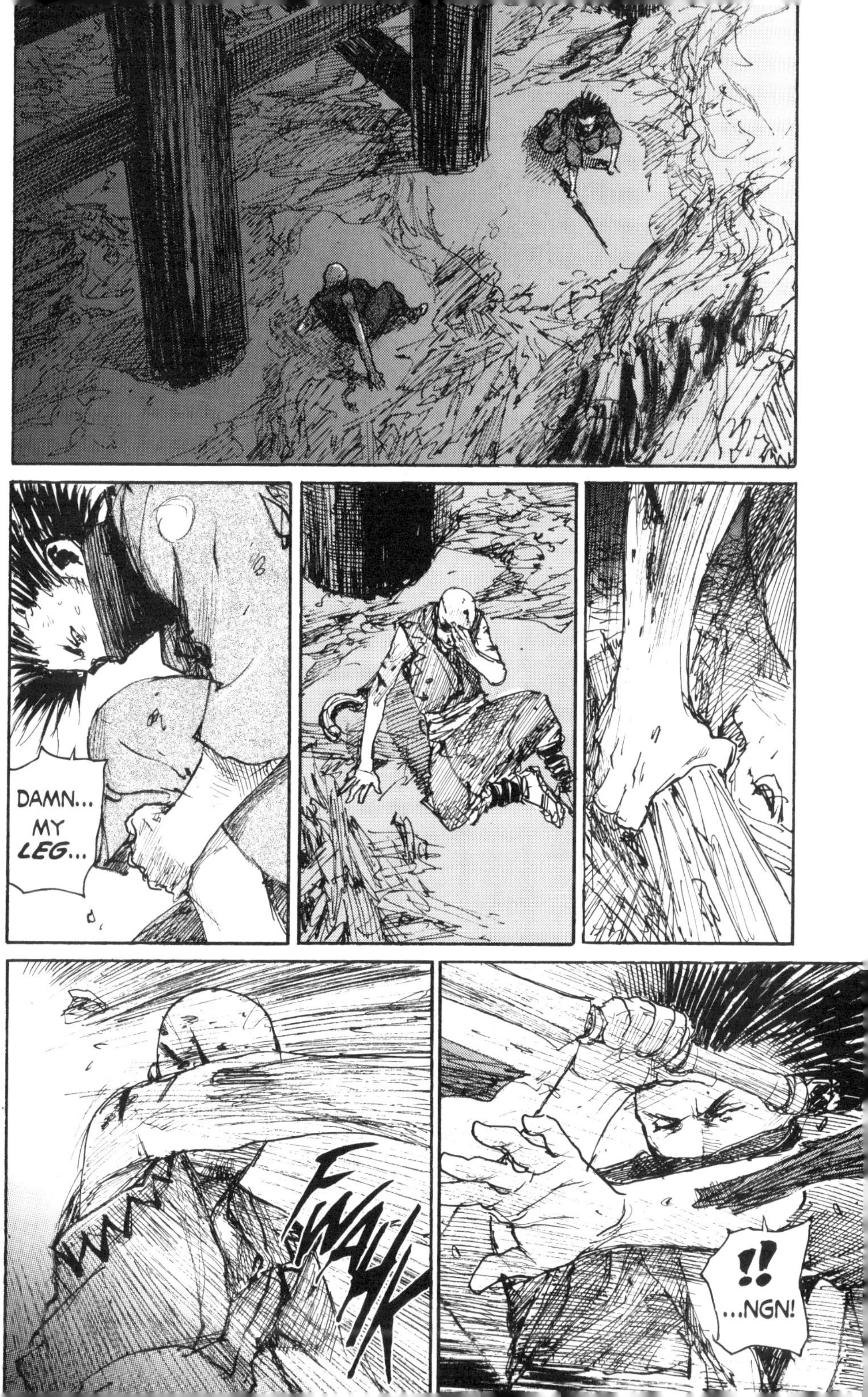
DAMN... MY LEG...
FWAK
!!
...NGN!

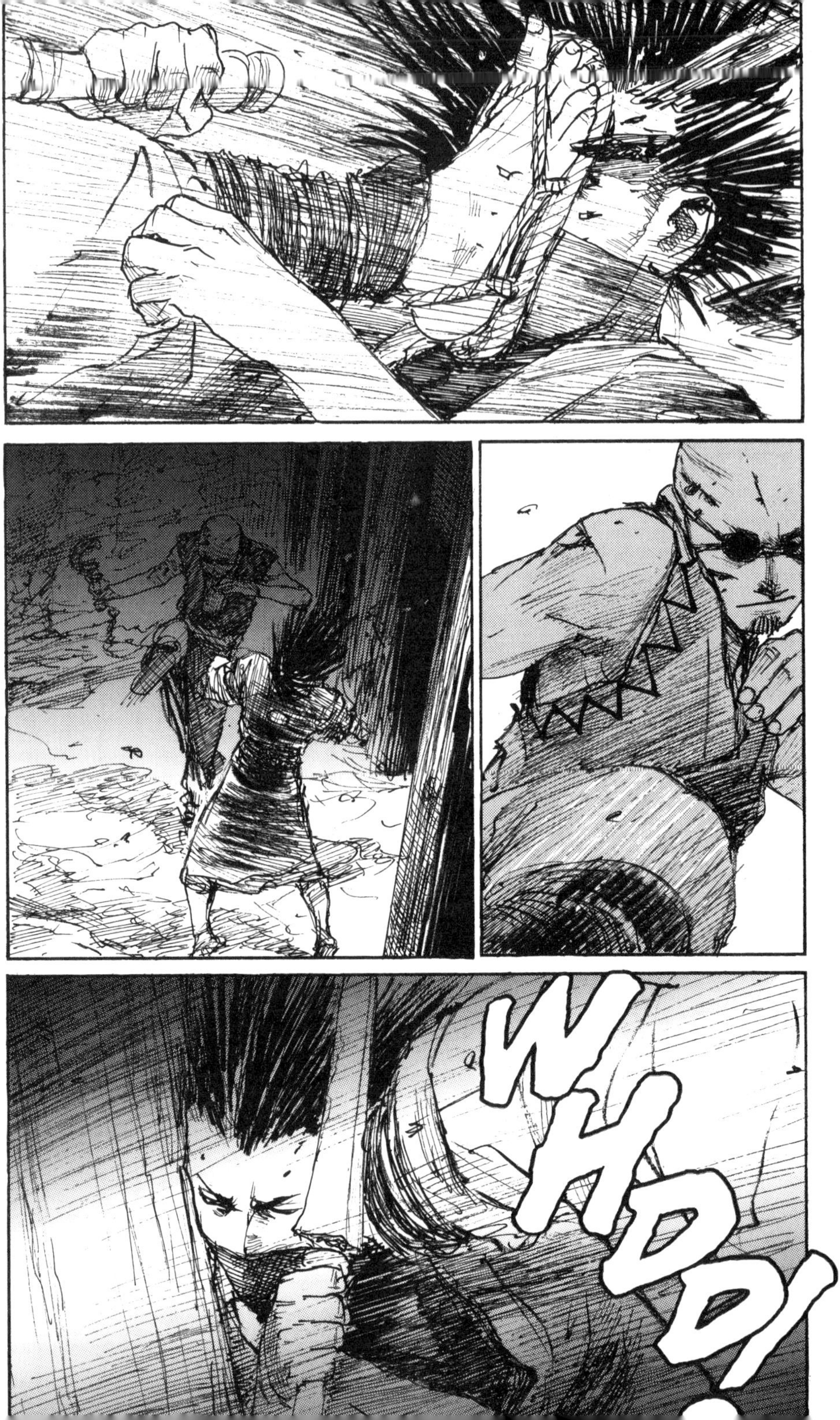
WHDD!

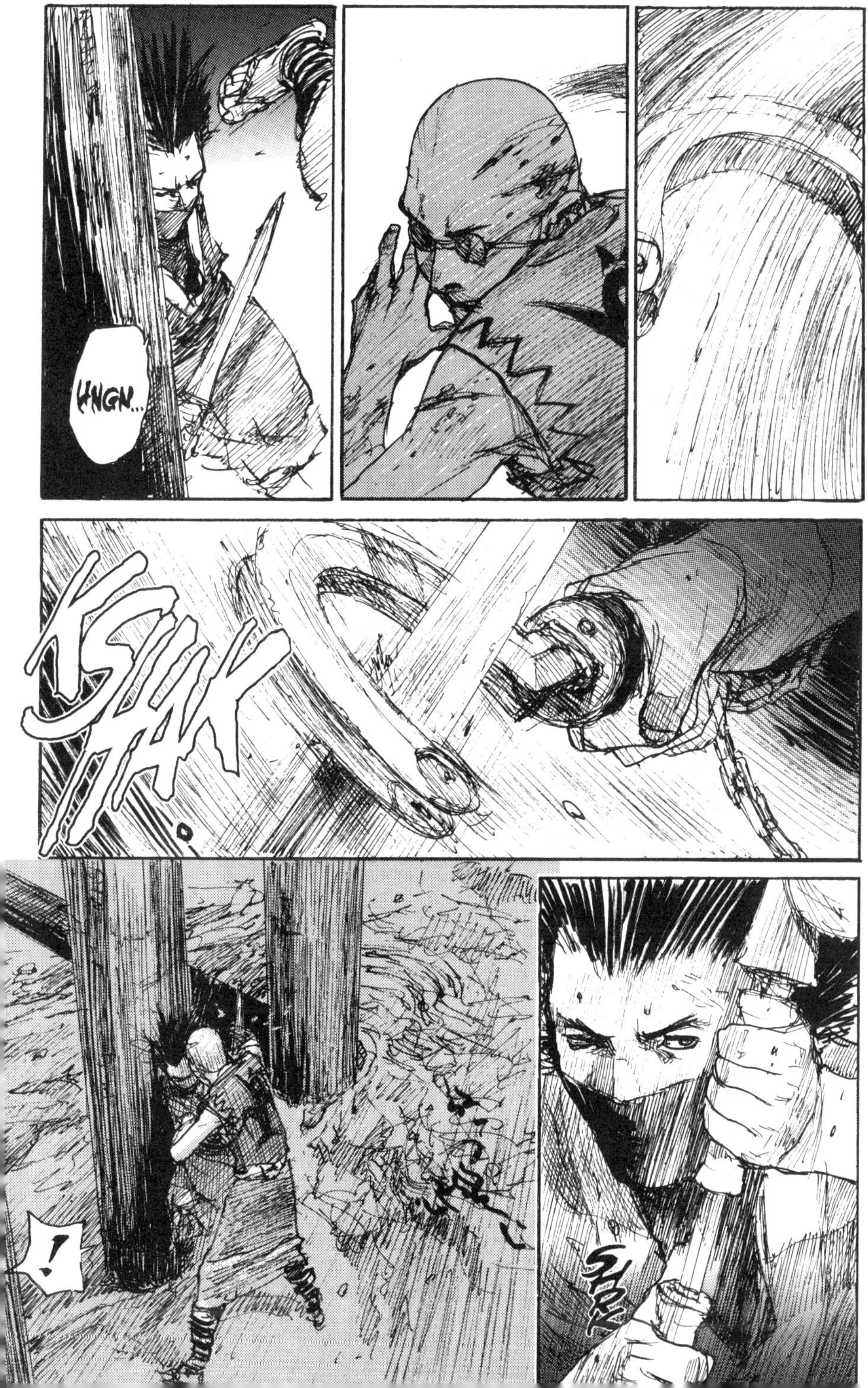
HNGN...
KSHK TAK
!
SHNK

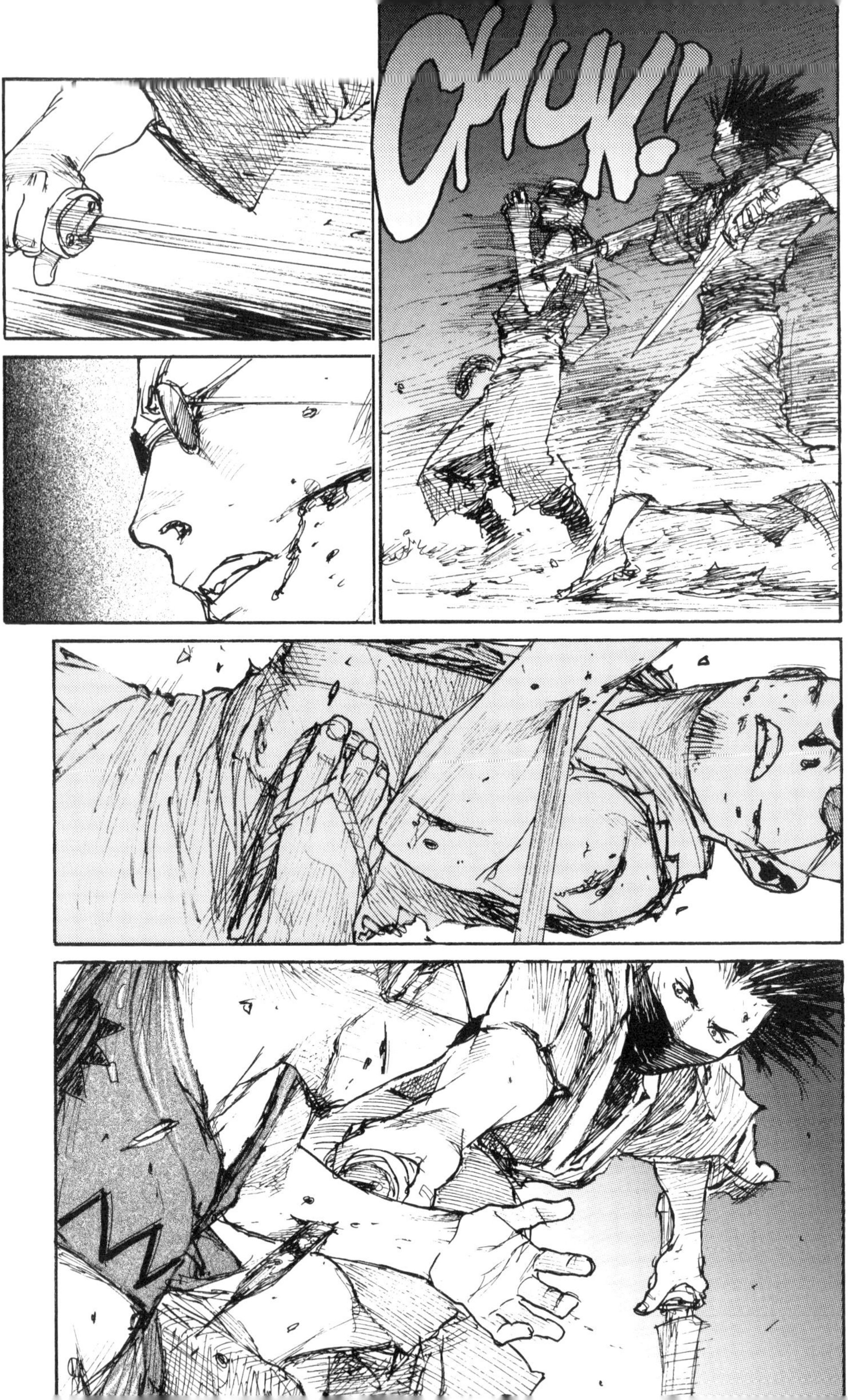
CHUK!

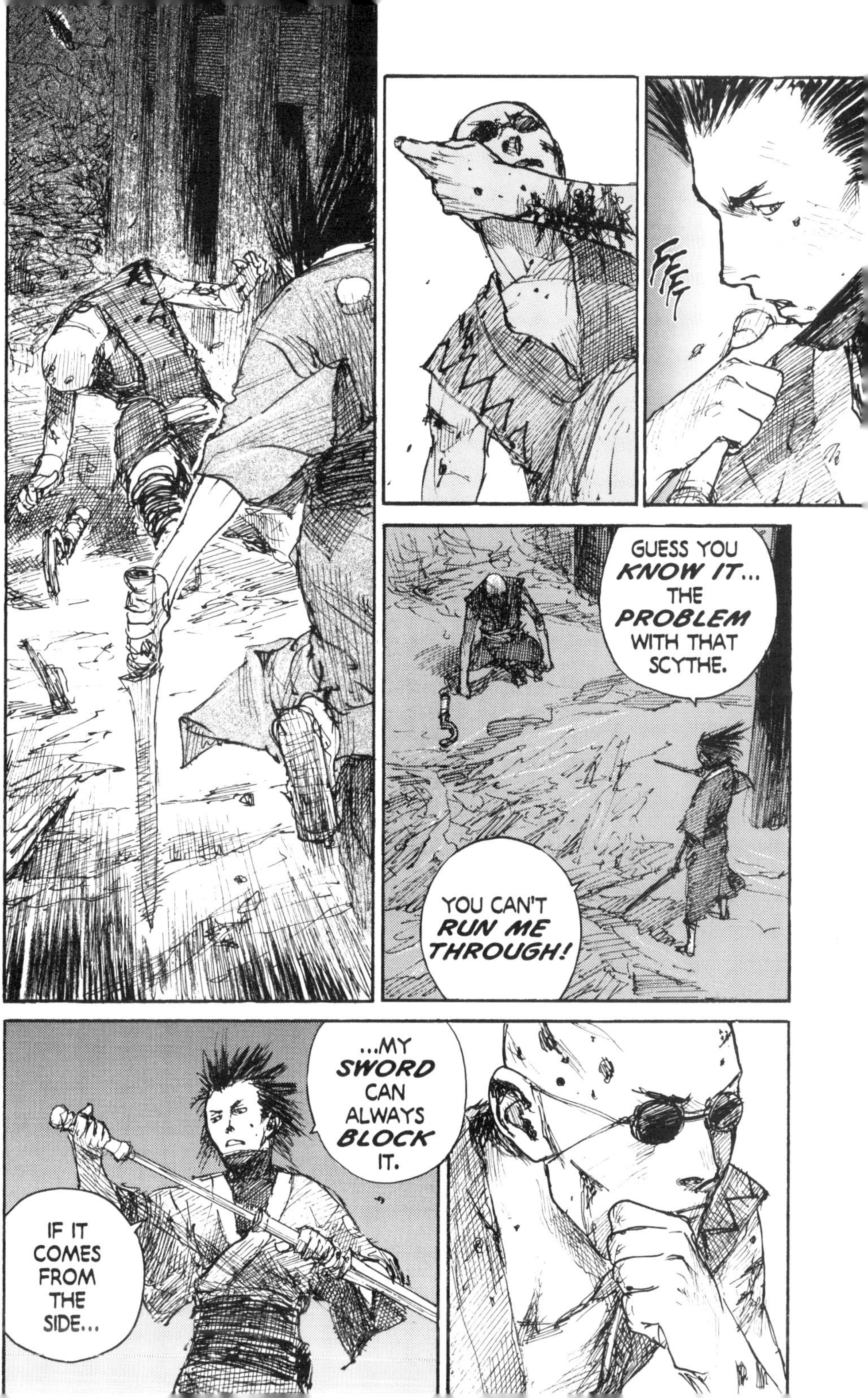
GUESS YOU *KNOW IT*... THE *PROBLEM* WITH THAT SCYTHE.
YOU CAN'T *RUN ME THROUGH!*
IF IT COMES FROM THE SIDE...
...MY *SWORD* CAN ALWAYS *BLOCK* IT.

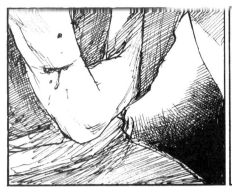

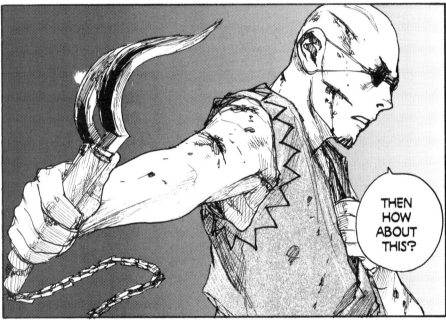

THEN HOW ABOUT THIS?

....

MANJI....! YOU *BASTARD!*

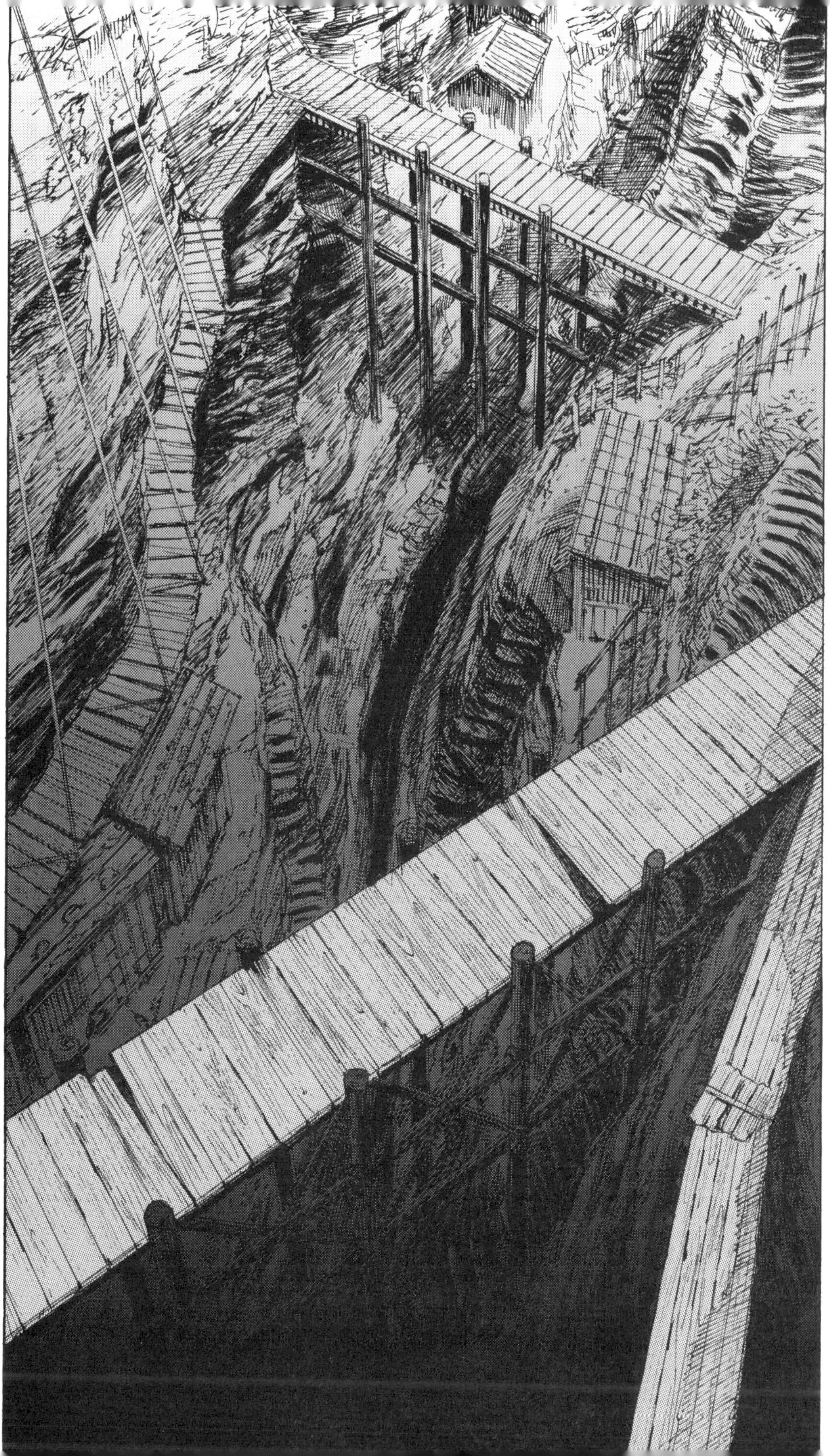

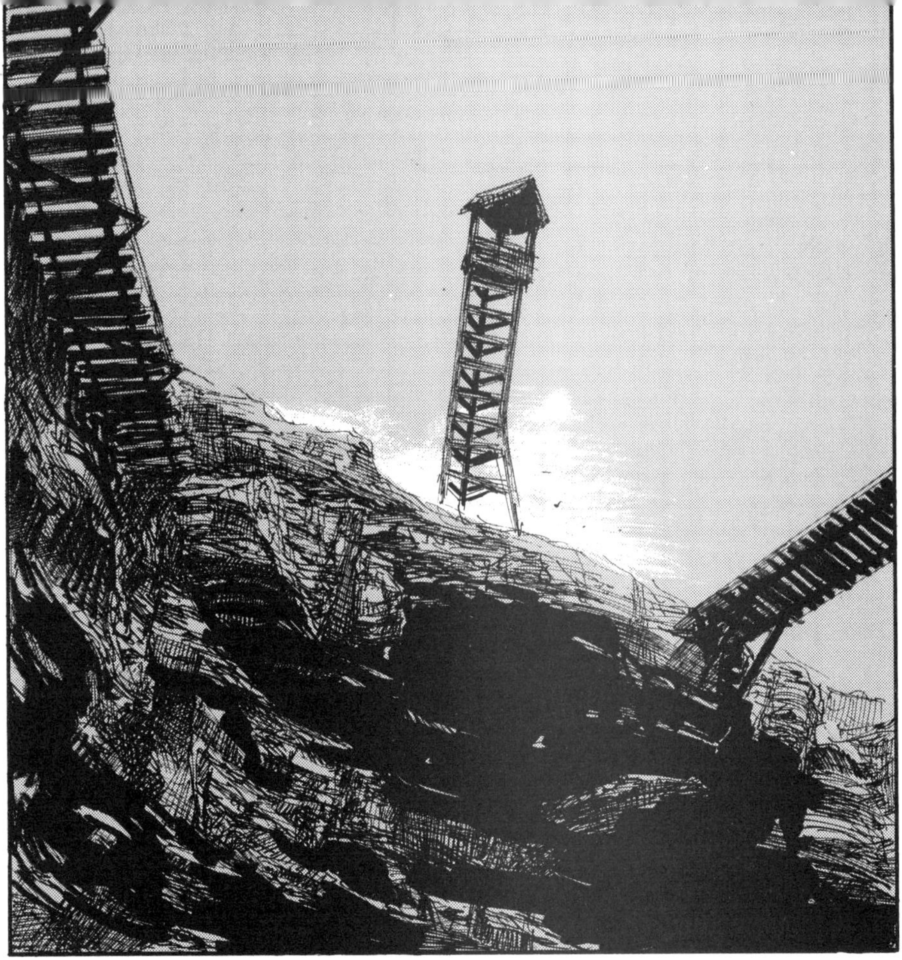
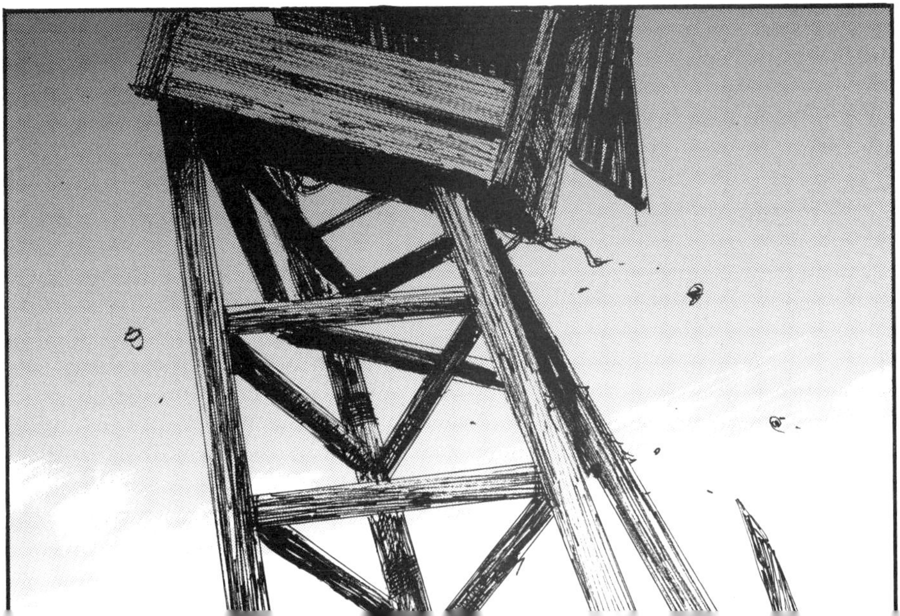

:hff:

:hahf:

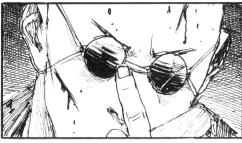

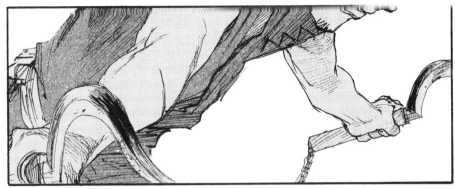

SHNNG

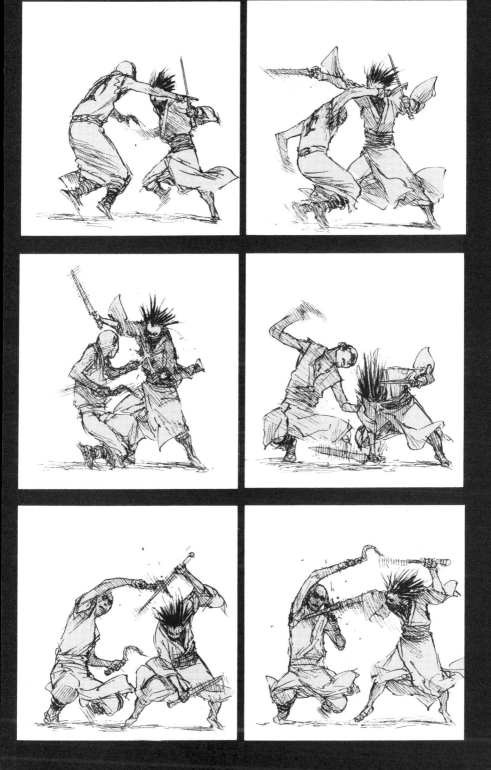

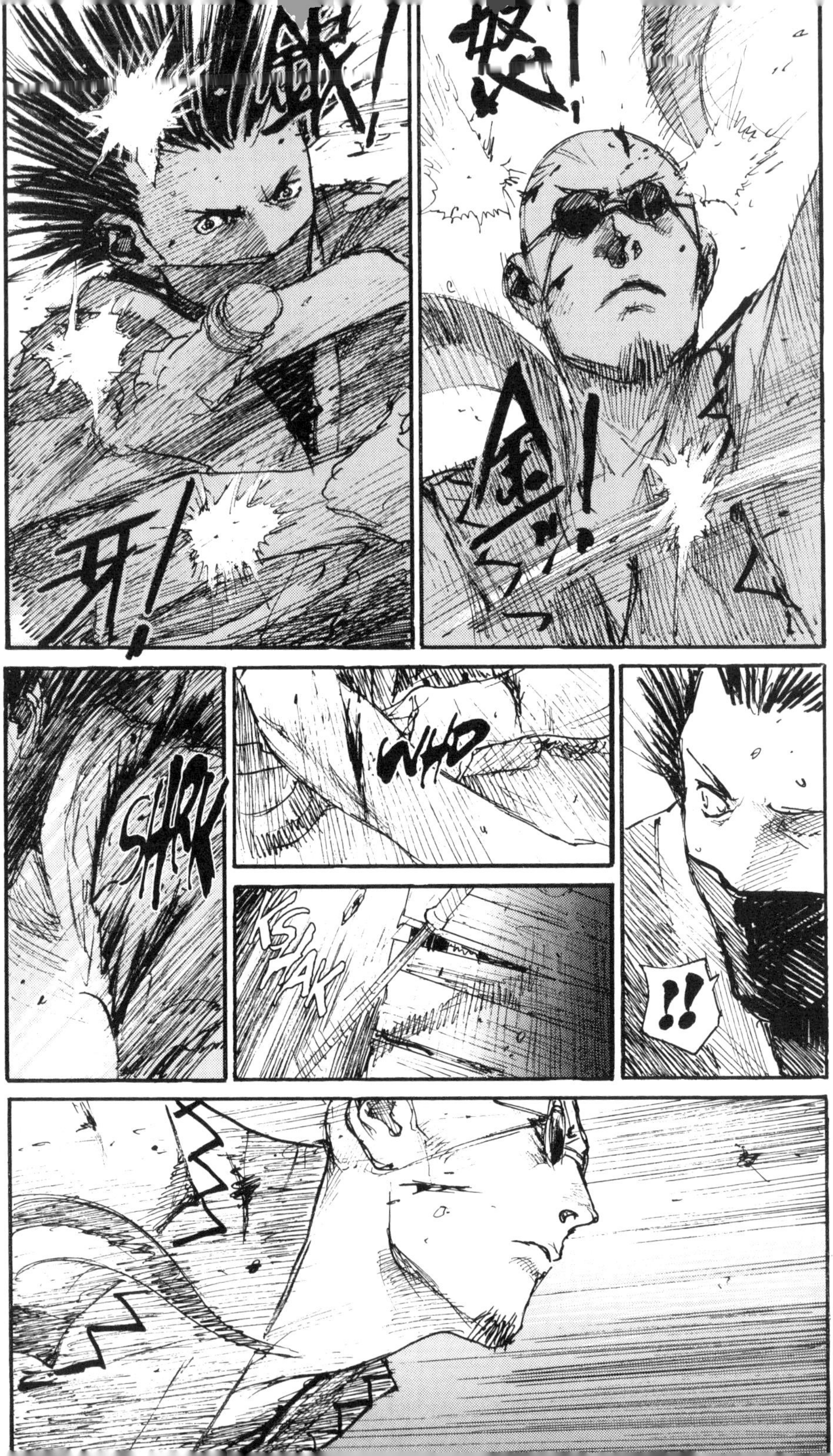
牙!
SHRK
WHO
KSHAK
!!

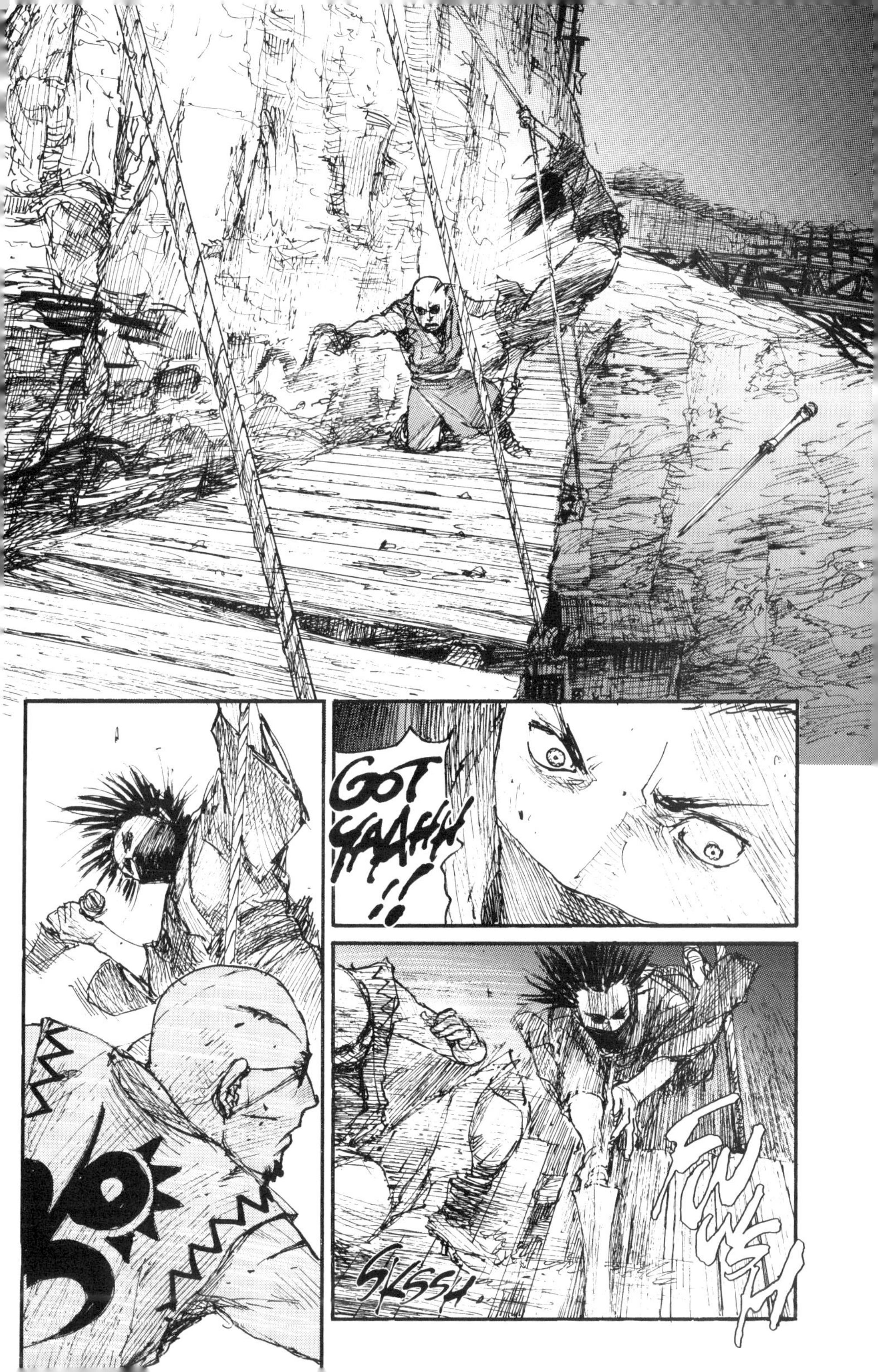
GOT YAAHH!!
SKSSH

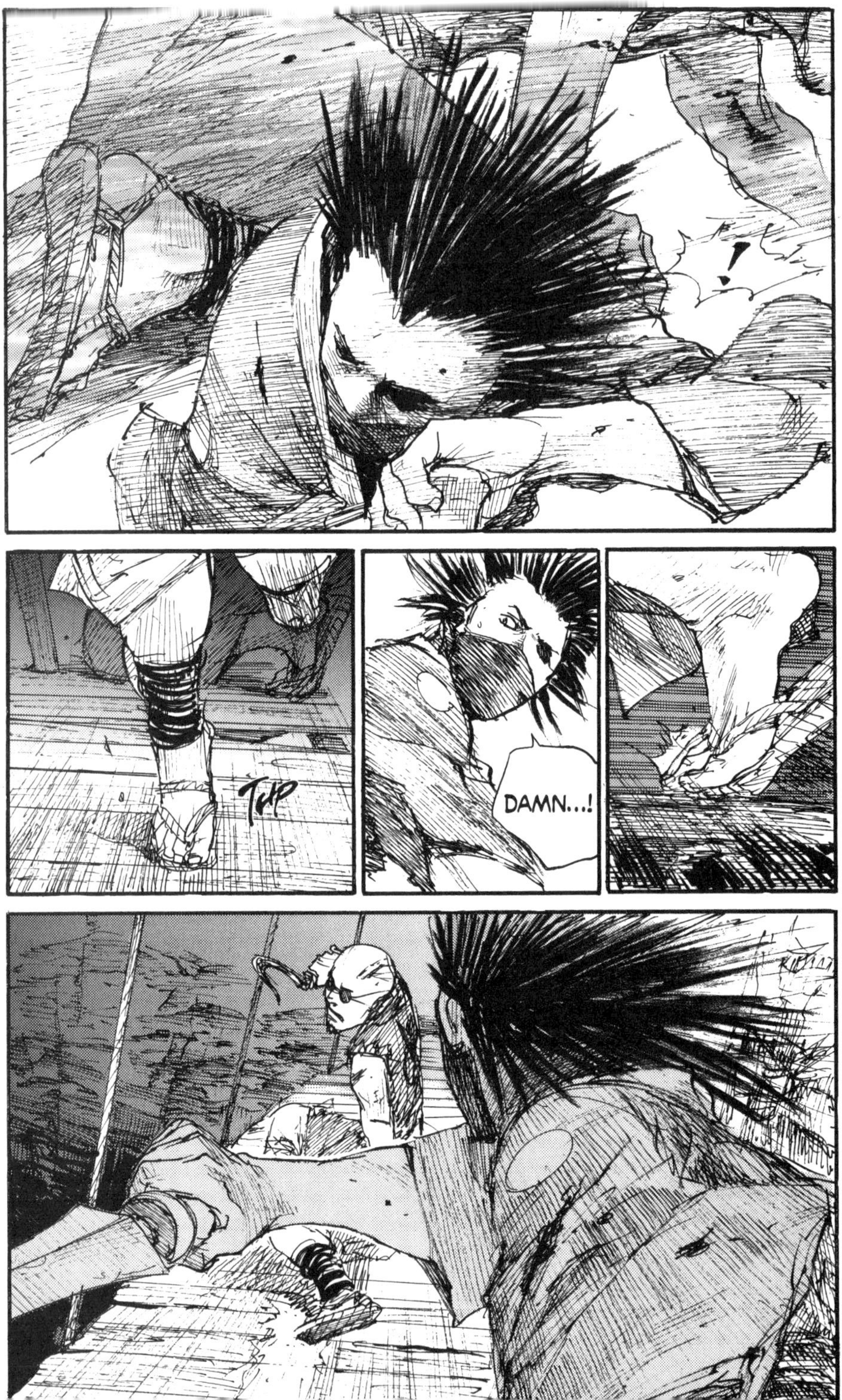
!
TUP
DAMN...!

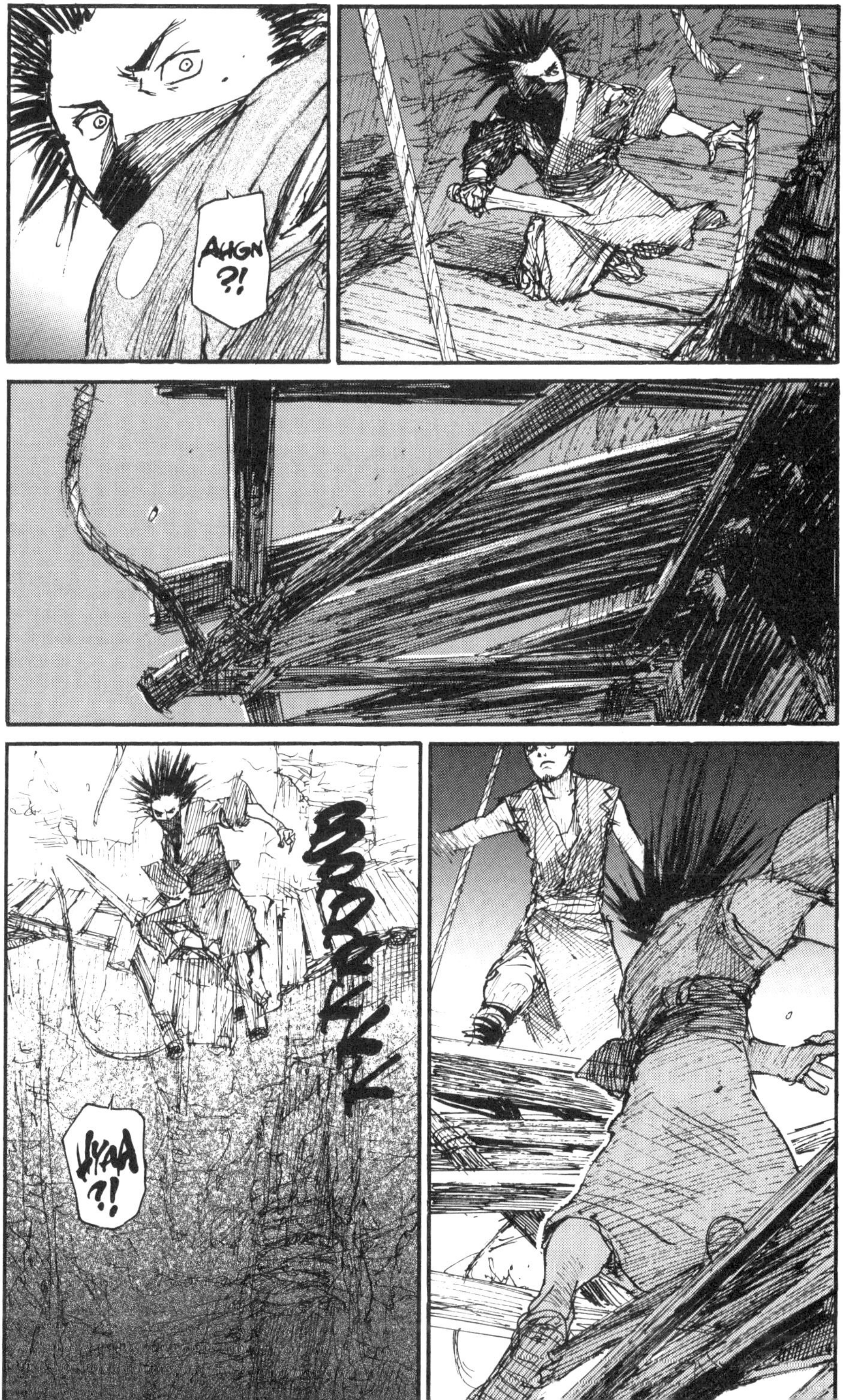
AHGN ?!
HYAA ?!

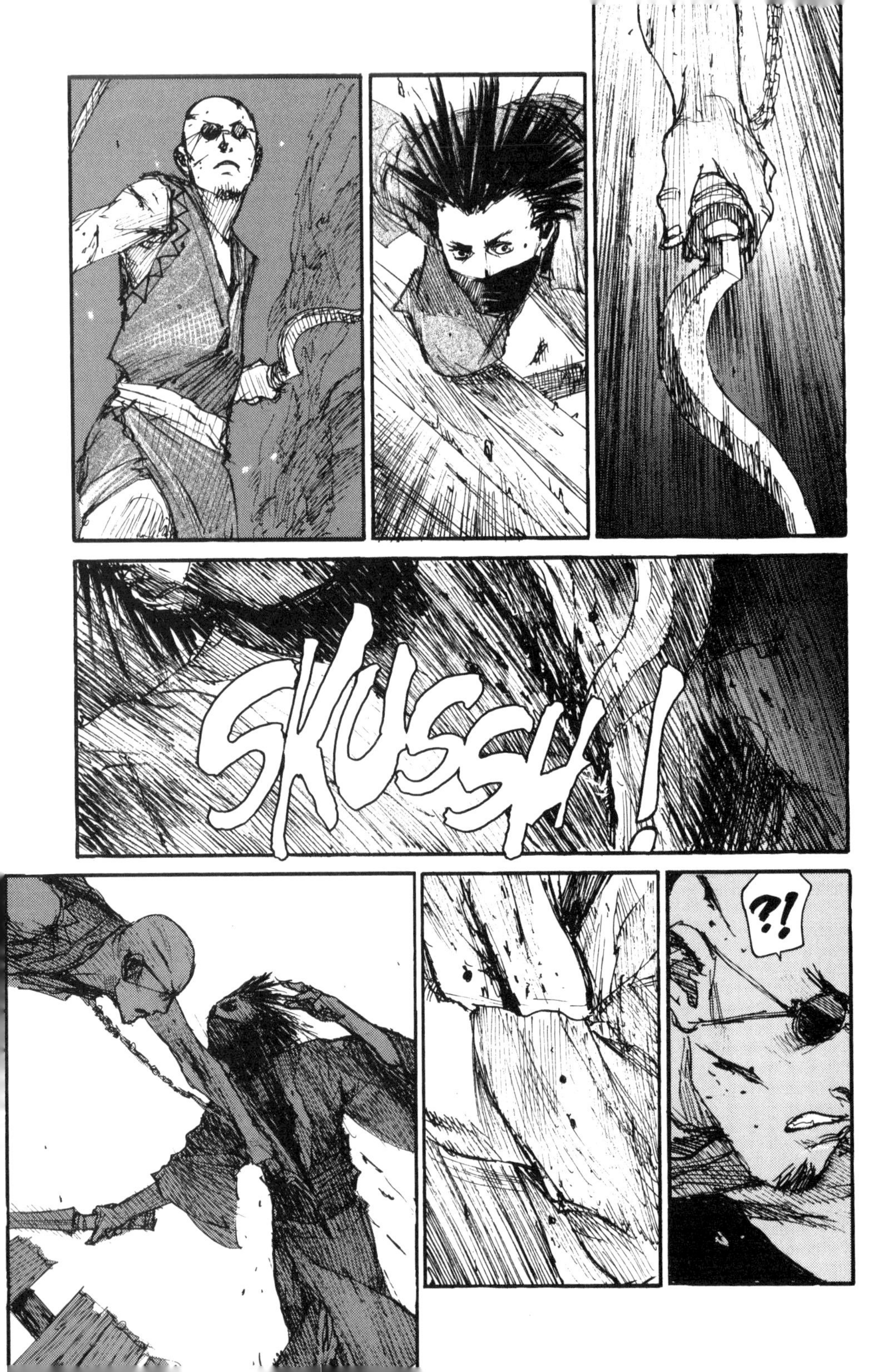
SKUSSH!
?!

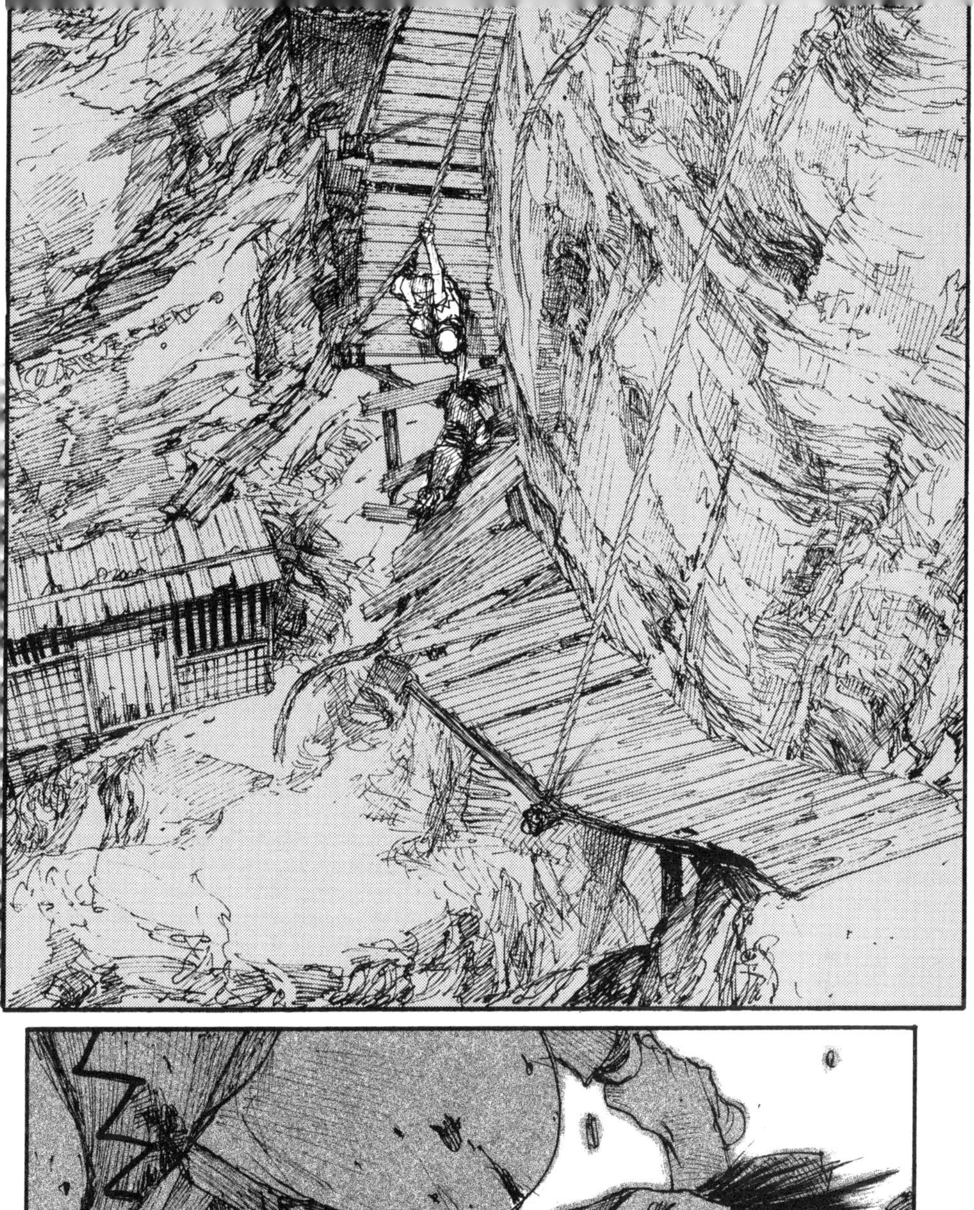
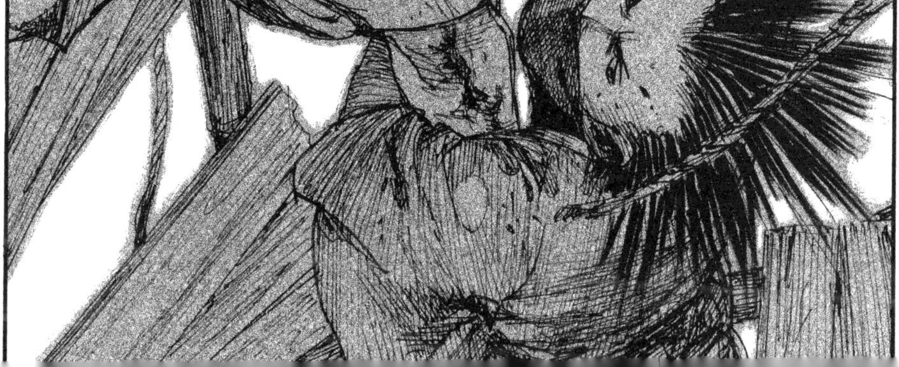

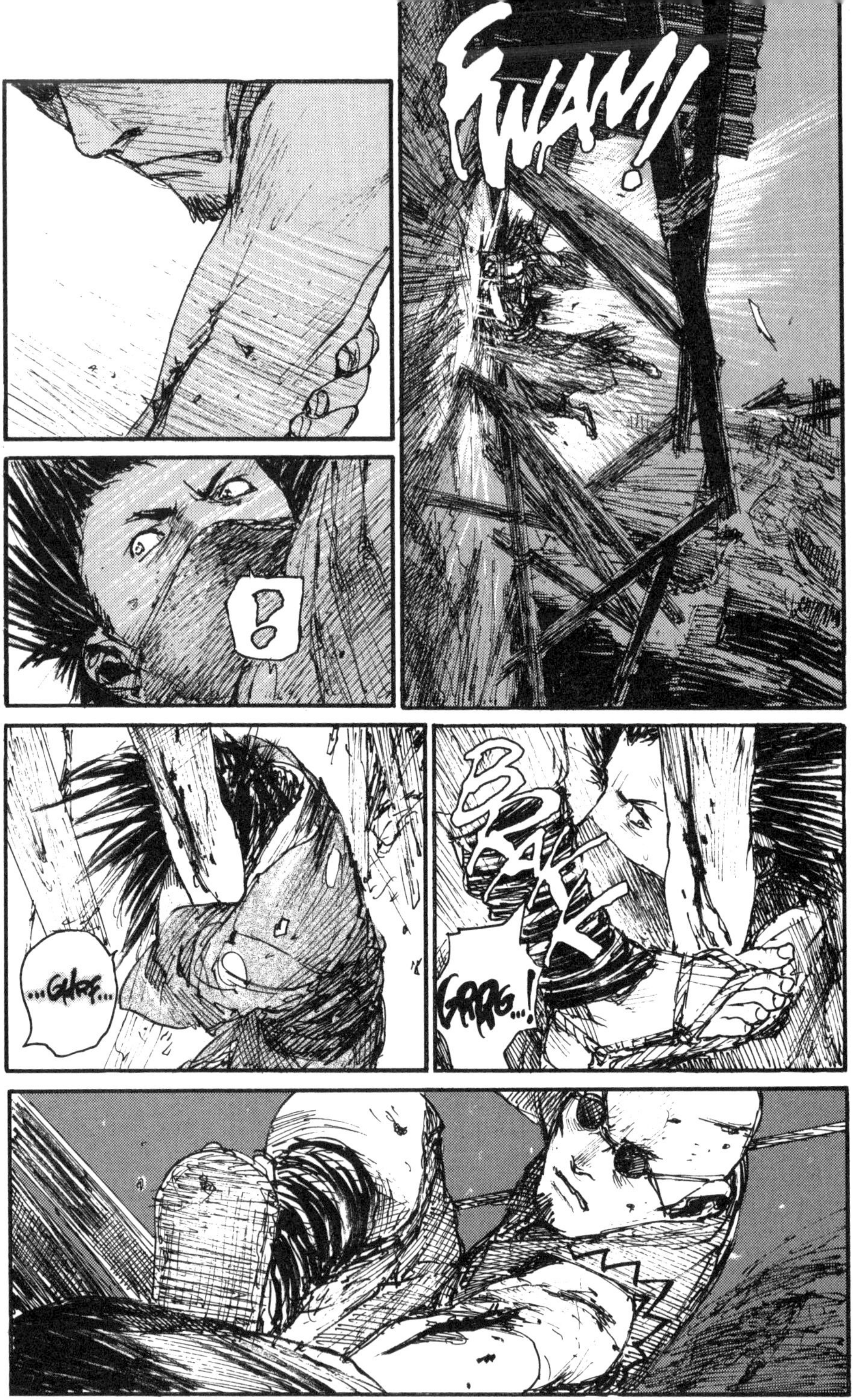
!
FWAM!
...GARF...
BAKK
GRRG...!

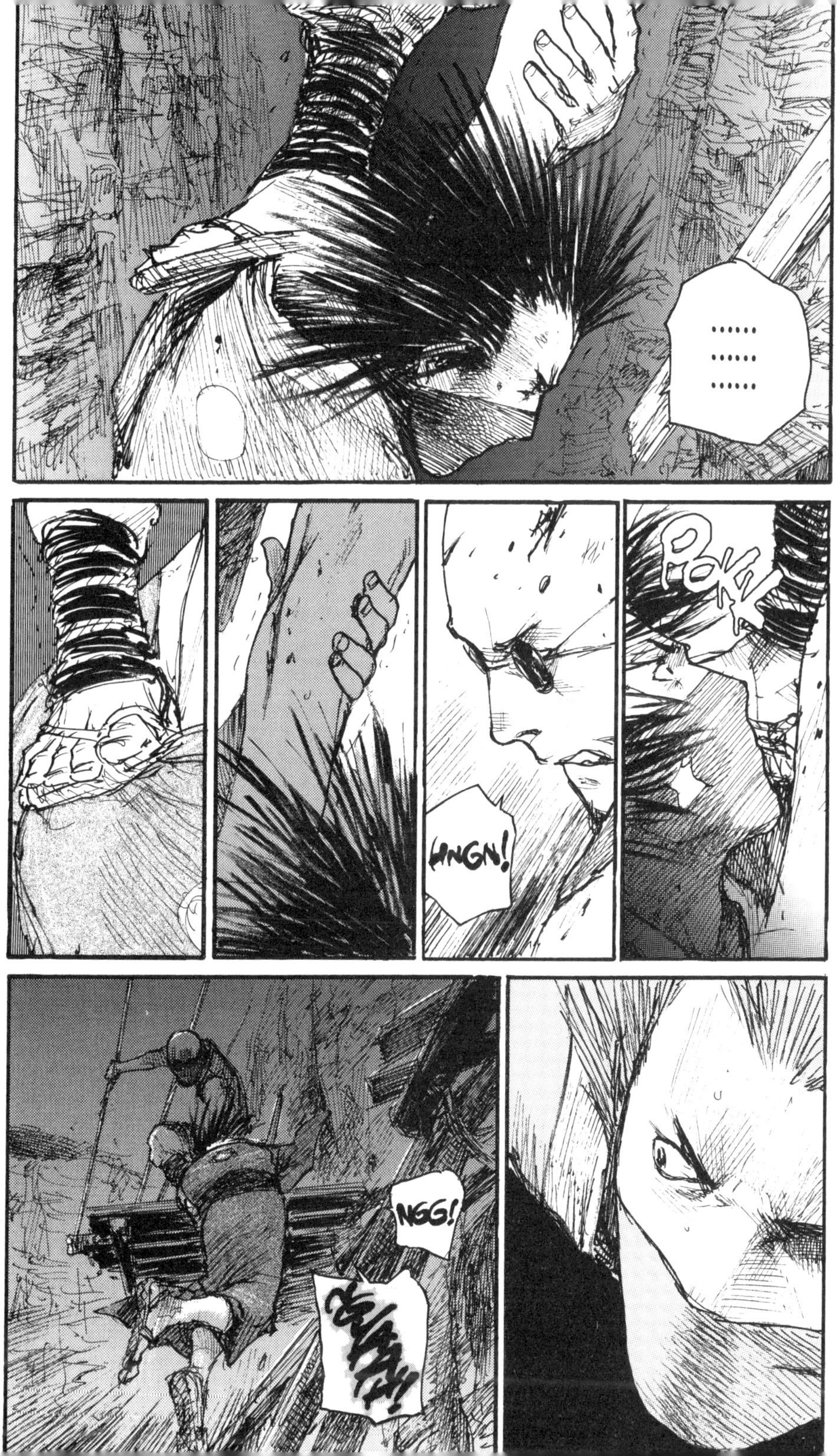
......
......
......
POK!
HNGN!
NGG!

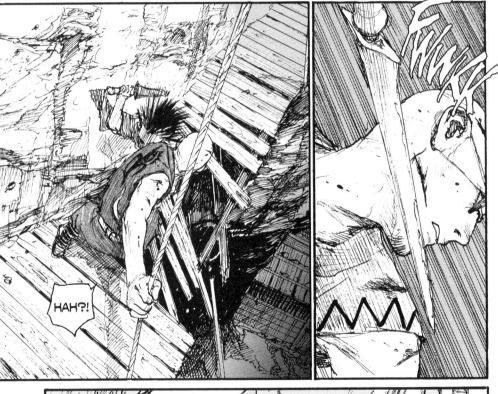

HAH?!

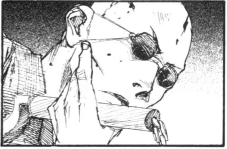

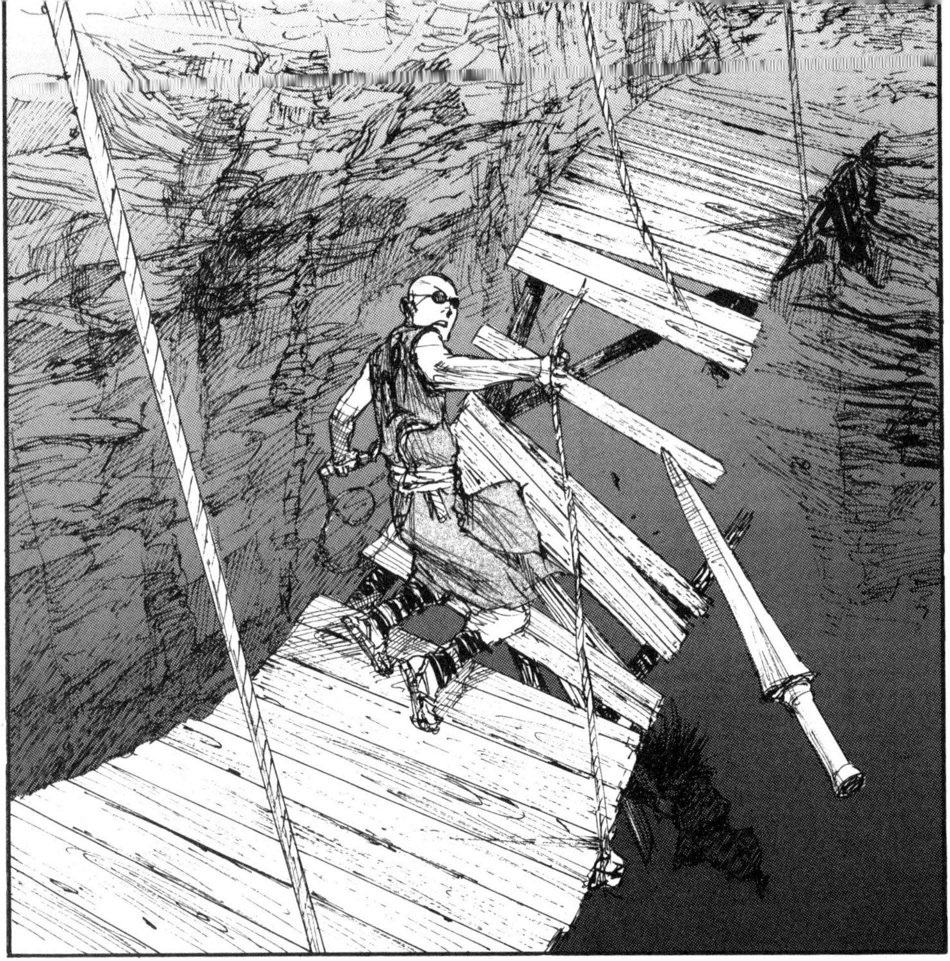
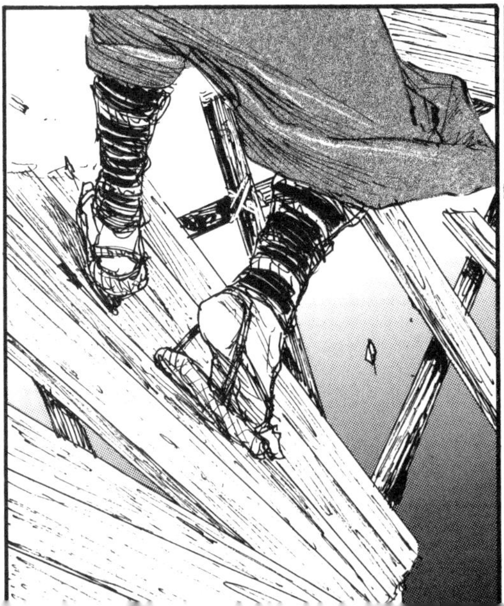
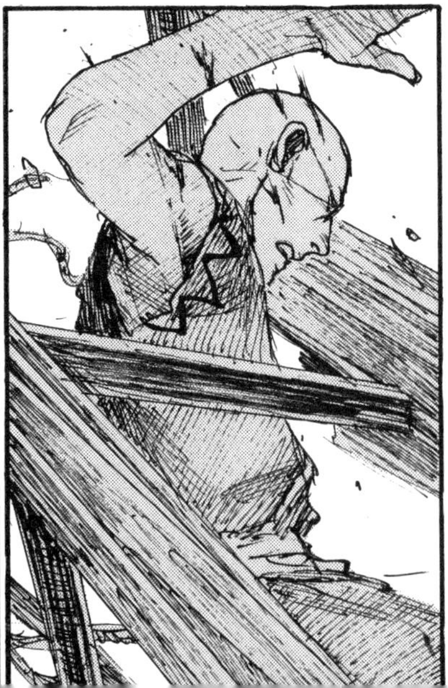

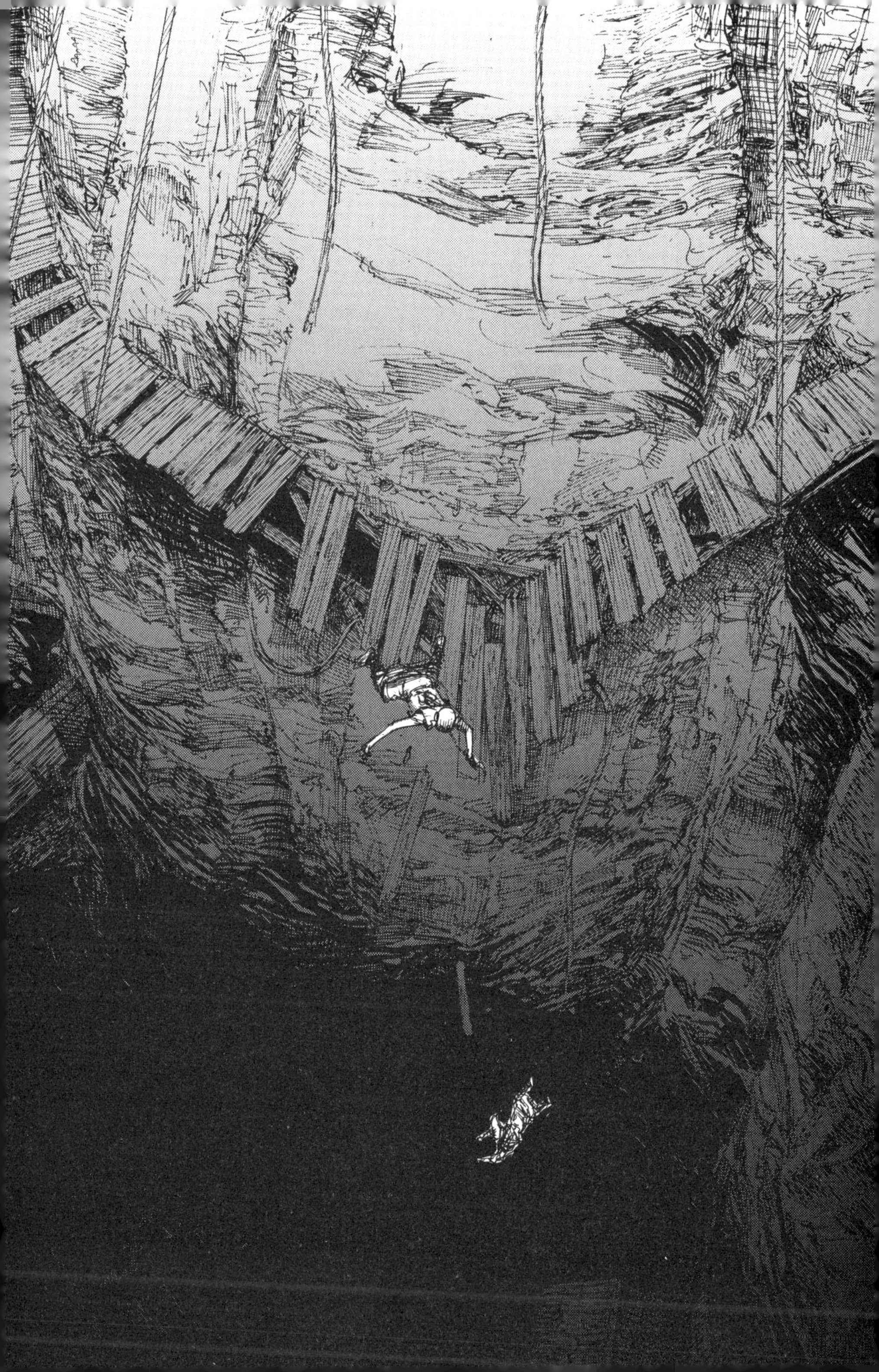

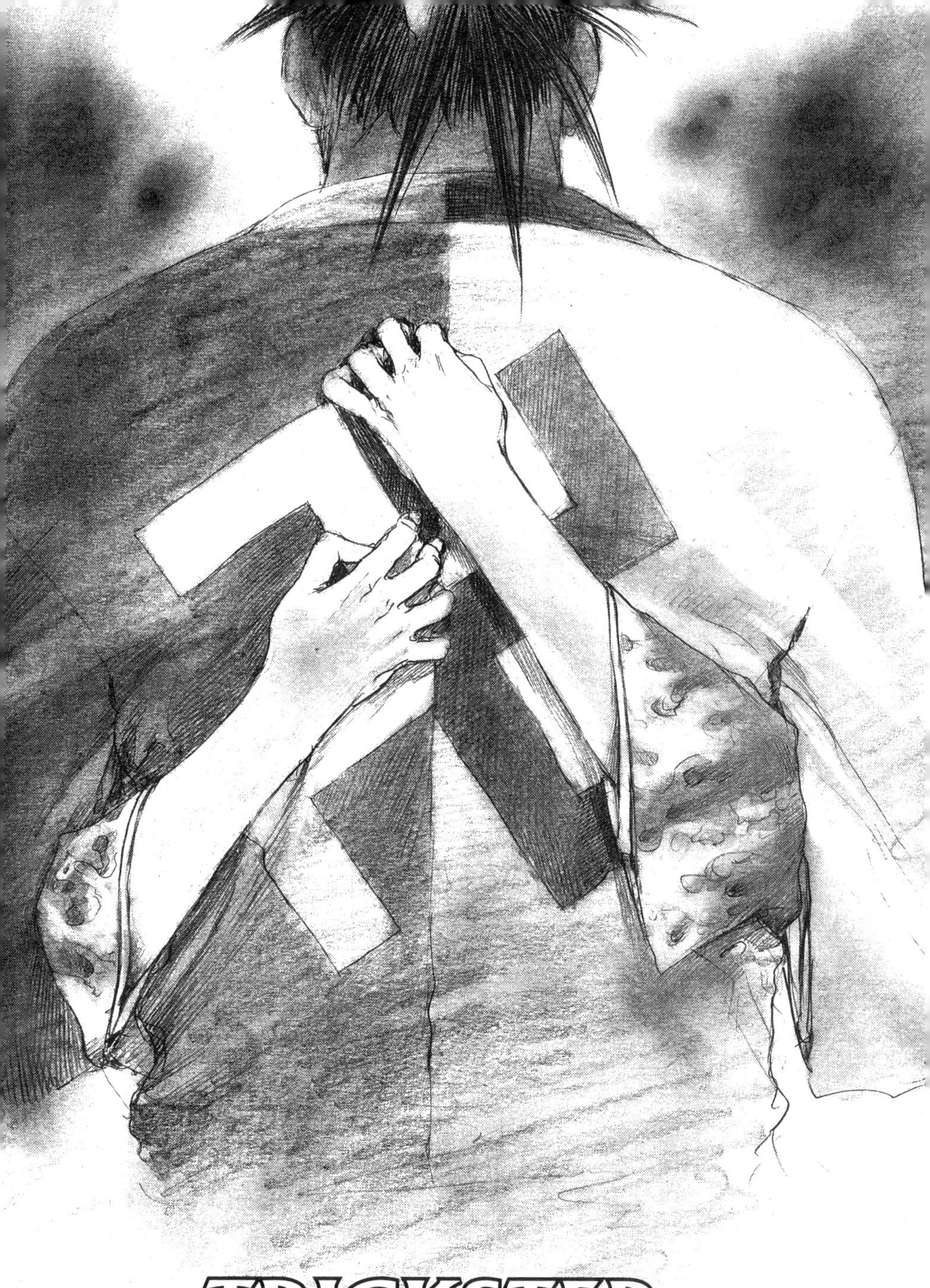

TRICKSTER
Part 5

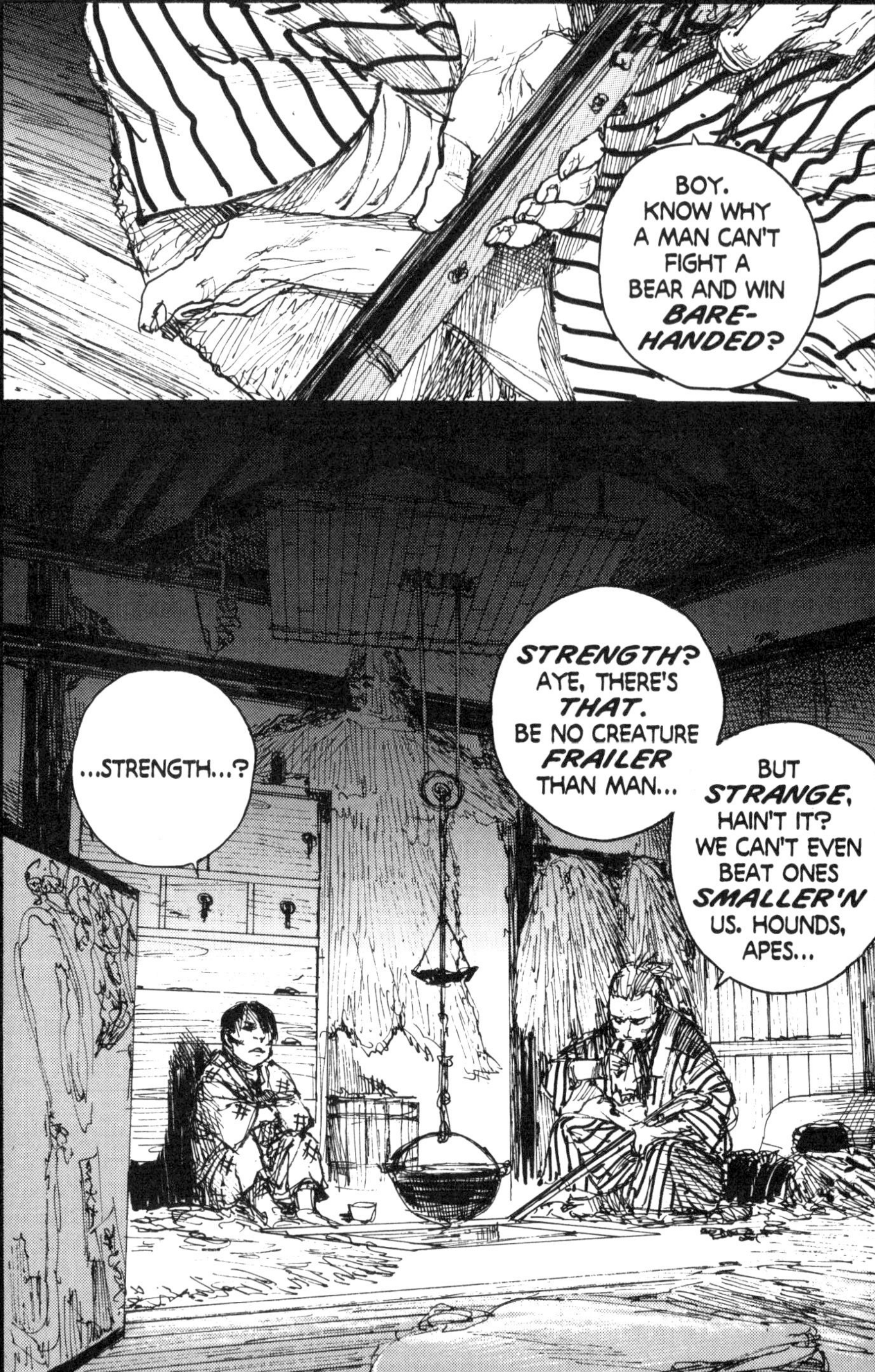
BOY. KNOW WHY A MAN CAN'T FIGHT A BEAR AND WIN BARE-HANDED?
...STRENGTH...?
STRENGTH? AYE, THERE'S THAT. BE NO CREATURE FRAILER THAN MAN...
BUT STRANGE, HAIN'T IT? WE CAN'T EVEN BEAT ONES SMALLER'N US. HOUNDS, APES...

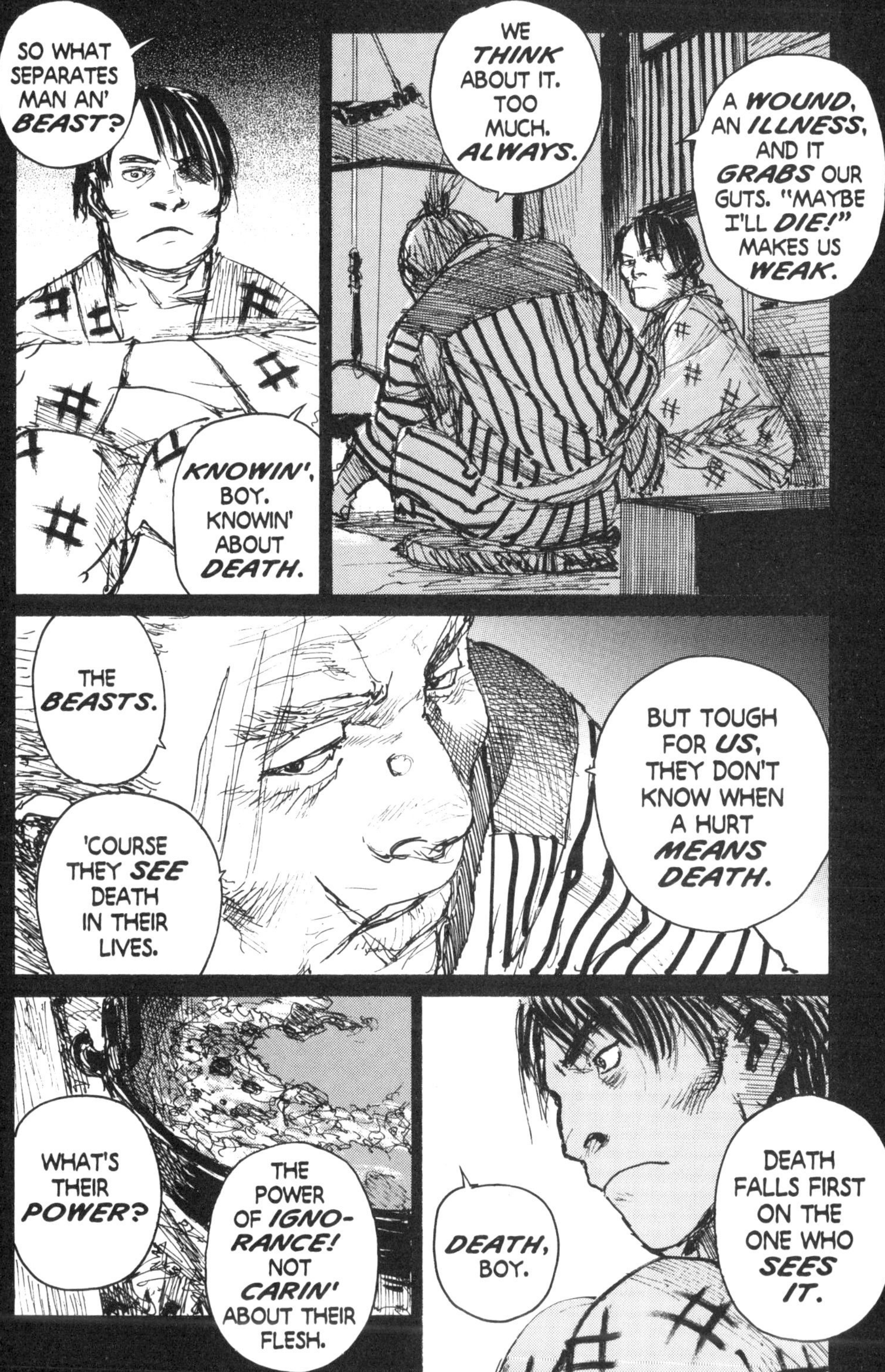
SO WHAT SEPARATES MAN AN' BEAST?
KNOWIN', BOY. KNOWIN' ABOUT DEATH.
WE THINK ABOUT IT. TOO MUCH. ALWAYS.
A WOUND, AN ILLNESS, AND IT GRABS OUR GUTS. "MAYBE I'LL DIE!" MAKES US WEAK.
THE BEASTS.
'COURSE THEY SEE DEATH IN THEIR LIVES.
BUT TOUGH FOR US, THEY DON'T KNOW WHEN A HURT MEANS DEATH.
WHAT'S THEIR POWER?
THE POWER OF IGNO-RANCE! NOT CARIN' ABOUT THEIR FLESH.
DEATH, BOY.
DEATH FALLS FIRST ON THE ONE WHO SEES IT.

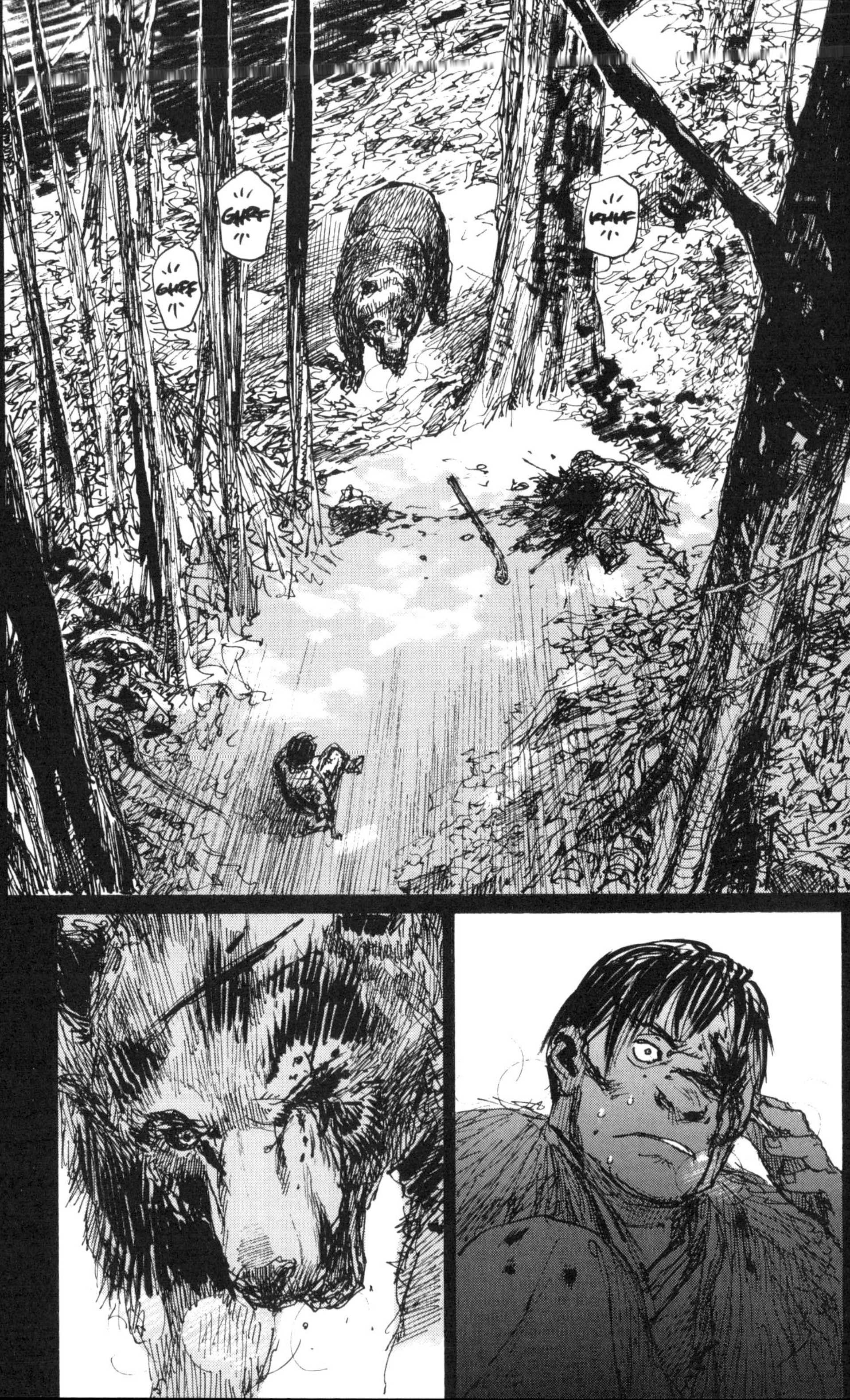
GARFF
KHUF
GARFF

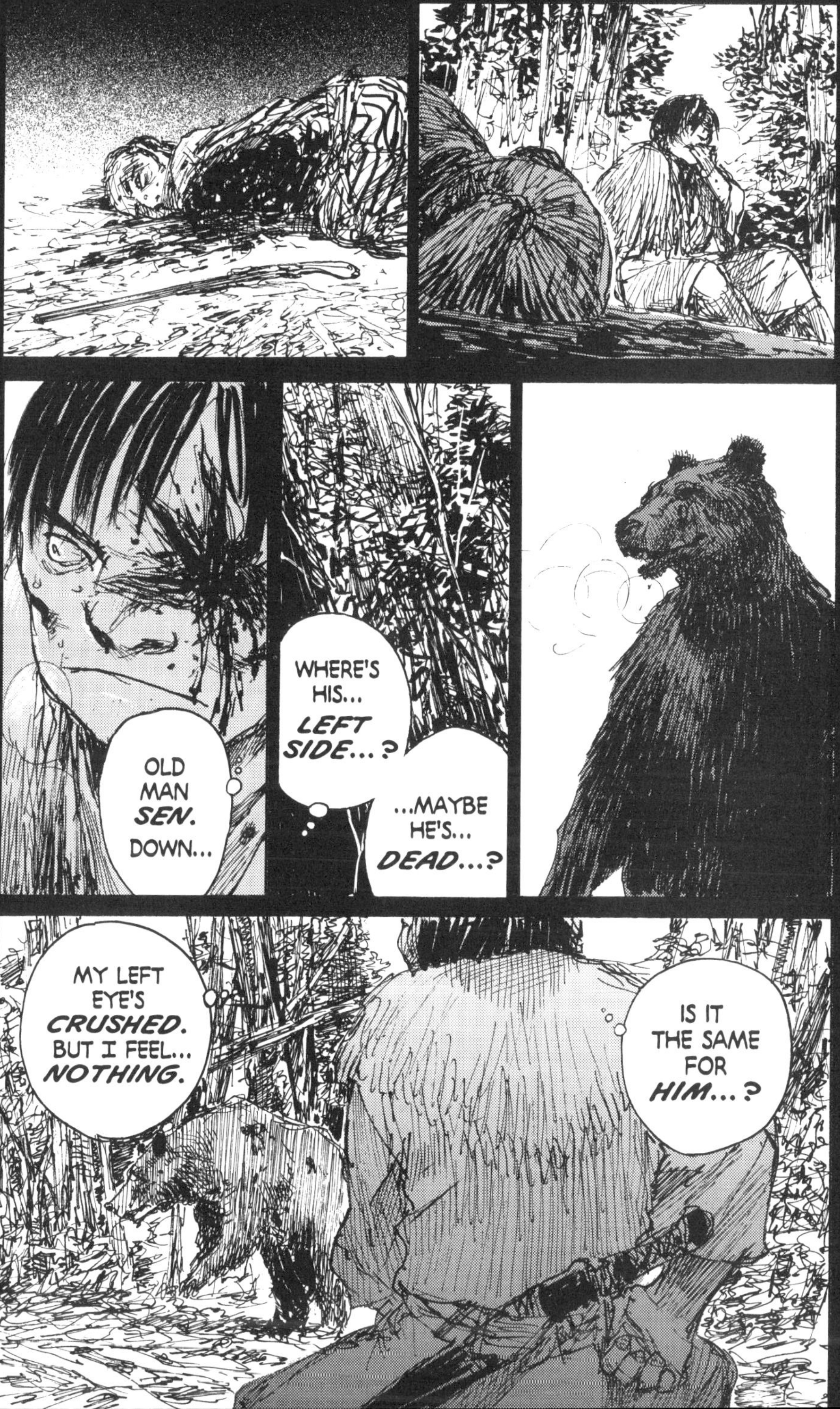
OLD MAN SEN. DOWN...
WHERE'S HIS... LEFT SIDE...?
...MAYBE HE'S... DEAD...?
MY LEFT EYE'S CRUSHED. BUT I FEEL... NOTHING.
IS IT THE SAME FOR HIM...?

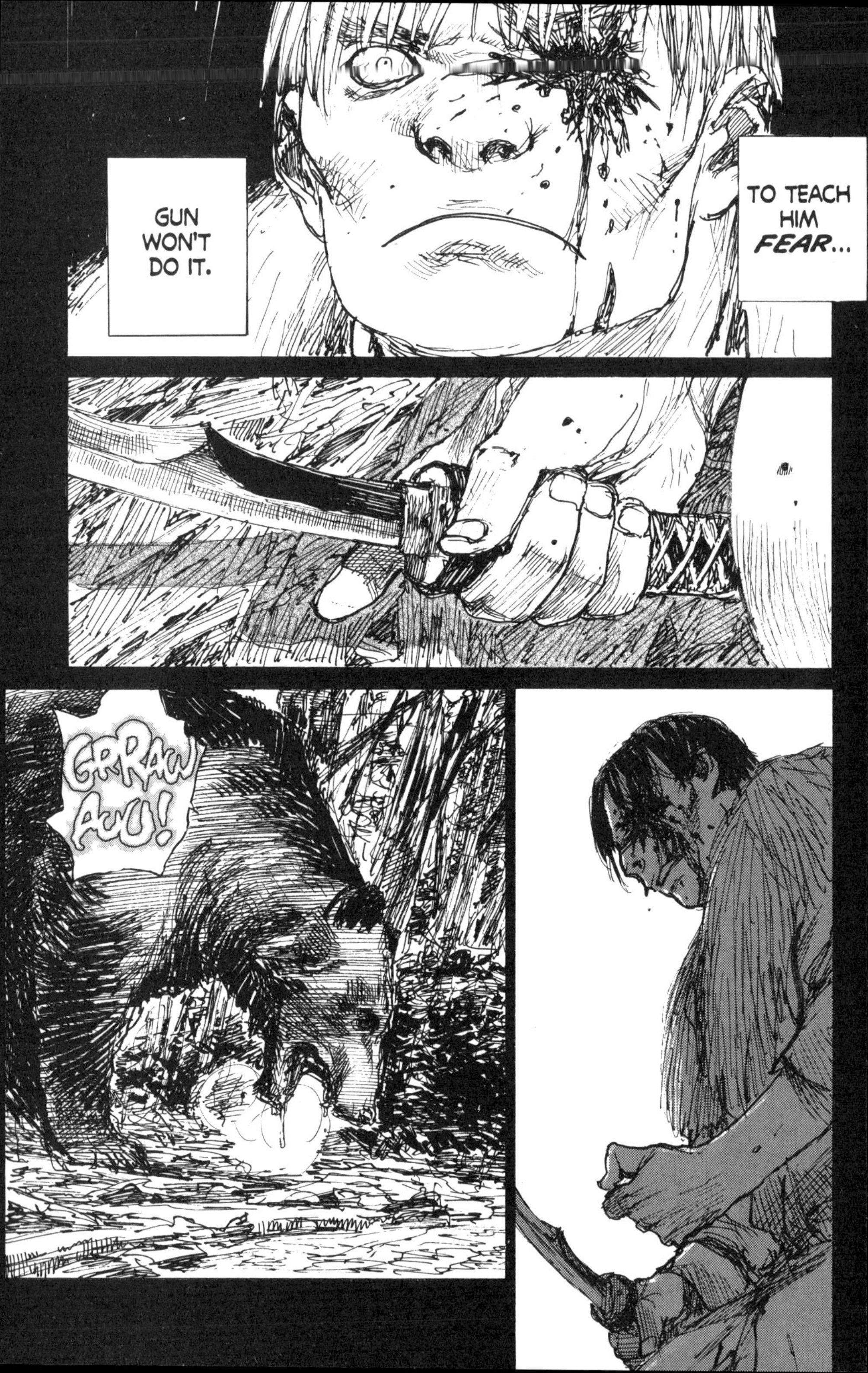
GUN WON'T DO IT.
TO TEACH HIM *FEAR*...
GRRAW AUU!

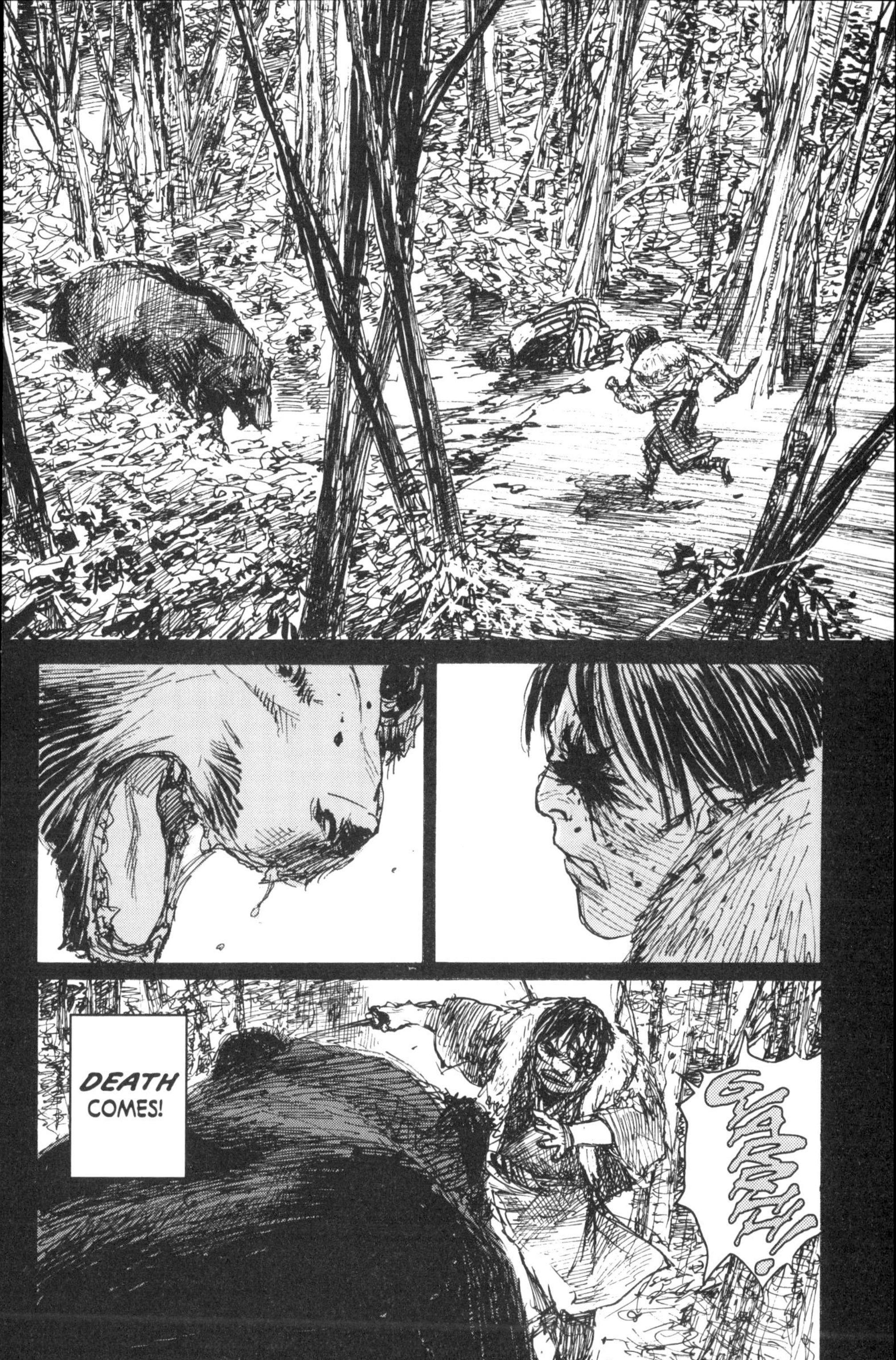
DEATH COMES!
GYAAAH!

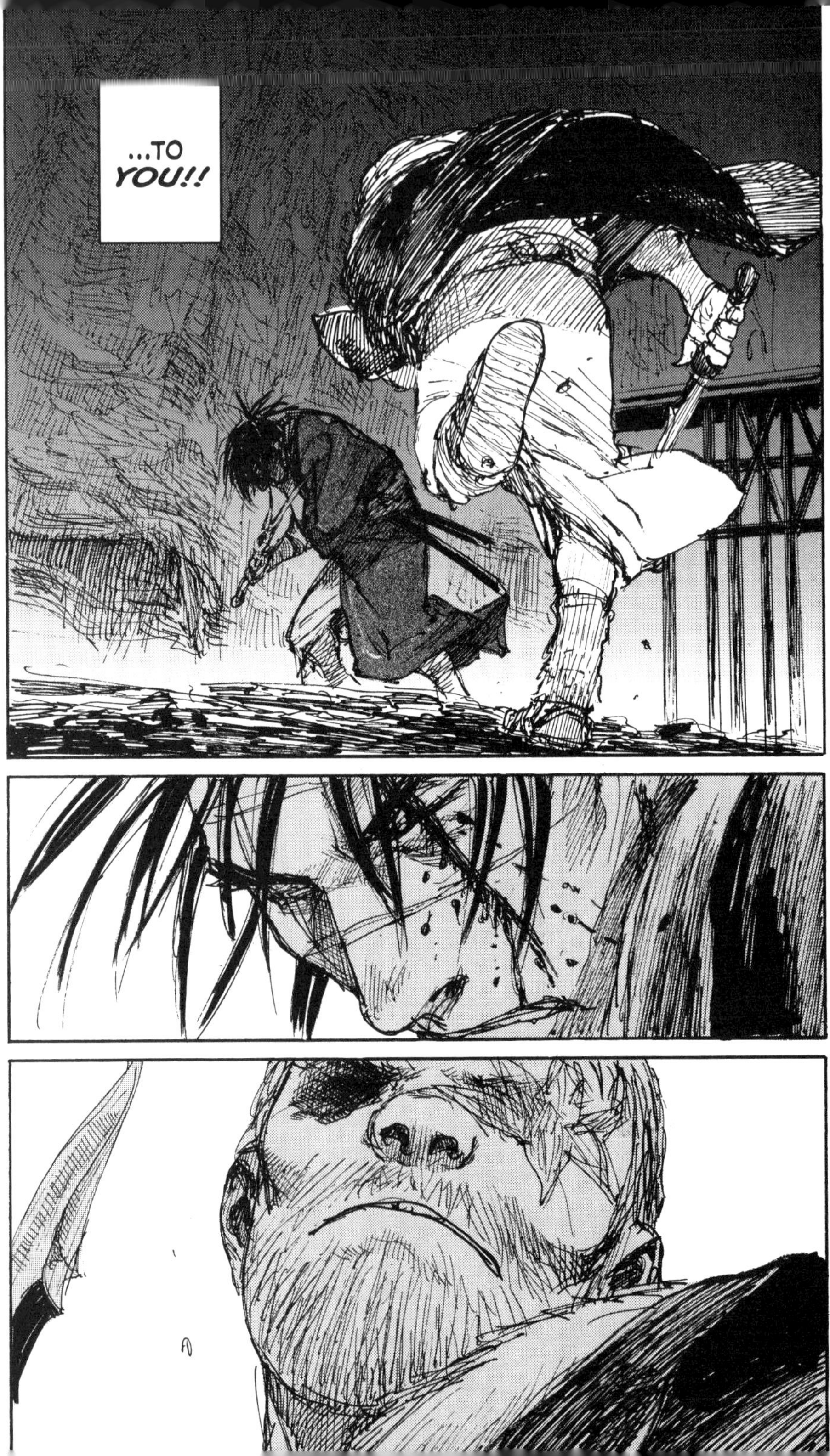
...TO
YOU!!

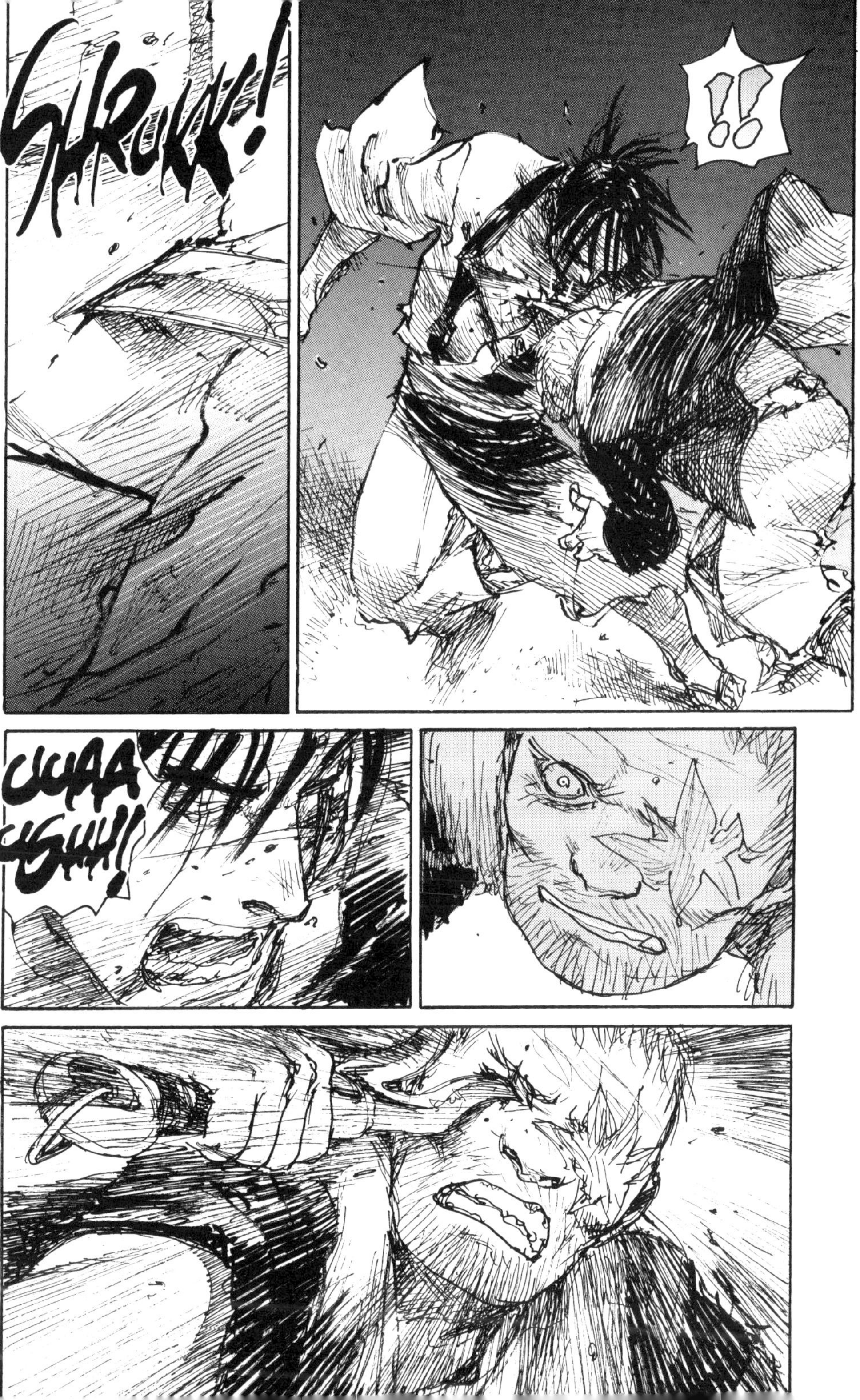
SHRUKK!
!!
UWAAGSHH!

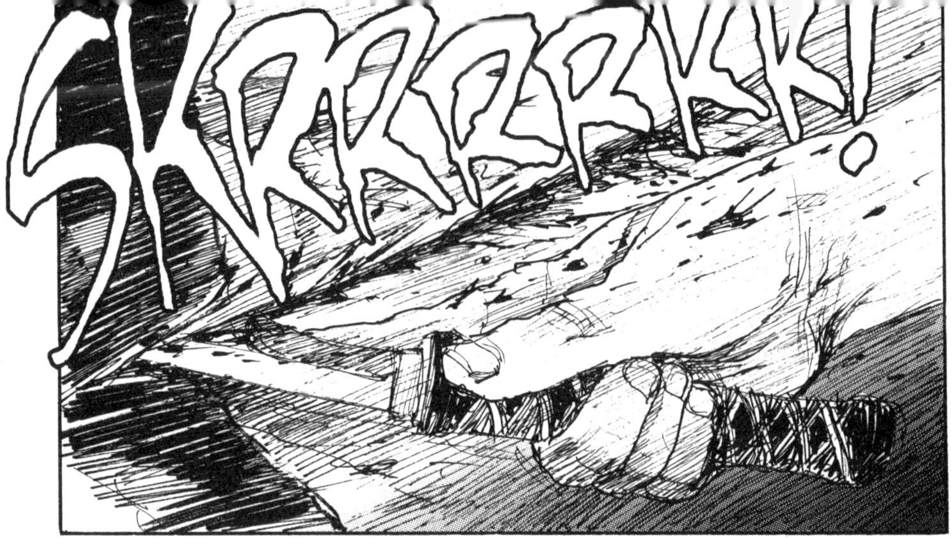
SKRRRRKK!

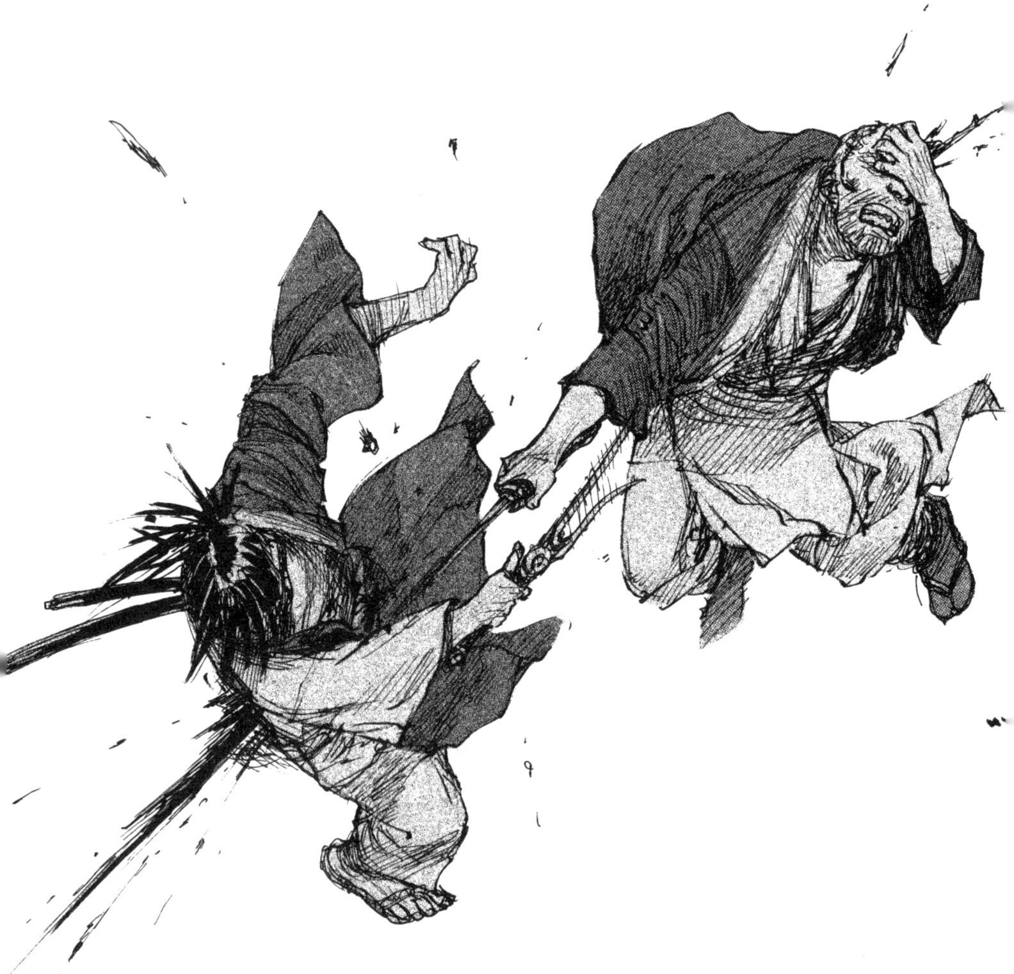

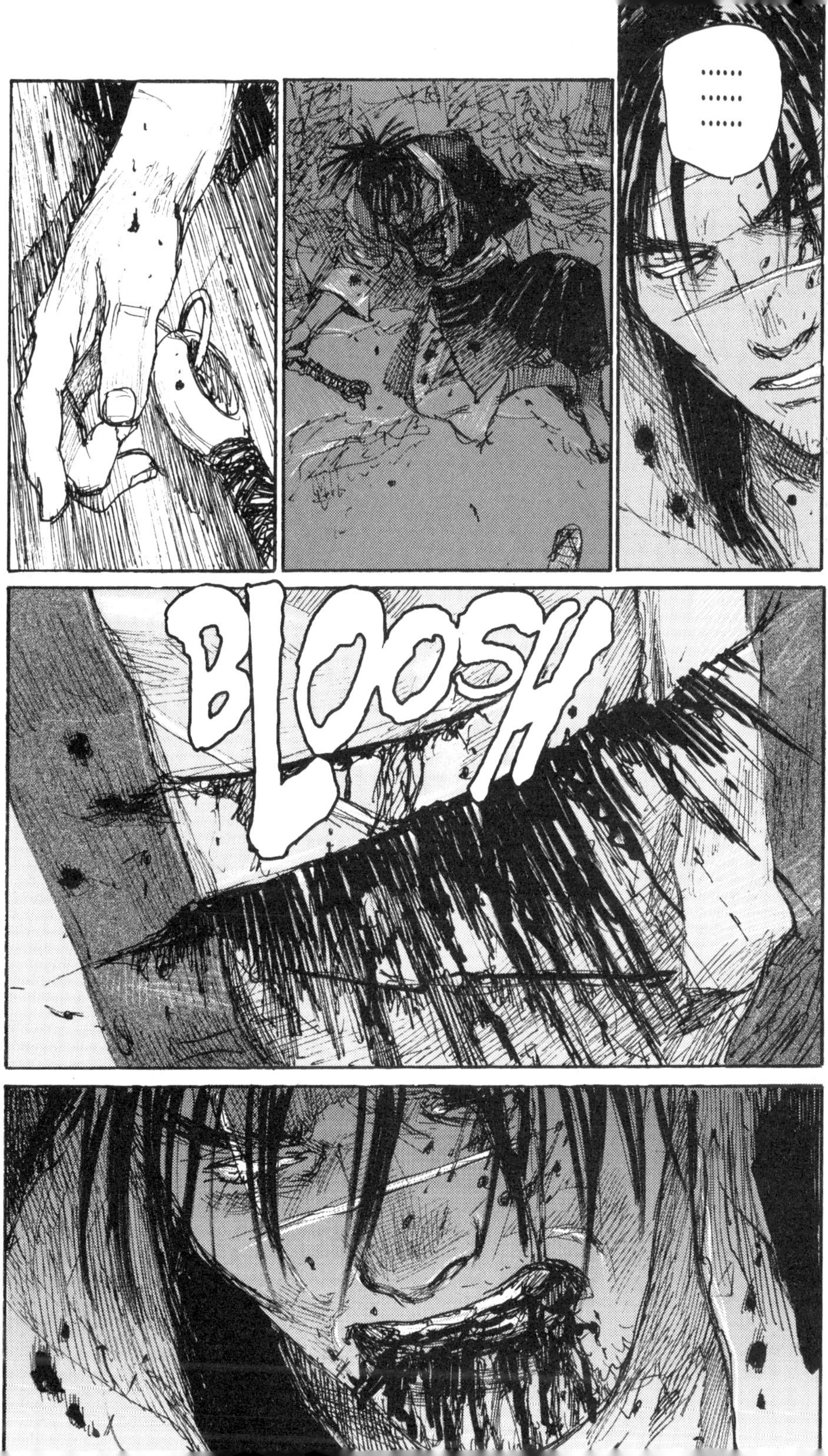

......
......
......
BLOOSH!

NNGH...

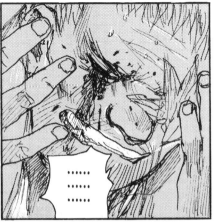

......
......
......

...AHNG...!

KILLER OF...

...A HUNDRED... HAVE I KILLED *YOU?!*

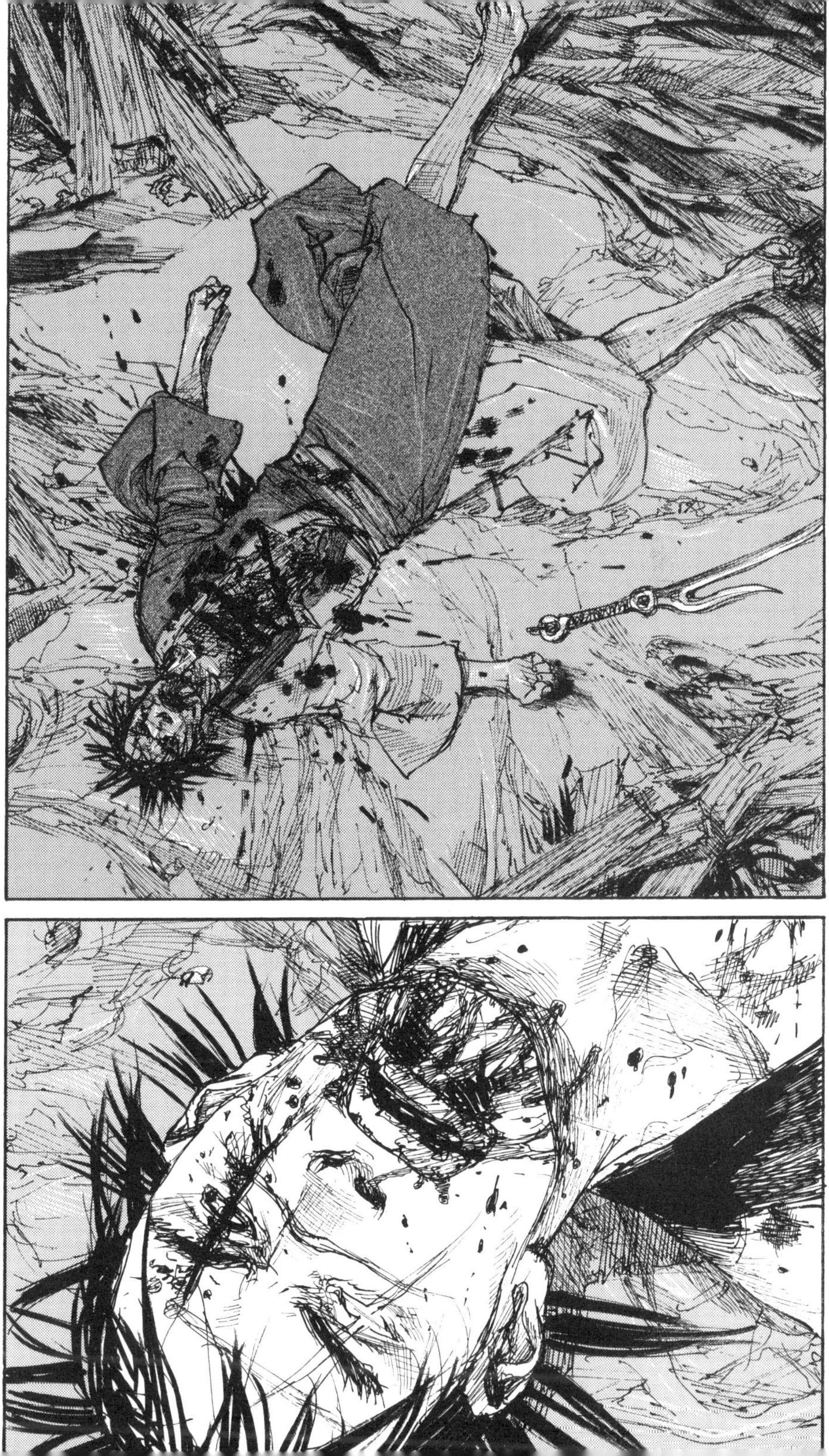

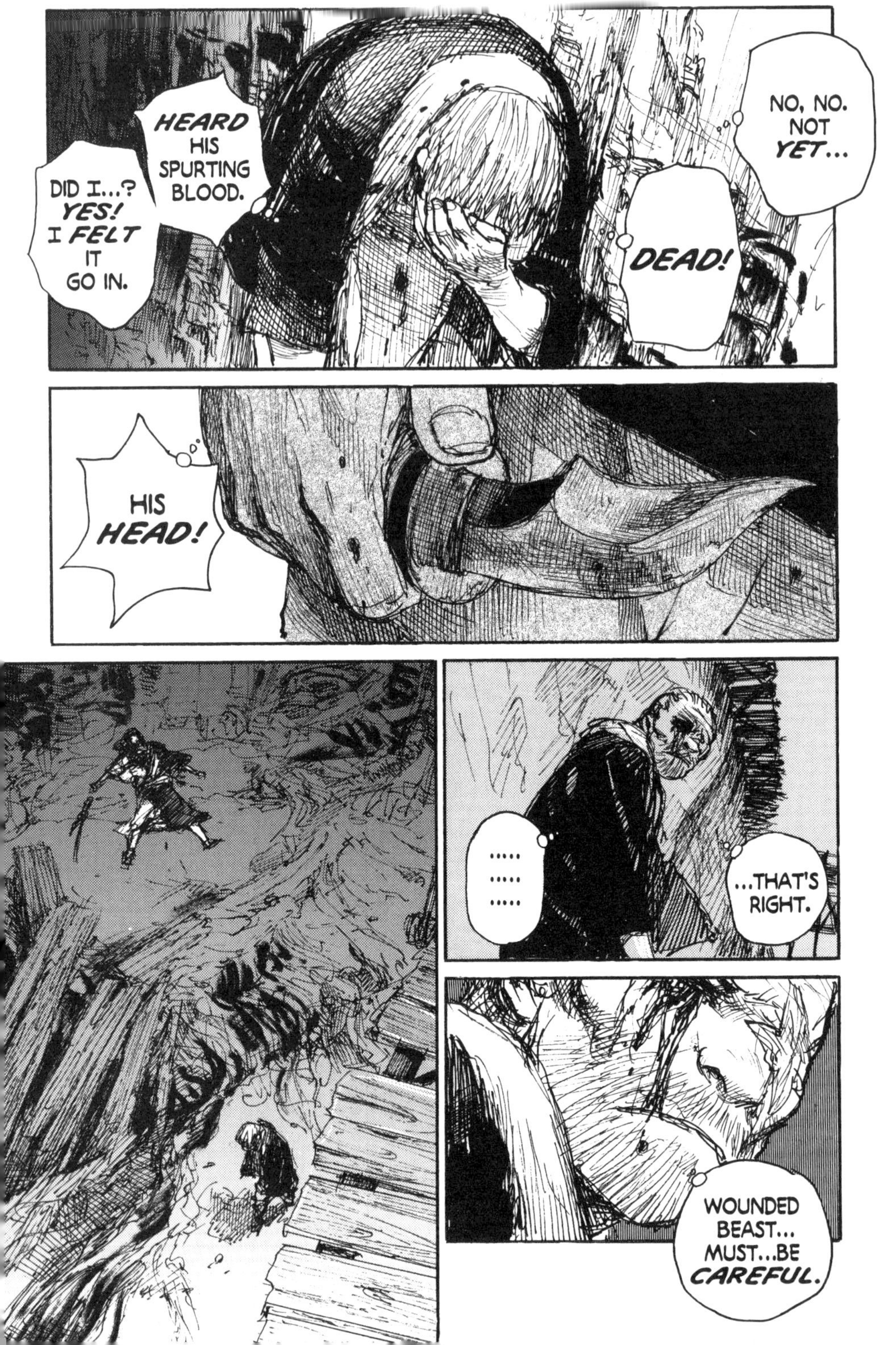
DID I...? YES! I FELT IT GO IN.
HEARD HIS SPURTING BLOOD.
DEAD!
NO, NO. NOT YET...
HIS HEAD!
....
...THAT'S RIGHT.
WOUNDED BEAST... MUST...BE CAREFUL.

~hahh~

~hff~

......
...GOOD IT WAS *NIGHT.*

THOUGHT I'D BE *DISORIENT-ED...*

BLIND-NESS, I CAN MANAGE...

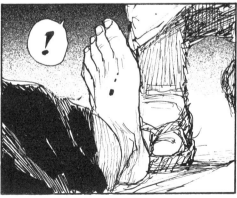

!

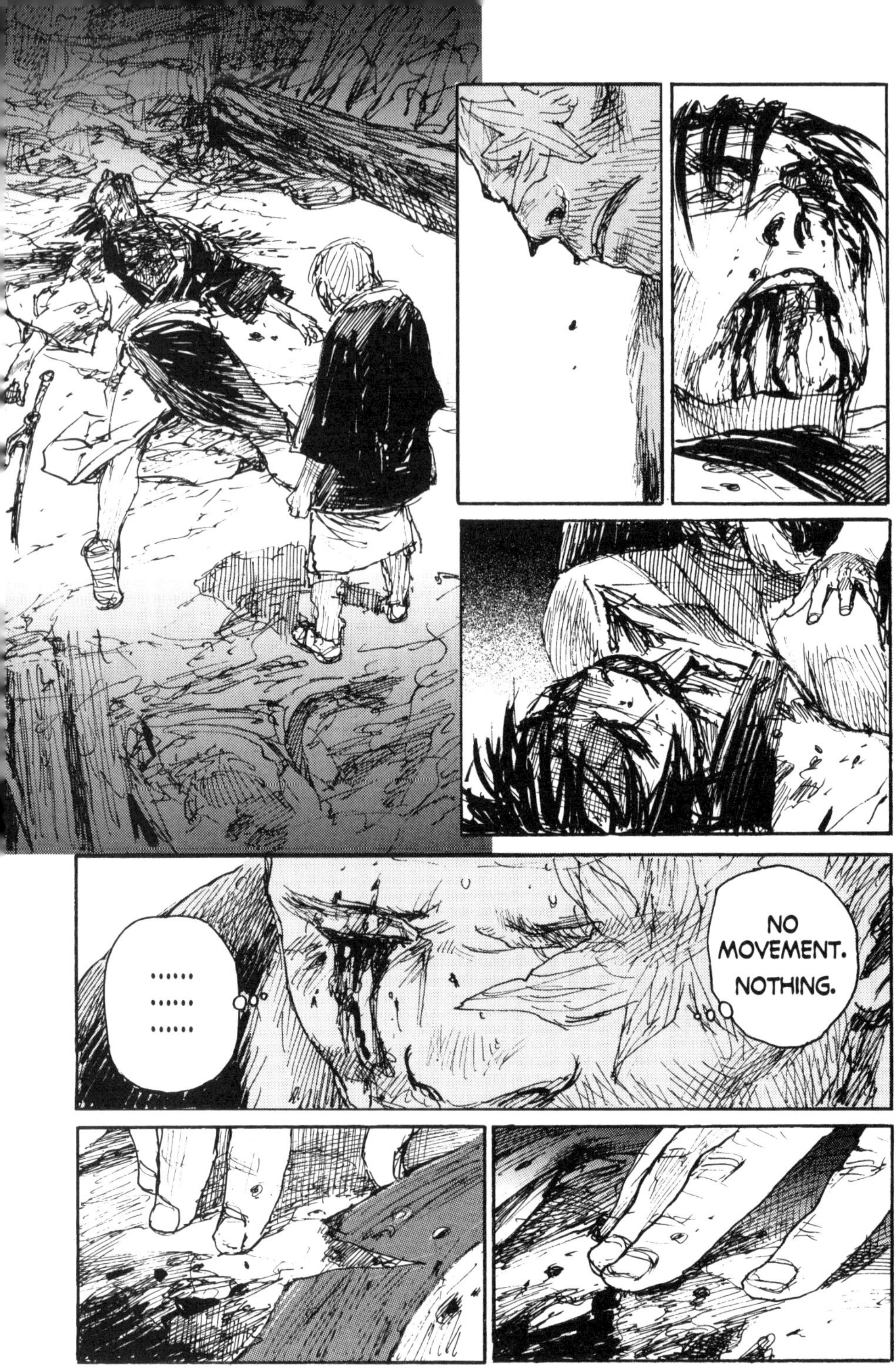
......
......
......
NO MOVEMENT. NOTHING.

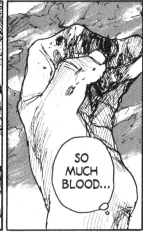

SO MUCH BLOOD...

THEN IT **WAS** HIS HEART...

...AND NOW...

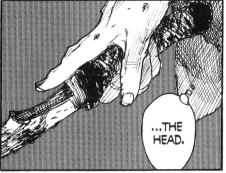

...THE HEAD.

WAIT...

hahf...!
hahh
haff
ahf
hahh
AFTER THE POISON, HALF AN HOUR AGO...
...OLD WOUNDS ACROSS HIS CHEST SPLIT OPEN.
THEN MINE. A THIRD.
THAT WOUND...
...SHOULD HAVE FINISHED HIM!

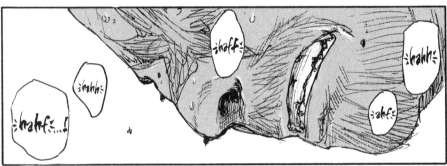

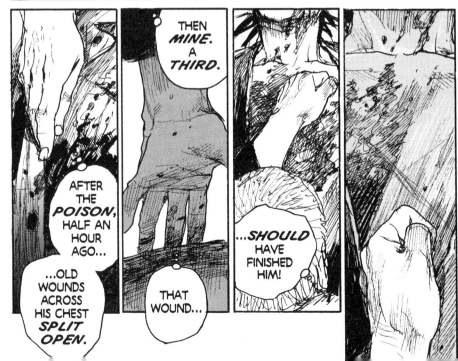

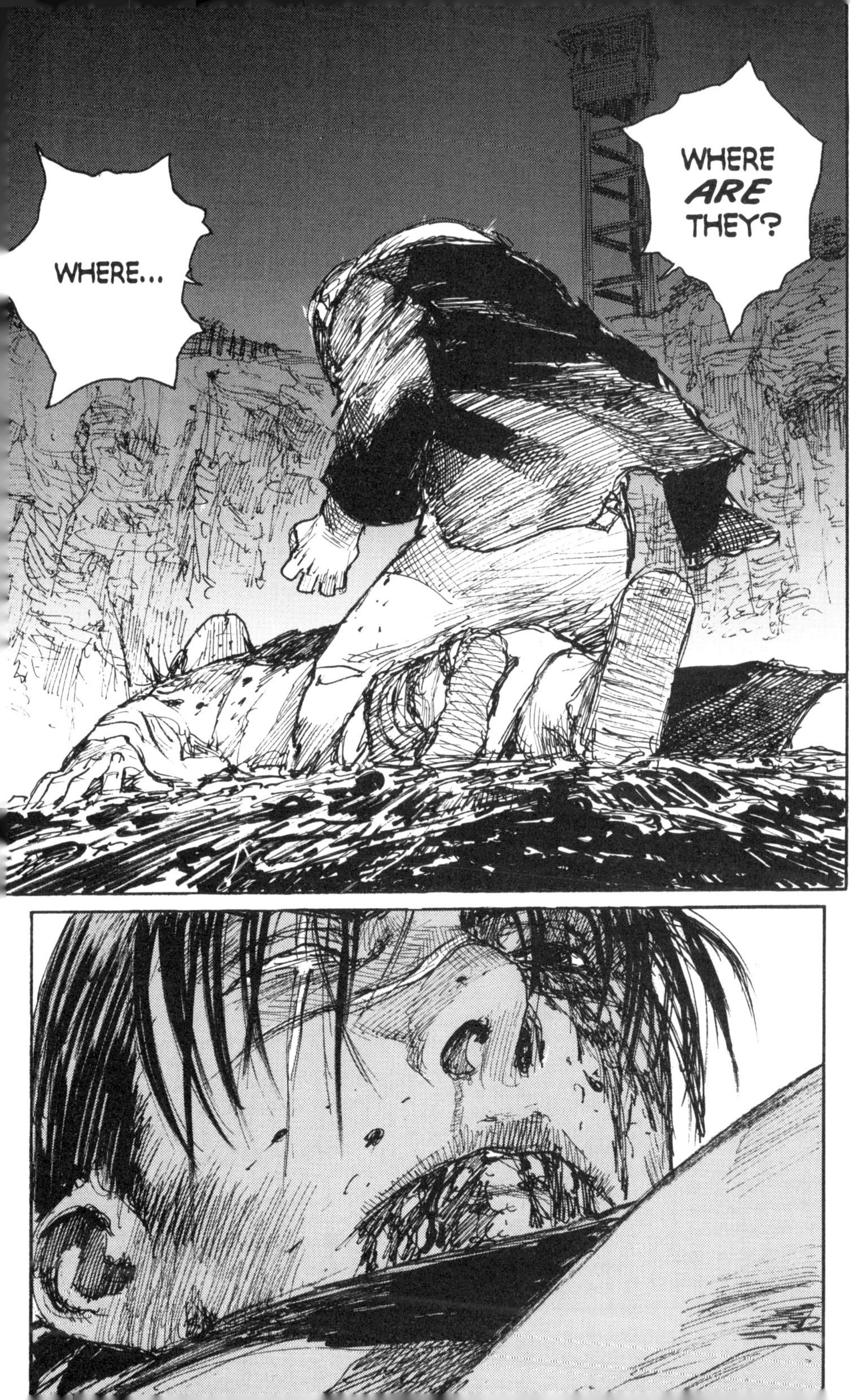
WHERE...
WHERE *ARE* THEY?

...GOD...

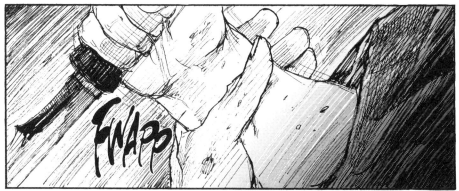

FNAPP

!

GULK

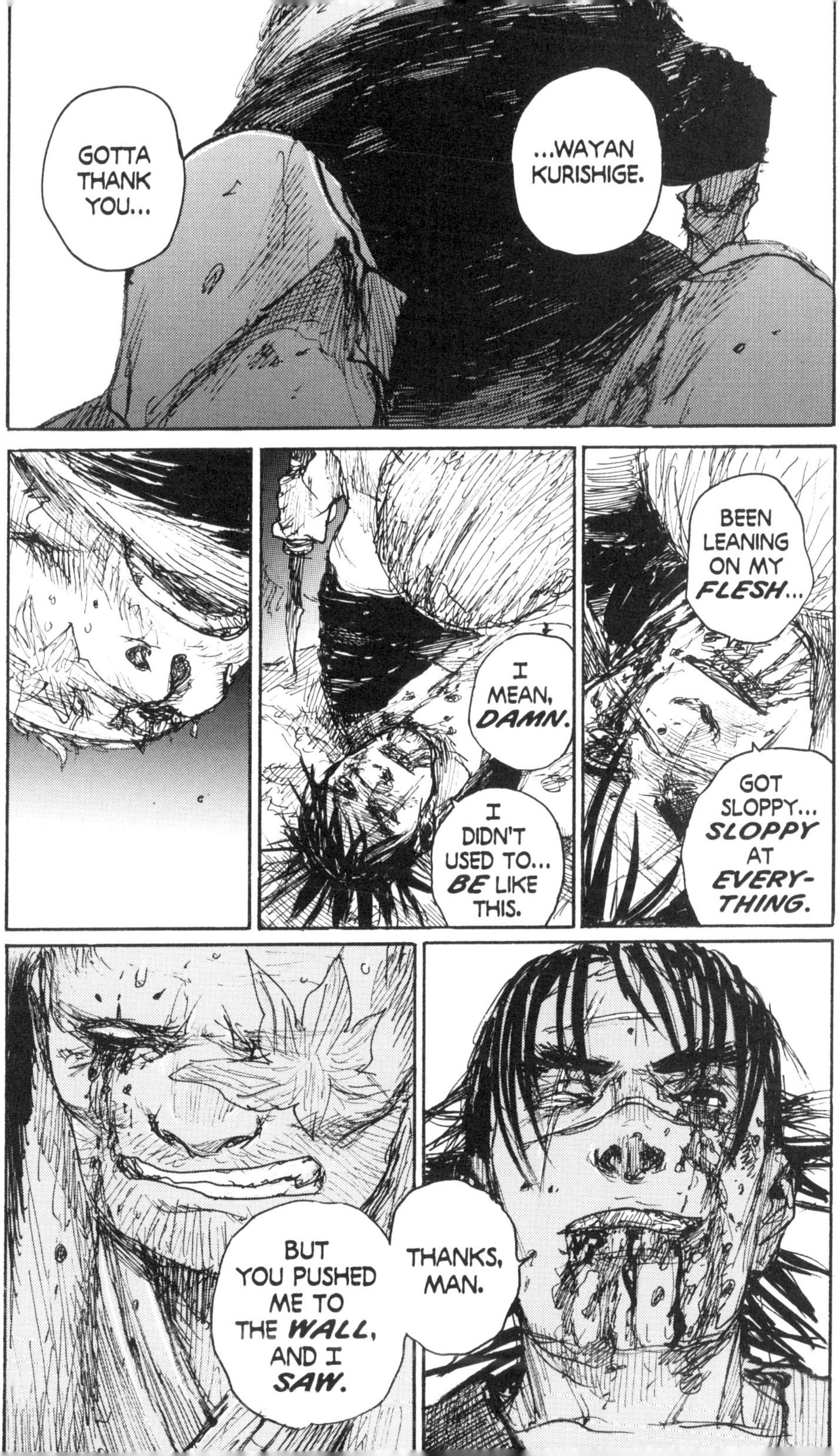
GOTTA THANK YOU...
...WAYAN KURISHIGE.
I MEAN, DAMN.
I DIDN'T USED TO... BE LIKE THIS.
BEEN LEANING ON MY FLESH...
GOT SLOPPY... SLOPPY AT EVERY-THING.
BUT YOU PUSHED ME TO THE WALL, AND I SAW.
THANKS, MAN.

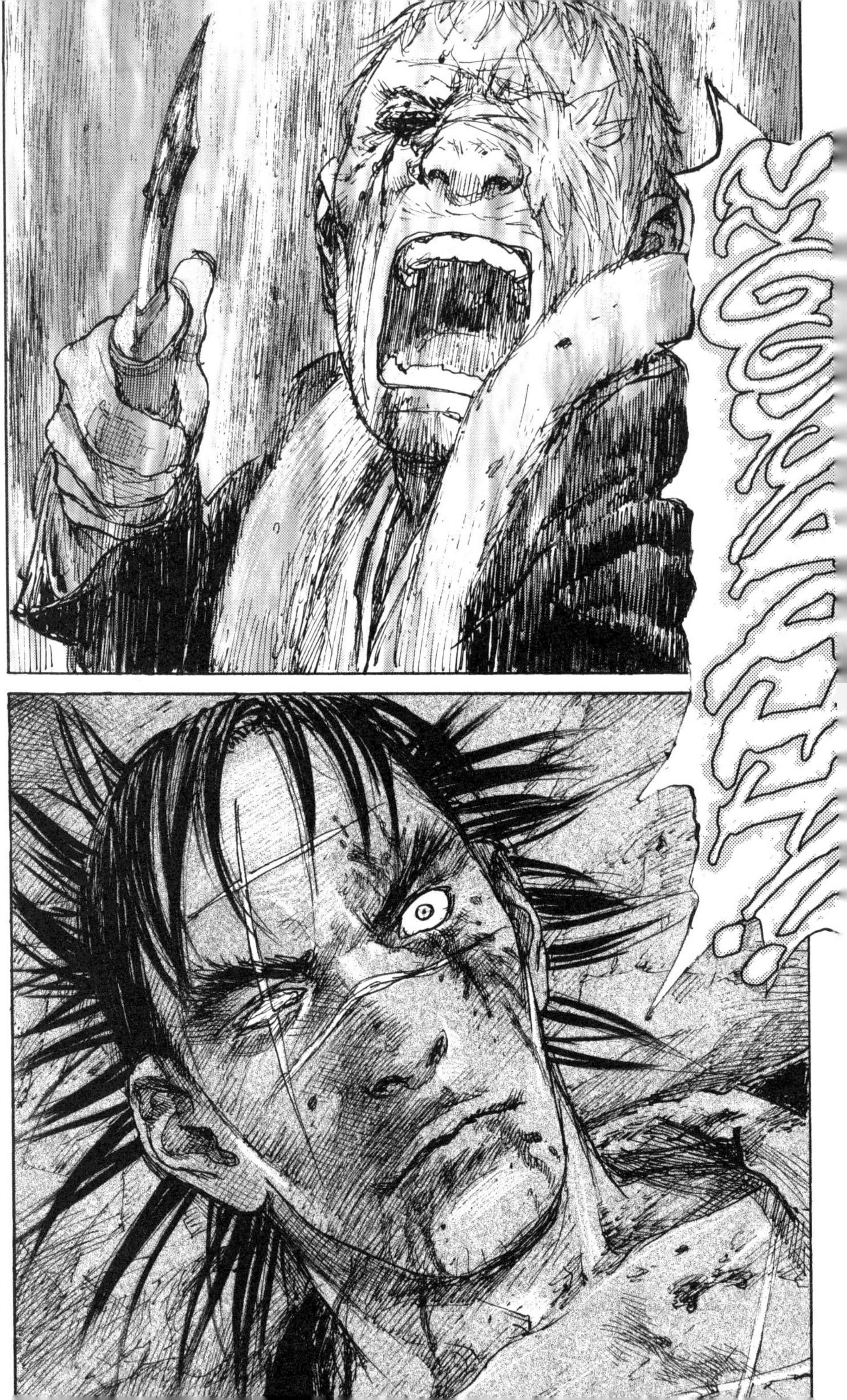

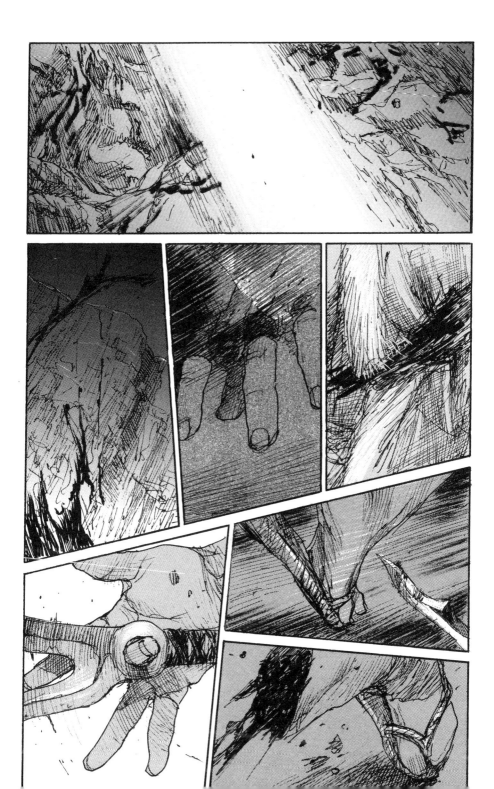

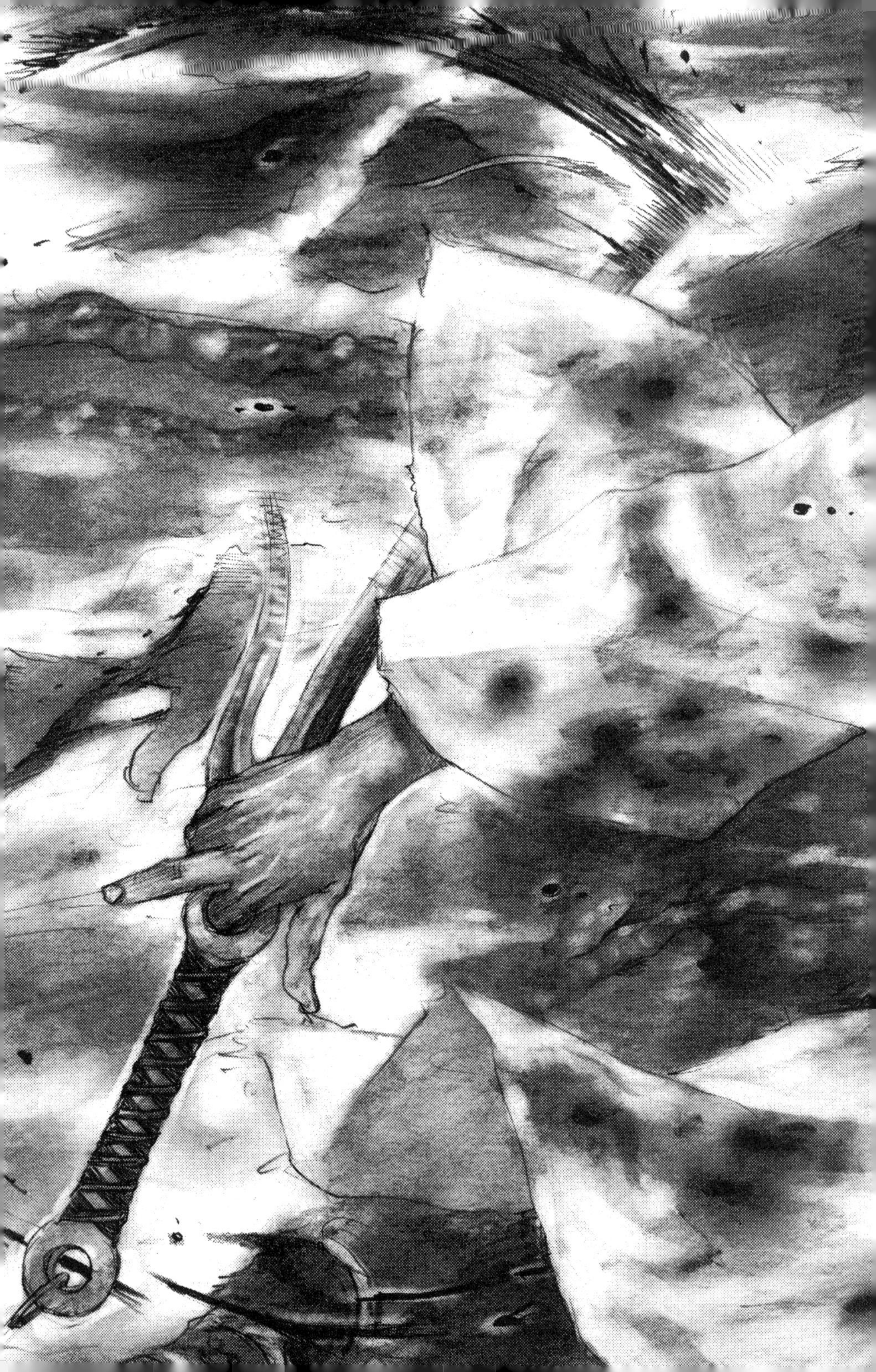

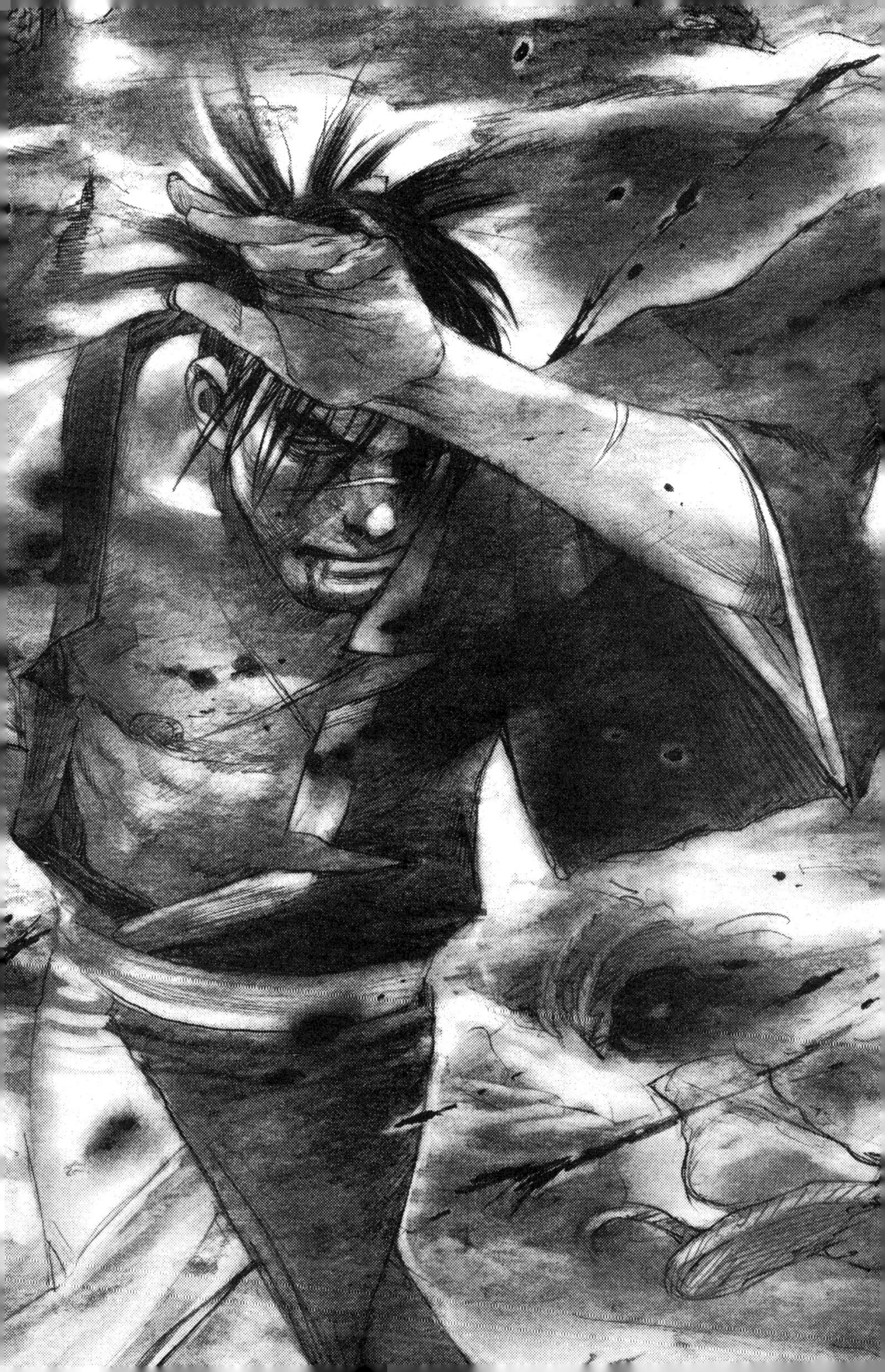

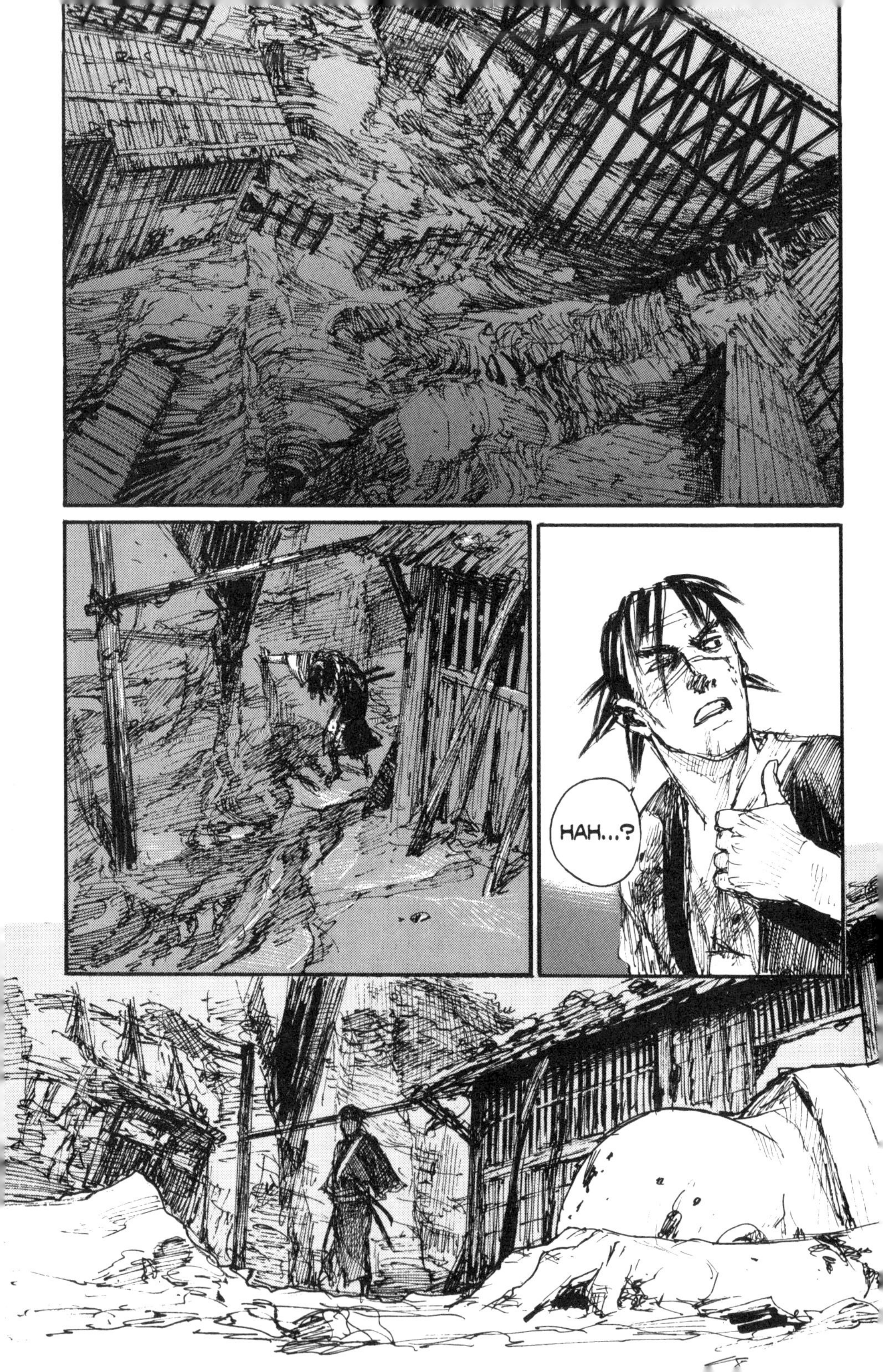
HAH...?

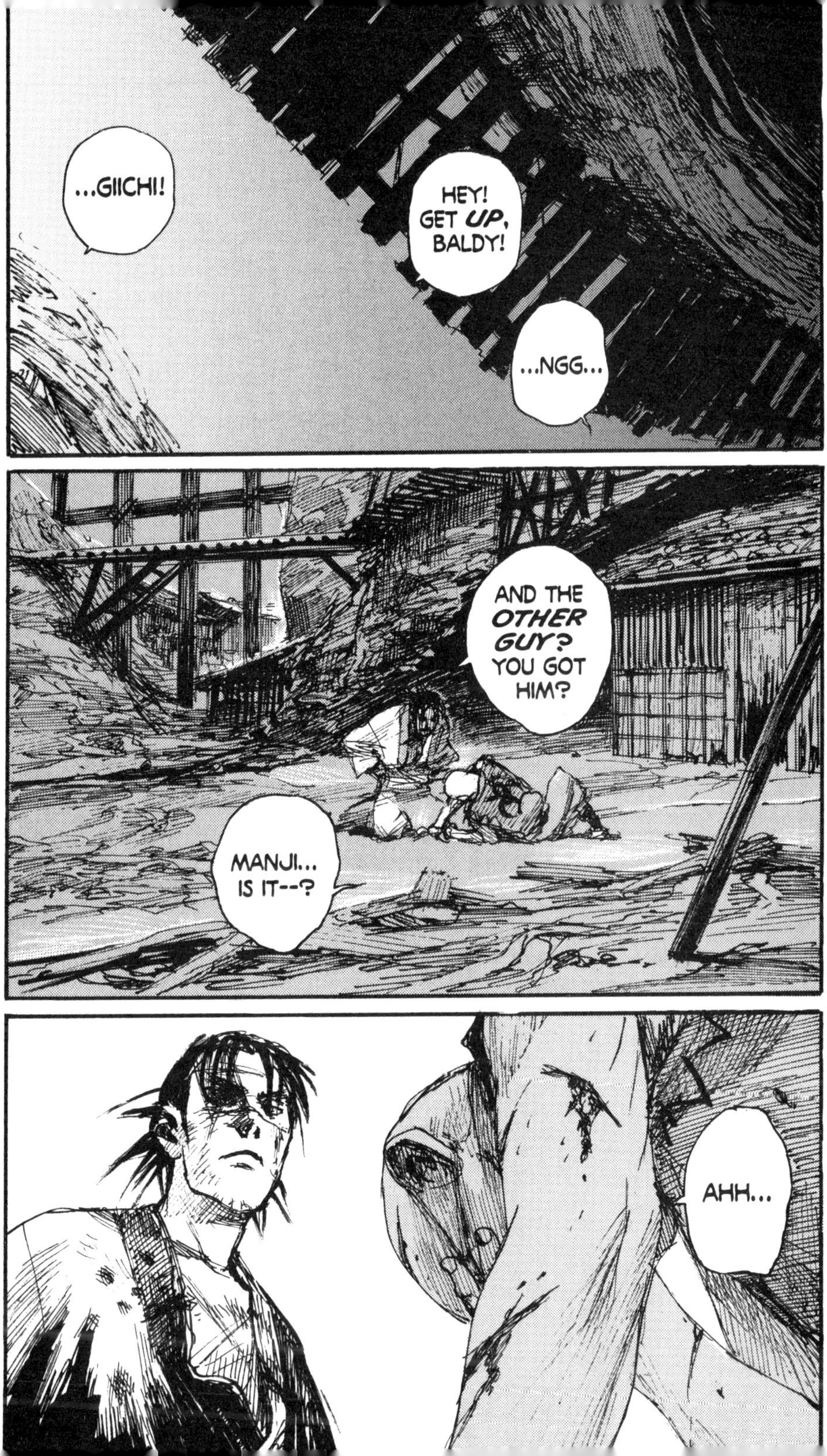
...GIICHI!
HEY! GET *UP*, BALDY!
...NGG...
AND THE *OTHER GUY*? YOU GOT HIM?
MANJI... IS IT--?
AHH...

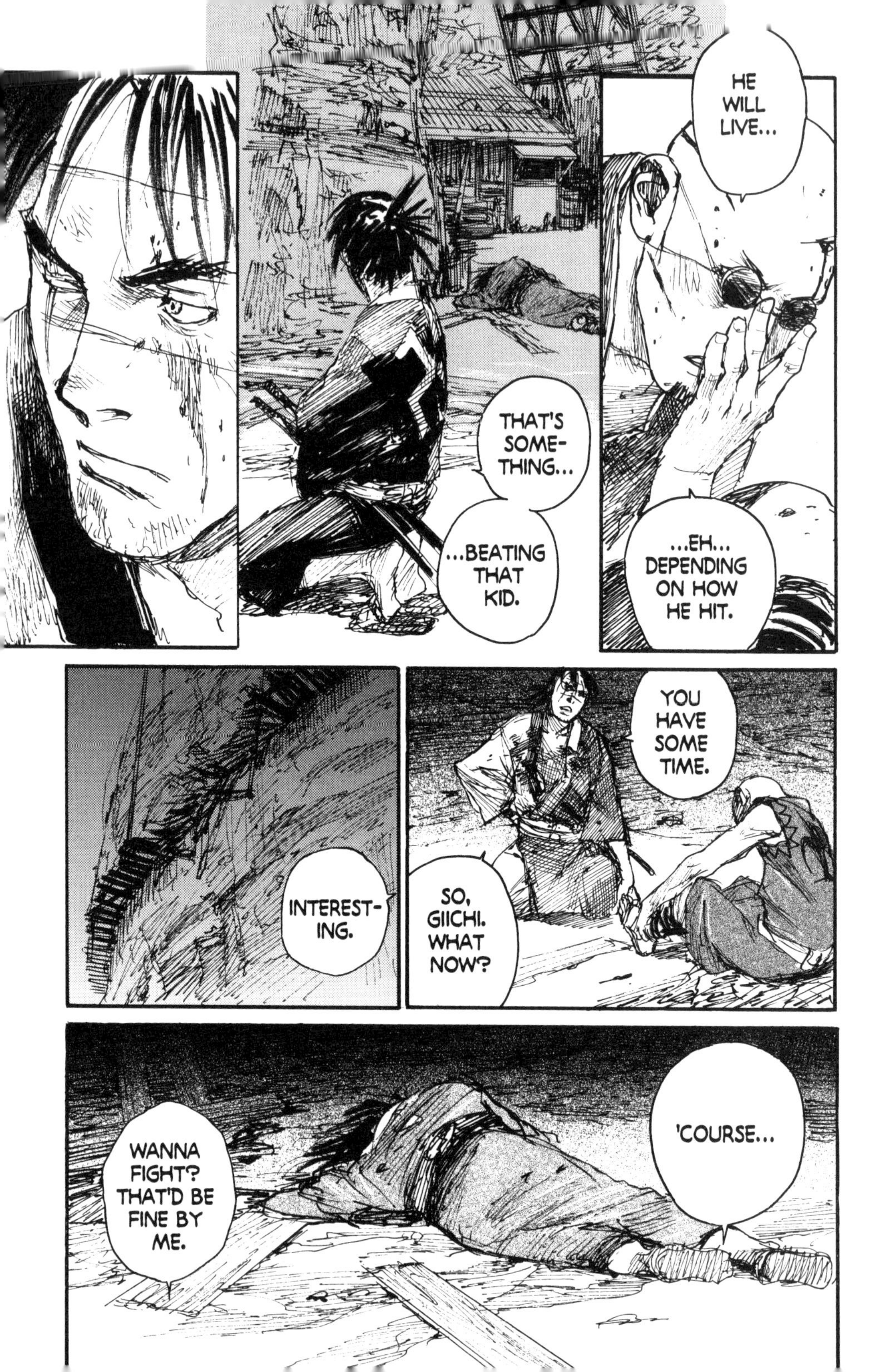
THAT'S SOME-THING...
...BEATING THAT KID.
HE WILL LIVE...
...EH... DEPENDING ON HOW HE HIT.
INTEREST-ING.
YOU HAVE SOME TIME.
SO, GIICHI. WHAT NOW?
'COURSE...
WANNA FIGHT? THAT'D BE FINE BY ME.

...IF YA DO, I'LL WAKE HIM UP.

THESE THINGS AIN'T *FUN* IF THEY'RE NOT *FAIR*... RIGHT?

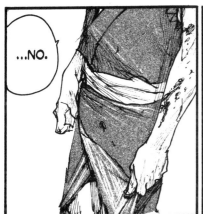

...NO.

ENOUGH. I DIDN'T COME TO DUEL. BESIDES...

...I DON'T WISH TO DEAL WITH HIM NOW. MY RIGHT ARM IS A WRECK.

GUESS SO...

MANJI.

AHNN?

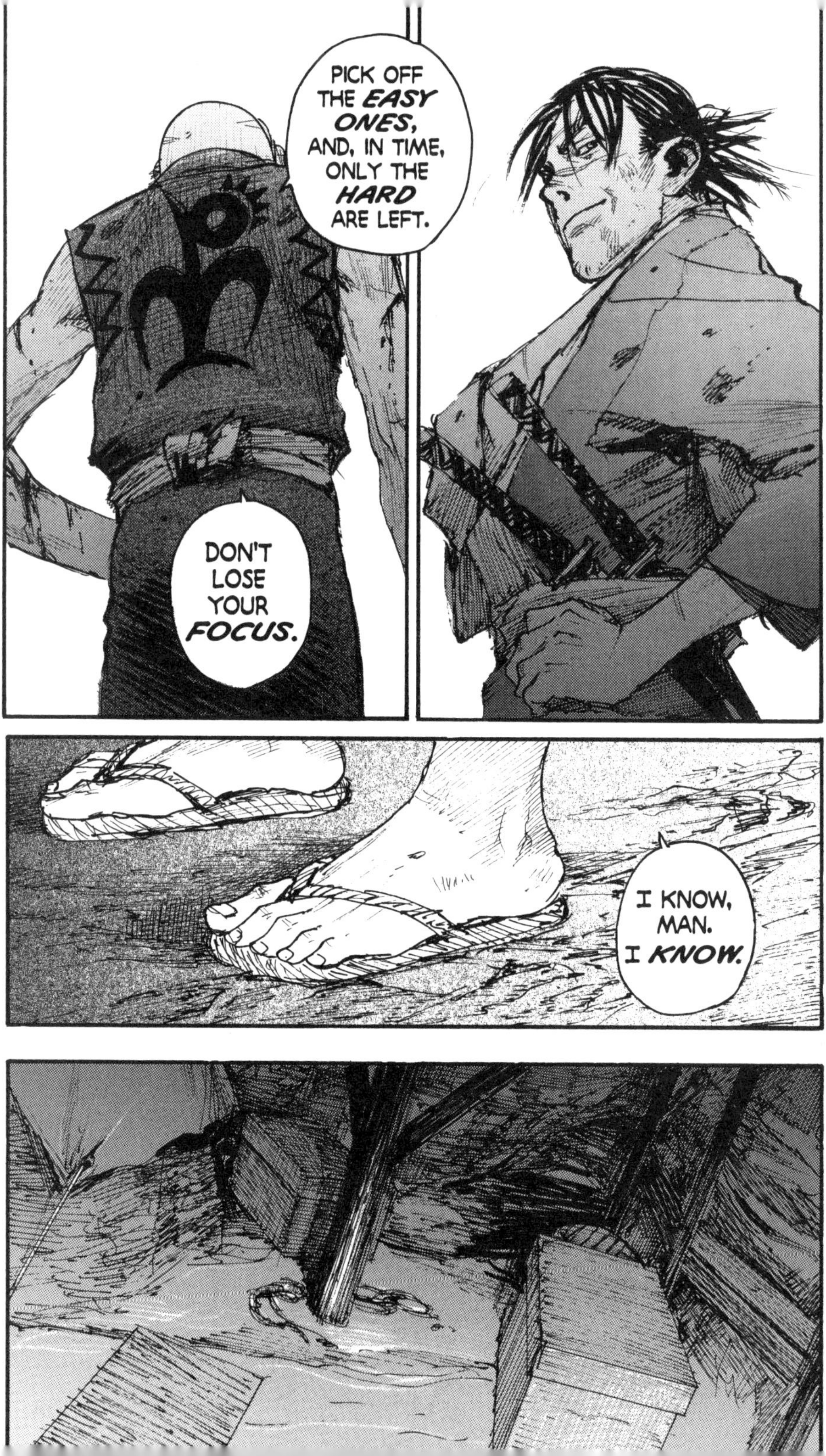
PICK OFF THE *EASY ONES*, AND, IN TIME, ONLY THE *HARD* ARE LEFT.
DON'T LOSE YOUR *FOCUS*.
I KNOW, MAN. I *KNOW*.

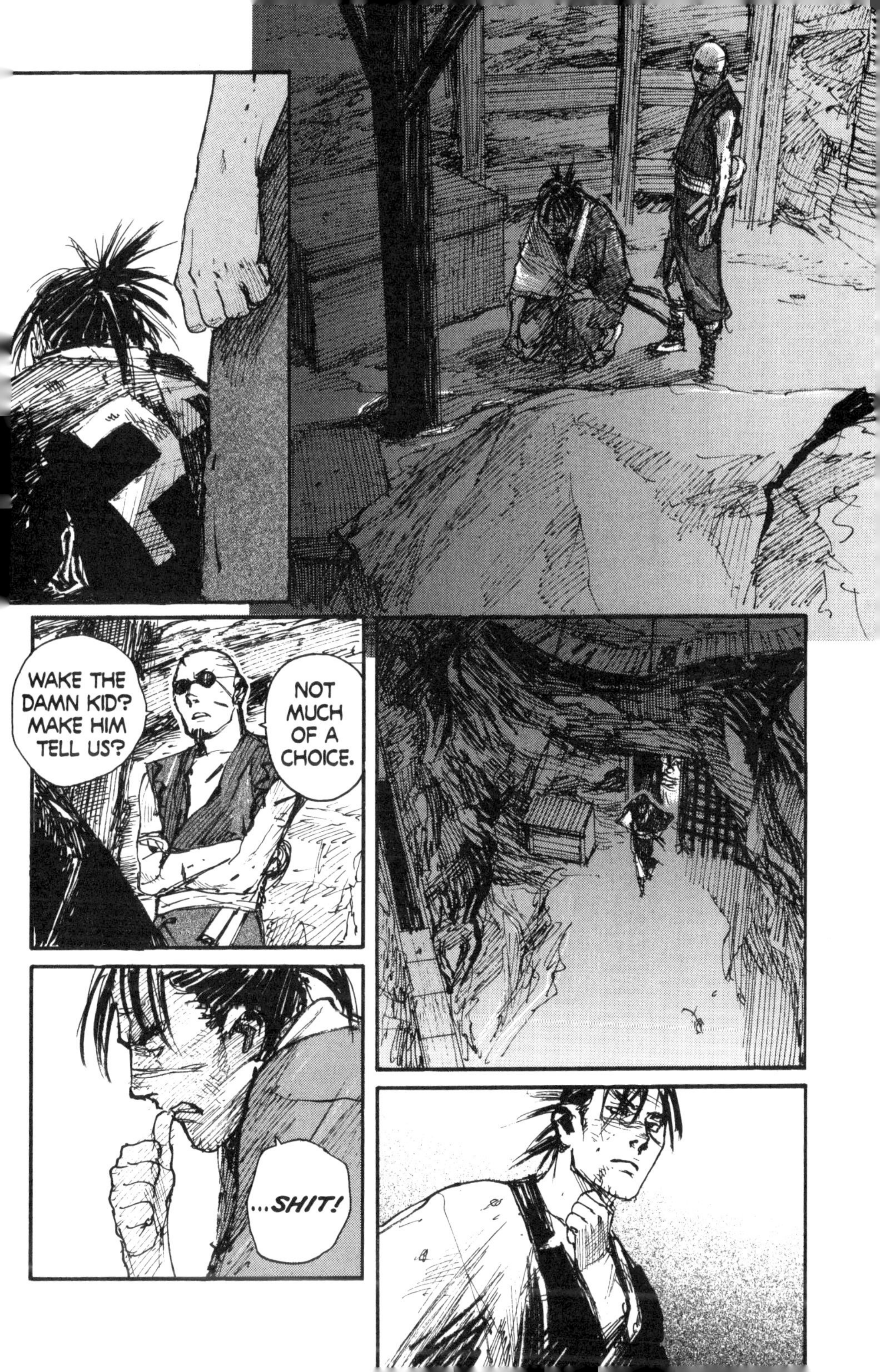
WAKE THE DAMN KID? MAKE HIM TELL US?
NOT MUCH OF A CHOICE.
...SHIT!

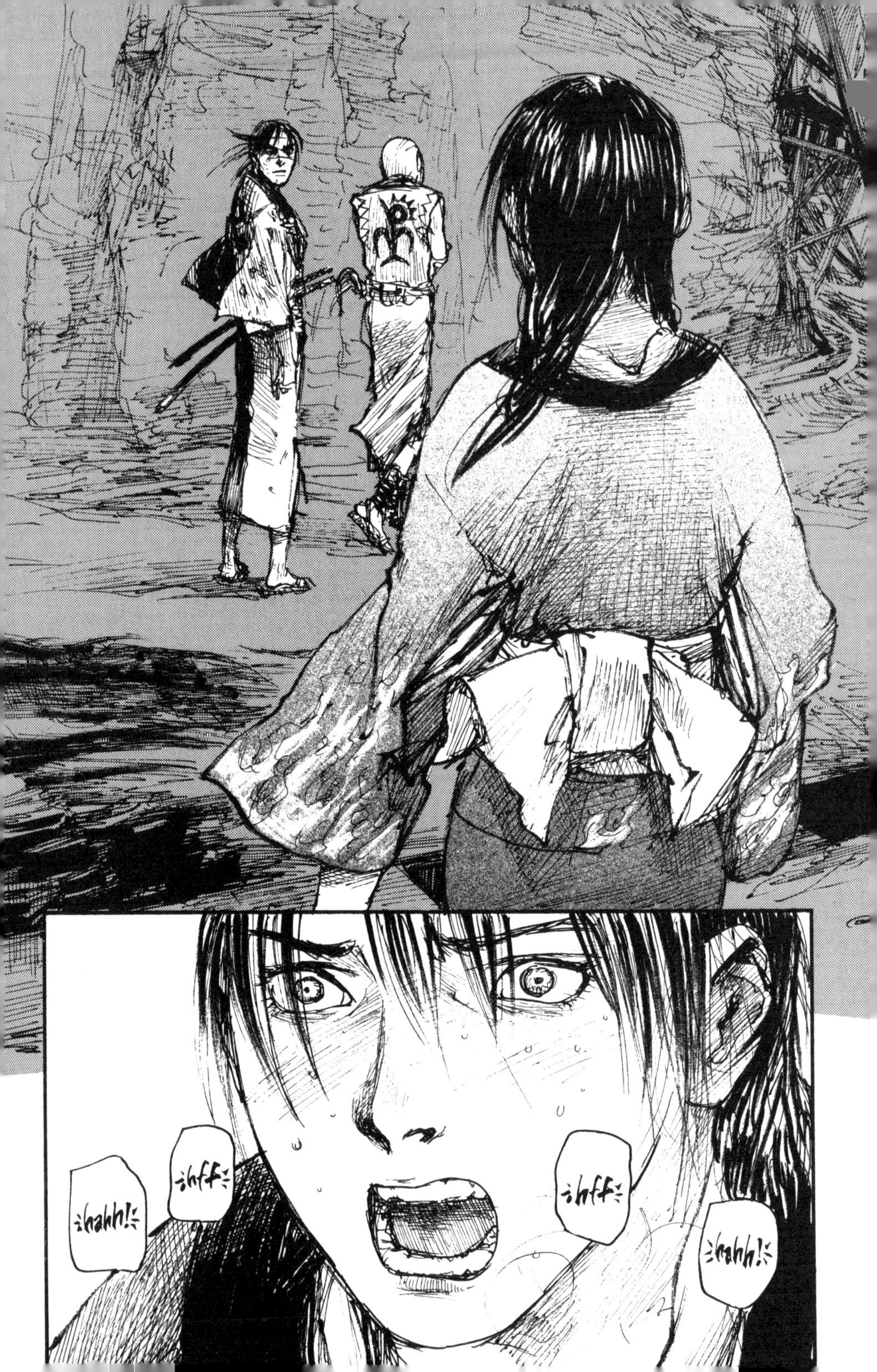

hahh!
hff
hff
hahh!

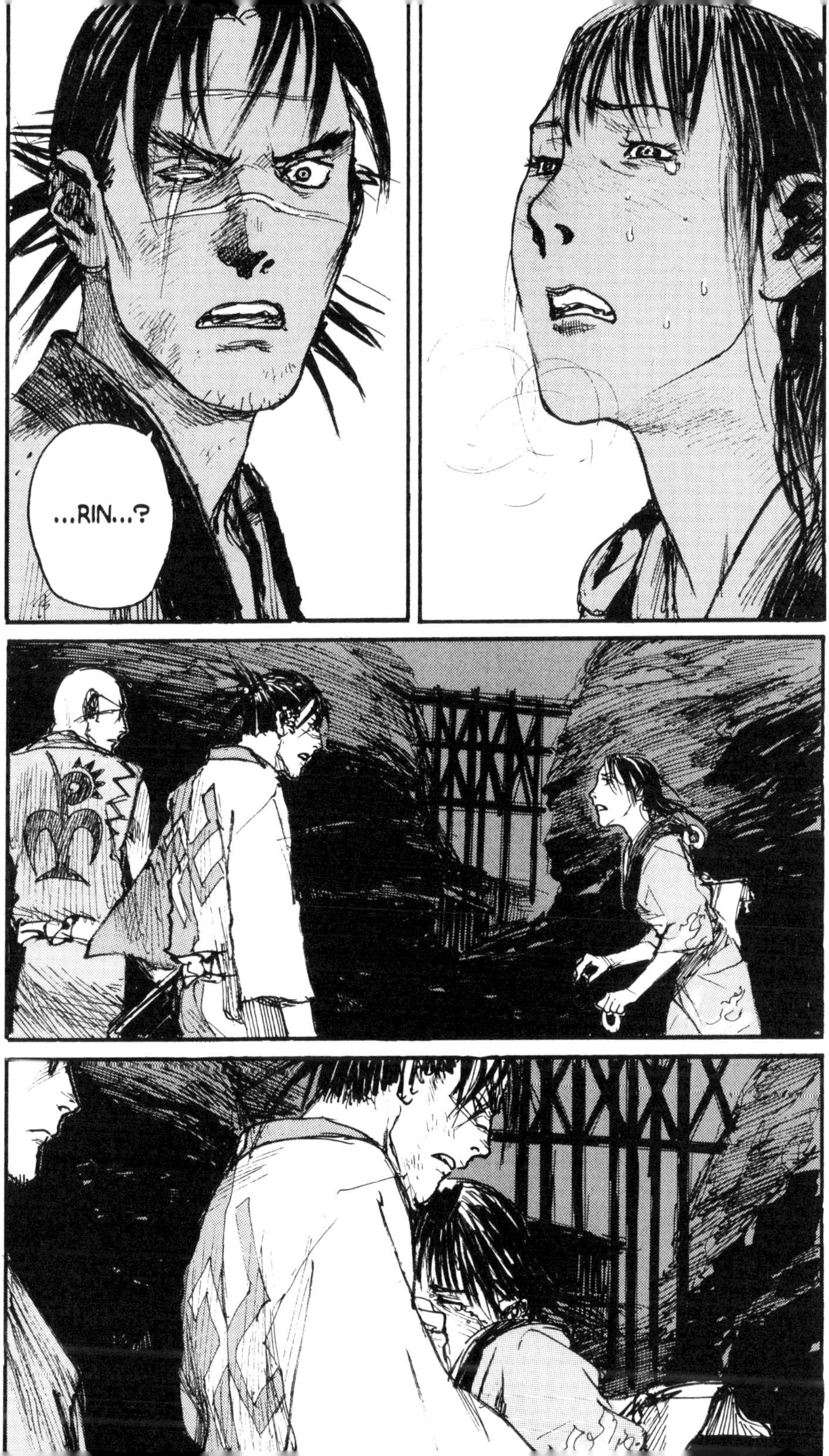
...RIN...?

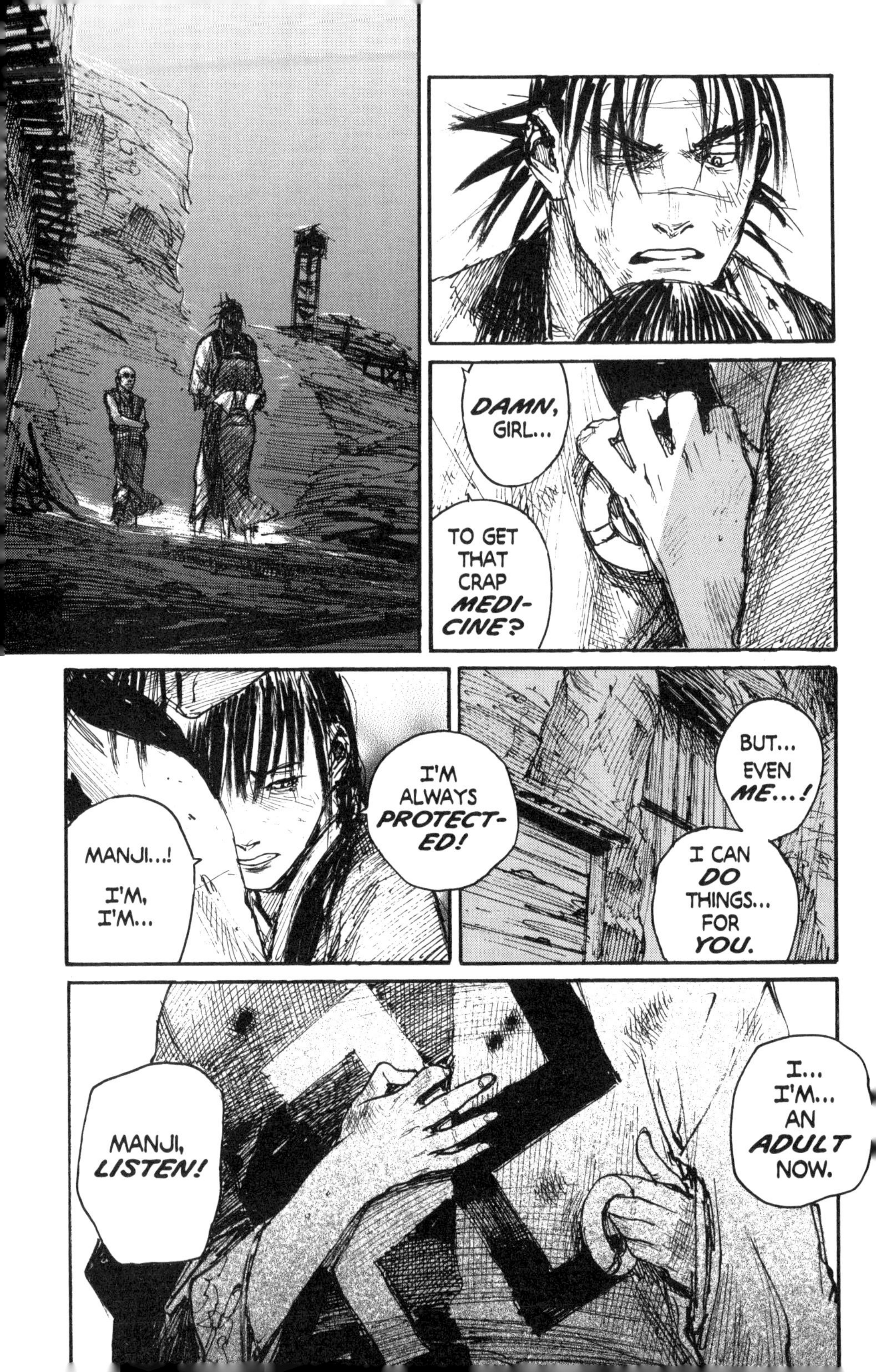
DAMN, GIRL...
TO GET THAT CRAP MEDICINE?
MANJI...! I'M, I'M...
I'M ALWAYS PROTECTED!
BUT... EVEN ME...!
I CAN DO THINGS... FOR YOU.
MANJI, LISTEN!
I... I'M... AN ADULT NOW.

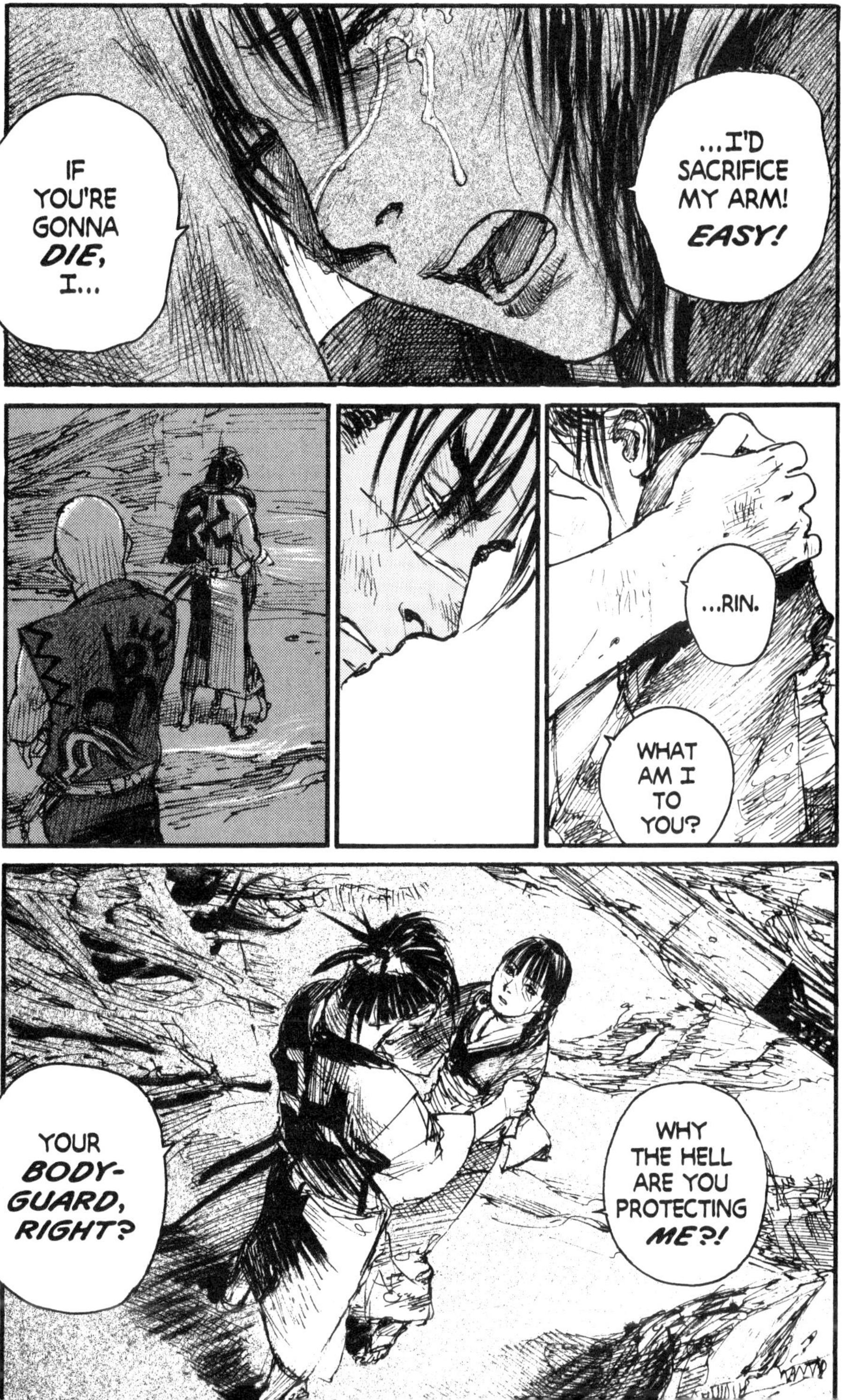
IF YOU'RE GONNA *DIE*, I...
...I'D SACRIFICE MY ARM! *EASY!*
...RIN.
WHAT AM I TO YOU?
YOUR *BODY-GUARD, RIGHT?*
WHY THE HELL ARE YOU PROTECTING *ME?!*

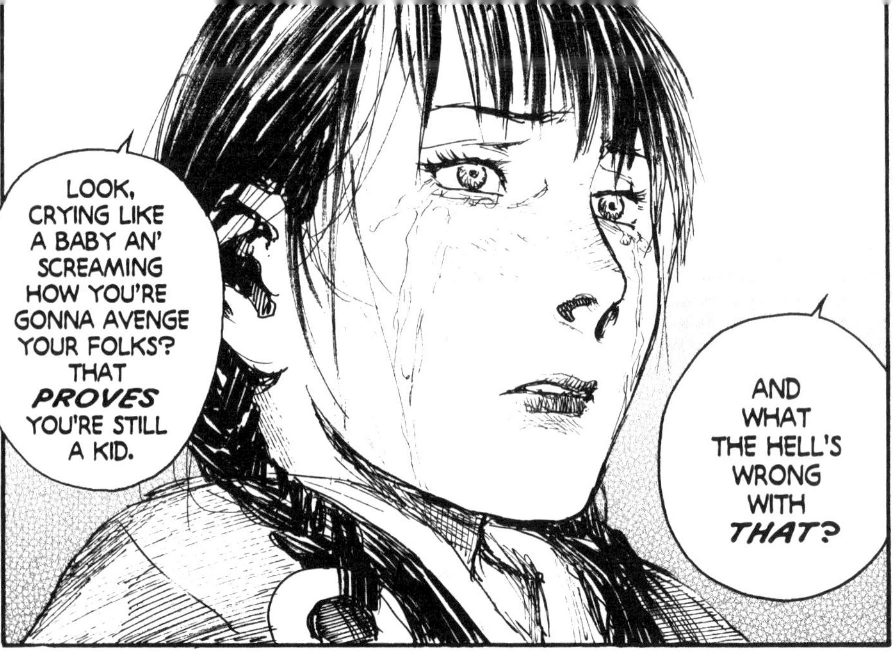
LOOK, CRYING LIKE A BABY AN' SCREAMING HOW YOU'RE GONNA AVENGE YOUR FOLKS? THAT *PROVES* YOU'RE STILL A KID.
AND WHAT THE HELL'S WRONG WITH *THAT?*
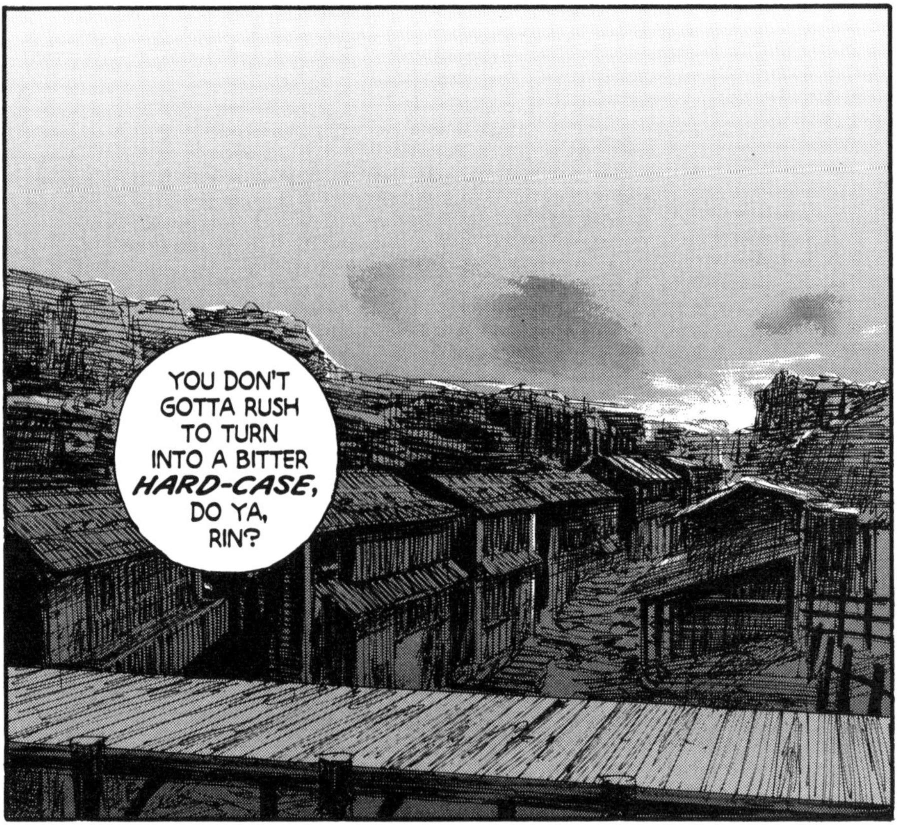
YOU DON'T GOTTA RUSH TO TURN INTO A BITTER *HARD-CASE,* DO YA, RIN?

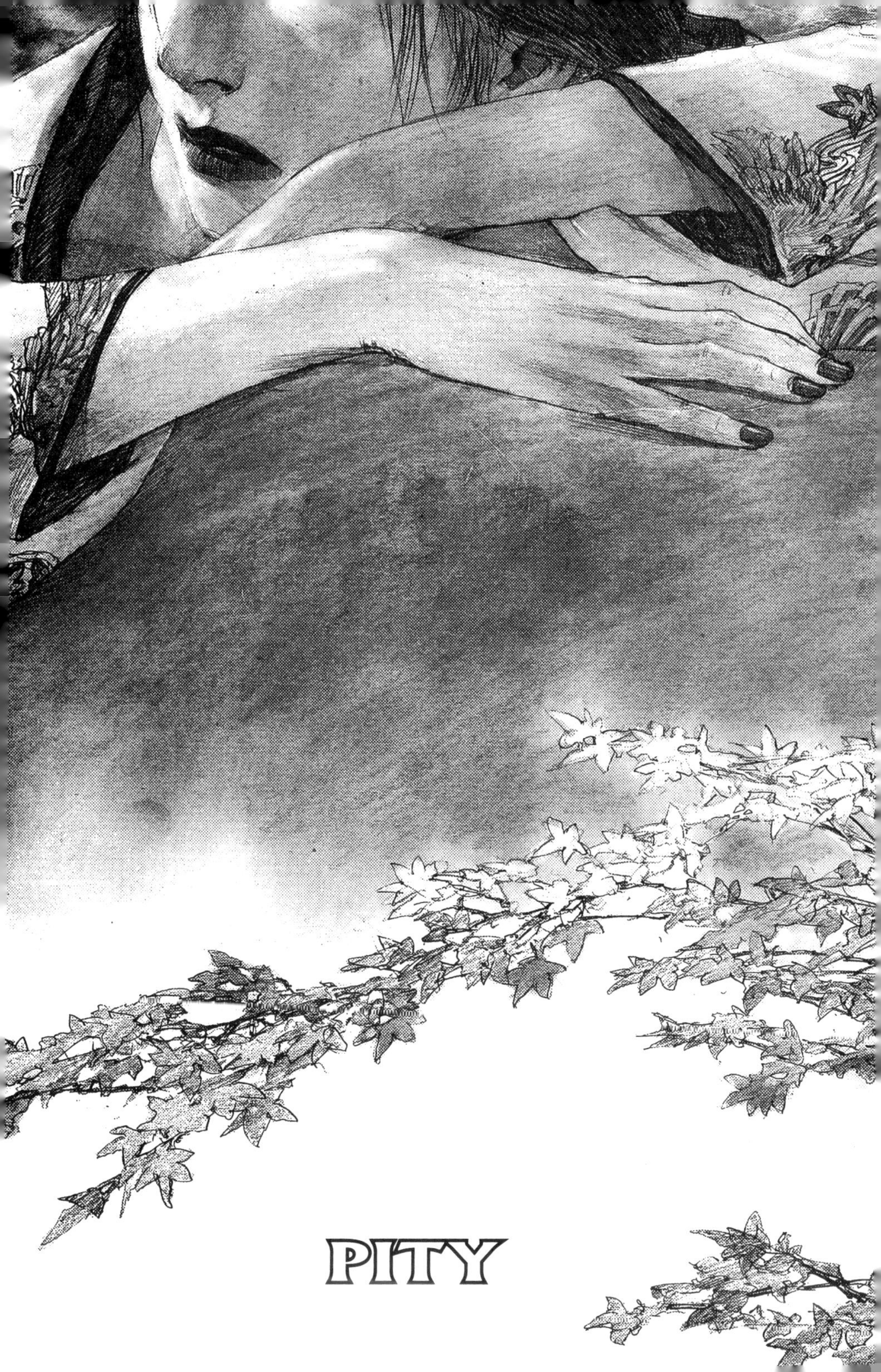

PITY

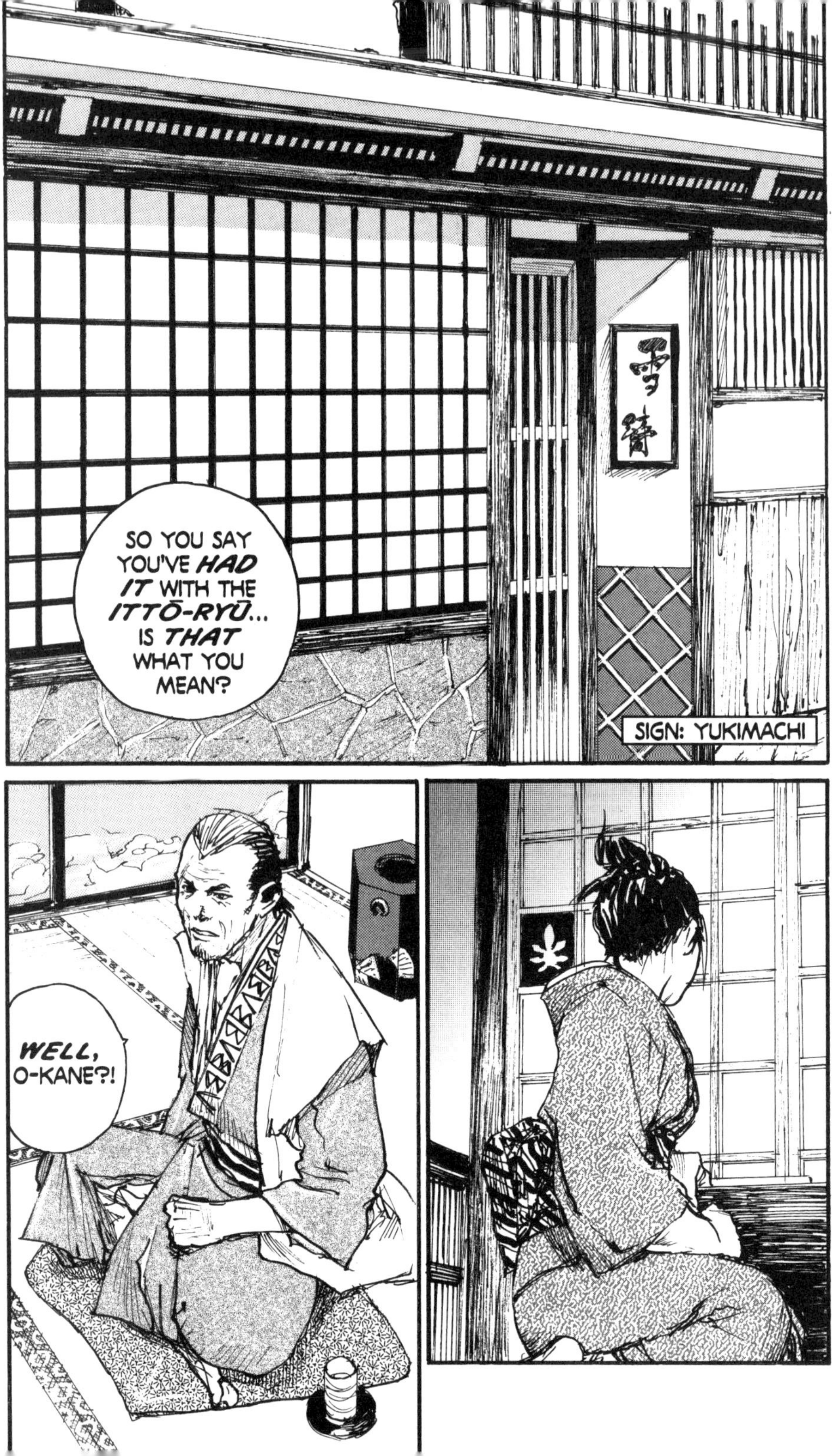
SO YOU SAY YOU'VE *HAD IT* WITH THE *ITTŌ-RYŪ*... IS *THAT* WHAT YOU MEAN?
SIGN: YUKIMACHI
WELL, O-KANE?!

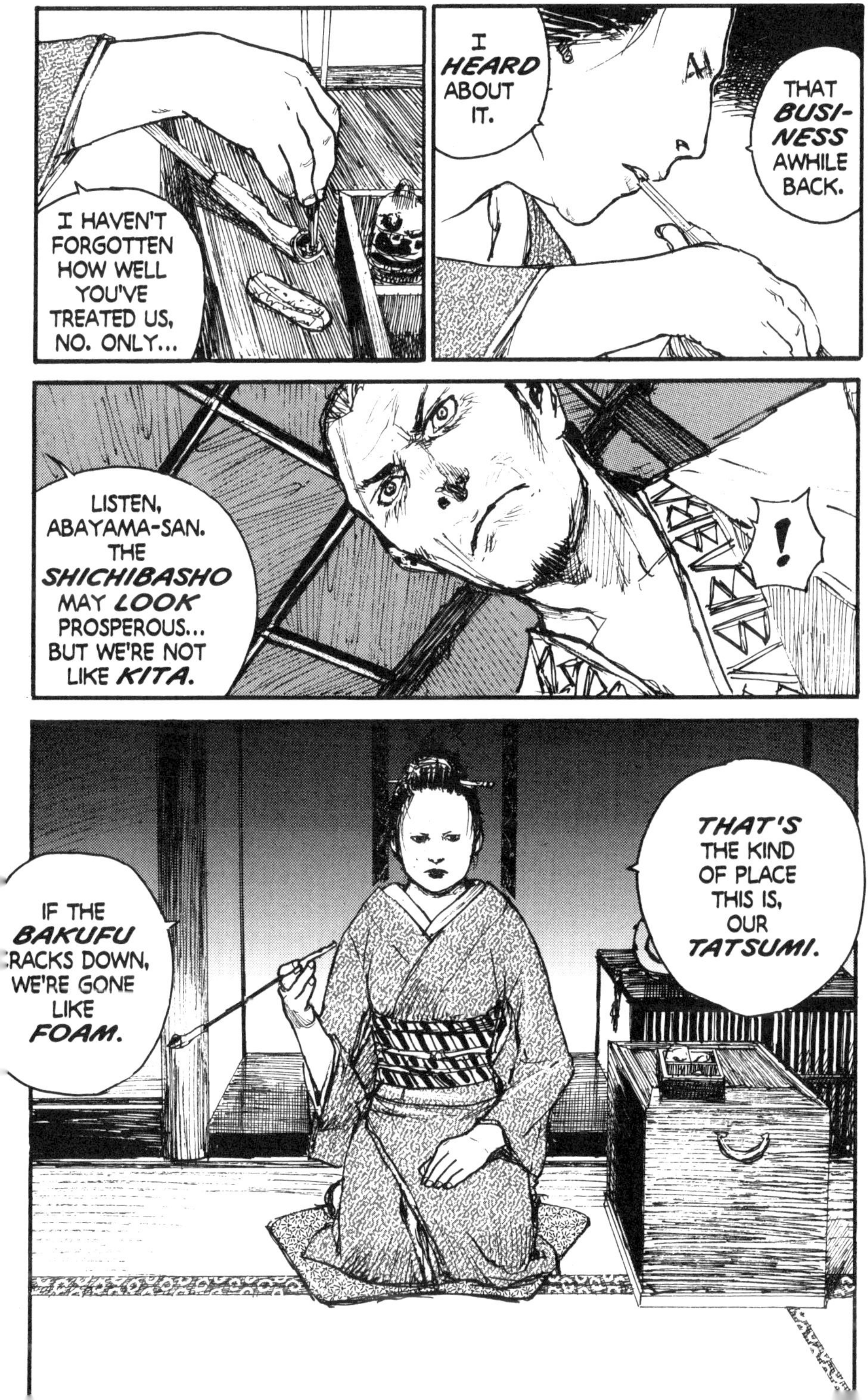
I HAVEN'T FORGOTTEN HOW WELL YOU'VE TREATED US, NO. ONLY...
I HEARD ABOUT IT.
THAT BUSINESS AWHILE BACK.
LISTEN, ABAYAMA-SAN. THE SHICHIBASHO MAY LOOK PROSPEROUS... BUT WE'RE NOT LIKE KITA.
!
IF THE BAKUFU CRACKS DOWN, WE'RE GONE LIKE FOAM.
THAT'S THE KIND OF PLACE THIS IS, OUR TATSUMI.

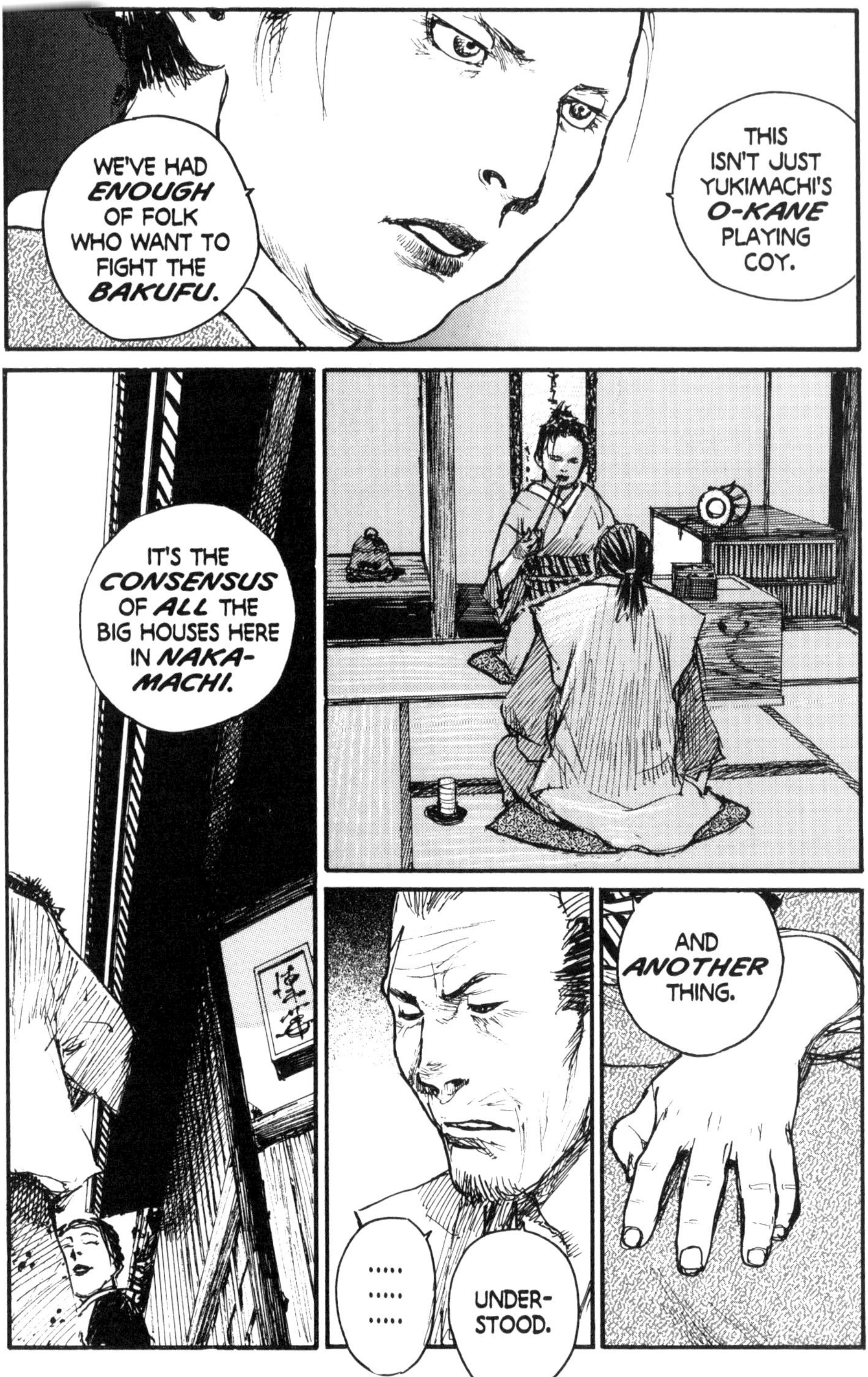
WE'VE HAD ENOUGH OF FOLK WHO WANT TO FIGHT THE BAKUFU.
THIS ISN'T JUST YUKIMACHI'S O-KANE PLAYING COY.
IT'S THE CONSENSUS OF ALL THE BIG HOUSES HERE IN NAKA-MACHI.
.....
UNDER-STOOD.
AND ANOTHER THING.

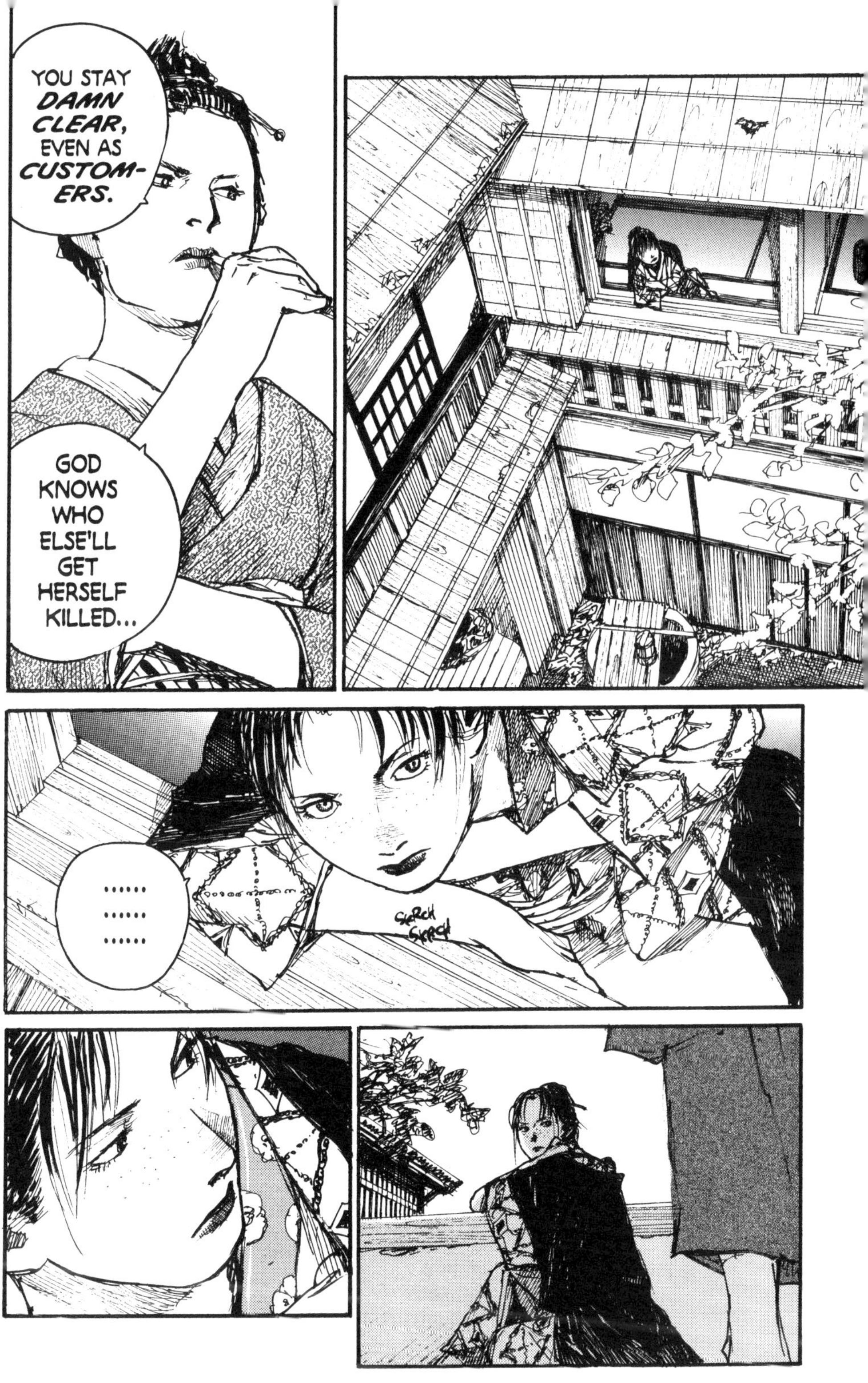
YOU STAY ***DAMN CLEAR,*** EVEN AS ***CUSTOMERS.***
GOD KNOWS WHO ELSE'LL GET HERSELF KILLED...
......
......
......
SKRCH
SKRCH

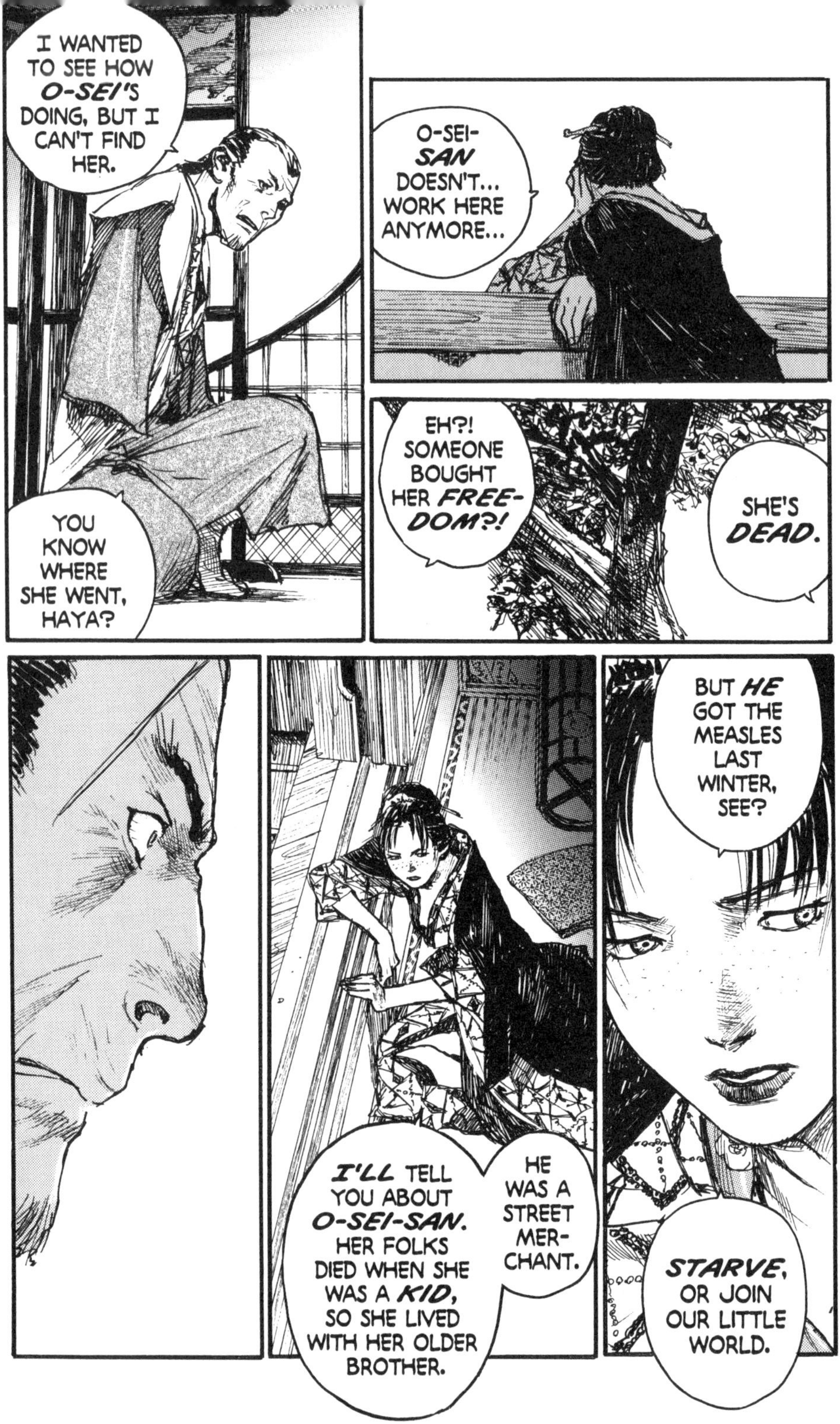
I WANTED TO SEE HOW O-SEI'S DOING, BUT I CAN'T FIND HER.
YOU KNOW WHERE SHE WENT, HAYA?
O-SEI-SAN DOESN'T... WORK HERE ANYMORE...
EH?! SOMEONE BOUGHT HER FREE-DOM?!
SHE'S DEAD.
I'LL TELL YOU ABOUT O-SEI-SAN. HER FOLKS DIED WHEN SHE WAS A KID, SO SHE LIVED WITH HER OLDER BROTHER.
HE WAS A STREET MER-CHANT.
BUT HE GOT THE MEASLES LAST WINTER, SEE?
STARVE, OR JOIN OUR LITTLE WORLD.

AND *THEN?* HER *BODY* HACKED UP LIKE THAT?

WHORE. *NO-THING.* ALL SHE COULD DO...

...WAS *HANG HER-SELF* WITH HIM.

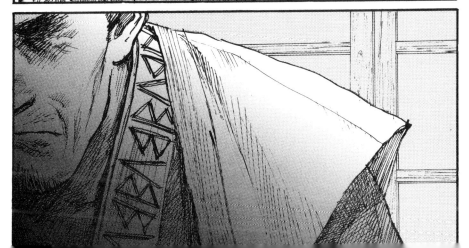

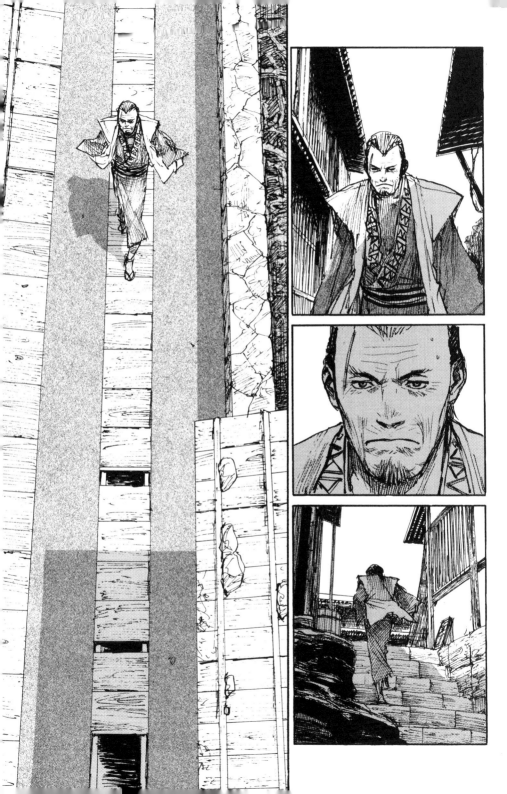

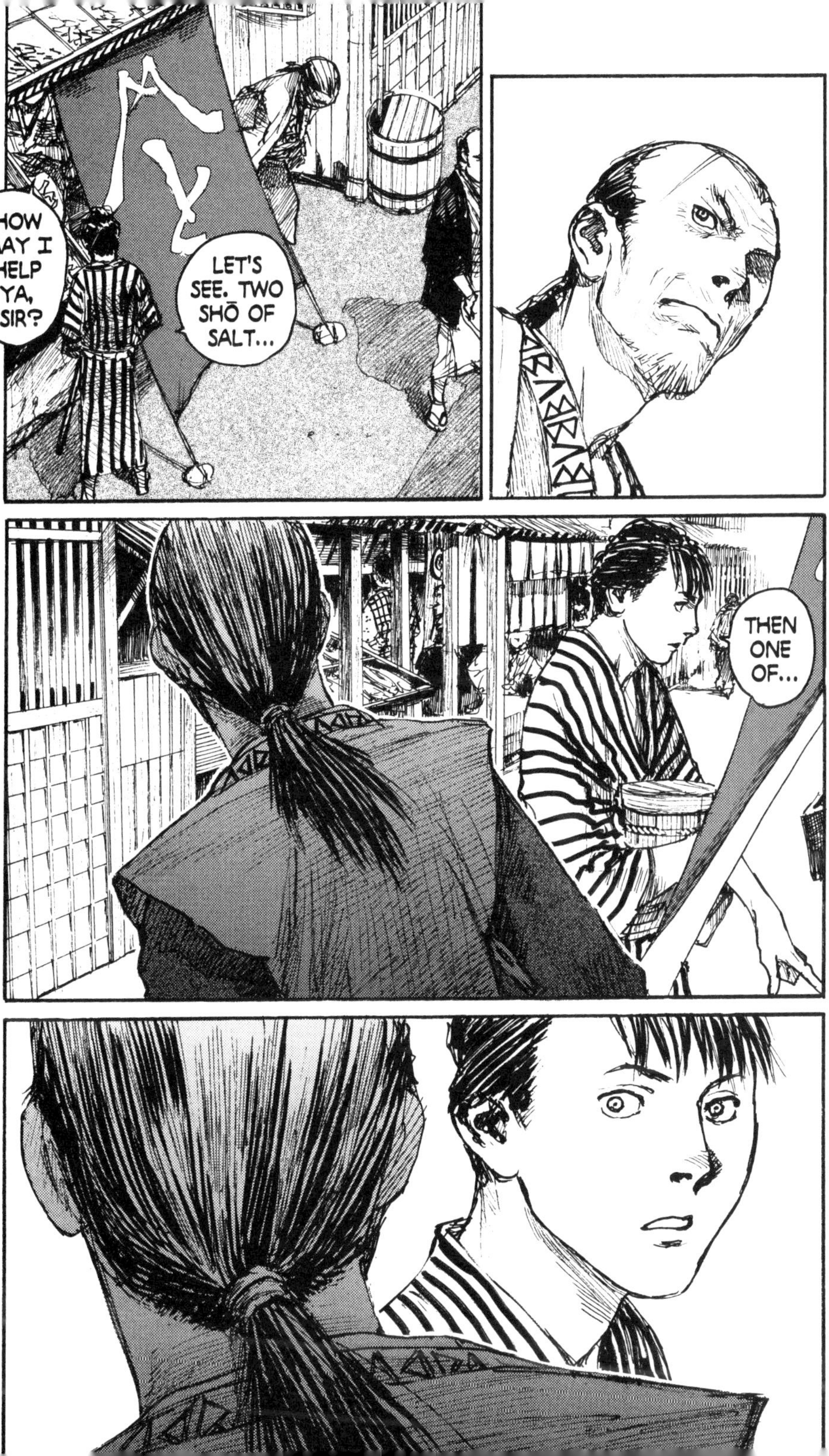
HOW MAY I HELP YA, SIR?
LET'S SEE. TWO SHŌ OF SALT...
THEN ONE OF...

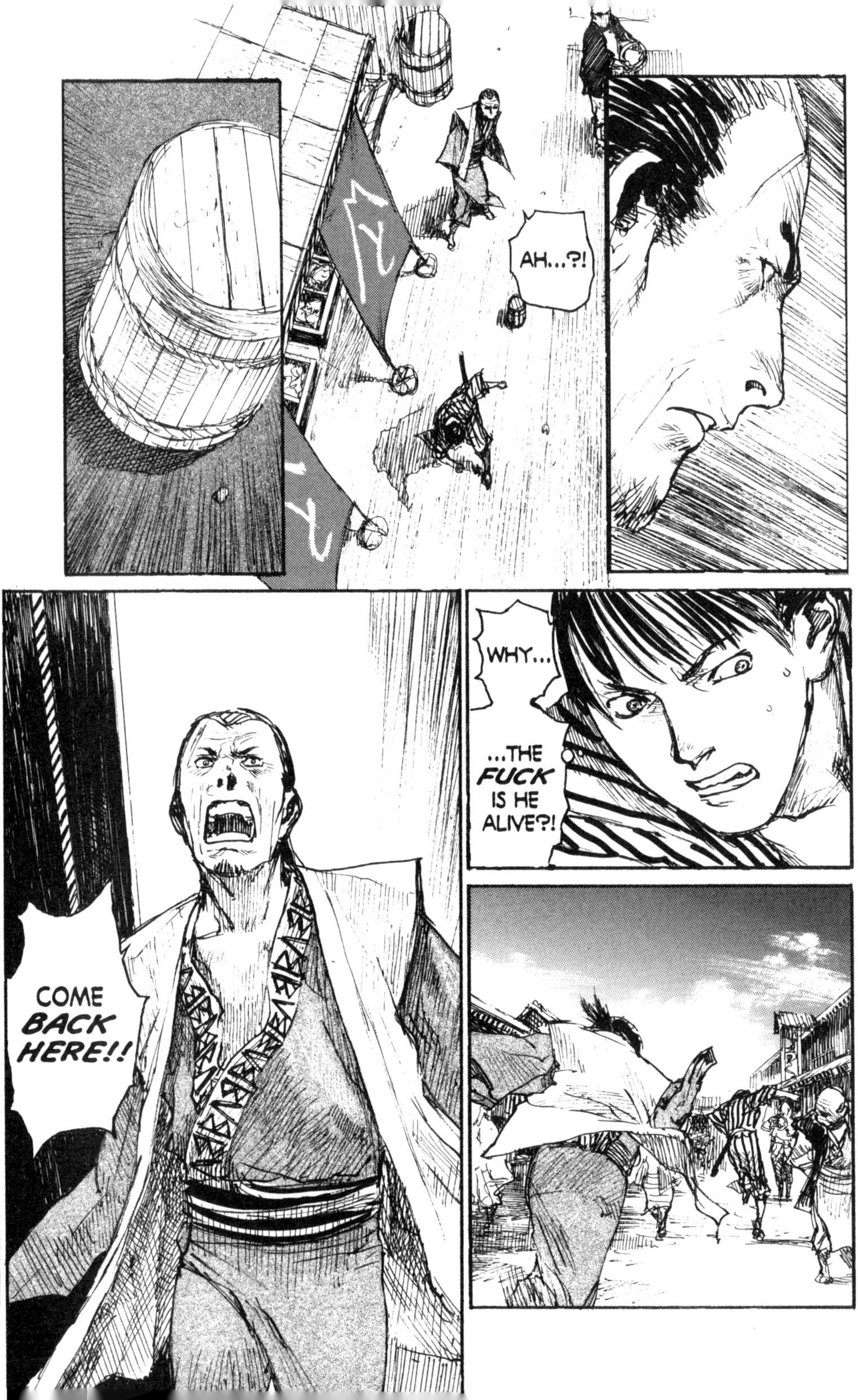
AH...?!
COME BACK HERE!!
WHY...
...THE FUCK IS HE ALIVE?!

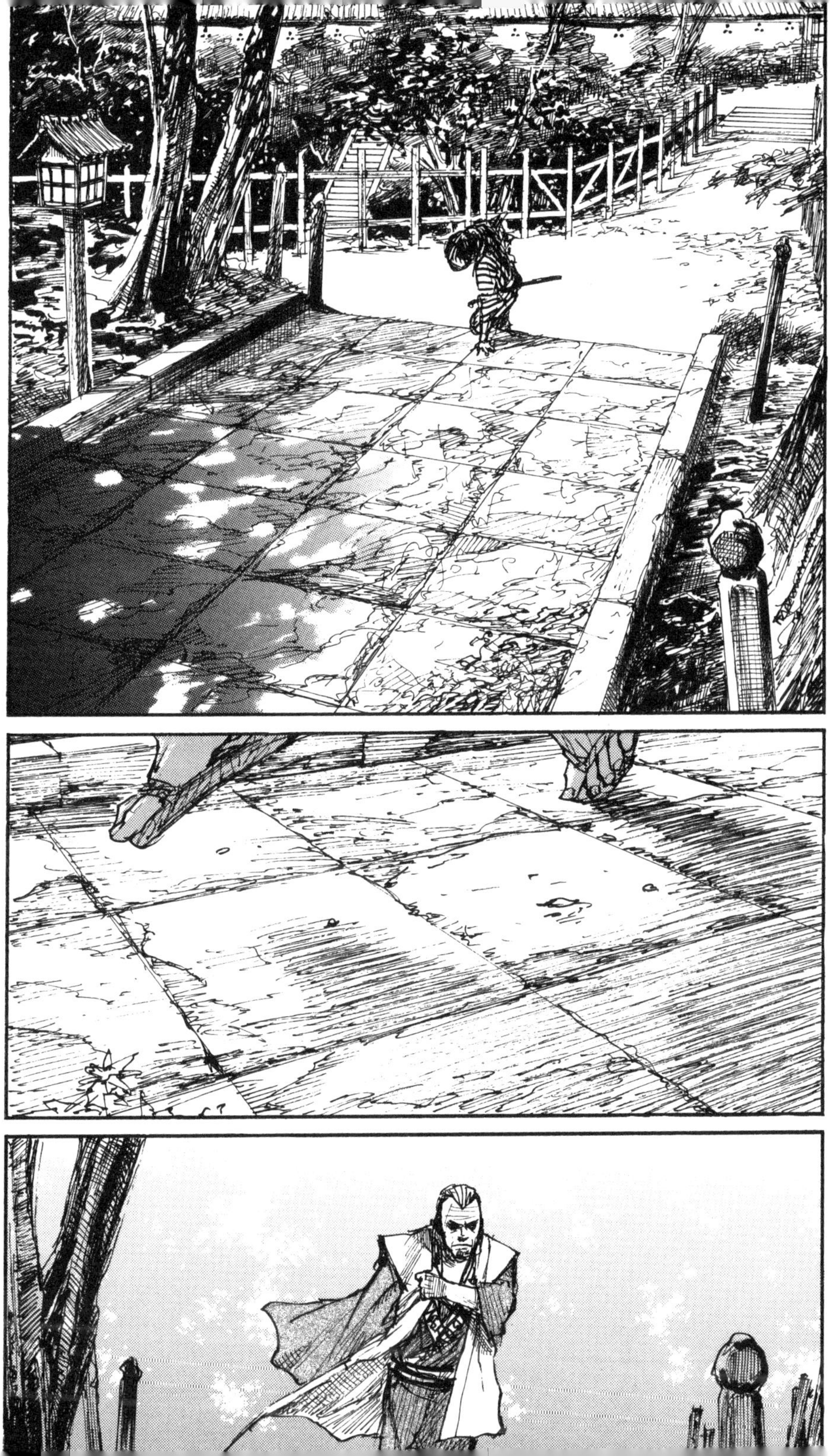

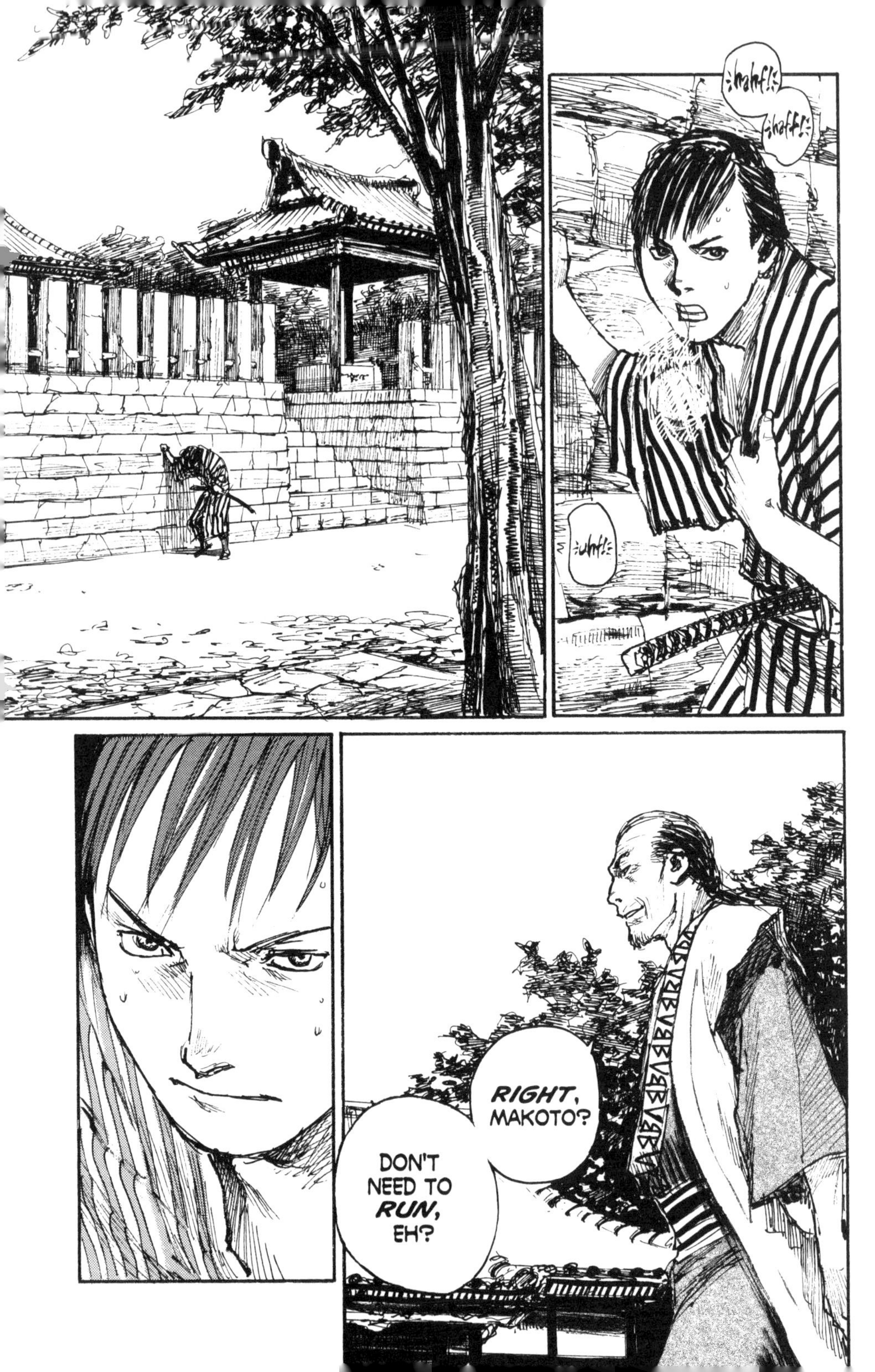
hahf!
haff!
uhf!
RIGHT, MAKOTO?
DON'T NEED TO RUN, EH?

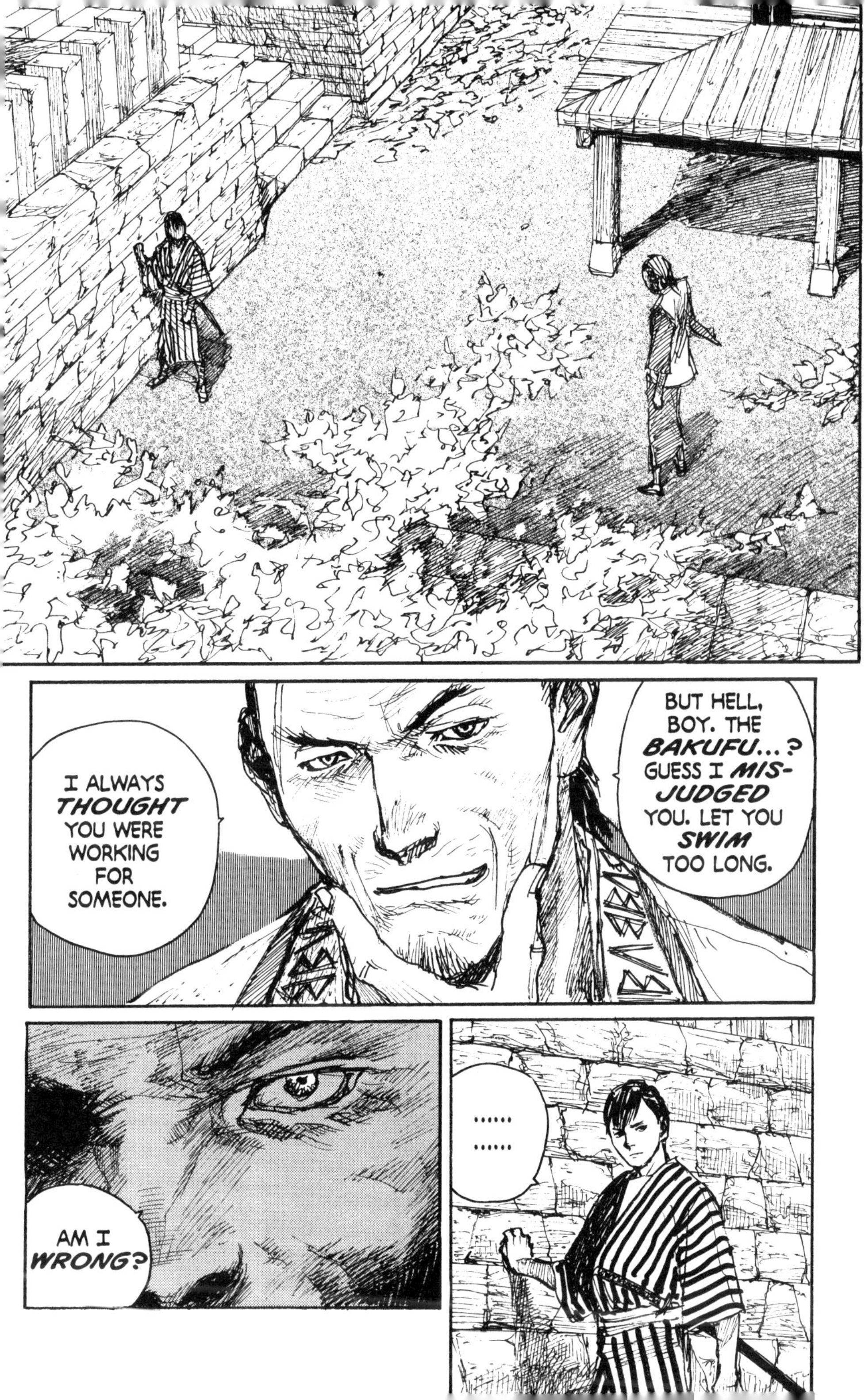
I ALWAYS THOUGHT YOU WERE WORKING FOR SOMEONE.
BUT HELL, BOY. THE BAKUFU...? GUESS I MIS-JUDGED YOU. LET YOU SWIM TOO LONG.
AM I WRONG?
......
......

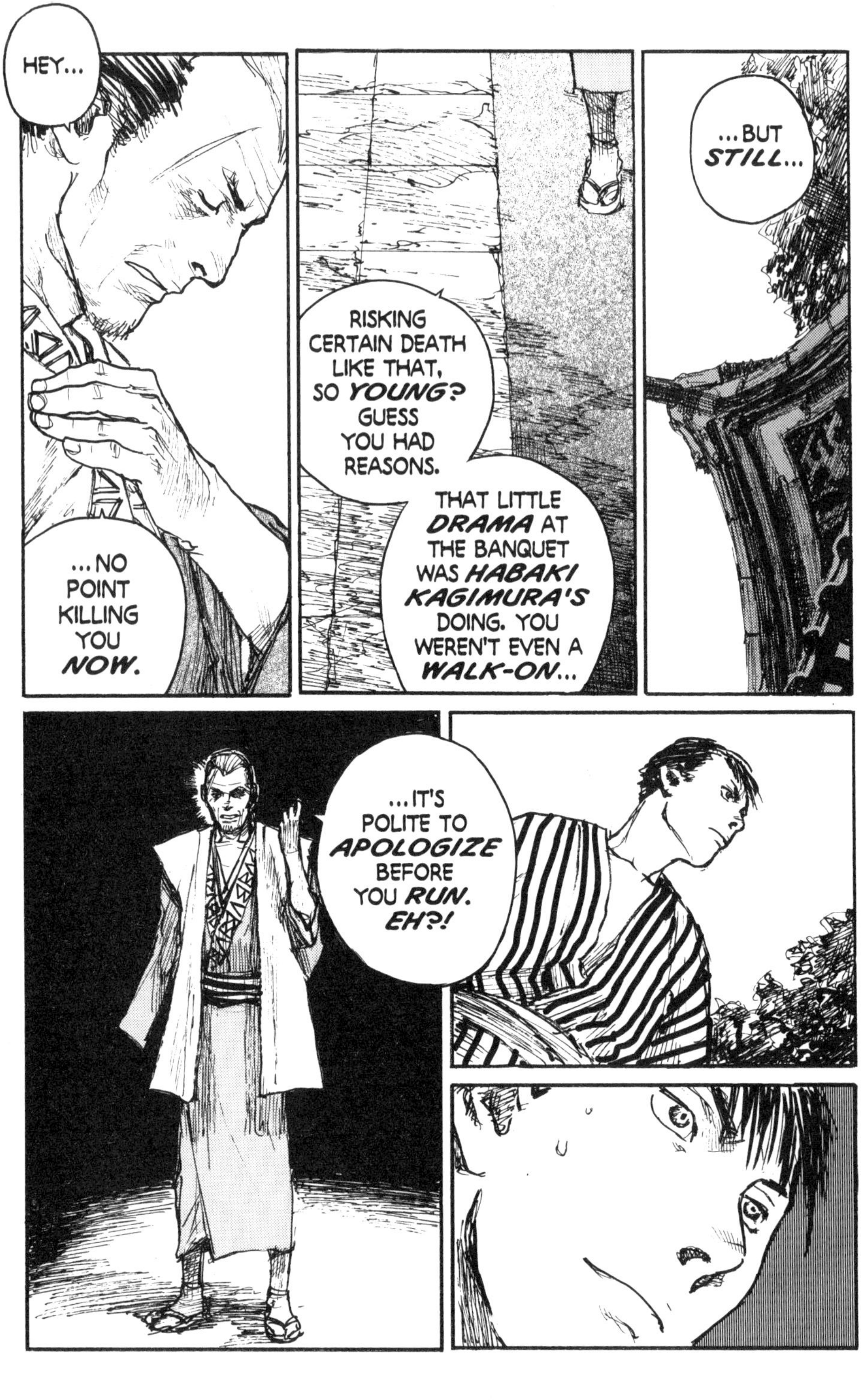
HEY...
...NO POINT KILLING YOU NOW.
RISKING CERTAIN DEATH LIKE THAT, SO YOUNG? GUESS YOU HAD REASONS.
THAT LITTLE DRAMA AT THE BANQUET WAS HABAKI KAGIMURA'S DOING. YOU WEREN'T EVEN A WALK-ON...
...BUT STILL...
...IT'S POLITE TO APOLOGIZE BEFORE YOU RUN. EH?!

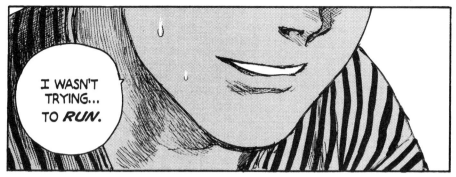

I WASN'T TRYING... TO *RUN*.

I CAME UP HERE, 'CUZ I COULDN'T *KILL YOU*...

...BACK THERE.

EVEN ONE OF YOU *ITTŌ-RYŪ* SHITS...

...KILLING AN UNARMED MAN WOULD JUST...

...*DISTURB* ANY ONLOOKERS.

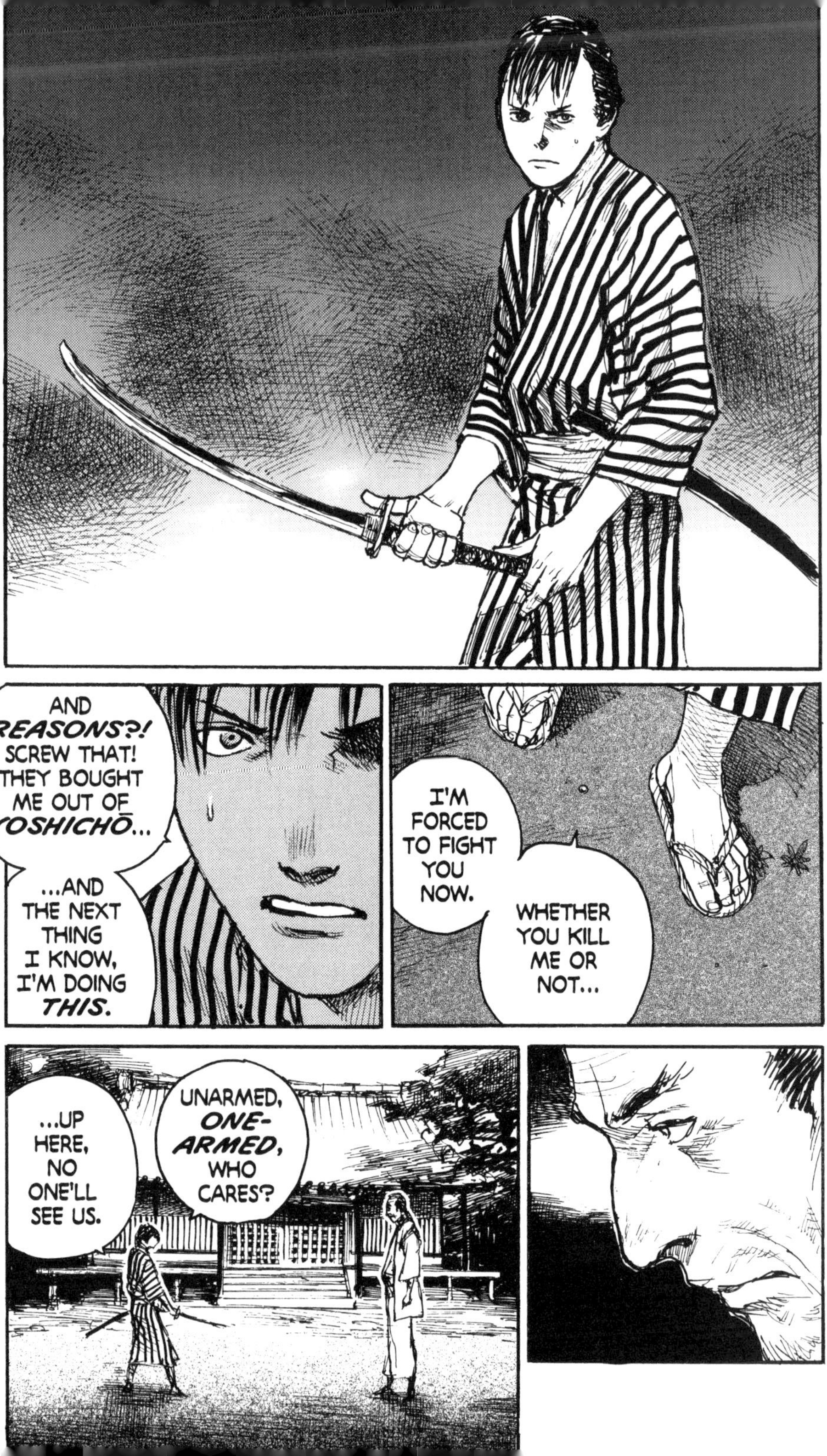
AND *REASONS?!* SCREW THAT! THEY BOUGHT ME OUT OF *YOSHICHŌ*...
...AND THE NEXT THING I KNOW, I'M DOING *THIS*.
I'M FORCED TO FIGHT YOU NOW.
WHETHER YOU KILL ME OR NOT...
...UP HERE, NO ONE'LL SEE US.
UNARMED, *ONE-ARMED*, WHO CARES?

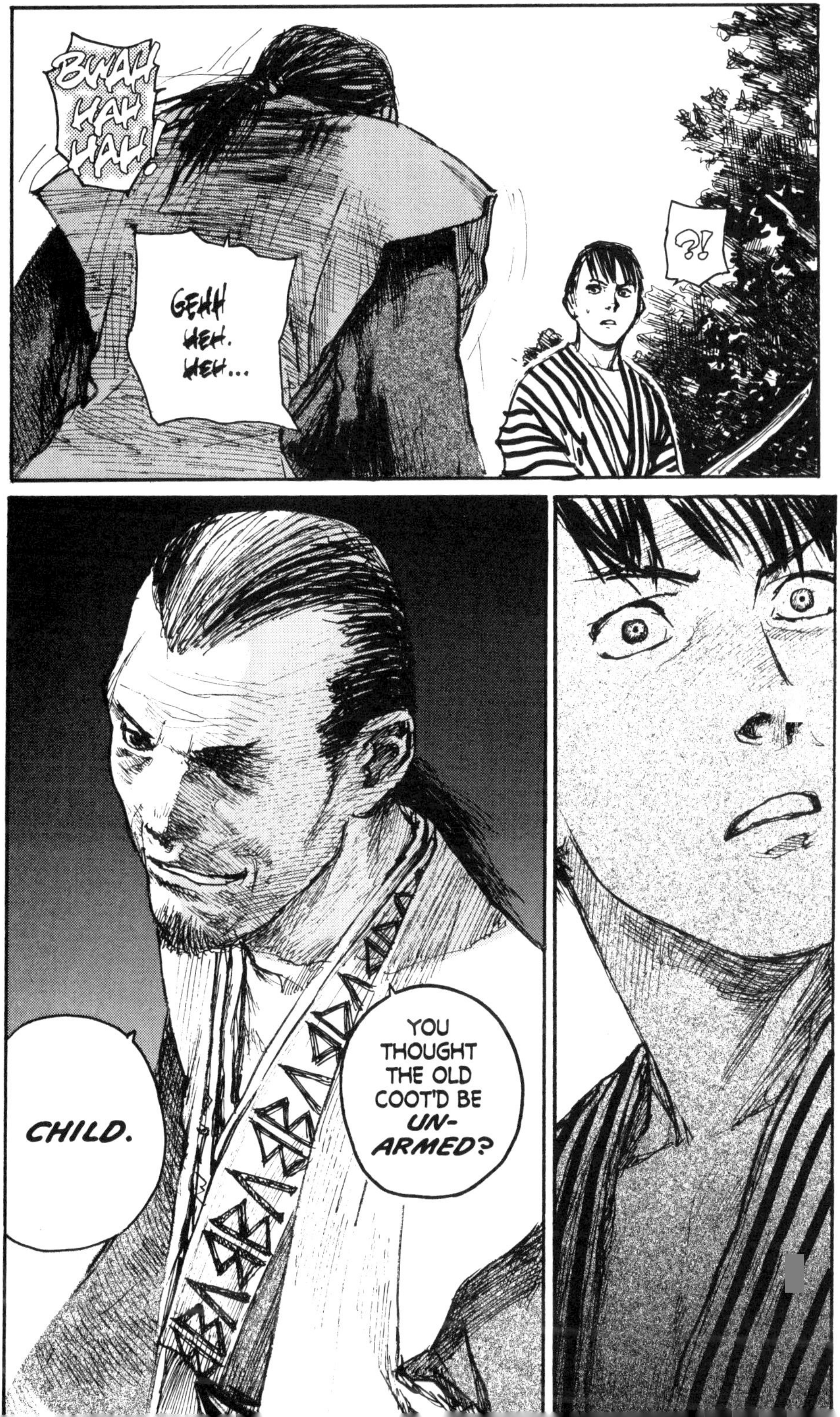
BWAH HAH HAH!
GEHH HEH. HEH...
?!
CHILD.
YOU THOUGHT THE OLD COOT'D BE UN-ARMED?

CARELESS, *CARE-LESS*, MAKOTO.

WE EAT OUTTA THE SAME POT FOR *THREE MONTHS*...

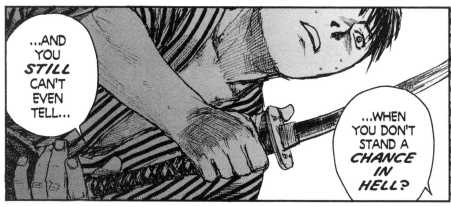

...AND YOU *STILL* CAN'T EVEN TELL...

...WHEN YOU DON'T STAND A *CHANCE IN HELL?*

MAKOTO, YOU NEVER BELONGED IN OUR WORLD.

SHUT UP!

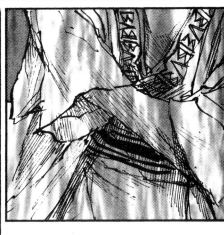

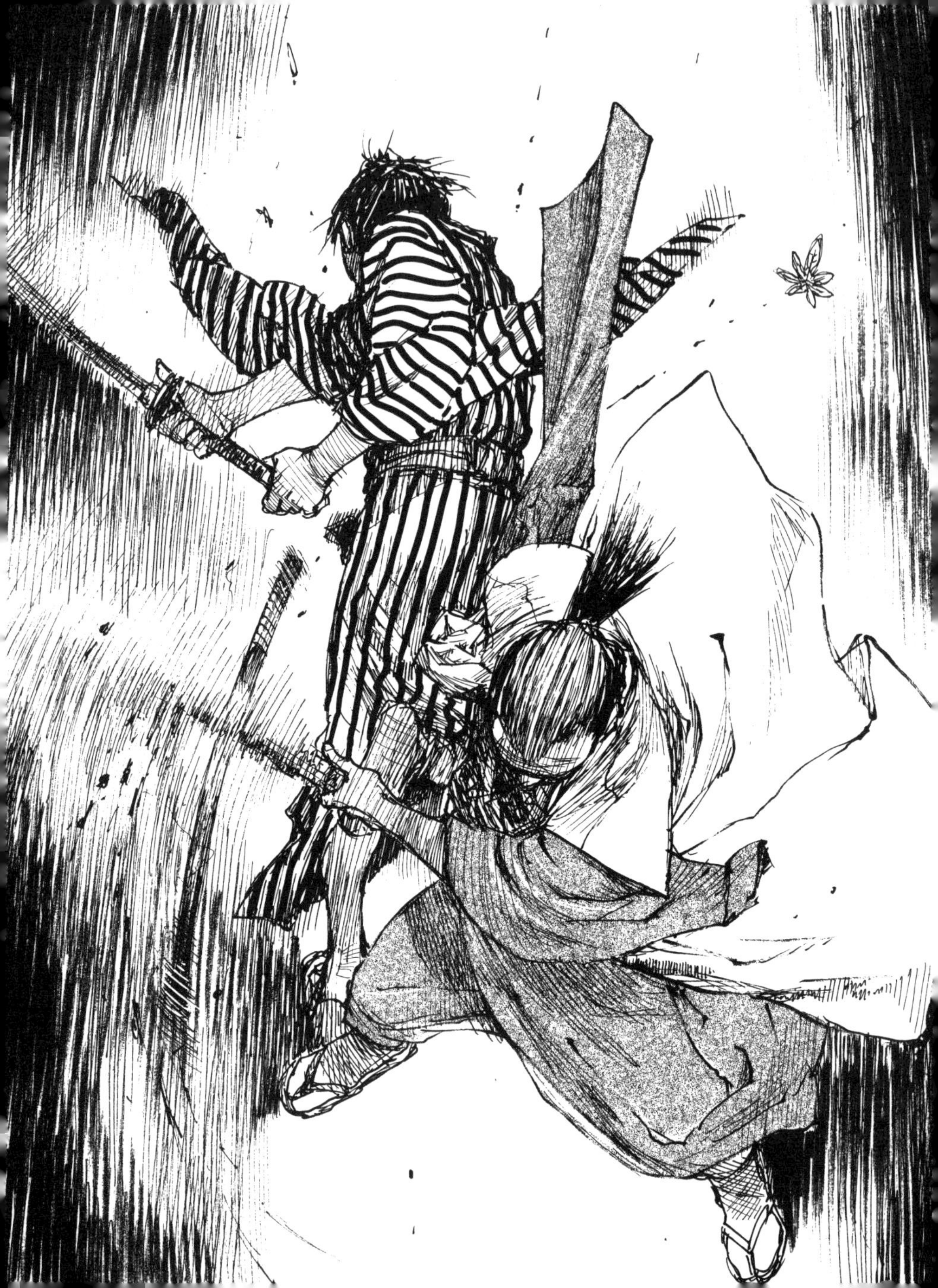

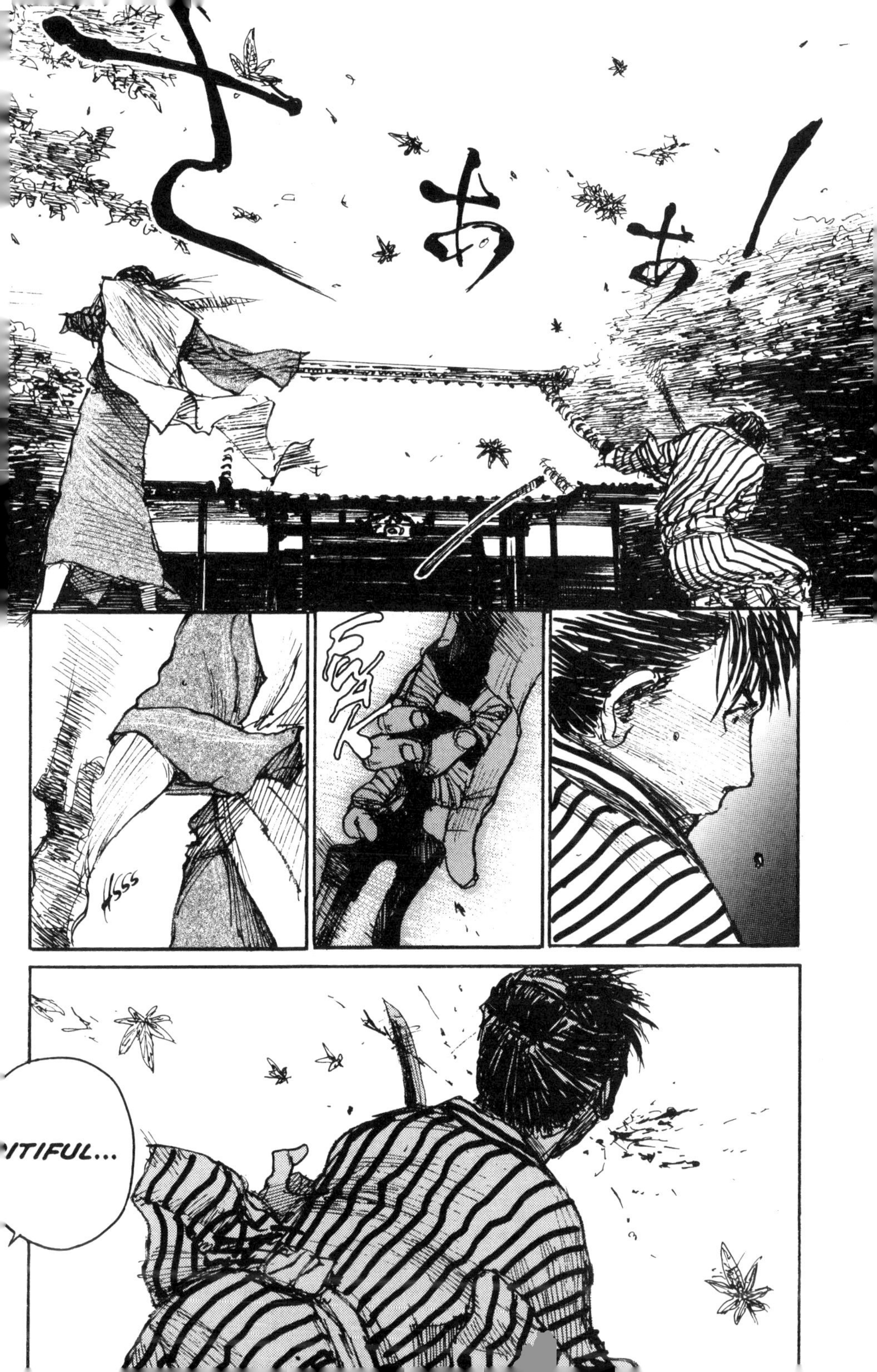
Hsss
ITIFUL...

HABAKI KAGIMURA!

MUST YOU MAKE THIS OLD MAN KILL A MERE *CHILD* LIKE HIM?

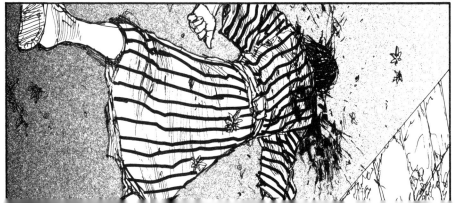

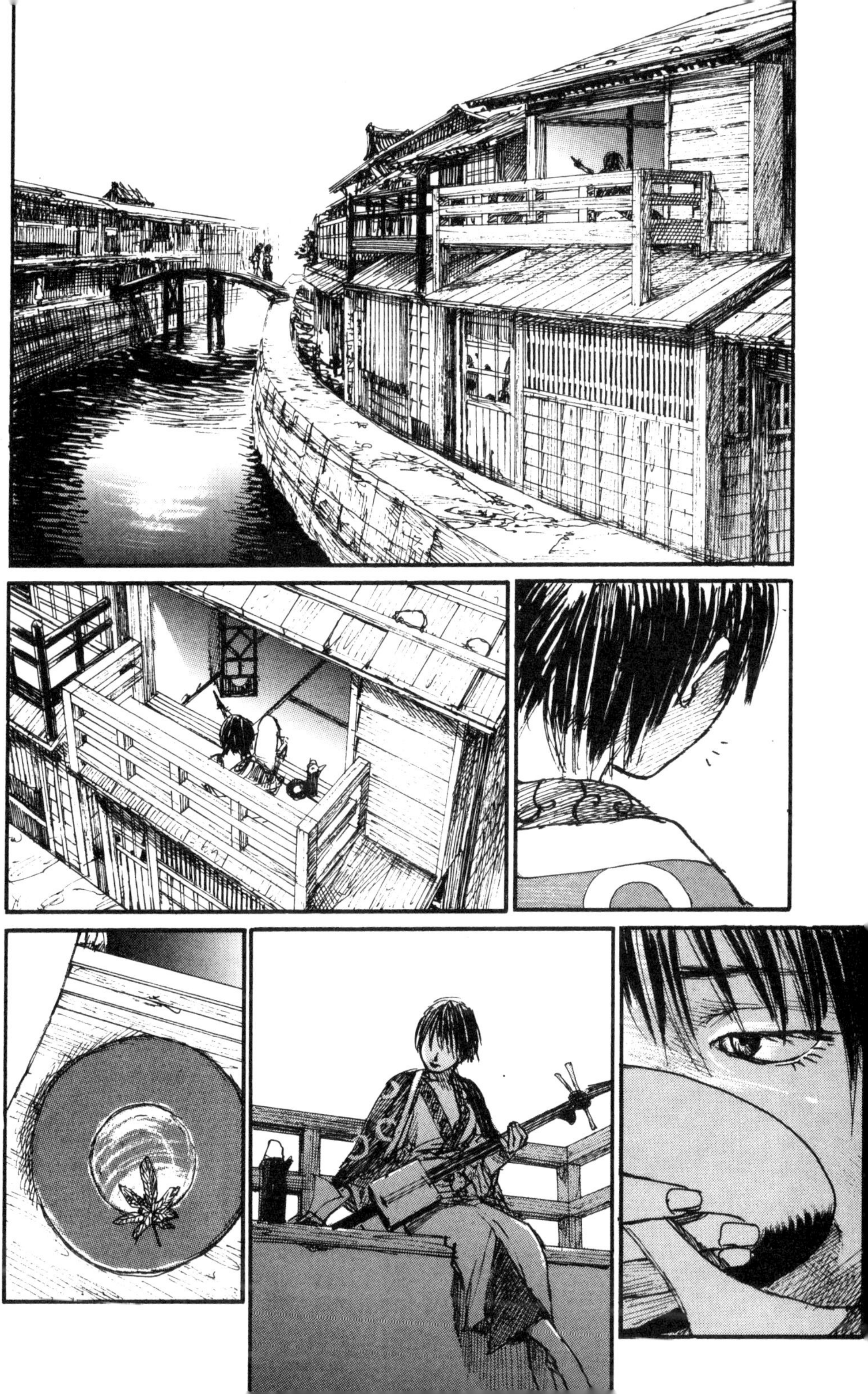

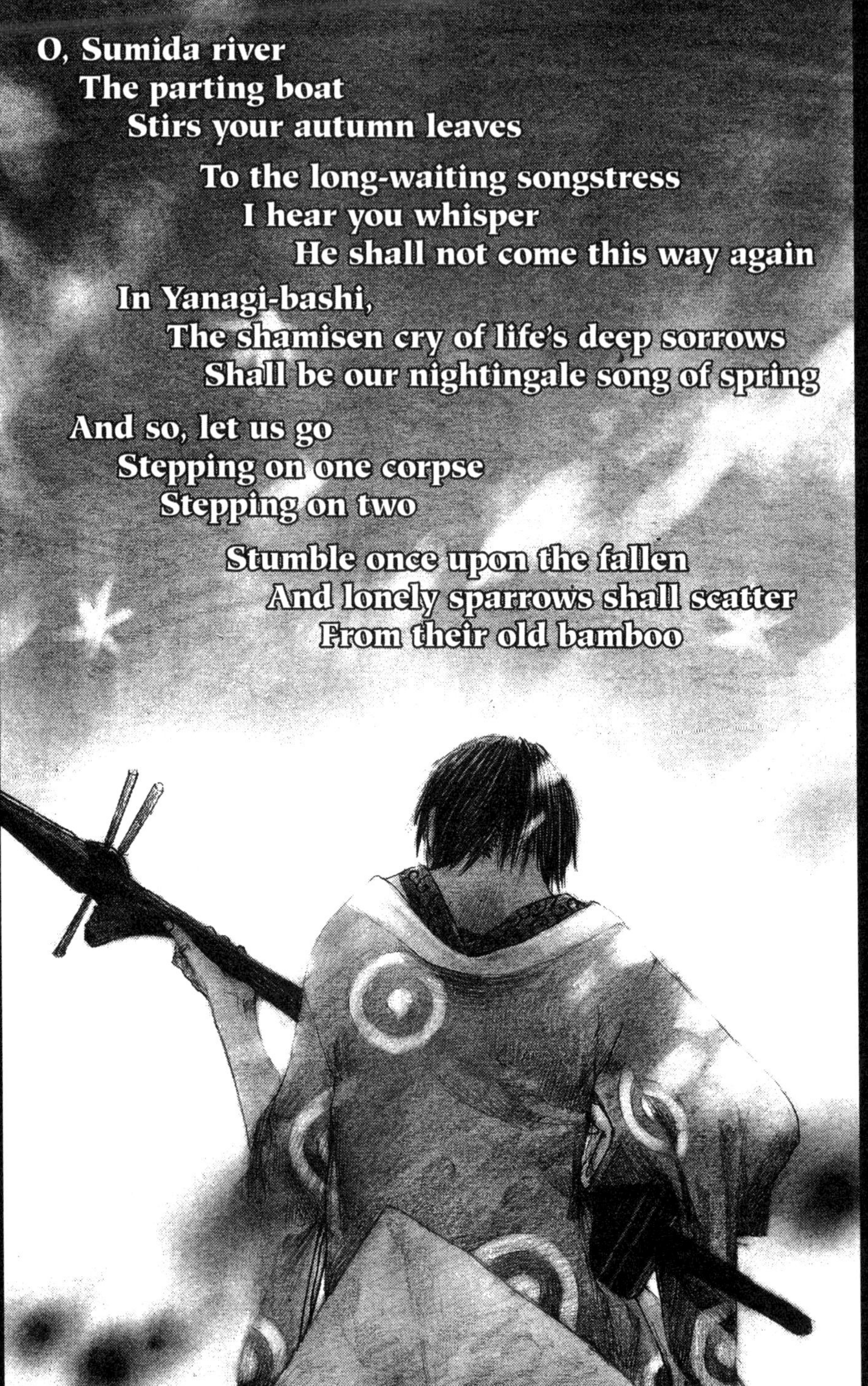
O, Sumida river
The parting boat
Stirs your autumn leaves
To the long-waiting songstress
I hear you whisper
He shall not come this way again
In Yanagi-bashi,
The shamisen cry of life's deep sorrows
Shall be our nightingale song of spring
And so, let us go
Stepping on one corpse
Stepping on two
Stumble once upon the fallen
And lonely sparrows shall scatter
From their old bamboo

FORSAKEN

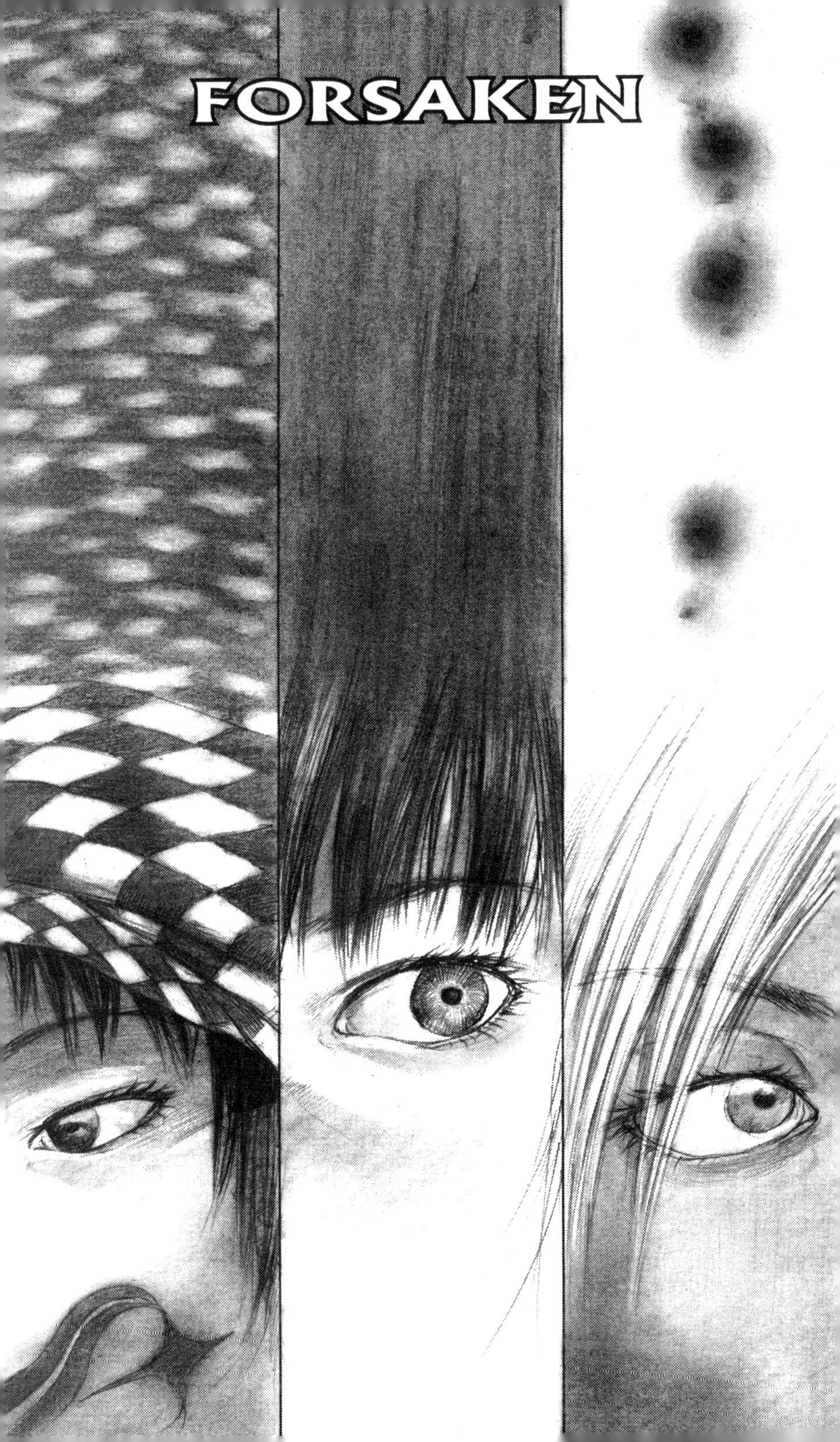

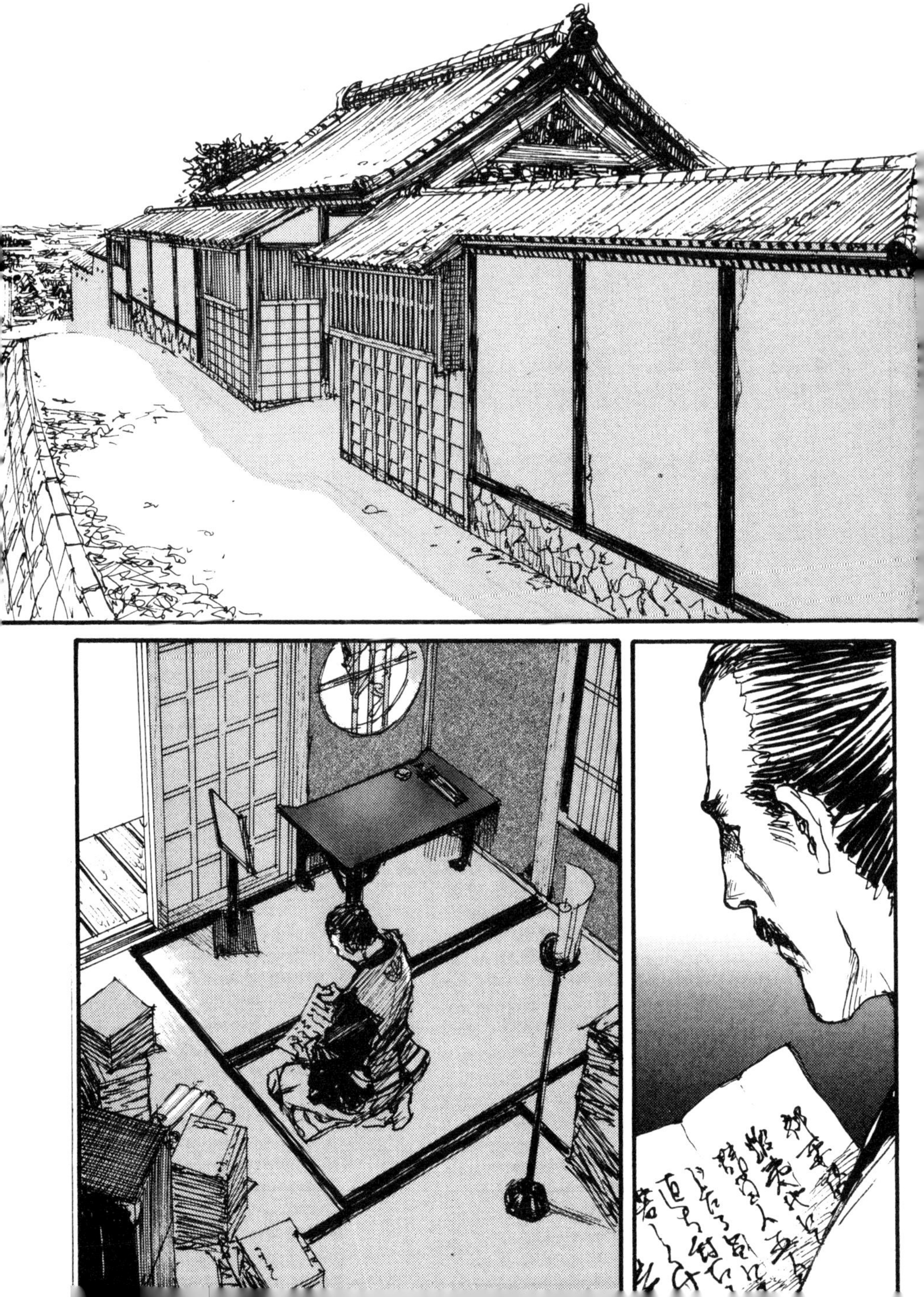

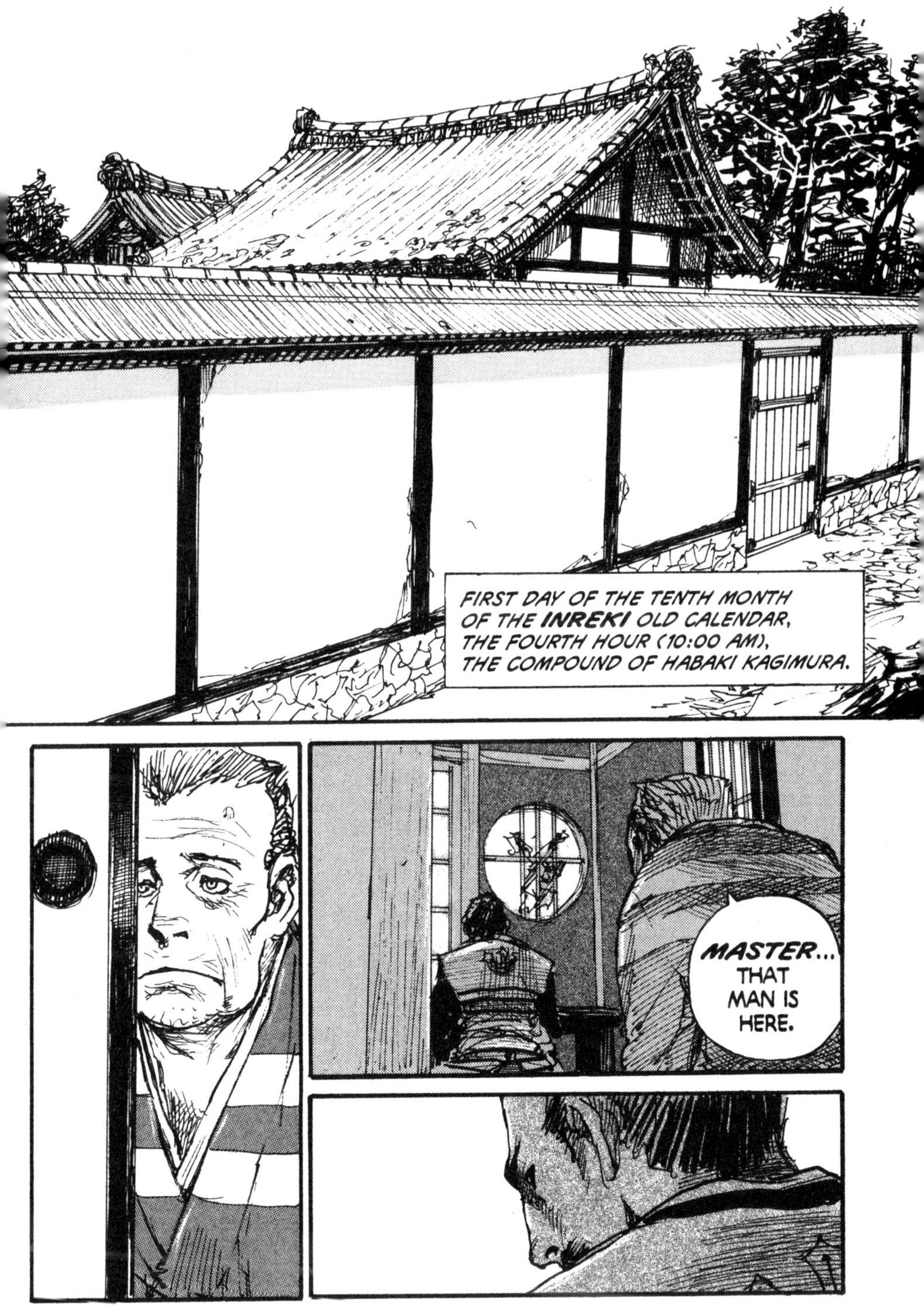
FIRST DAY OF THE TENTH MONTH OF THE **INREKI** OLD CALENDAR, THE FOURTH HOUR (10:00 AM), THE COMPOUND OF HABAKI KAGIMURA.
MASTER... THAT MAN IS HERE.

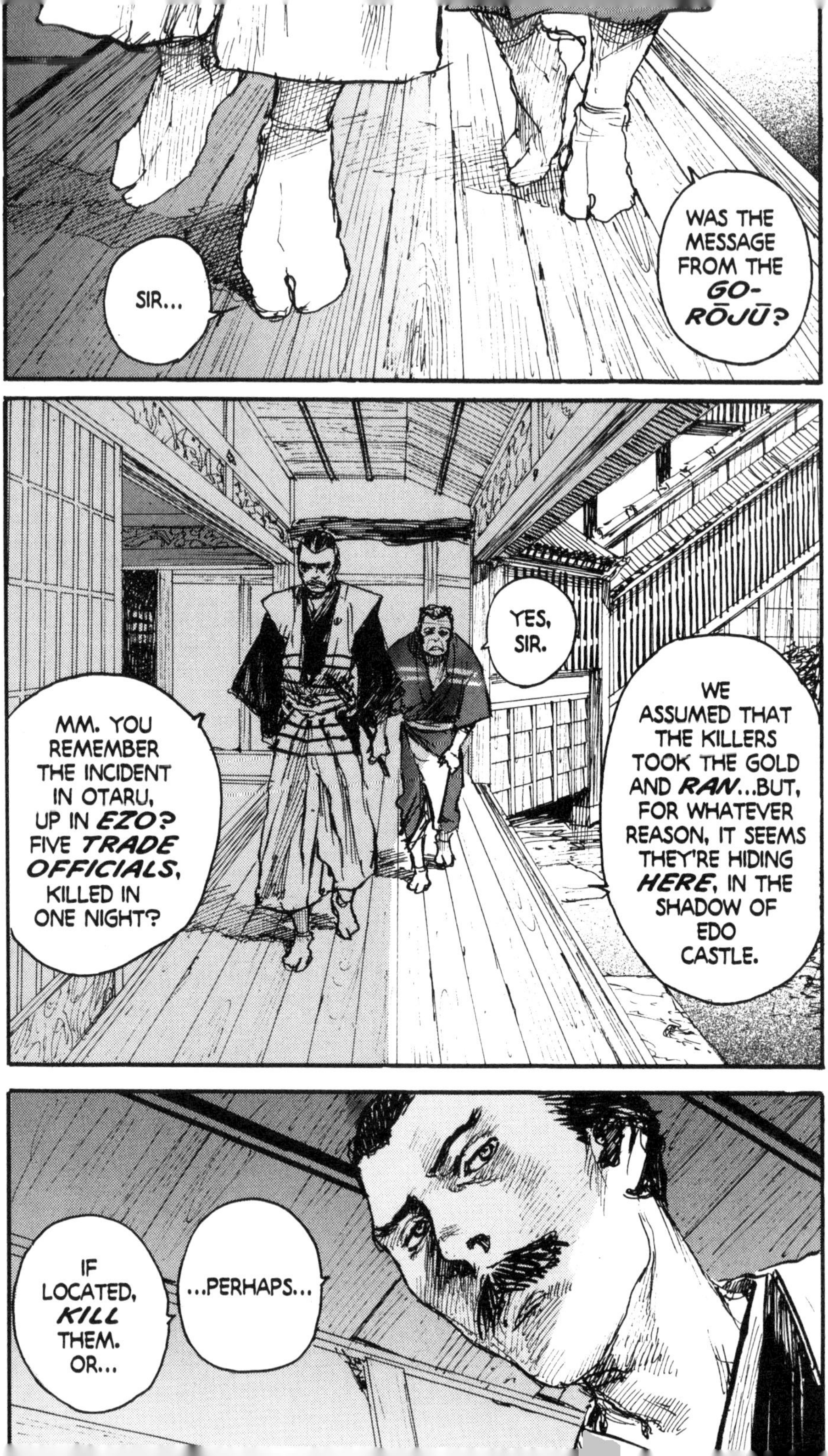
SIR...
WAS THE MESSAGE FROM THE GO-RŌJŪ?
YES, SIR.
MM. YOU REMEMBER THE INCIDENT IN OTARU, UP IN EZO? FIVE TRADE OFFICIALS, KILLED IN ONE NIGHT?
WE ASSUMED THAT THE KILLERS TOOK THE GOLD AND RAN...BUT, FOR WHATEVER REASON, IT SEEMS THEY'RE HIDING HERE, IN THE SHADOW OF EDO CASTLE.
IF LOCATED, KILL THEM. OR...
...PERHAPS...

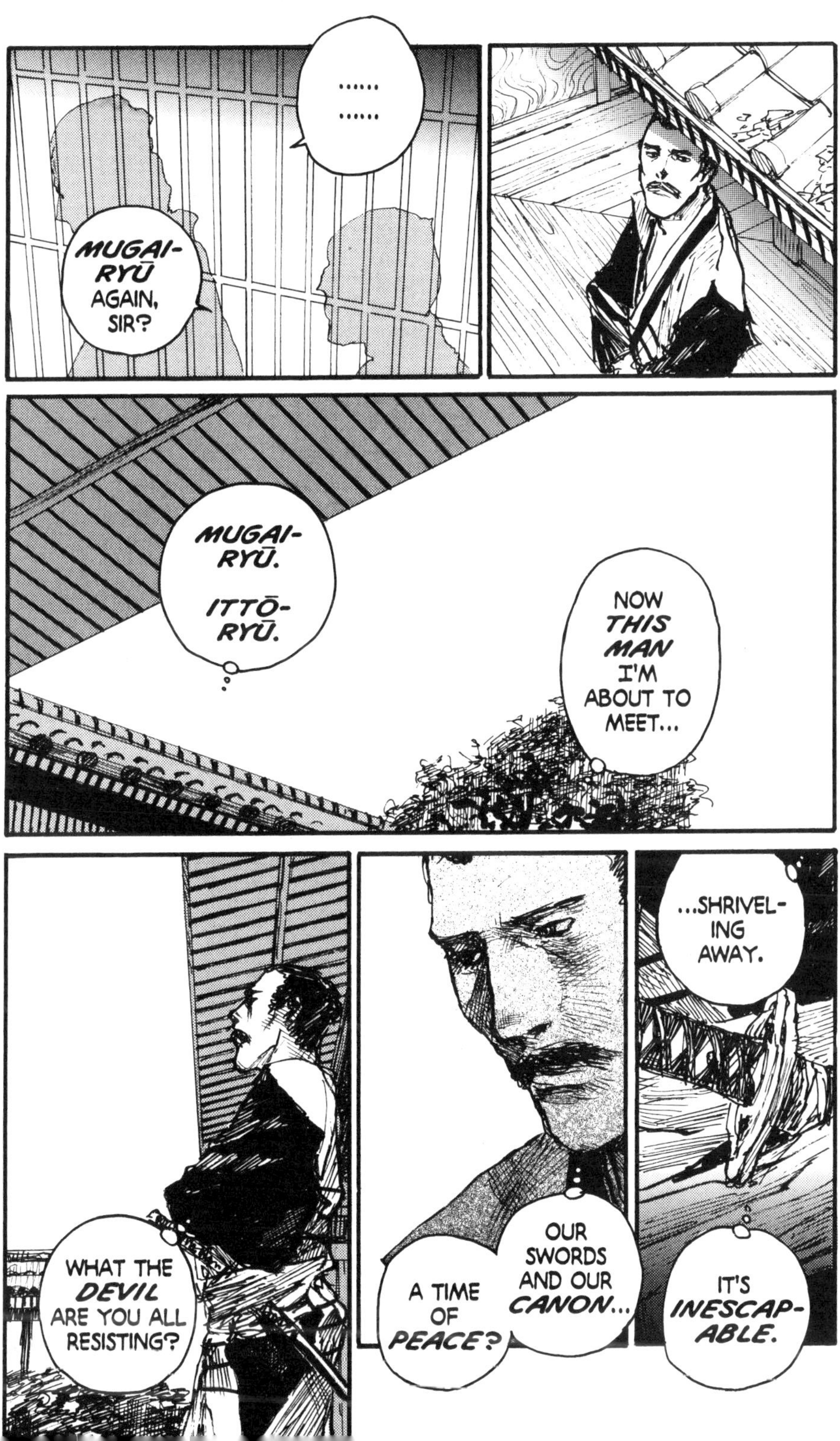
......
......
MUGAI-RYŪ AGAIN, SIR?
MUGAI-RYŪ.
ITTŌ-RYŪ.
NOW THIS MAN I'M ABOUT TO MEET...
WHAT THE DEVIL ARE YOU ALL RESISTING?
A TIME OF PEACE?
OUR SWORDS AND OUR CANON...
...SHRIVEL-ING AWAY.
IT'S INESCAP-ABLE.

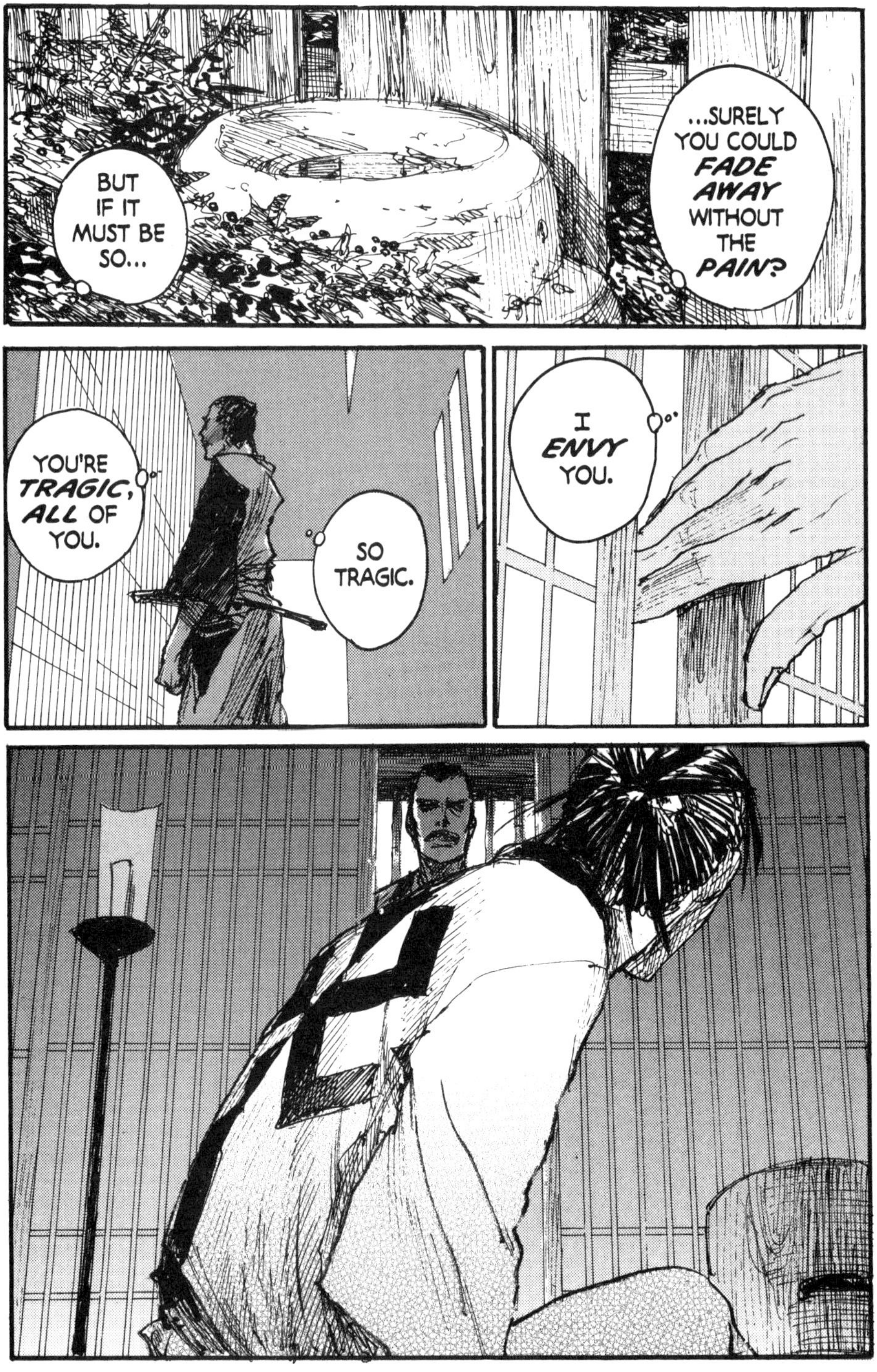
BUT IF IT MUST BE SO...
...SURELY YOU COULD FADE AWAY WITHOUT THE PAIN?
YOU'RE TRAGIC, ALL OF YOU.
SO TRAGIC.
I ENVY YOU.

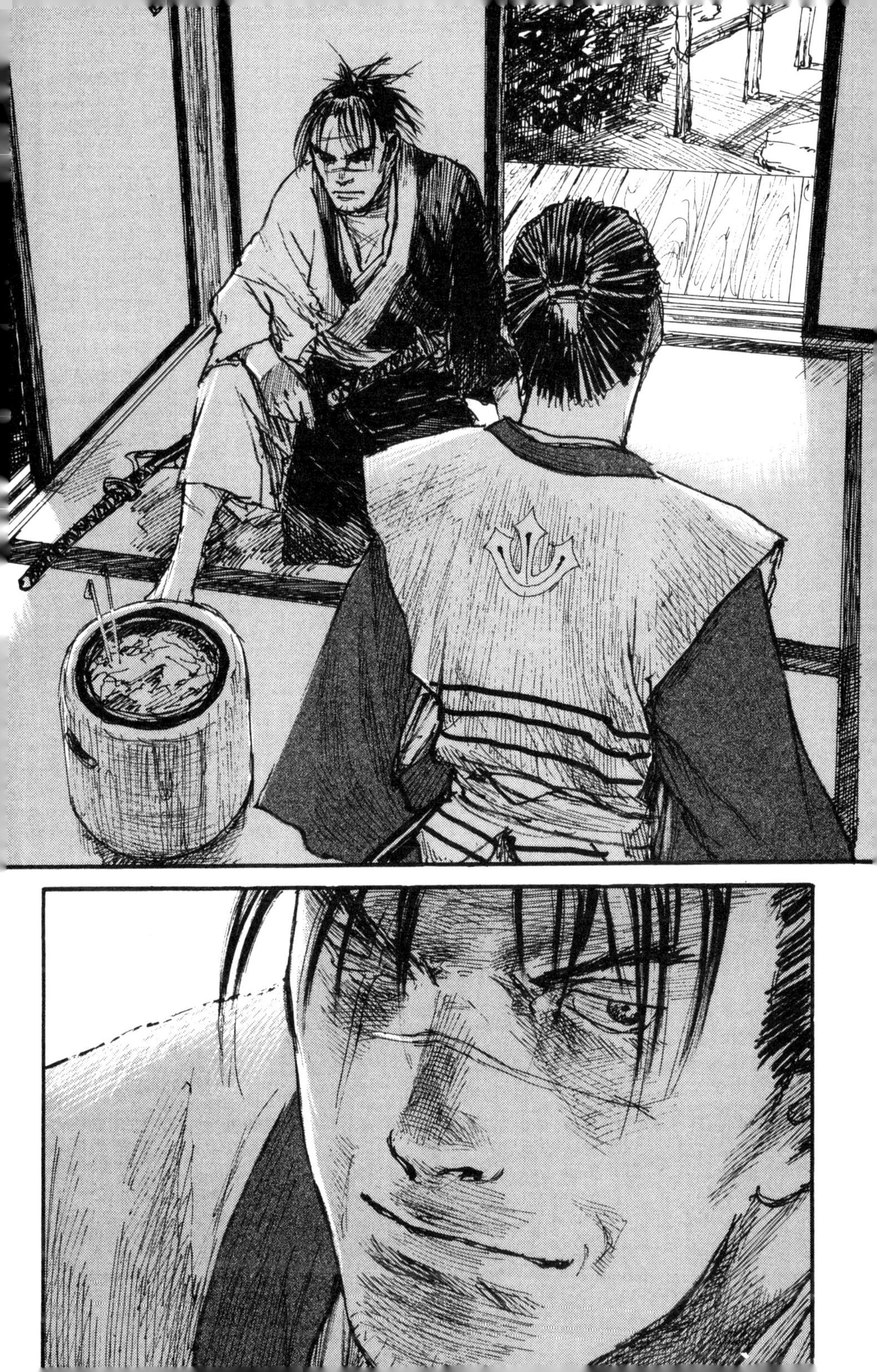

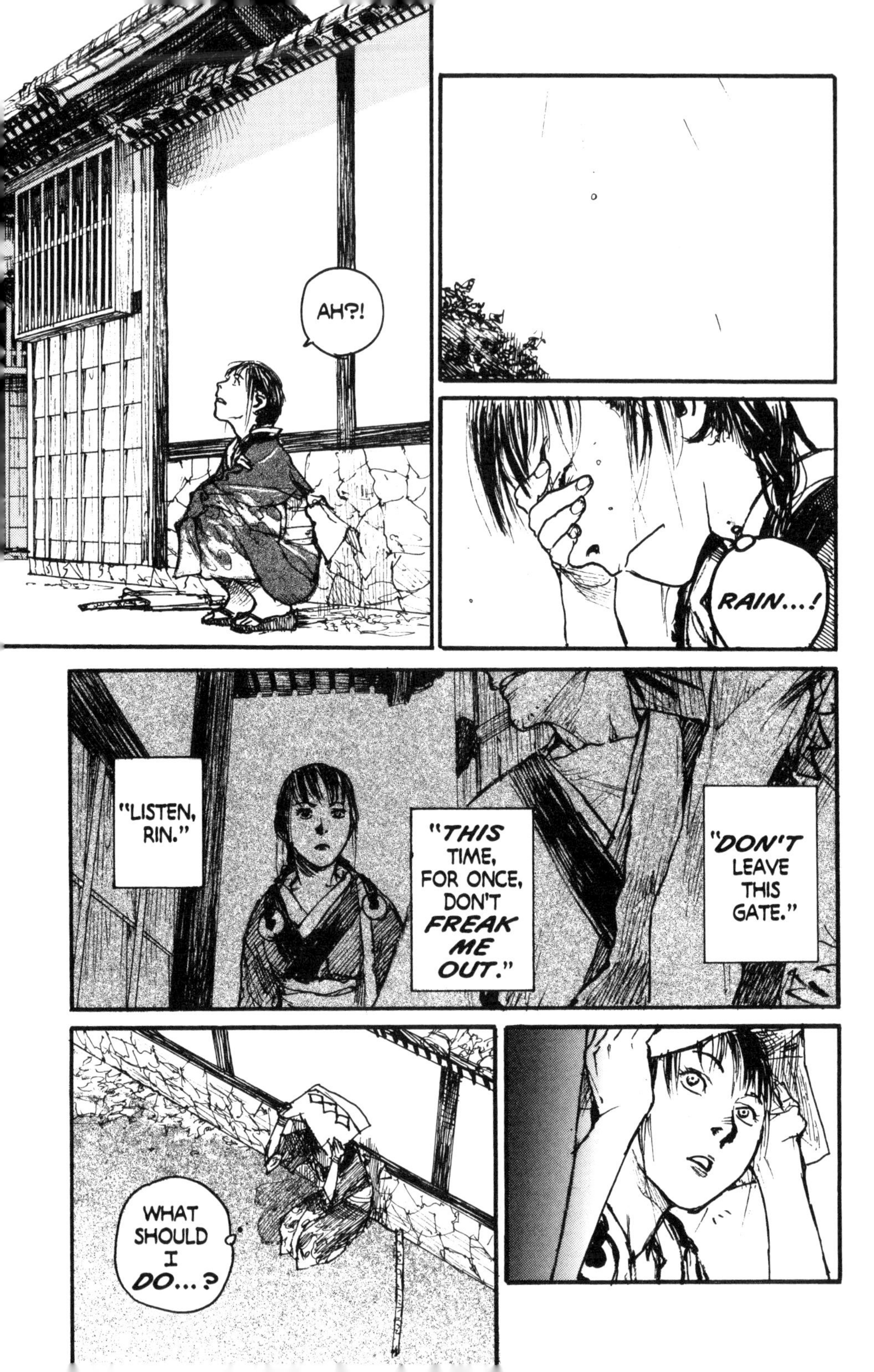
AH?!
RAIN...!
"LISTEN, RIN."
"THIS TIME, FOR ONCE, DON'T FREAK ME OUT."
"DON'T LEAVE THIS GATE."
WHAT SHOULD I DO...?

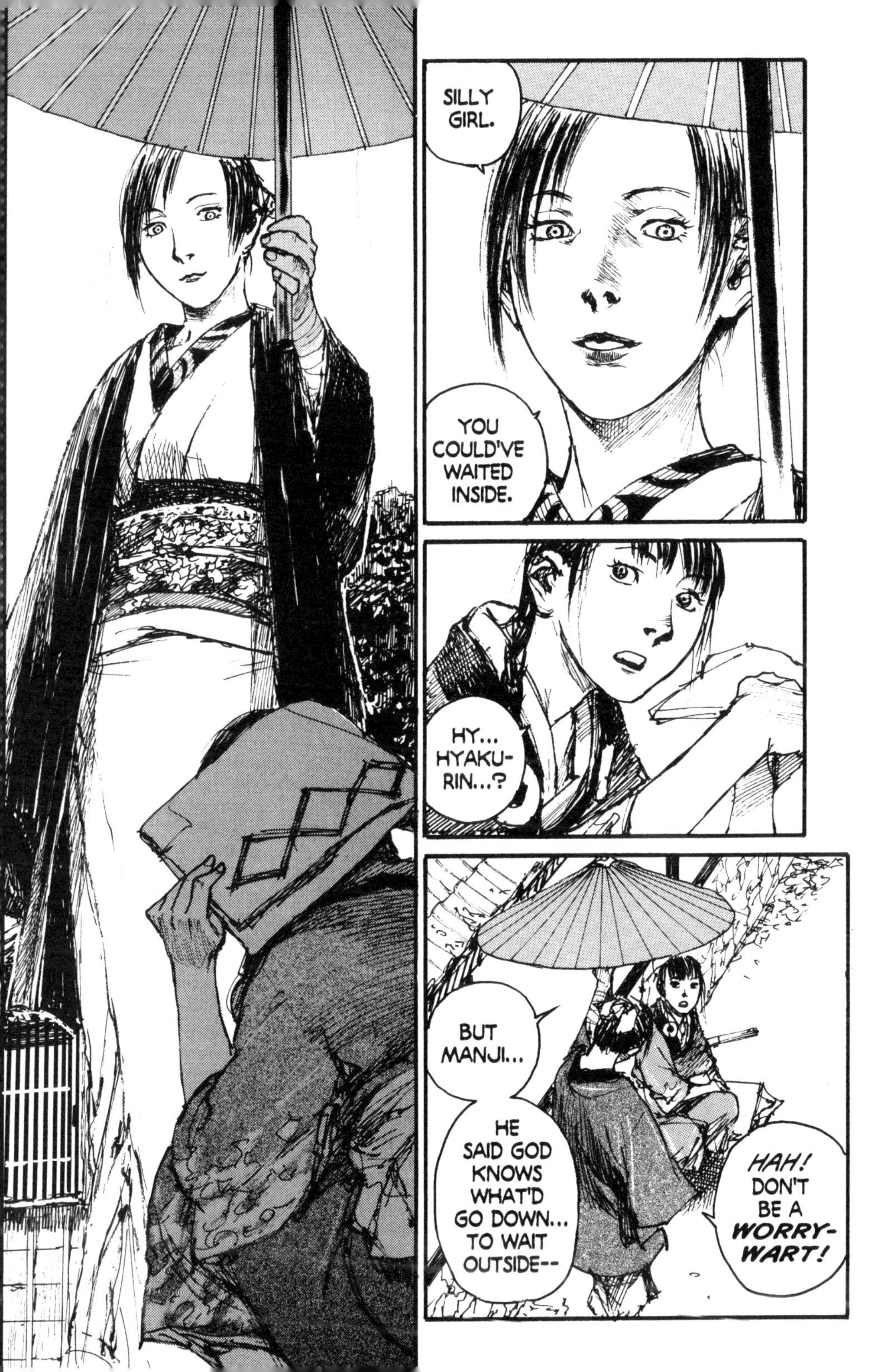
SILLY GIRL.
YOU COULD'VE WAITED INSIDE.
HY... HYAKU-RIN...?
BUT MANJI...
HE SAID GOD KNOWS WHAT'D GO DOWN... TO WAIT OUTSIDE--
HAH! DON'T BE A ***WORRY-WART!***

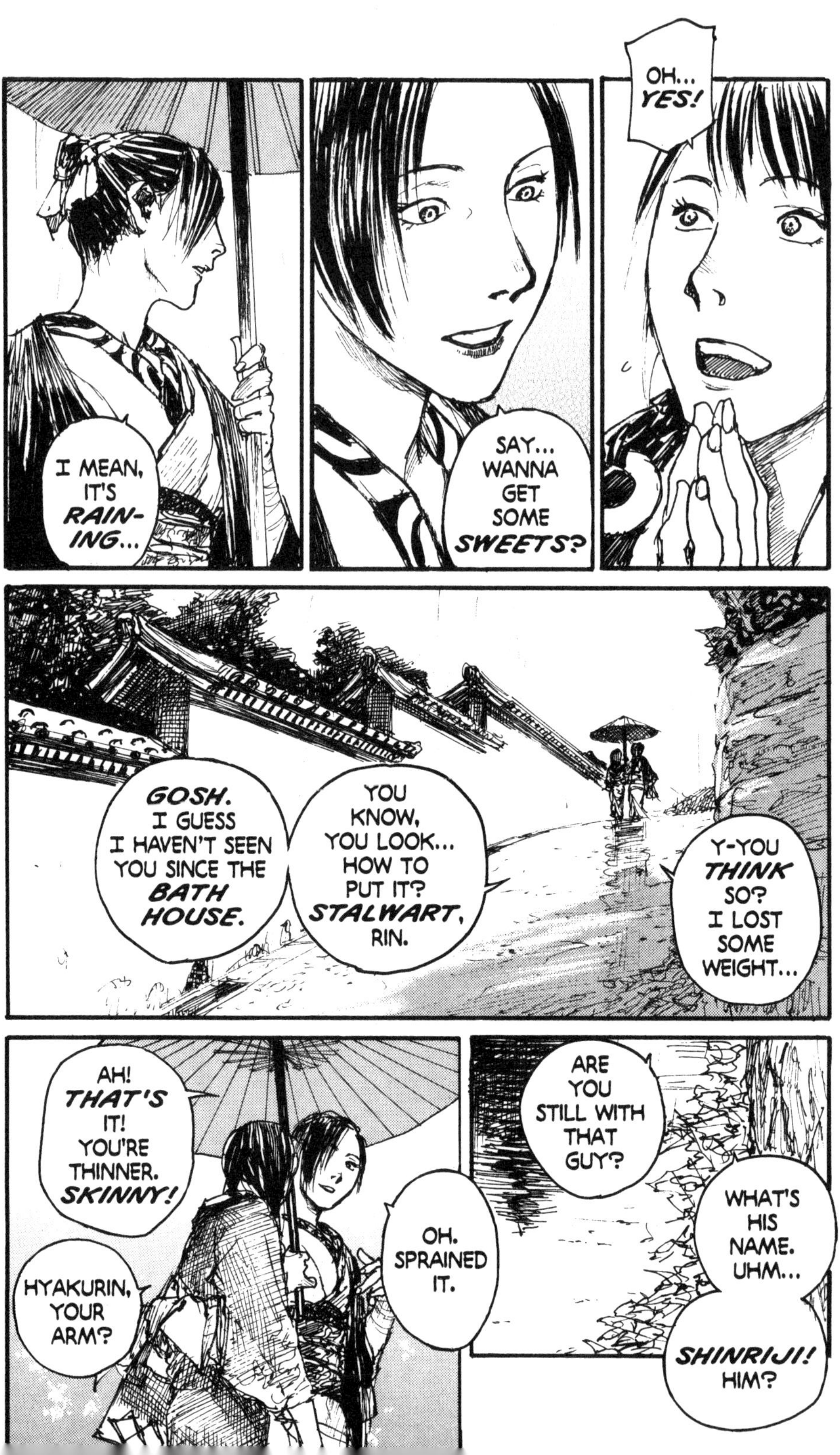
I MEAN, IT'S RAINING...
SAY... WANNA GET SOME SWEETS?
OH... YES!
GOSH. I GUESS I HAVEN'T SEEN YOU SINCE THE BATH HOUSE.
YOU KNOW, YOU LOOK... HOW TO PUT IT? STALWART, RIN.
Y-YOU THINK SO? I LOST SOME WEIGHT...
AH! THAT'S IT! YOU'RE THINNER. SKINNY!
HYAKURIN, YOUR ARM?
OH. SPRAINED IT.
ARE YOU STILL WITH THAT GUY?
WHAT'S HIS NAME. UHM...
SHINRIJI! HIM?

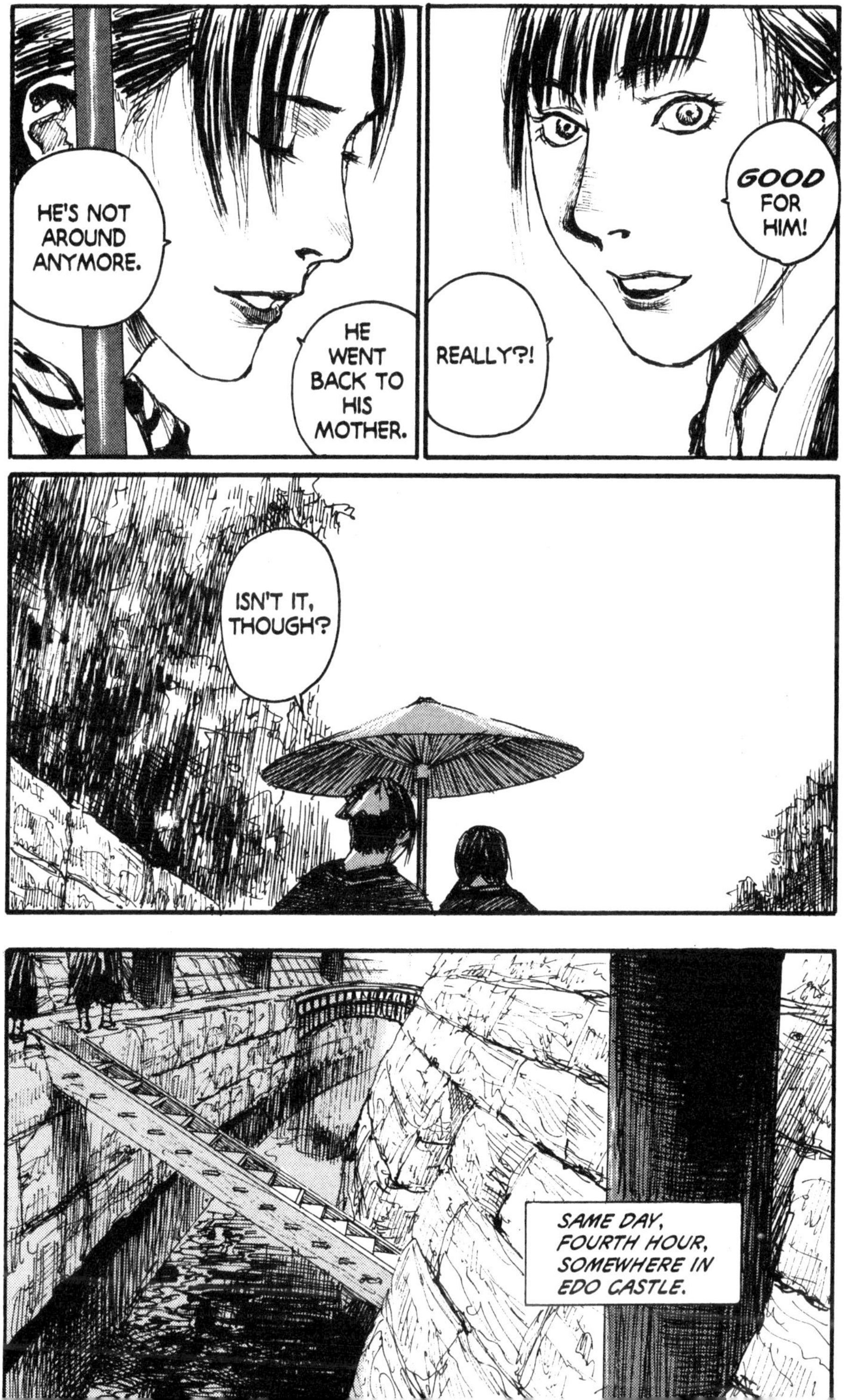
HE'S NOT AROUND ANYMORE.
HE WENT BACK TO HIS MOTHER.
REALLY?!
GOOD FOR HIM!
ISN'T IT, THOUGH?
SAME DAY, FOURTH HOUR, SOMEWHERE IN EDO CASTLE.

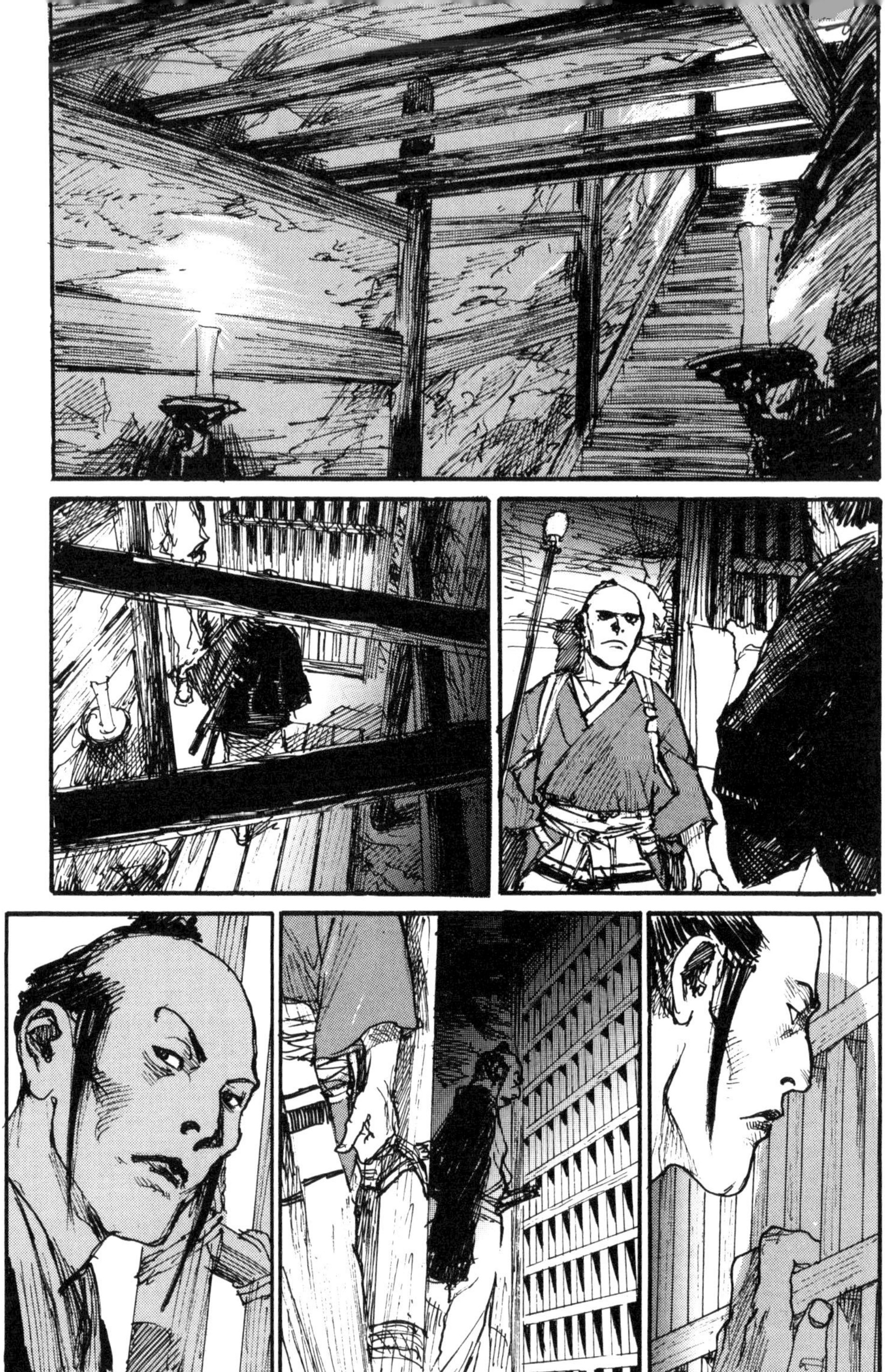

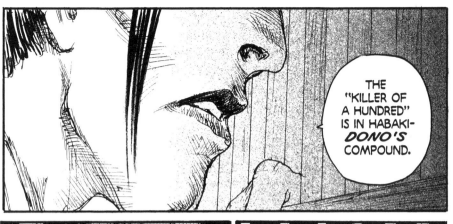

THE "KILLER OF A HUNDRED" IS IN HABAKI-*DONO'S* COMPOUND.

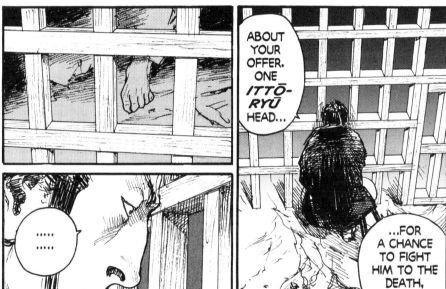

ABOUT YOUR OFFER. ONE *ITTŌ-RYŪ* HEAD...

.....
.....

...FOR A CHANCE TO FIGHT HIM TO THE DEATH, *HMM?*

IT WON'T FLY.

SO SORRY.

NOT *TASTY* ENOUGH.

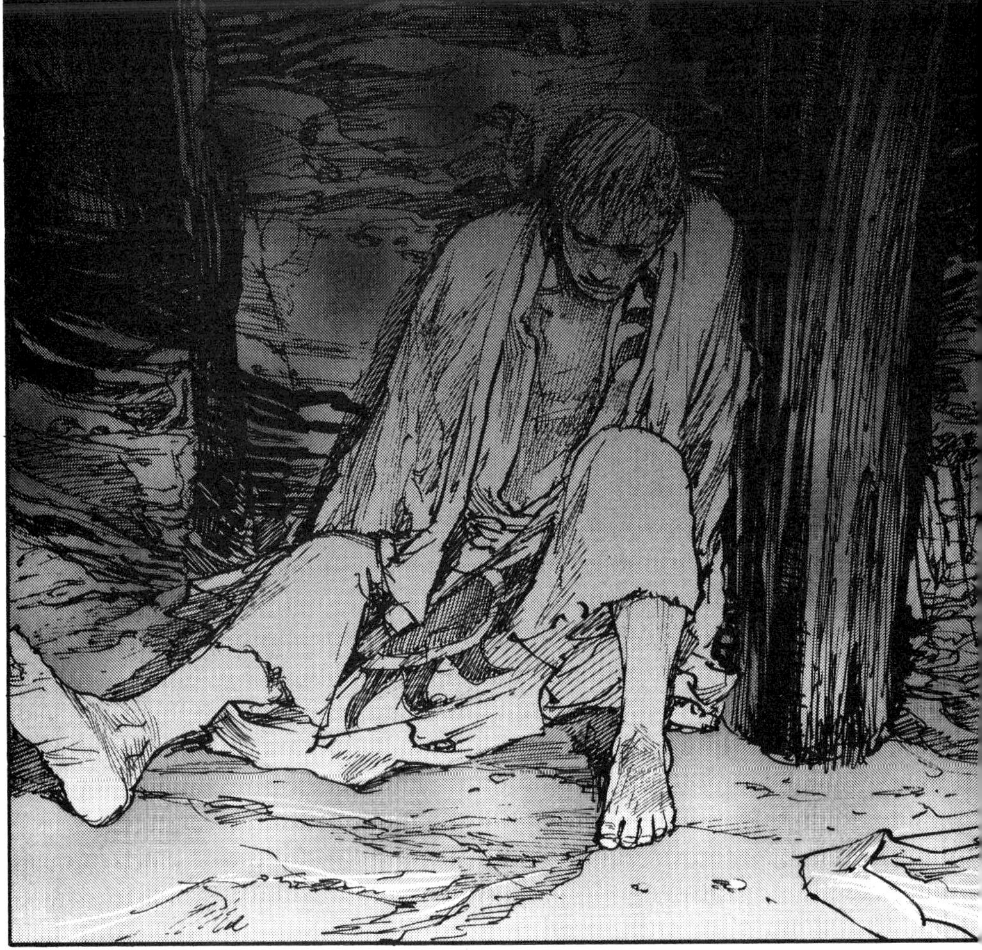
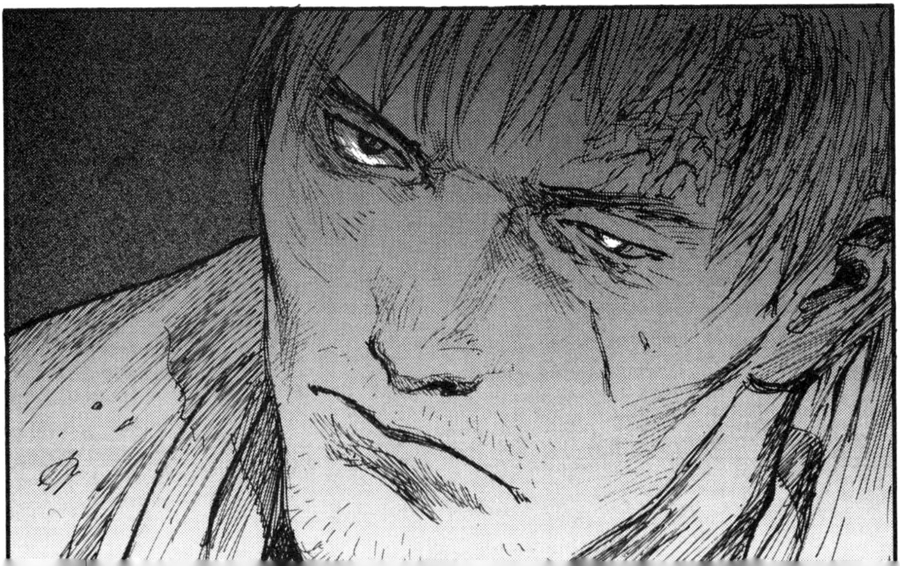

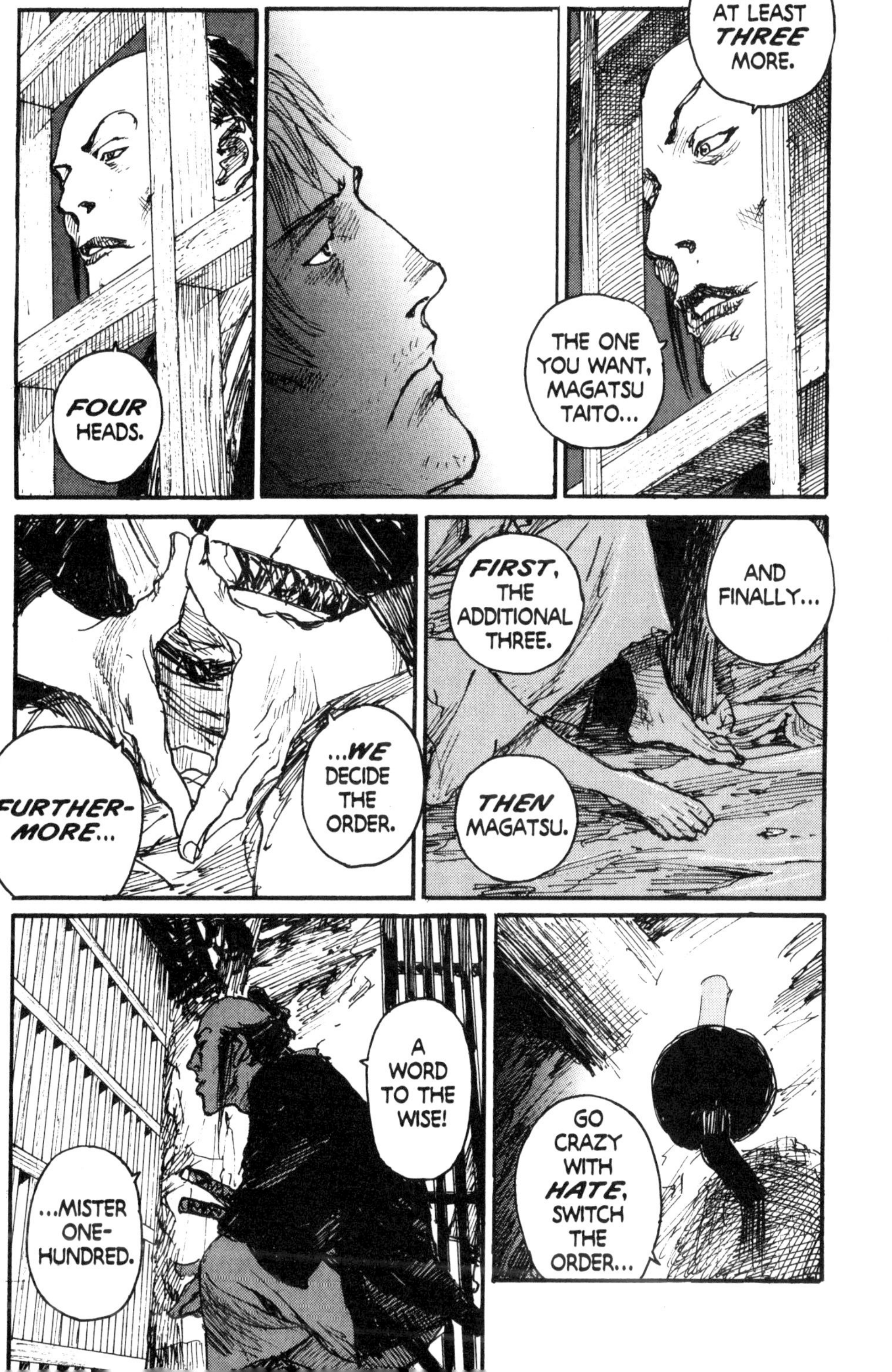
FOUR HEADS.
...AND AT LEAST THREE MORE.
THE ONE YOU WANT, MAGATSU TAITO...
FURTHER-MORE...
...WE DECIDE THE ORDER.
FIRST, THE ADDITIONAL THREE.
THEN MAGATSU.
AND FINALLY...
...MISTER ONE-HUNDRED.
A WORD TO THE WISE!
GO CRAZY WITH HATE, SWITCH THE ORDER...

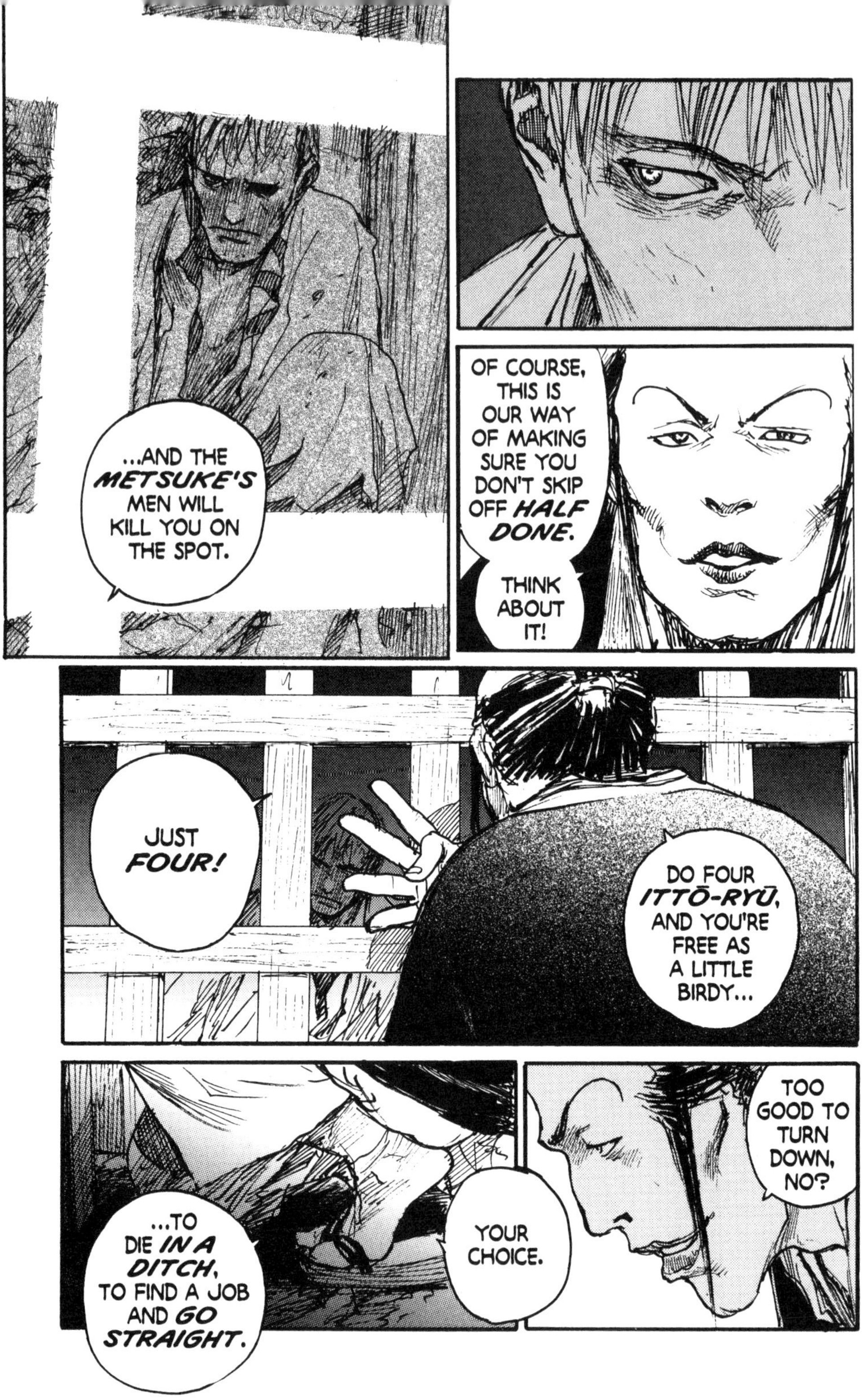
...AND THE METSUKE'S MEN WILL KILL YOU ON THE SPOT.
OF COURSE, THIS IS OUR WAY OF MAKING SURE YOU DON'T SKIP OFF HALF DONE.
THINK ABOUT IT!
JUST FOUR!
DO FOUR ITTŌ-RYŪ, AND YOU'RE FREE AS A LITTLE BIRDY...
...TO DIE IN A DITCH, TO FIND A JOB AND GO STRAIGHT.
YOUR CHOICE.
TOO GOOD TO TURN DOWN, NO?

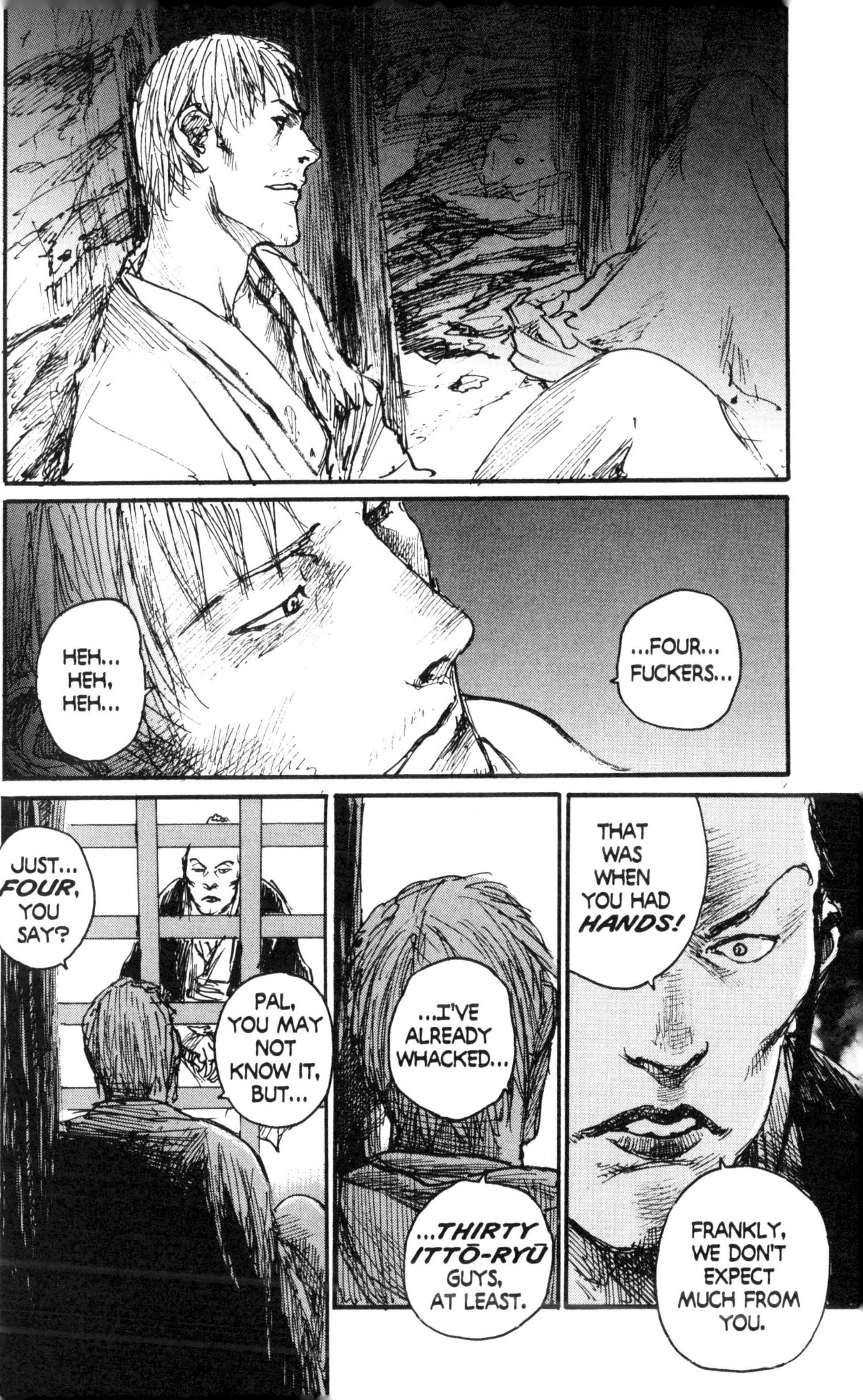
HEH... HEH, HEH...
...FOUR... FUCKERS...
JUST... FOUR, YOU SAY?
PAL, YOU MAY NOT KNOW IT, BUT...
...I'VE ALREADY WHACKED...
...THIRTY ITTŌ-RYŪ GUYS, AT LEAST.
THAT WAS WHEN YOU HAD HANDS!
FRANKLY, WE DON'T EXPECT MUCH FROM YOU.

THE ONLY REASON WE *HARBOR* A WRECK LIKE YOU, IS BECAUSE HABAKI-*DONO* SAID TO.

EVEN A *MAD DOG*, A CORNERED *RAT*, IF PUSHED...

...HAS CRAZY STRENGTH. OR SO SAYS HE.

BUT, IF YOU QUERY *ME*...

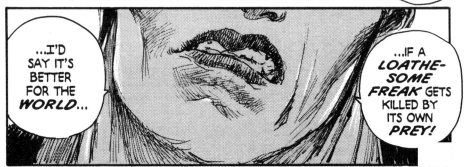

...I'D SAY IT'S BETTER FOR THE *WORLD*...

...IF A *LOATHE- SOME FREAK* GETS KILLED BY ITS OWN *PREY!*

AFTER I... WENT DOWN THE FALLS...

...I... LOST... MY LEFT *EYE.*

IN IT'S PLACE...

...THERE'S A NEW *WEAPON*...

A *WEAPON...* ?!

CAN'T... TELL YOU.

HOH! ONE CAN *HARDLY* WAIT!

BUT, AS FOR *NOW*...

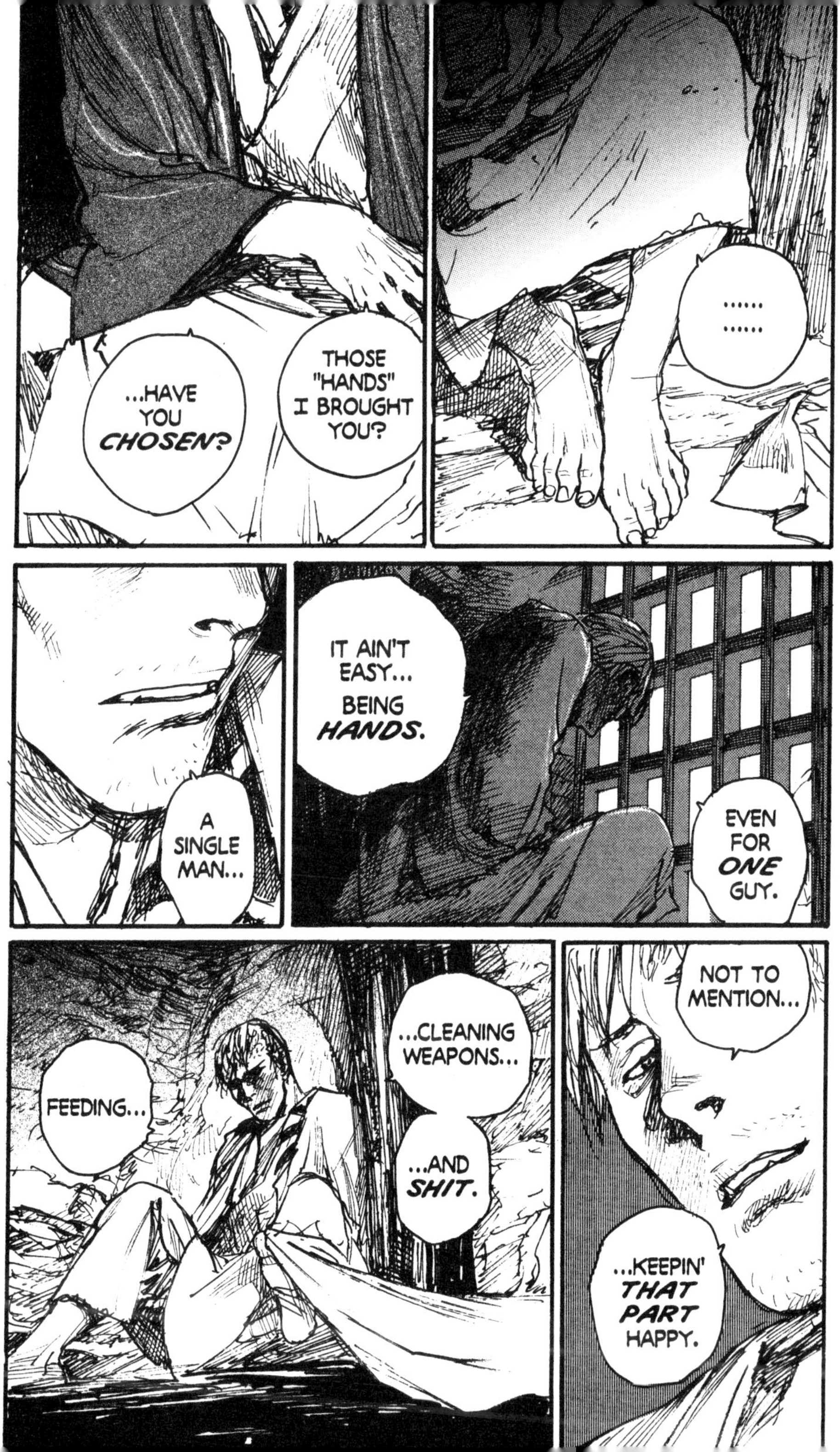
...HAVE YOU *CHOSEN?*
THOSE "HANDS" I BROUGHT YOU?
......
......
A SINGLE MAN...
IT AIN'T EASY... BEING *HANDS*.
EVEN FOR *ONE* GUY.
FEEDING...
...CLEANING WEAPONS...
...AND *SHIT*.
NOT TO MENTION...
...KEEPIN' *THAT PART* HAPPY.

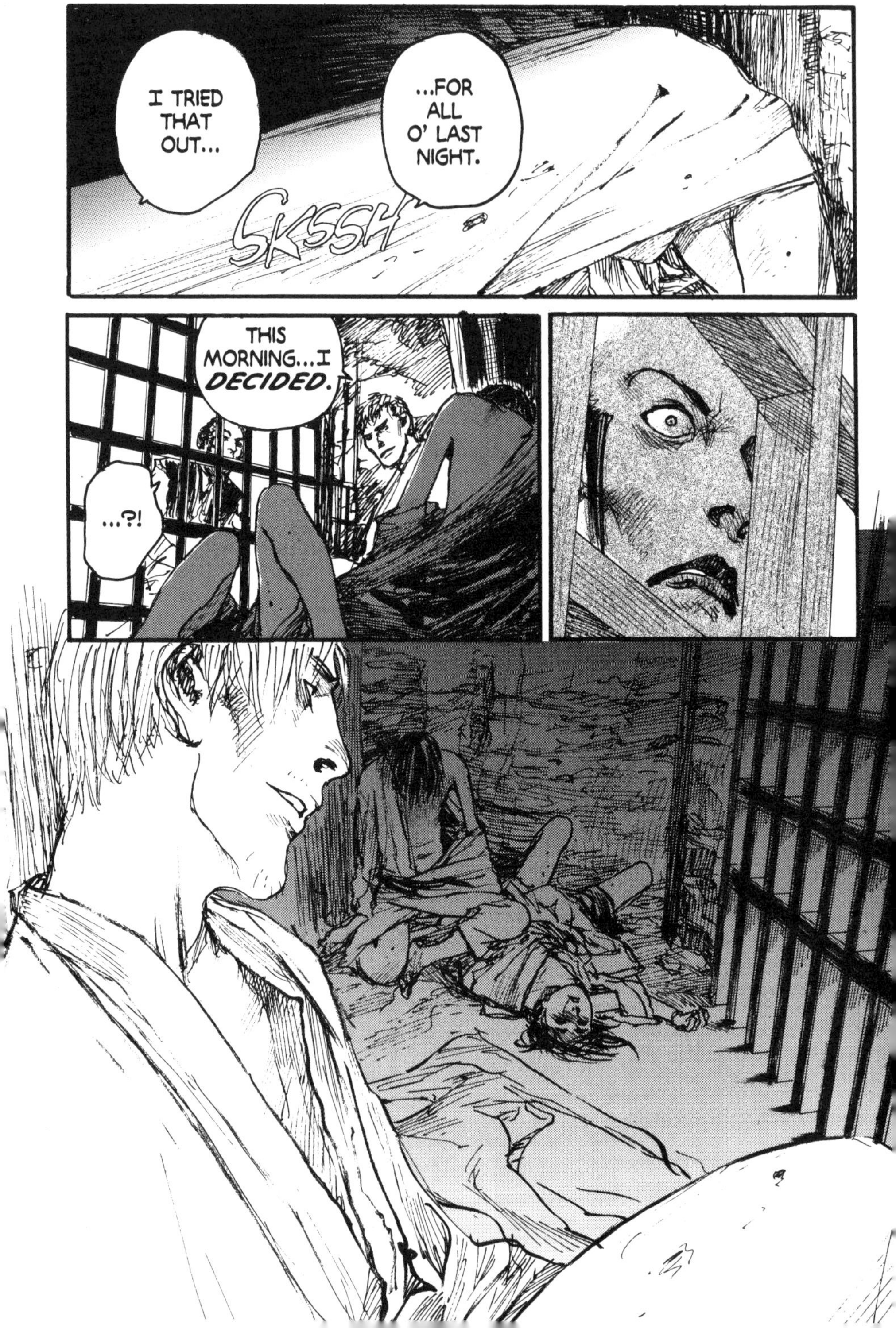
I TRIED THAT OUT...
...FOR ALL O' LAST NIGHT.
SKSSH
THIS MORNING...I *DECIDED*.
...?!

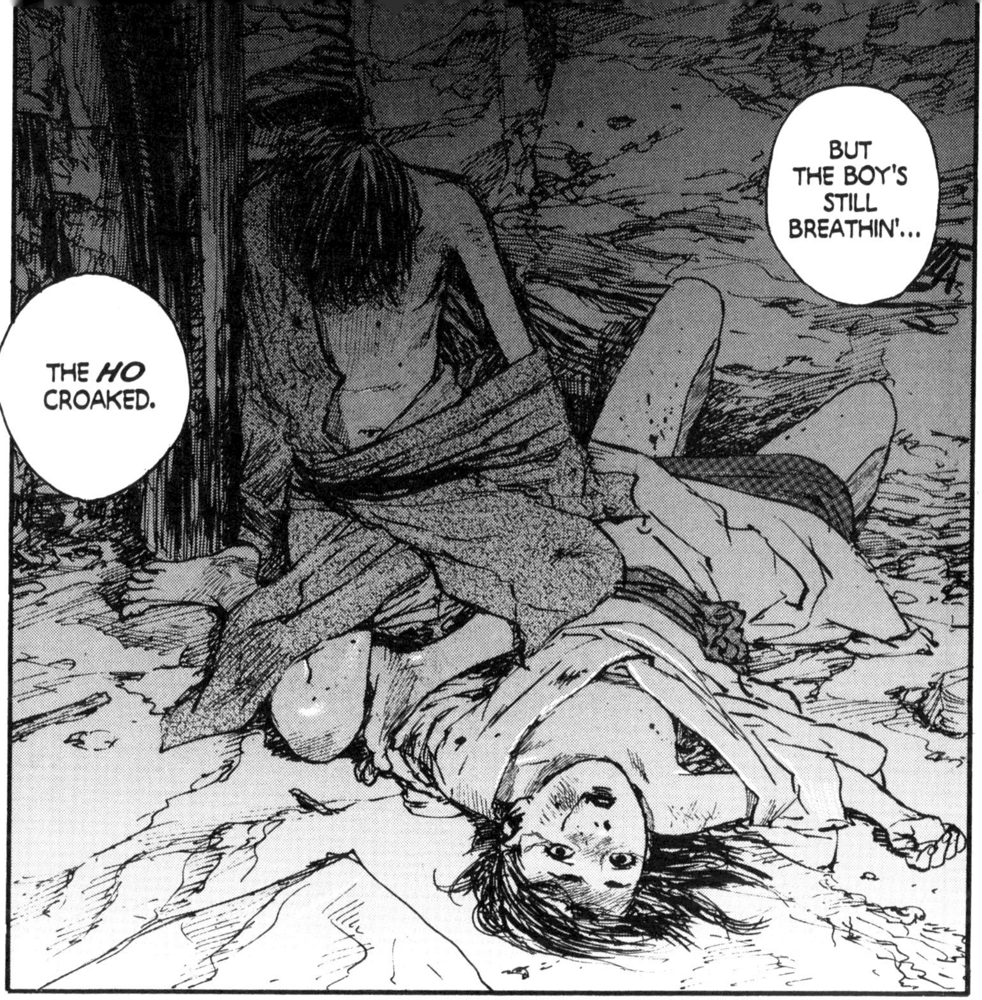
THE *HO* CROAKED.
BUT THE BOY'S STILL BREATHIN'...

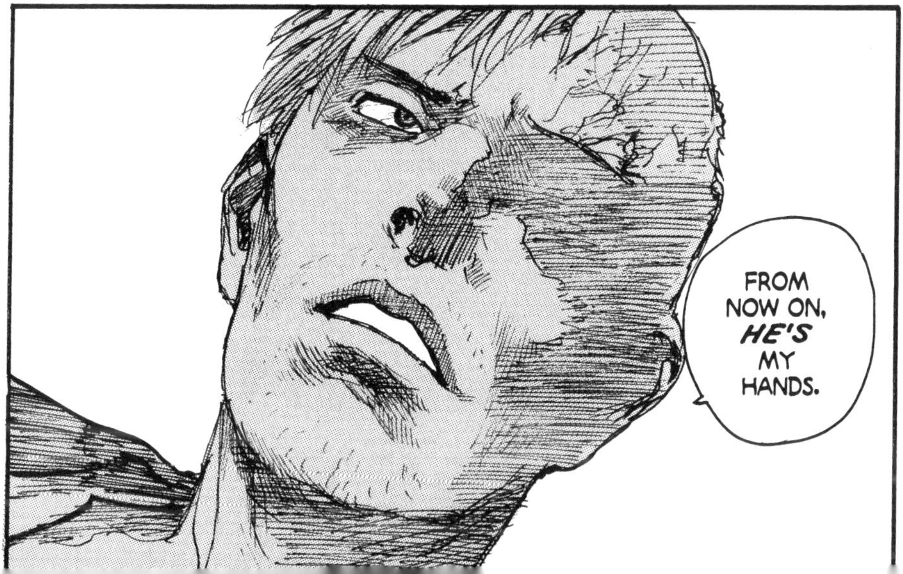
FROM NOW ON, ***HE'S*** MY HANDS.

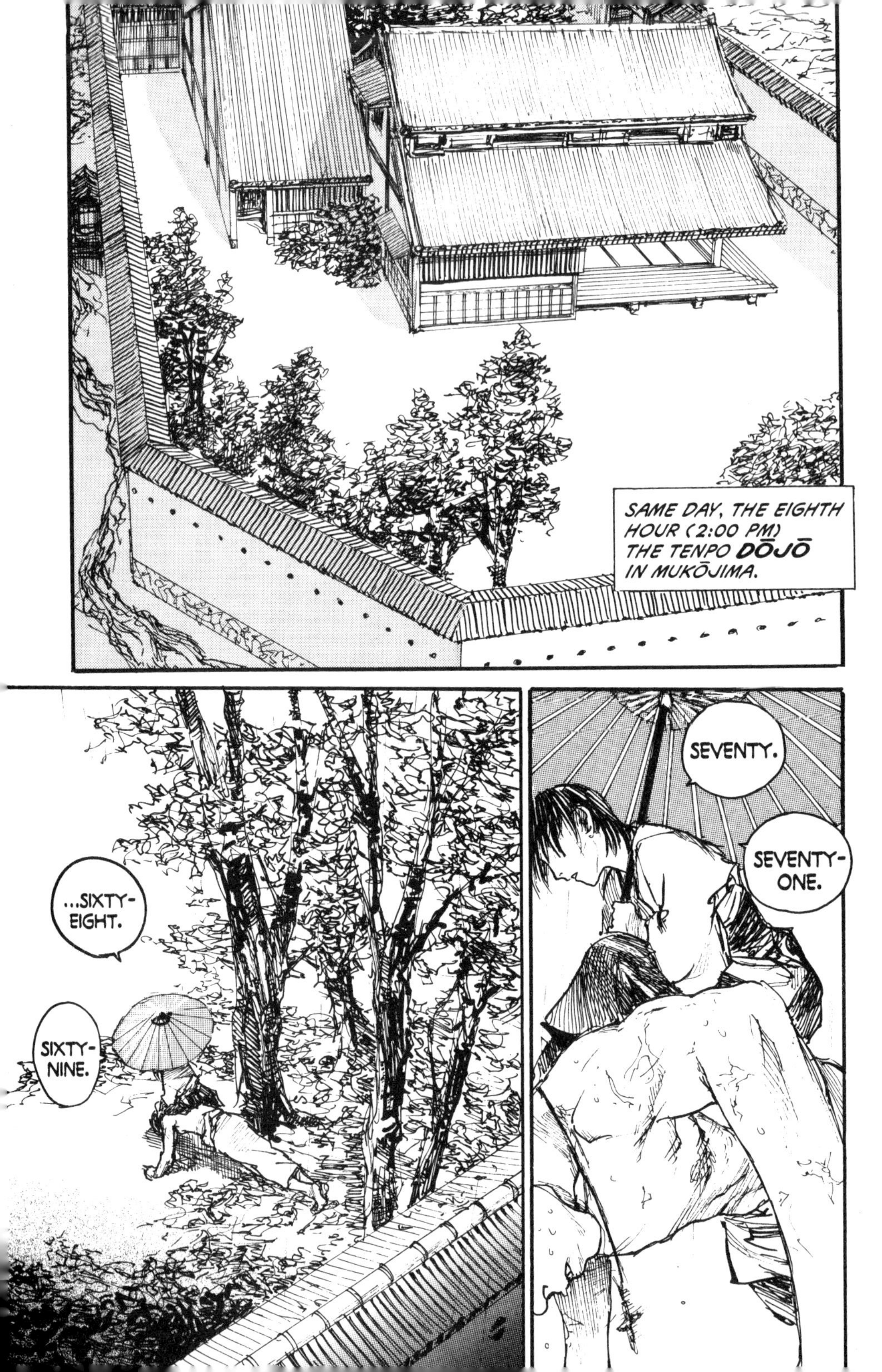
SAME DAY, THE EIGHTH HOUR (2:00 PM) THE TENPO DŌJŌ IN MUKŌJIMA.
...SIXTY-EIGHT.
SIXTY-NINE.
SEVENTY.
SEVENTY-ONE.

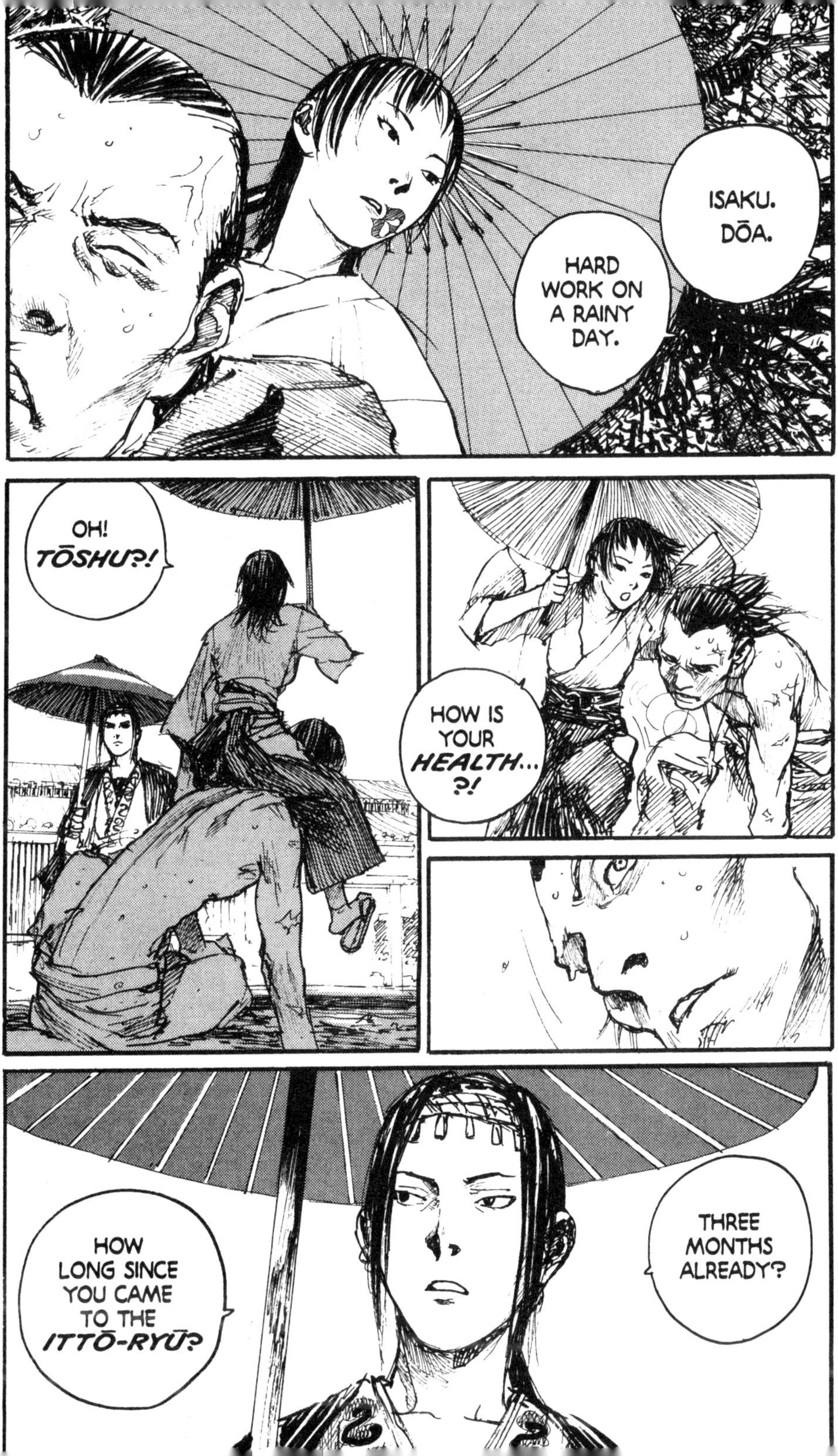
ISAKU. DŌA.
HARD WORK ON A RAINY DAY.
OH! TŌSHU?!
HOW IS YOUR HEALTH...?!
HOW LONG SINCE YOU CAME TO THE ITTŌ-RYŪ?
THREE MONTHS ALREADY?

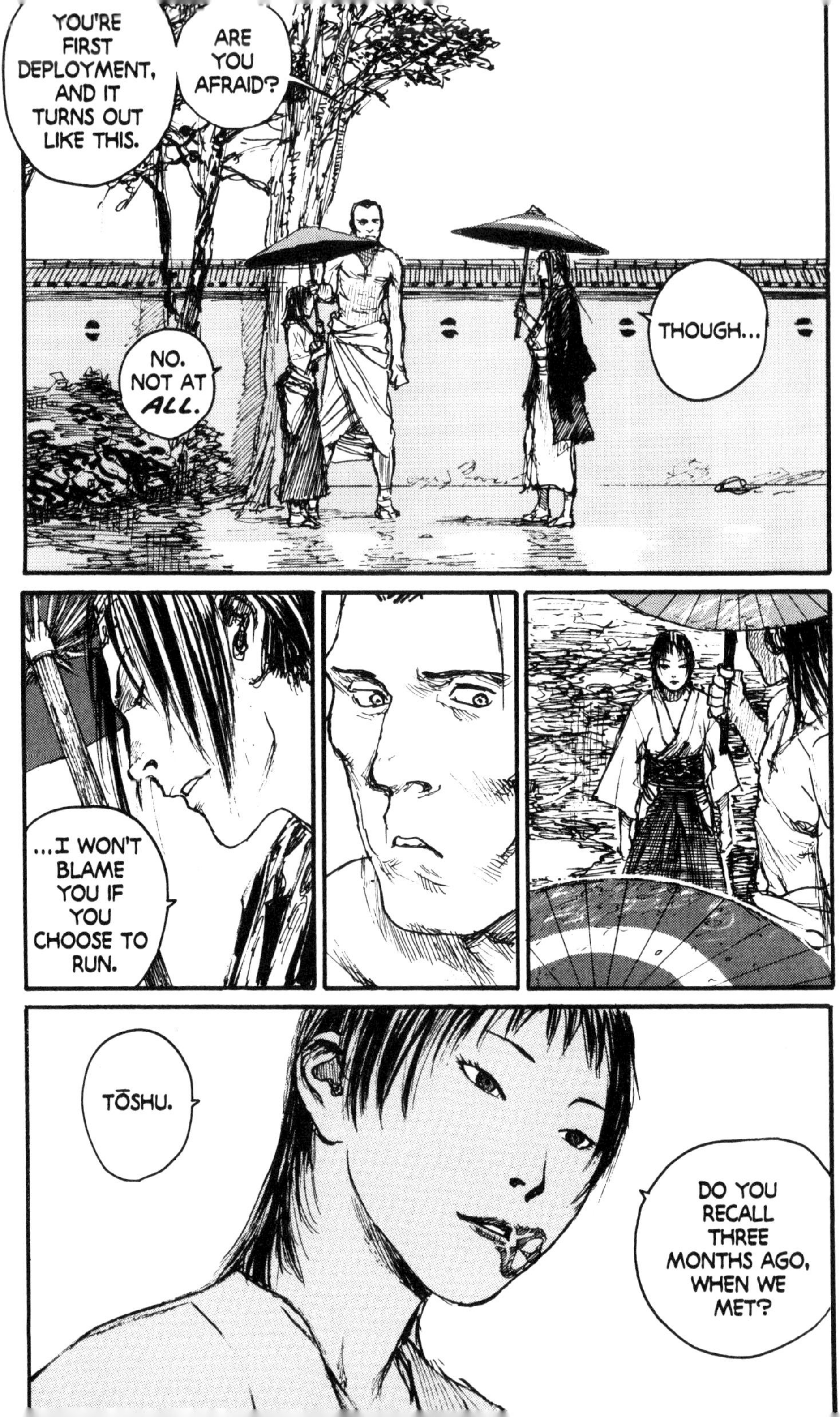
YOU'RE FIRST DEPLOYMENT, AND IT TURNS OUT LIKE THIS.
ARE YOU AFRAID?
NO. NOT AT ALL.
THOUGH...
...I WON'T BLAME YOU IF YOU CHOOSE TO RUN.
TŌSHU.
DO YOU RECALL THREE MONTHS AGO, WHEN WE MET?

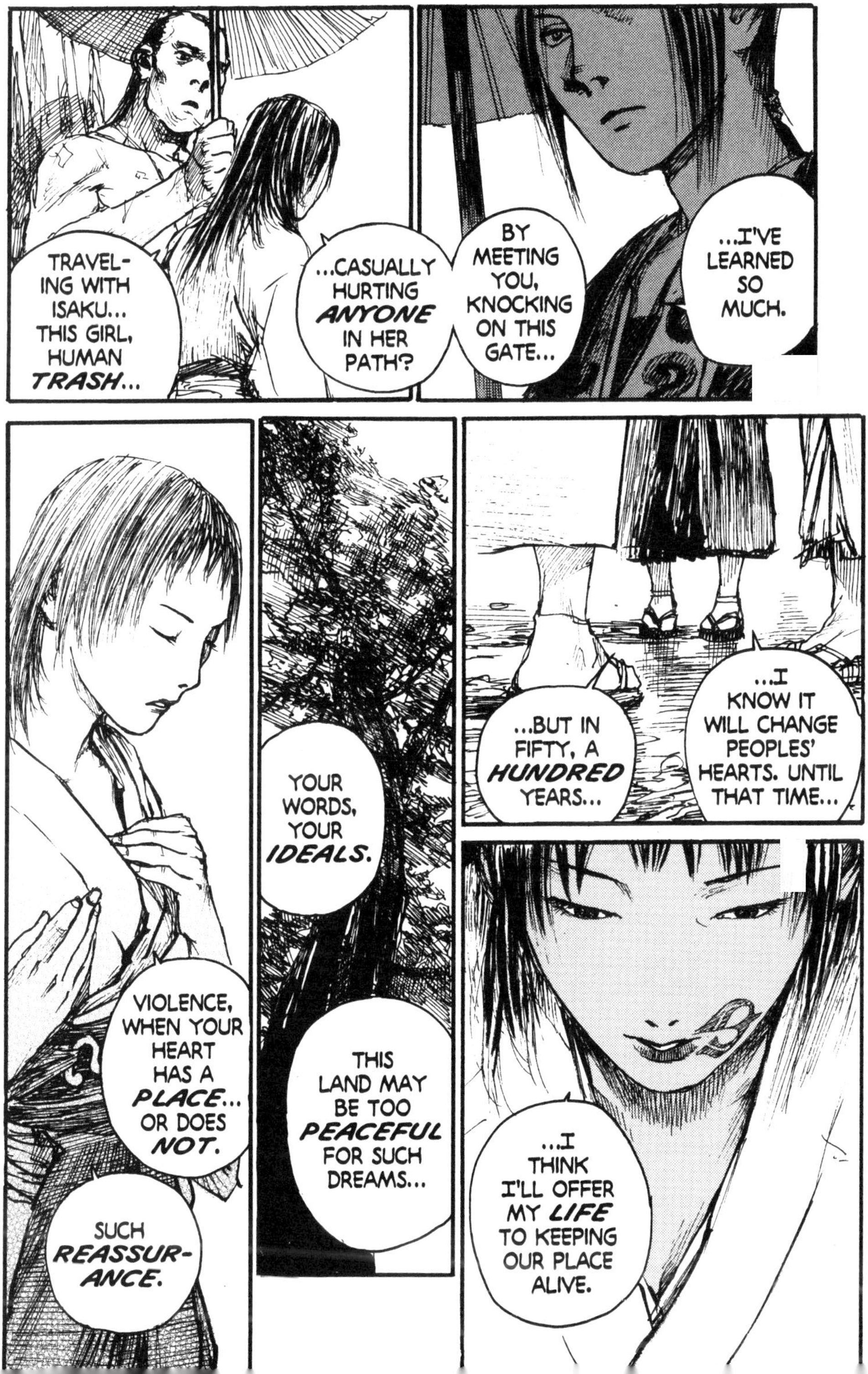
TRAVEL-ING WITH ISAKU... THIS GIRL, HUMAN *TRASH*...
...CASUALLY HURTING *ANYONE* IN HER PATH?
BY MEETING YOU, KNOCKING ON THIS GATE...
...I'VE LEARNED SO MUCH.
VIOLENCE, WHEN YOUR HEART HAS A *PLACE*... OR DOES *NOT*.
SUCH *REASSUR-ANCE*.
YOUR WORDS, YOUR *IDEALS*.
THIS LAND MAY BE TOO *PEACEFUL* FOR SUCH DREAMS...
...BUT IN FIFTY, A *HUNDRED* YEARS...
...I KNOW IT WILL CHANGE PEOPLES' HEARTS. UNTIL THAT TIME...
...I THINK I'LL OFFER MY *LIFE* TO KEEPING OUR PLACE ALIVE.

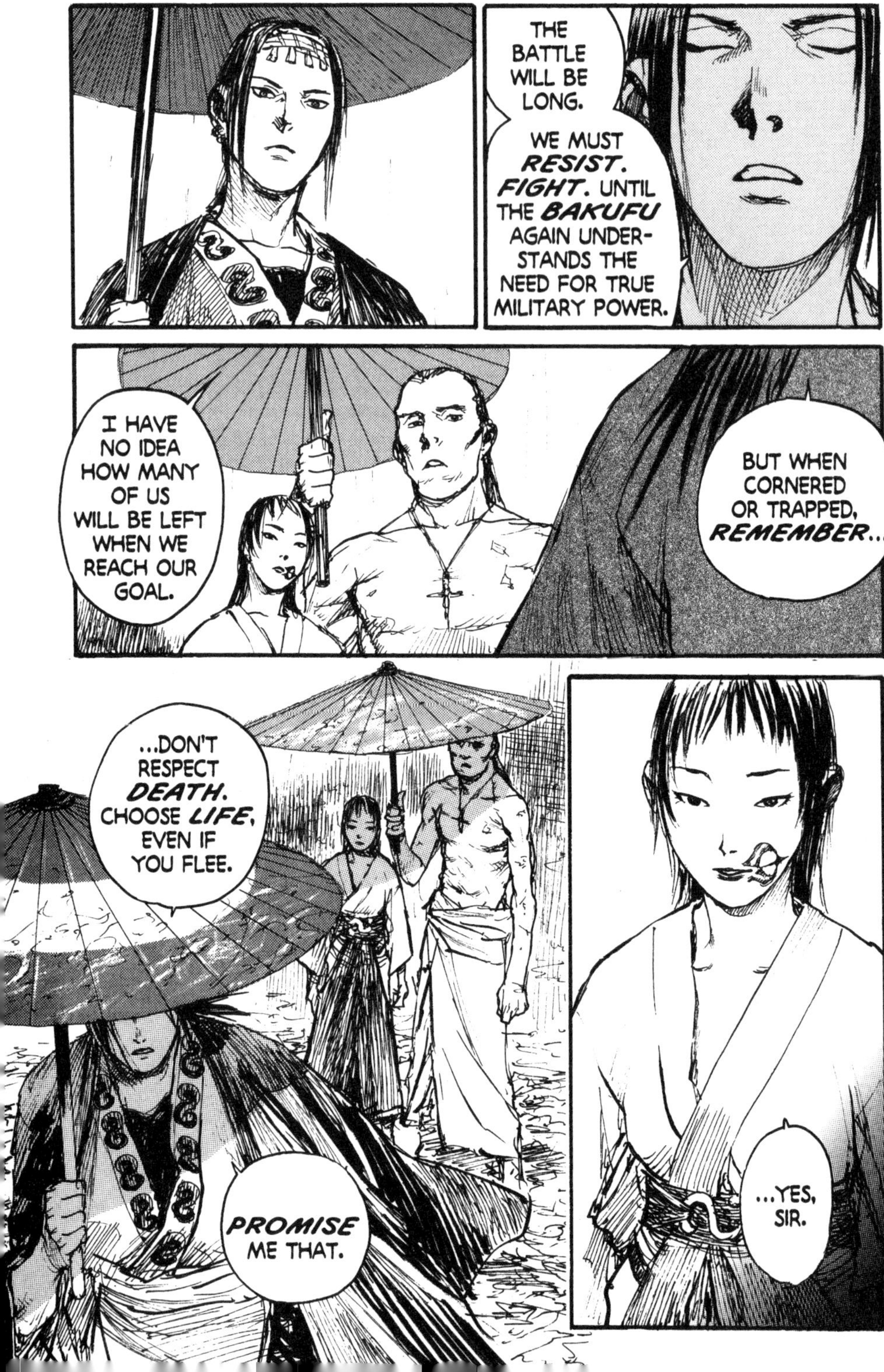
THE BATTLE WILL BE LONG.
WE MUST *RESIST*. *FIGHT*. UNTIL THE *BAKUFU* AGAIN UNDER-STANDS THE NEED FOR TRUE MILITARY POWER.
I HAVE NO IDEA HOW MANY OF US WILL BE LEFT WHEN WE REACH OUR GOAL.
BUT WHEN CORNERED OR TRAPPED, *REMEMBER*...
...DON'T RESPECT *DEATH*. CHOOSE *LIFE*, EVEN IF YOU FLEE.
PROMISE ME THAT.
...YES, SIR.

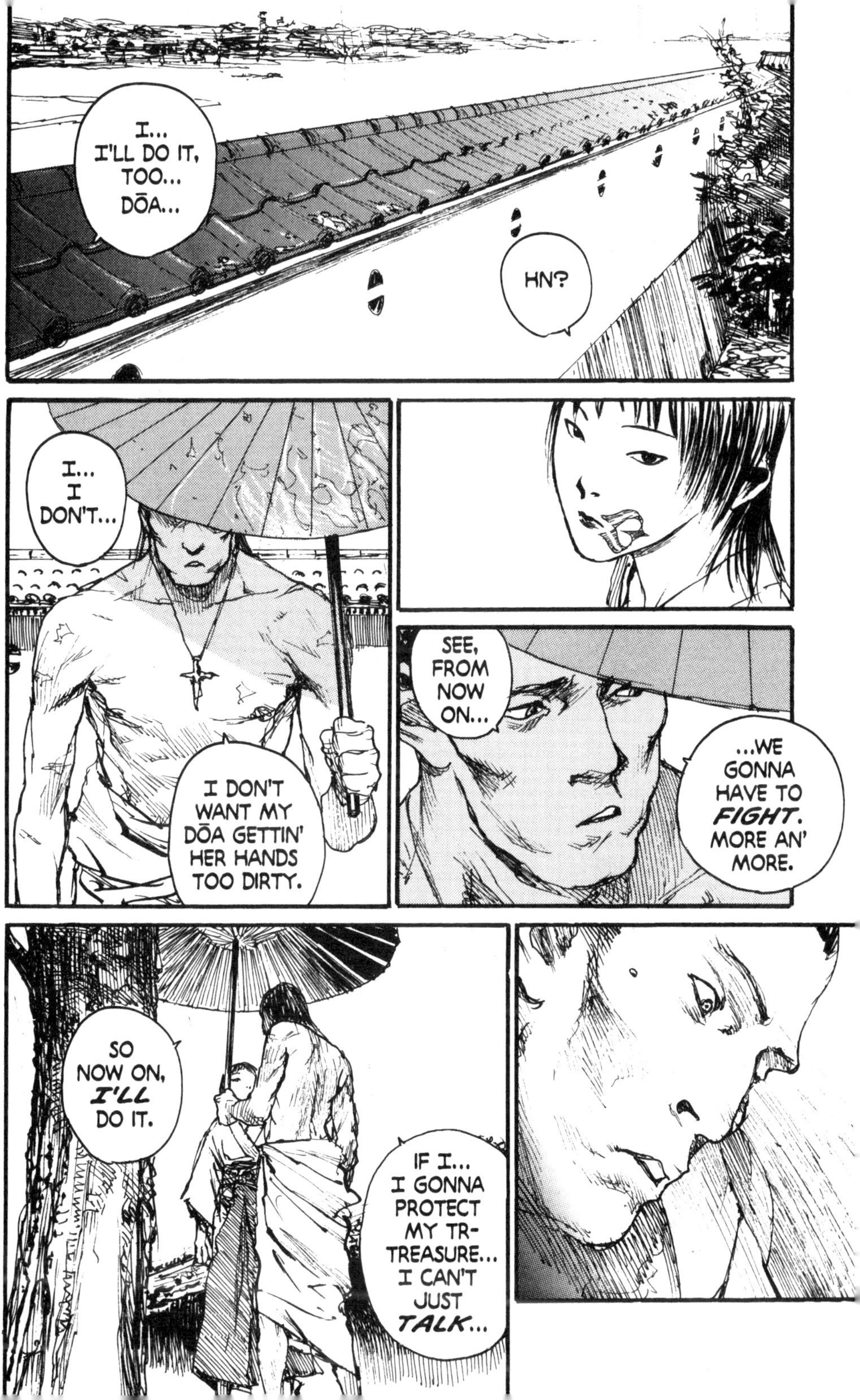
I... I'LL DO IT, TOO... DŌA...
HN?
I... I DON'T...
I DON'T WANT MY DŌA GETTIN' HER HANDS TOO DIRTY.
SEE, FROM NOW ON...
...WE GONNA HAVE TO FIGHT. MORE AN' MORE.
SO NOW ON, I'LL DO IT.
IF I... I GONNA PROTECT MY TR-TREASURE... I CAN'T JUST TALK...

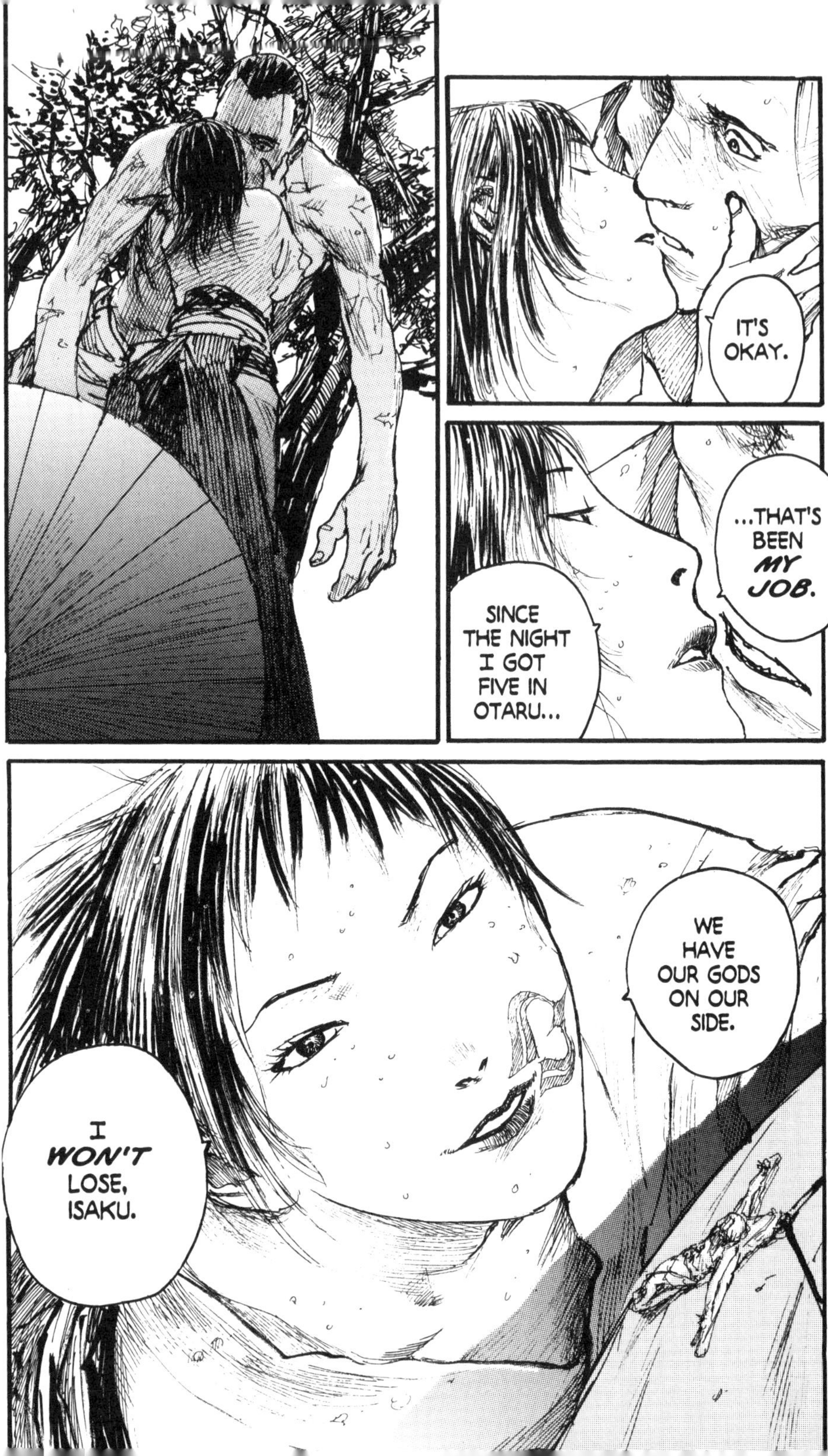
IT'S OKAY.
SINCE THE NIGHT I GOT FIVE IN OTARU...
...THAT'S BEEN *MY JOB*.
WE HAVE OUR GODS ON OUR SIDE.
I *WON'T* LOSE, ISAKU.

DUET

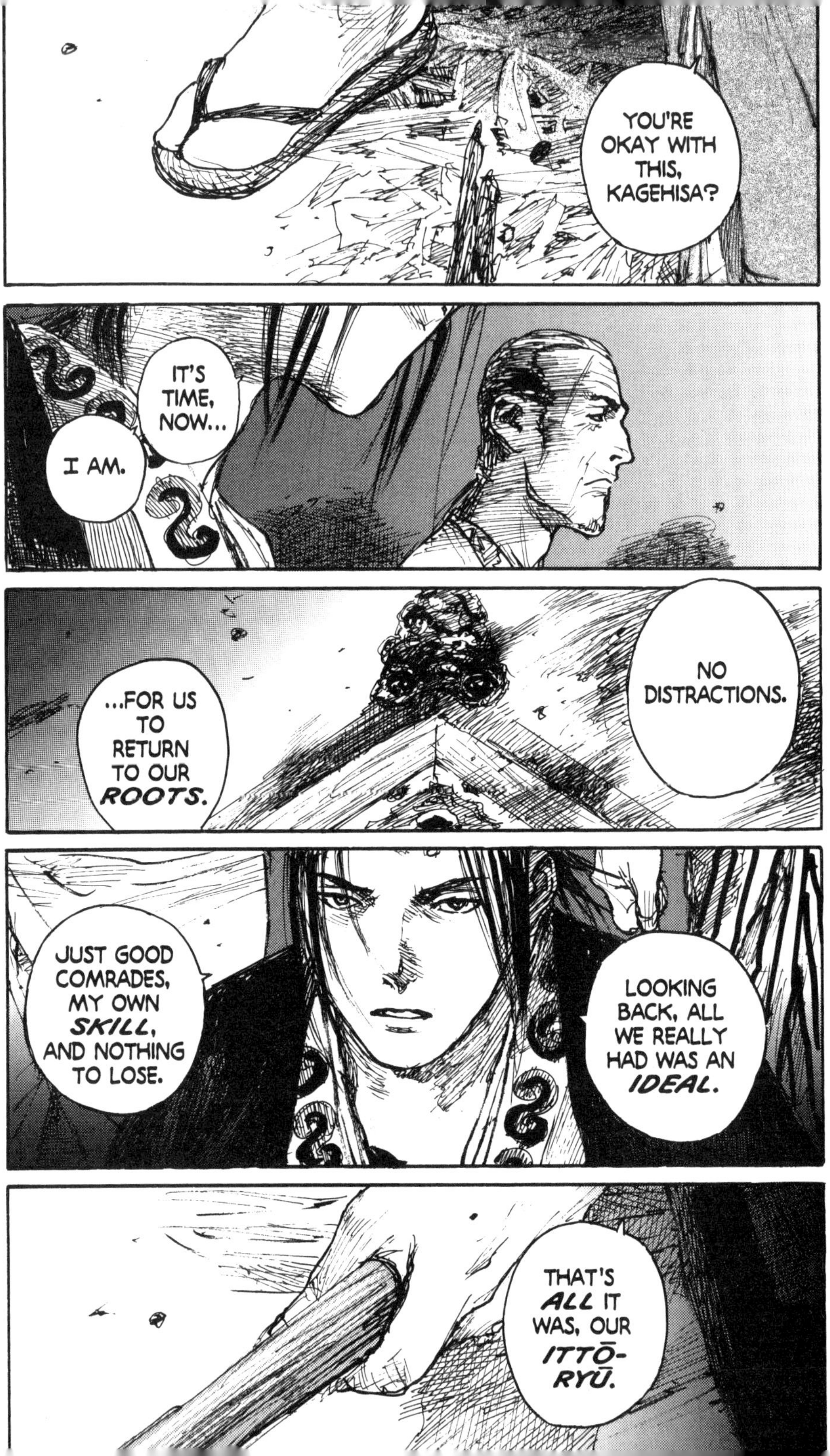
YOU'RE OKAY WITH THIS, KAGEHISA?
I AM.
IT'S TIME, NOW...
...FOR US TO RETURN TO OUR *ROOTS*.
NO DISTRACTIONS.
JUST GOOD COMRADES, MY OWN *SKILL*, AND NOTHING TO LOSE.
LOOKING BACK, ALL WE REALLY HAD WAS AN *IDEAL*.
THAT'S *ALL* IT WAS, OUR *ITTŌ-RYŪ*.

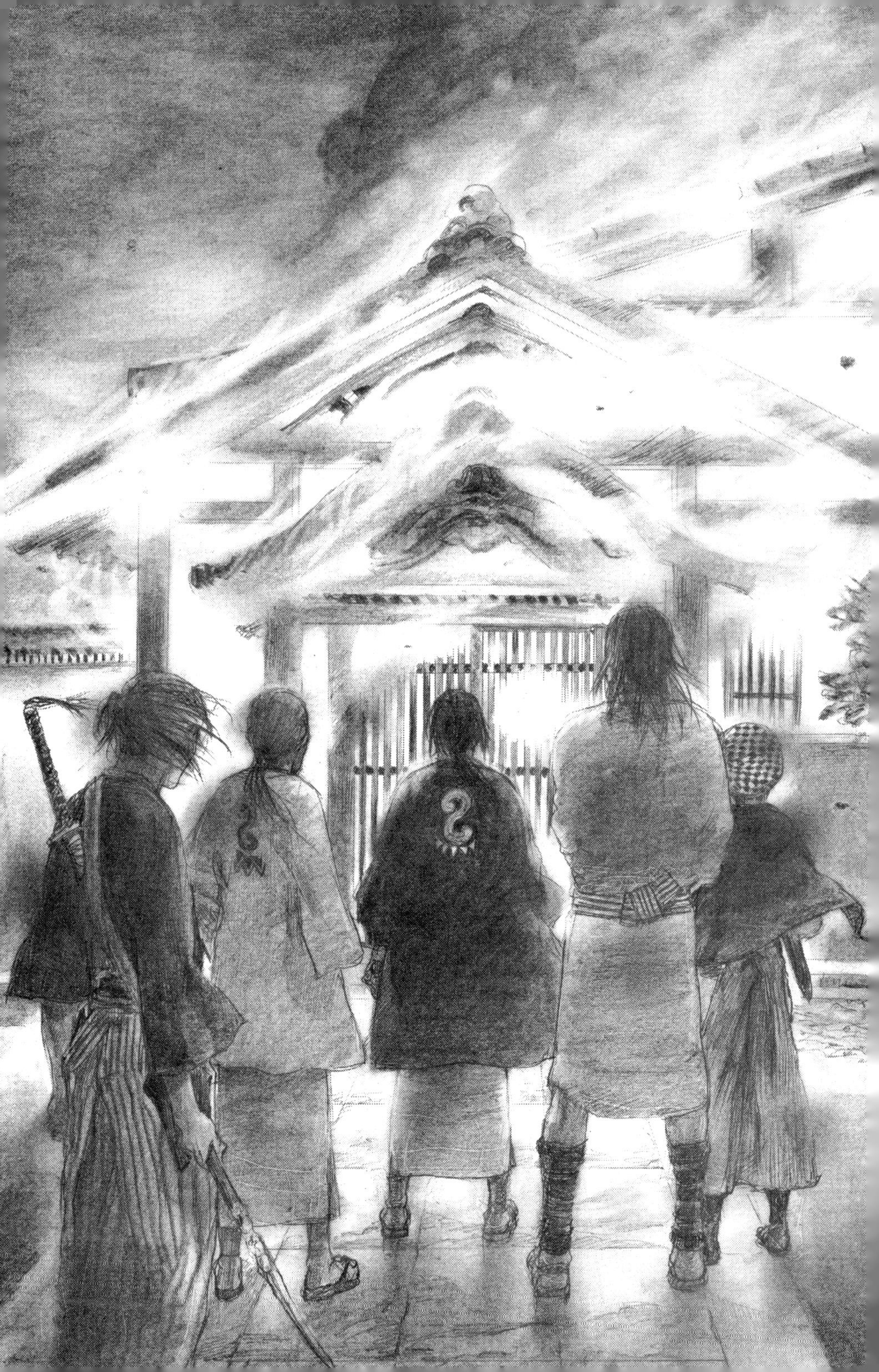

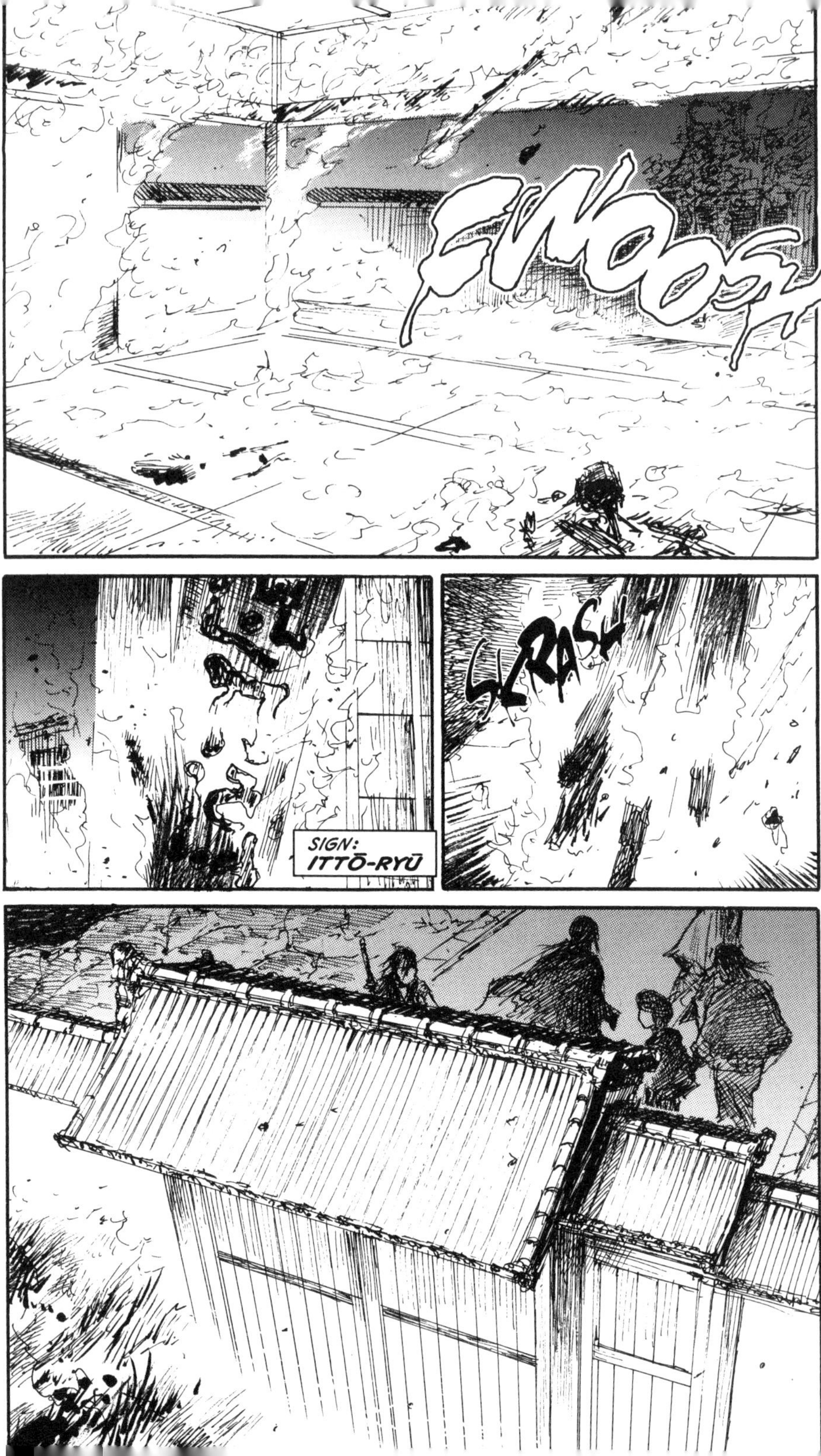

SWOOSH
SIGN:
ITTŌ-RYŪ
SLRASH

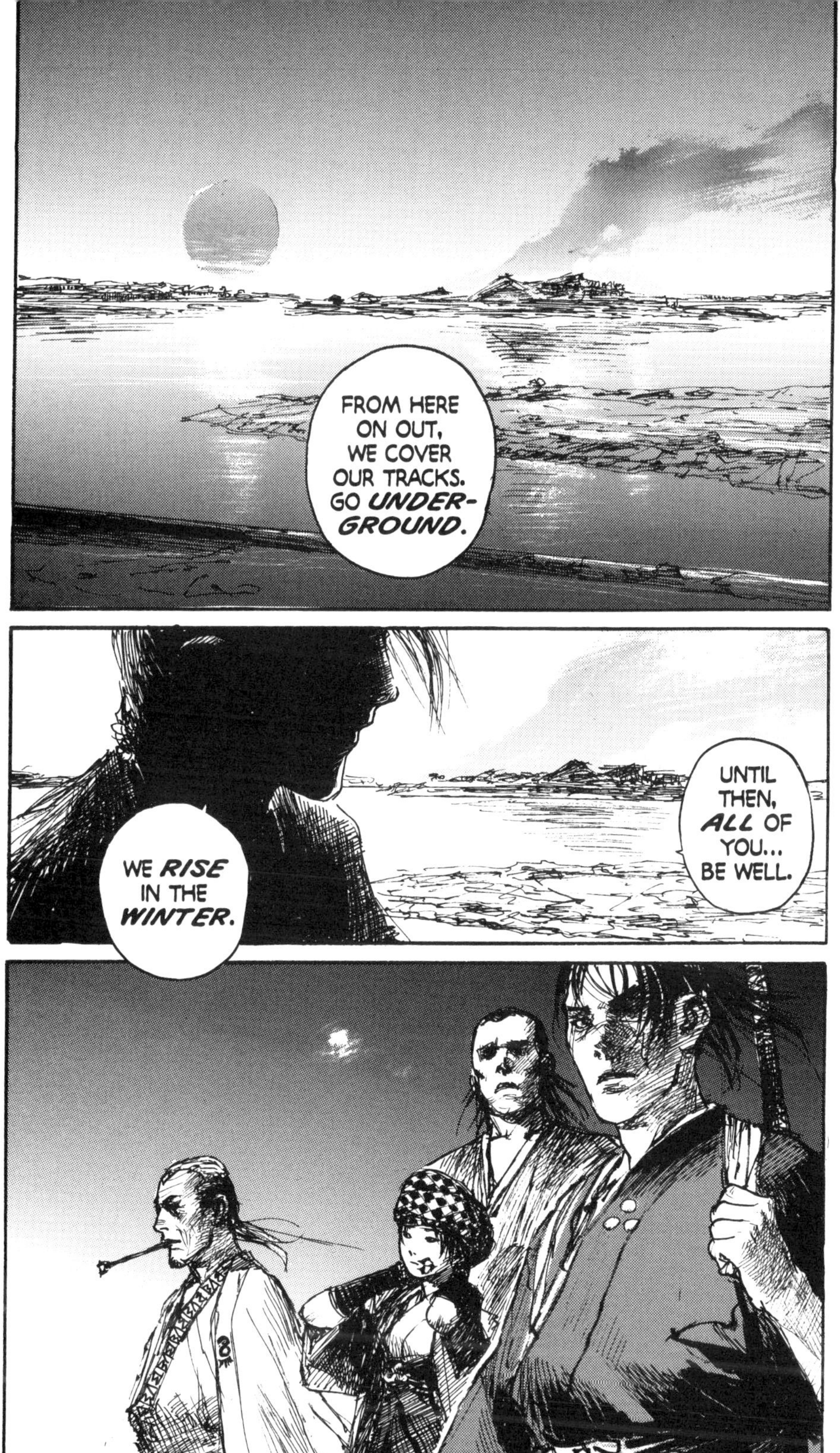
FROM HERE ON OUT, WE COVER OUR TRACKS. GO UNDERGROUND.
WE RISE IN THE WINTER.
UNTIL THEN, ALL OF YOU... BE WELL.

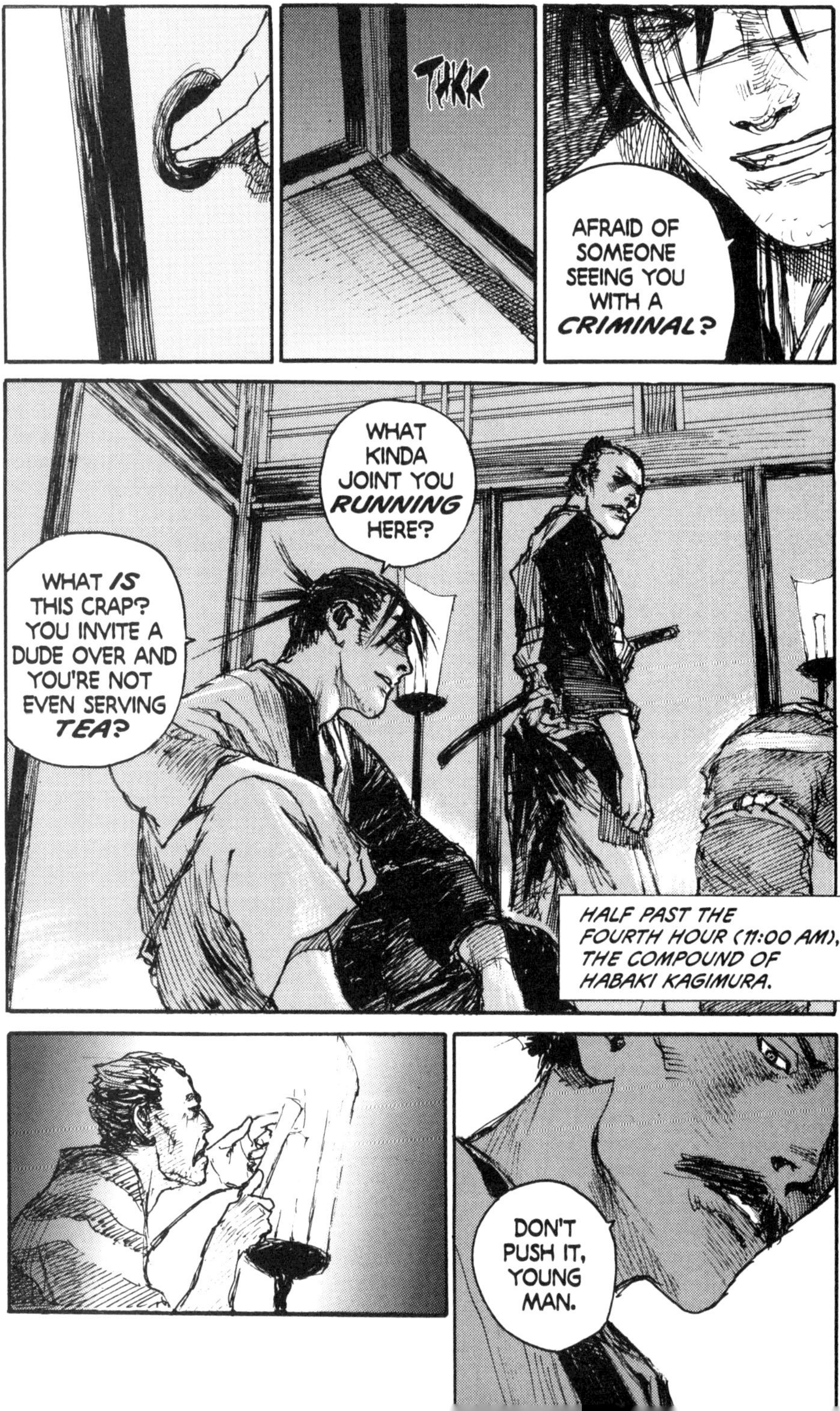
THKK
AFRAID OF SOMEONE SEEING YOU WITH A *CRIMINAL?*
WHAT *IS* THIS CRAP? YOU INVITE A DUDE OVER AND YOU'RE NOT EVEN SERVING *TEA?*
WHAT KINDA JOINT YOU *RUNNING* HERE?
HALF PAST THE FOURTH HOUR (11:00 AM), THE COMPOUND OF HABAKI KAGIMURA.
DON'T PUSH IT, YOUNG MAN.

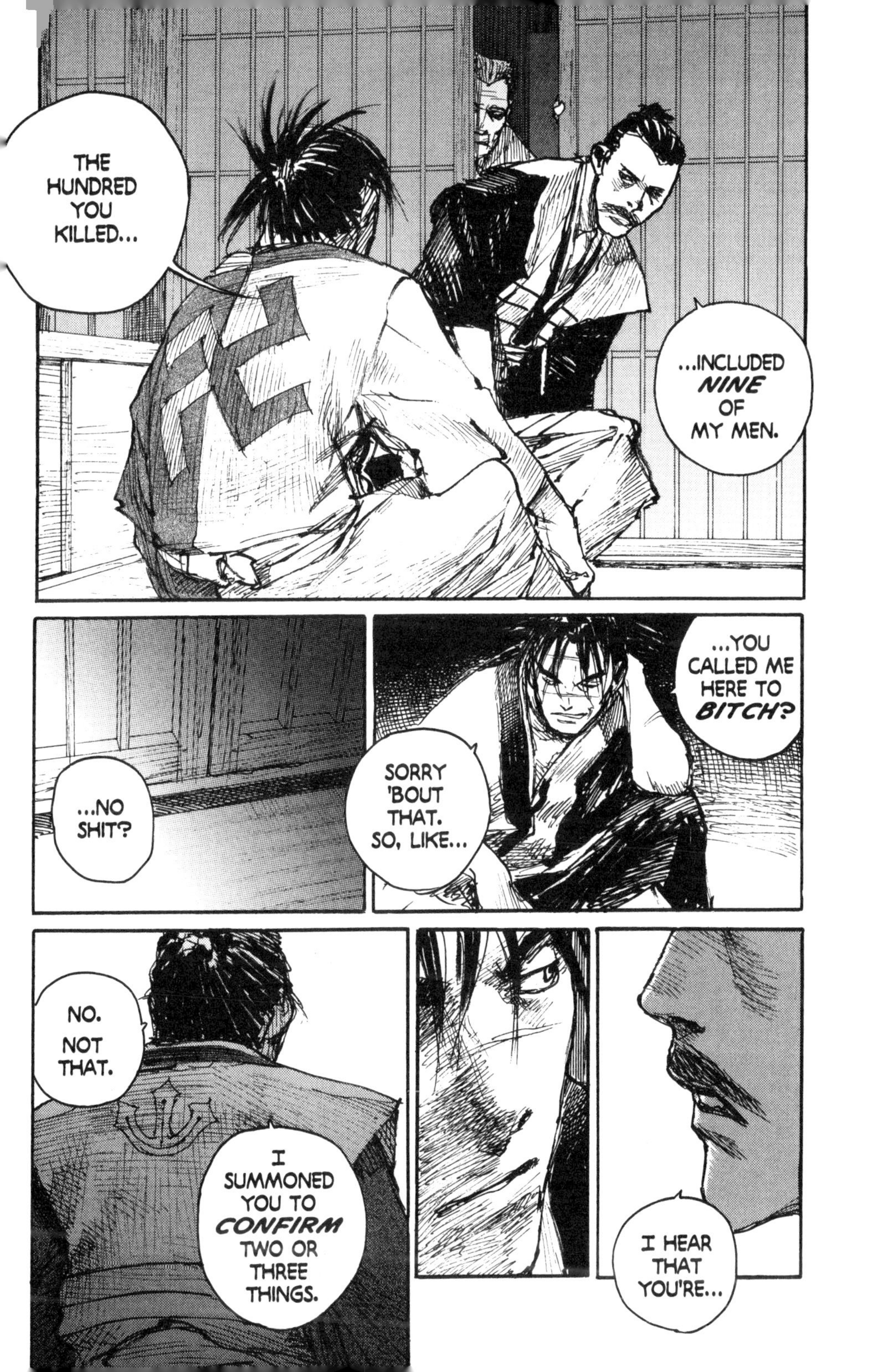
THE HUNDRED YOU KILLED...
...INCLUDED NINE OF MY MEN.
...NO SHIT?
...YOU CALLED ME HERE TO BITCH?
SORRY 'BOUT THAT. SO, LIKE...
NO. NOT THAT.
I SUMMONED YOU TO CONFIRM TWO OR THREE THINGS.
I HEAR THAT YOU'RE...

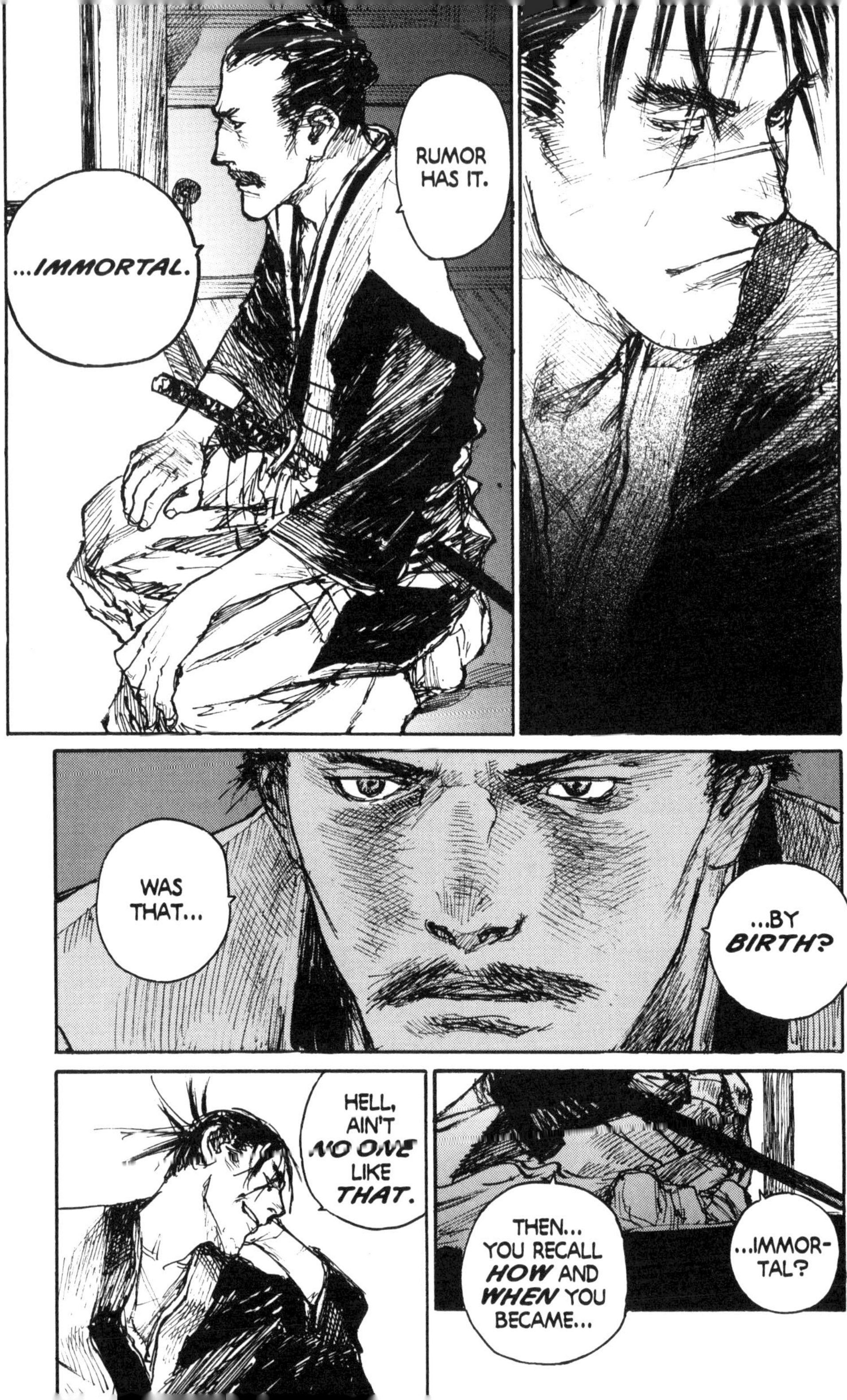
RUMOR HAS IT.
...IMMORTAL.
WAS THAT...
...BY BIRTH?
HELL, AIN'T NO ONE LIKE THAT.
THEN... YOU RECALL HOW AND WHEN YOU BECAME...
...IMMOR-TAL?

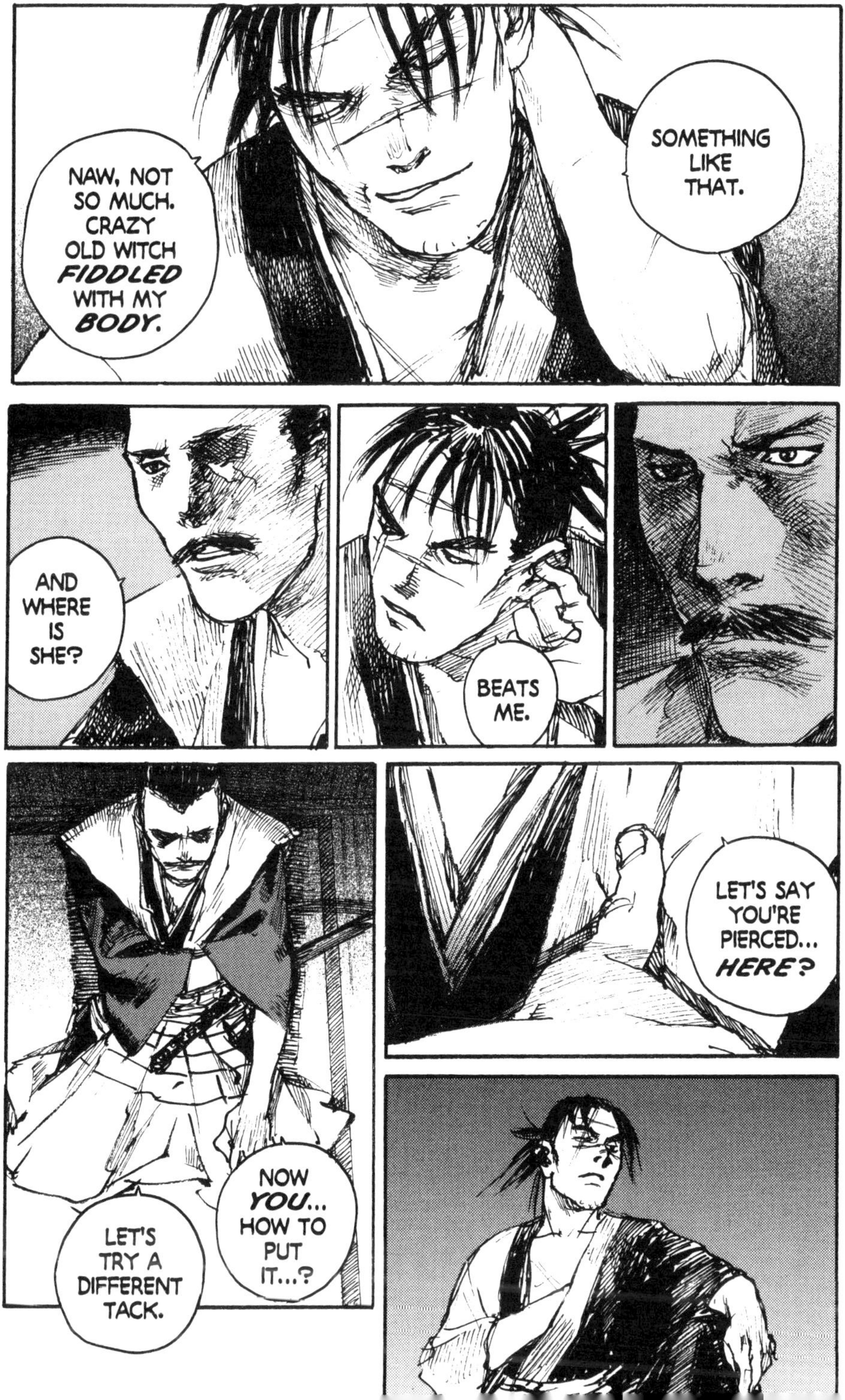
NAW, NOT SO MUCH. CRAZY OLD WITCH FIDDLED WITH MY BODY.
SOMETHING LIKE THAT.
AND WHERE IS SHE?
BEATS ME.
LET'S TRY A DIFFERENT TACK.
NOW YOU... HOW TO PUT IT...?
LET'S SAY YOU'RE PIERCED... HERE?

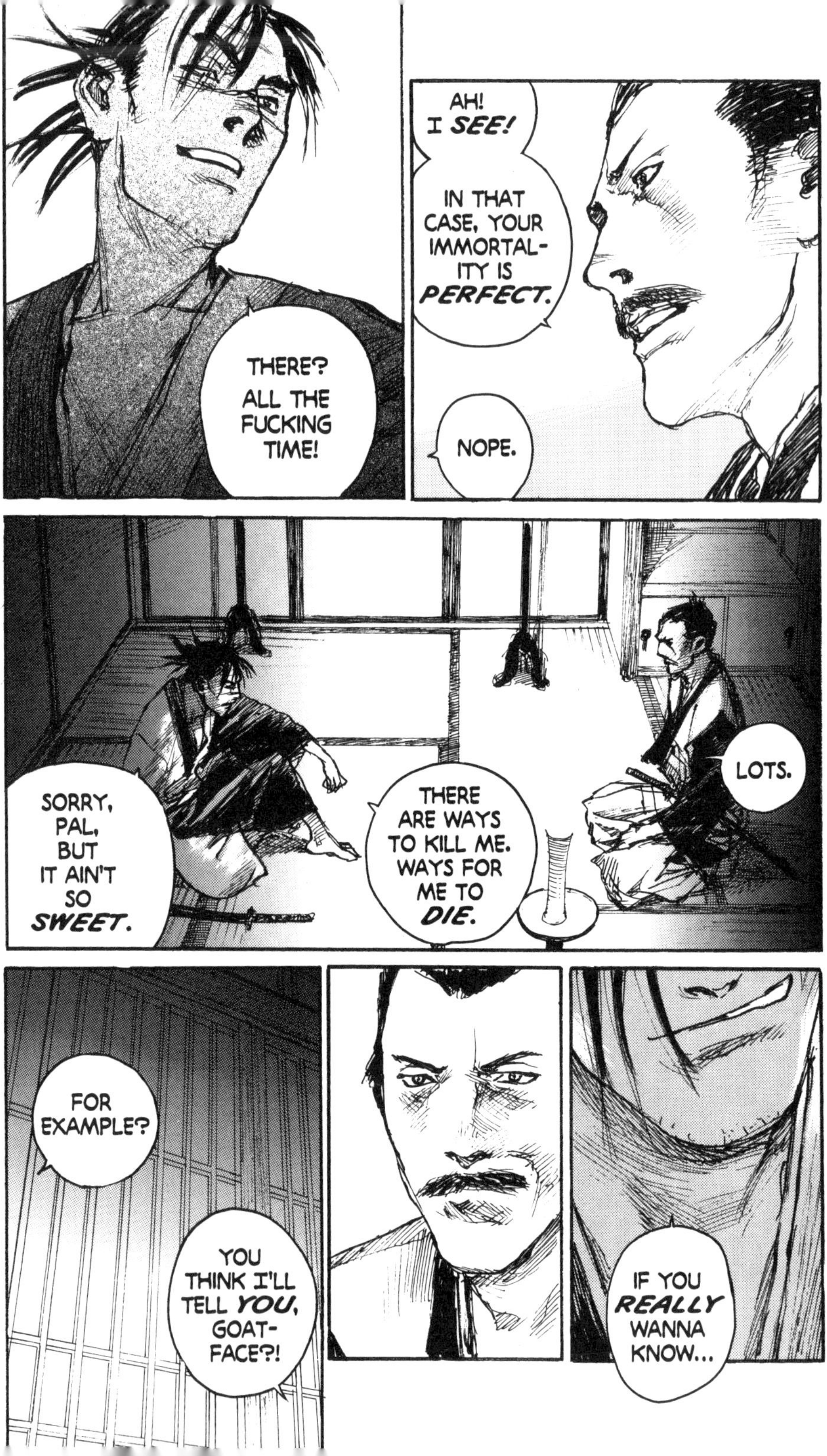
THERE? ALL THE FUCKING TIME!
AH! I *SEE!*
IN THAT CASE, YOUR IMMORTALITY IS *PERFECT.*
NOPE.
SORRY, PAL, BUT IT AIN'T SO *SWEET*.
THERE ARE WAYS TO KILL ME. WAYS FOR ME TO *DIE.*
LOTS.
FOR EXAMPLE?
YOU THINK I'LL TELL *YOU*, GOAT-FACE?!
IF YOU *REALLY* WANNA KNOW...

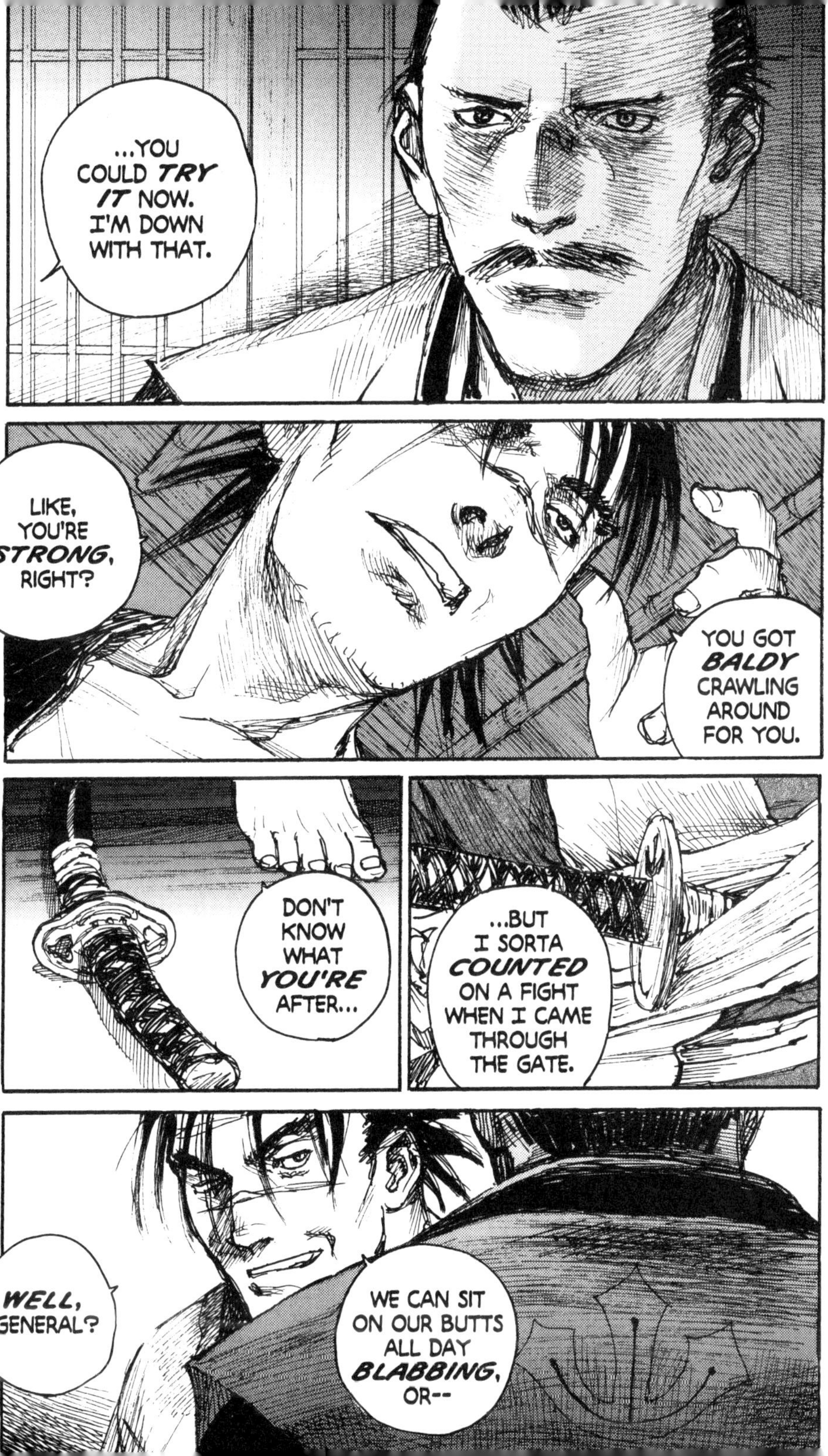
...YOU COULD *TRY IT* NOW. I'M DOWN WITH THAT.
LIKE, YOU'RE *STRONG*, RIGHT?
YOU GOT *BALDY* CRAWLING AROUND FOR YOU.
DON'T KNOW WHAT *YOU'RE* AFTER...
...BUT I SORTA *COUNTED* ON A FIGHT WHEN I CAME THROUGH THE GATE.
WELL, GENERAL?
WE CAN SIT ON OUR BUTTS ALL DAY *BLABBING*, OR--

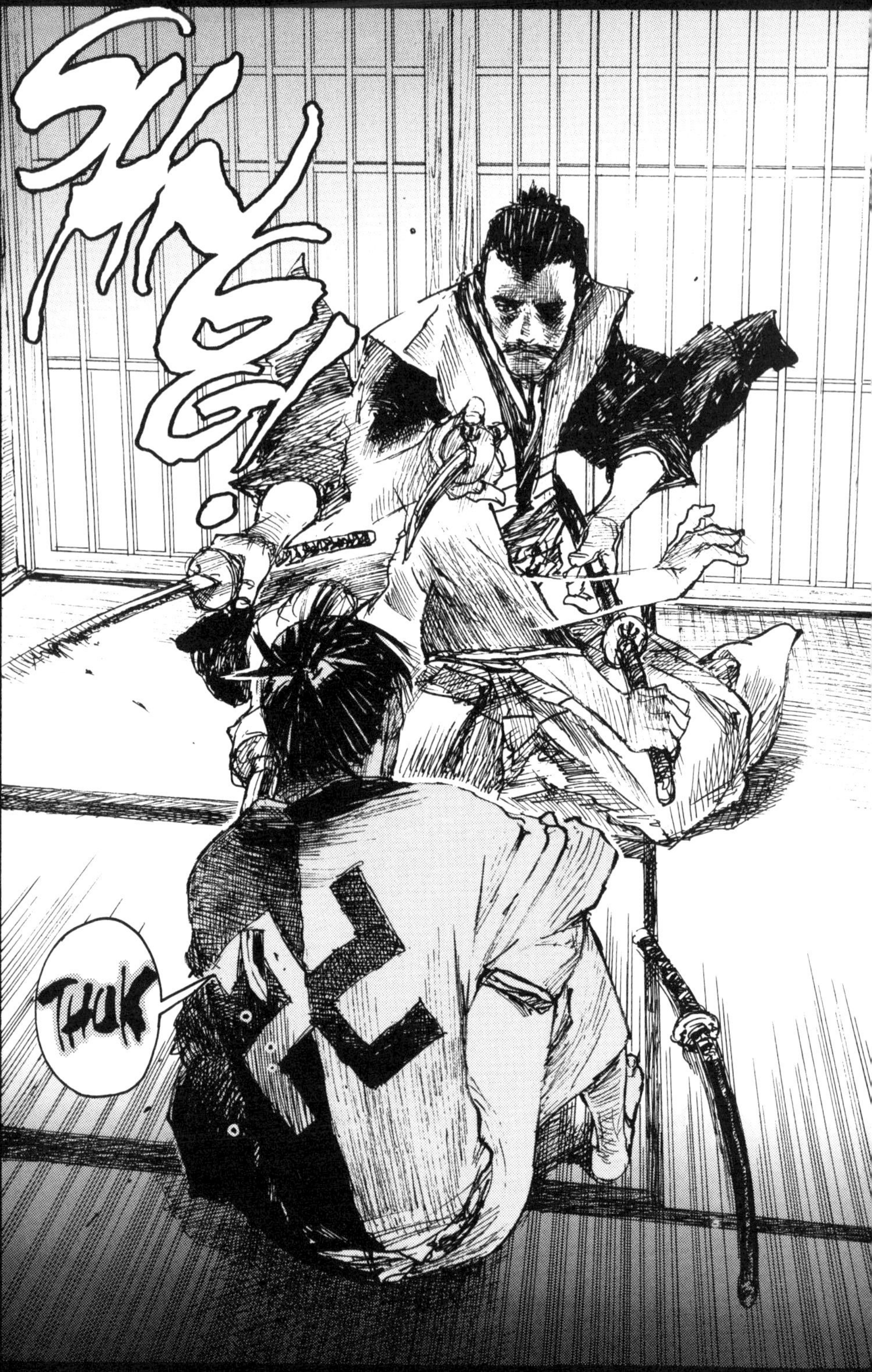
SHING!
THUK

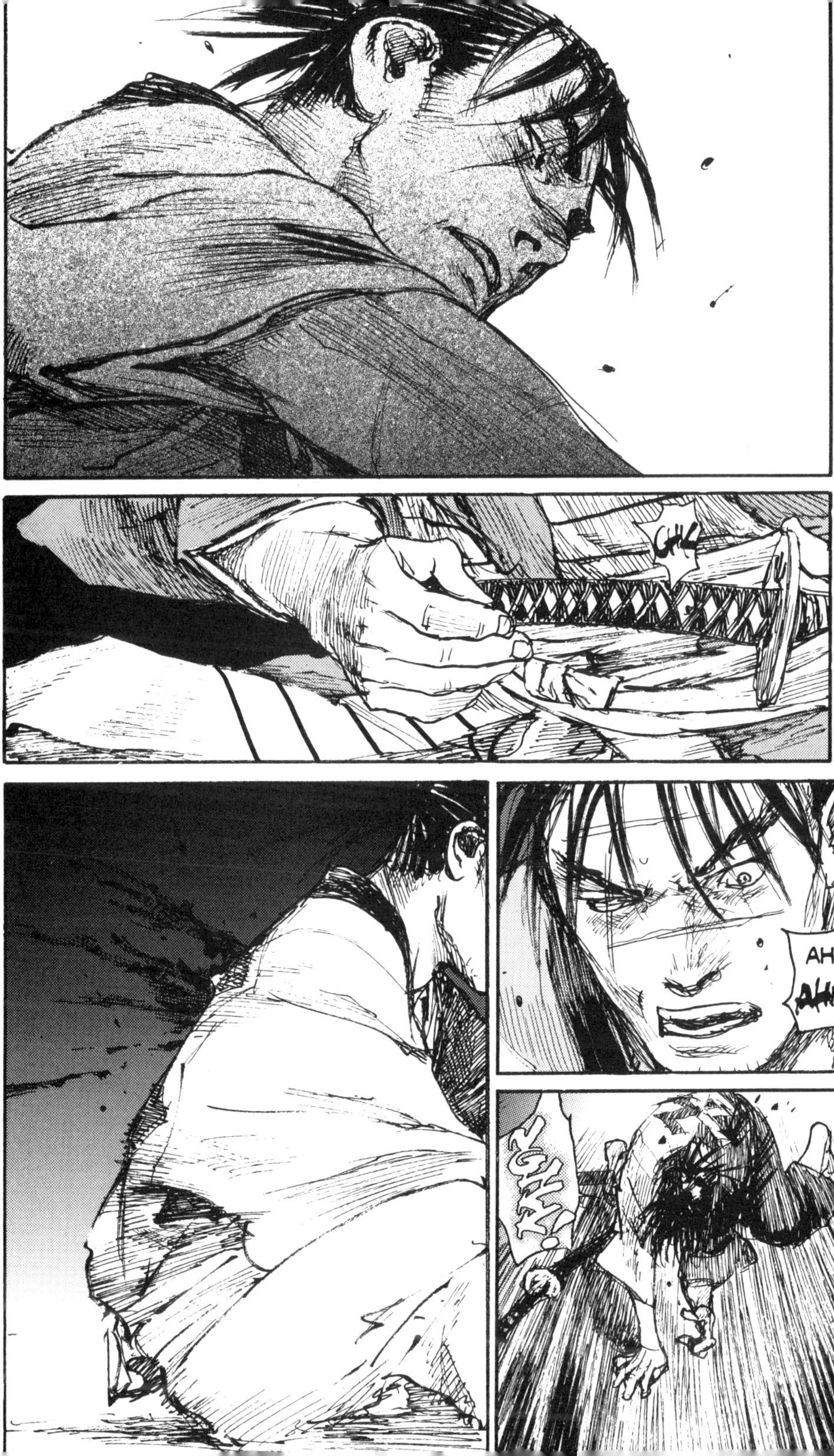
GHK
AH... AHN?!

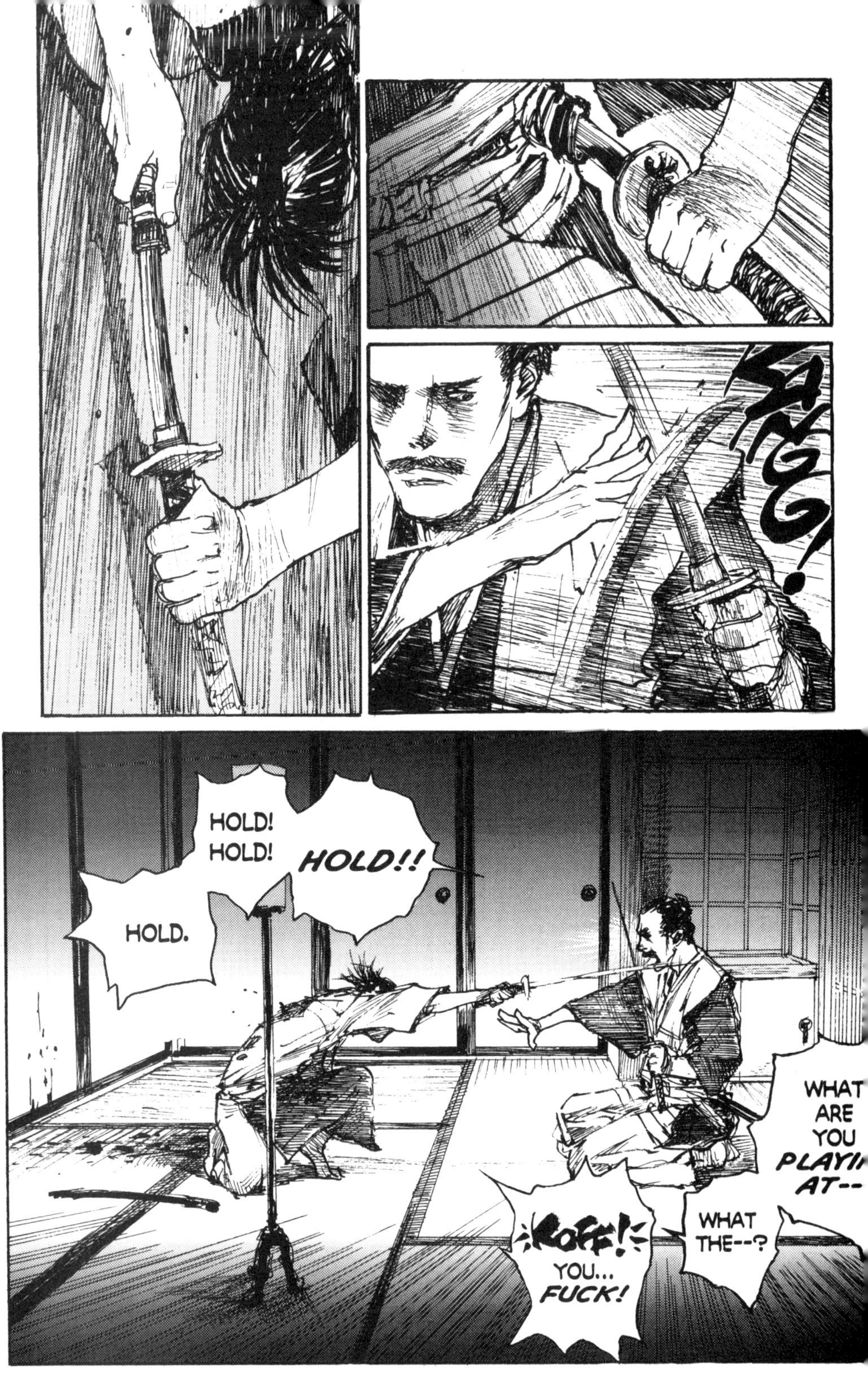
HOLD! HOLD!
HOLD!!
HOLD.
WHAT ARE YOU PLAYI AT--
KOFF! YOU... FUCK!
WHAT THE--?

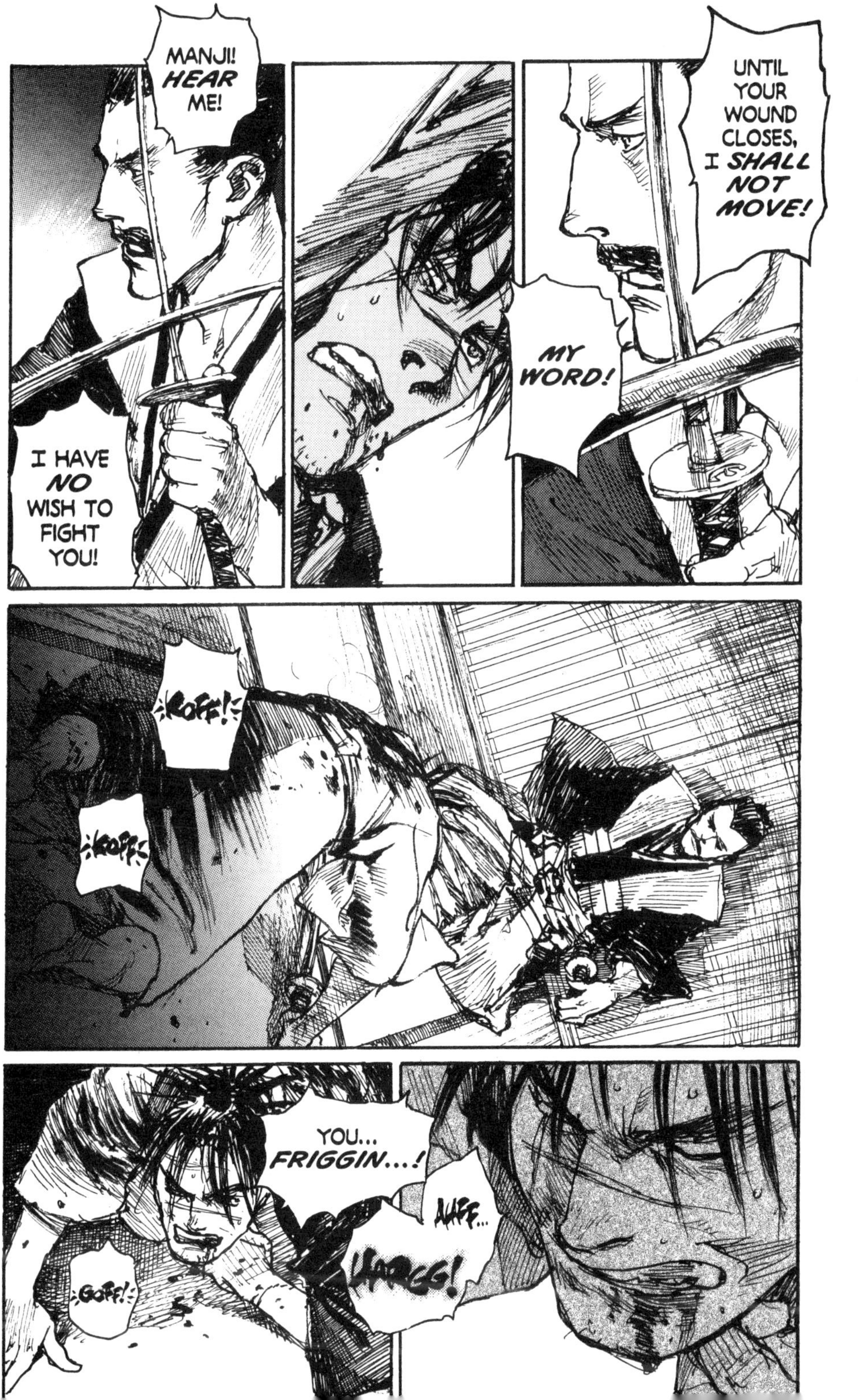
MANJI! HEAR ME!
I HAVE NO WISH TO FIGHT YOU!
UNTIL YOUR WOUND CLOSES, I SHALL NOT MOVE!
MY WORD!
KOFF!
KOFF!
GOFF!
YOU... FRIGGIN...!
AUAFF...
UARGG!

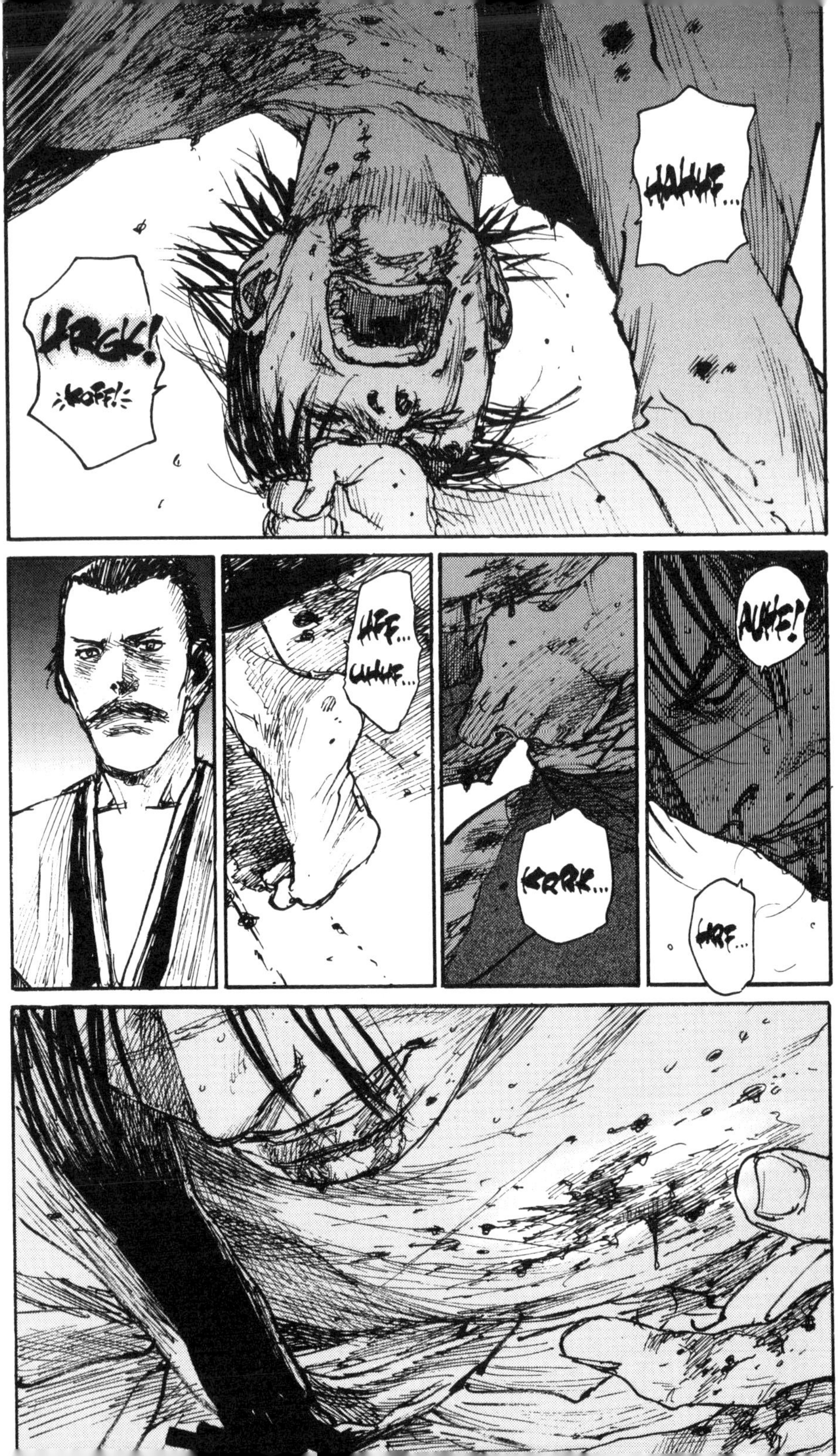
URGK!
KOFF!
HAHUF...
HFF...
UHUF...
KRRRK...
AUHE!
HRF...

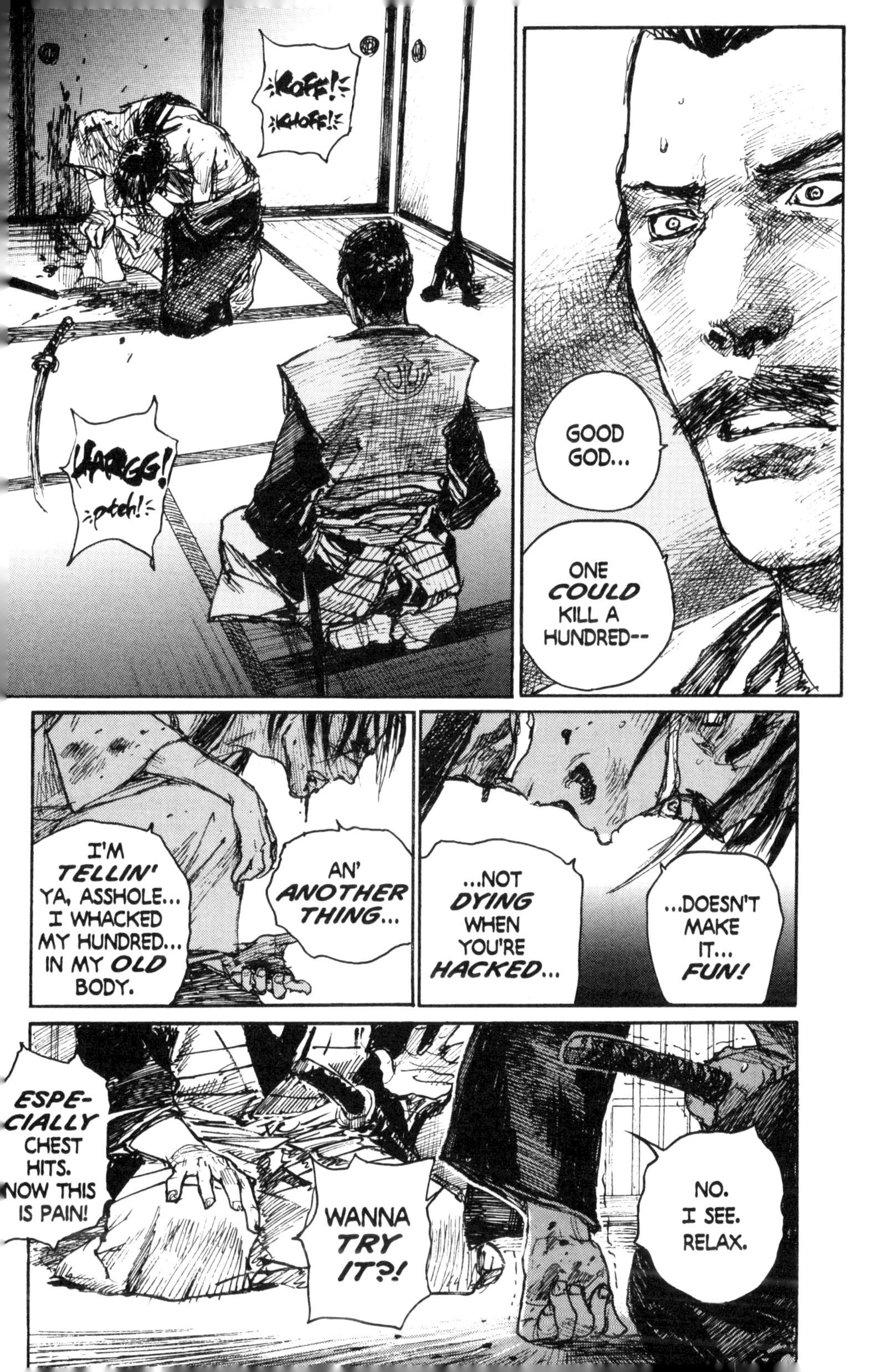
KOFF! KHOFF!
UHRGG! pteh!
GOOD GOD...
ONE COULD KILL A HUNDRED--
I'M TELLIN' YA, ASSHOLE... I WHACKED MY HUNDRED... IN MY OLD BODY.
AN' ANOTHER THING...
...NOT DYING WHEN YOU'RE HACKED...
...DOESN'T MAKE IT... FUN!
ESPECIALLY CHEST HITS. NOW THIS IS PAIN!
WANNA TRY IT?!
NO. I SEE. RELAX.

THAT WAS BAD OF ME.

ACTUALLY, I SUPPOSE I SHOULD CONFESS. FROM THE START, JUST AS YOU INTENDED TO TEST MY SWORD... I INTENDED TO *EXPLORE* YOUR IMMORTALITY.

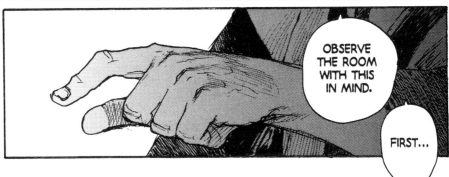

OBSERVE THE ROOM WITH THIS IN MIND.

FIRST...

...YOU WERE NOT TAKEN TO THE GUEST ROOM. IT'S BAD LUCK TO BLOODY THE *TOKONO-MA.*

I REPLACED THE SLIDING DOORS BEHIND YOU WITH PAPER SCREENS. IT'S ANNOYING TO SCRAPE GORE FROM THE FRAMES.

WELL, SCREW ME...

FURTHER, THE CLOSED DOORS. BLOOD SPATTER IN A GARDEN ATTRACTS ATTENTION.

SO MANY WAYS TO KEEP *MY BLOOD* OFF YOUR PRECIOUS *HOUSE.* JUST LOVELY.

WORTH THE TROUBLE. TO BE HONEST, AN *UNBELIEV-ABLE* SIGHT.

EASILY WORTH ONE HUNDRED LIVES.

HABAKI KAGIMURA. *BAN-GASHIRA.*

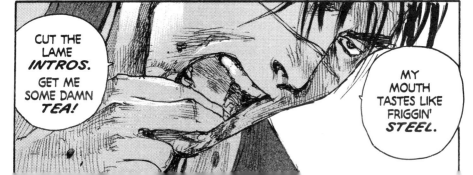

CUT THE LAME *INTROS.* GET ME SOME DAMN *TEA!*

MY MOUTH TASTES LIKE FRIGGIN' *STEEL.*

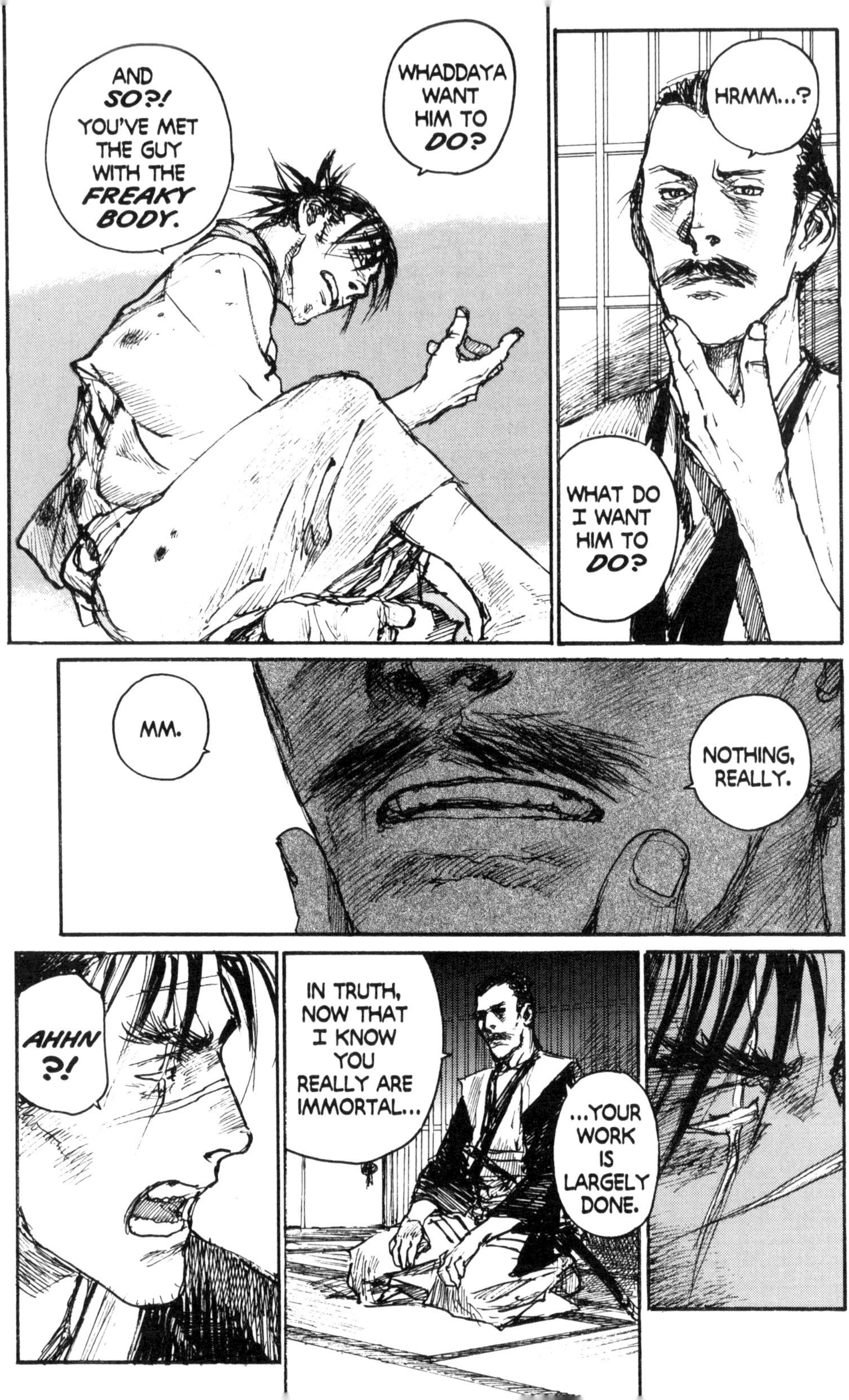
AND *SO?!* YOU'VE MET THE GUY WITH THE *FREAKY BODY*.
WHADDAYA WANT HIM TO *DO?*
HRMM...?
WHAT DO I WANT HIM TO *DO?*
MM.
NOTHING, REALLY.
AHHN ?!
IN TRUTH, NOW THAT I KNOW YOU REALLY ARE IMMORTAL...
...YOUR WORK IS LARGELY DONE.

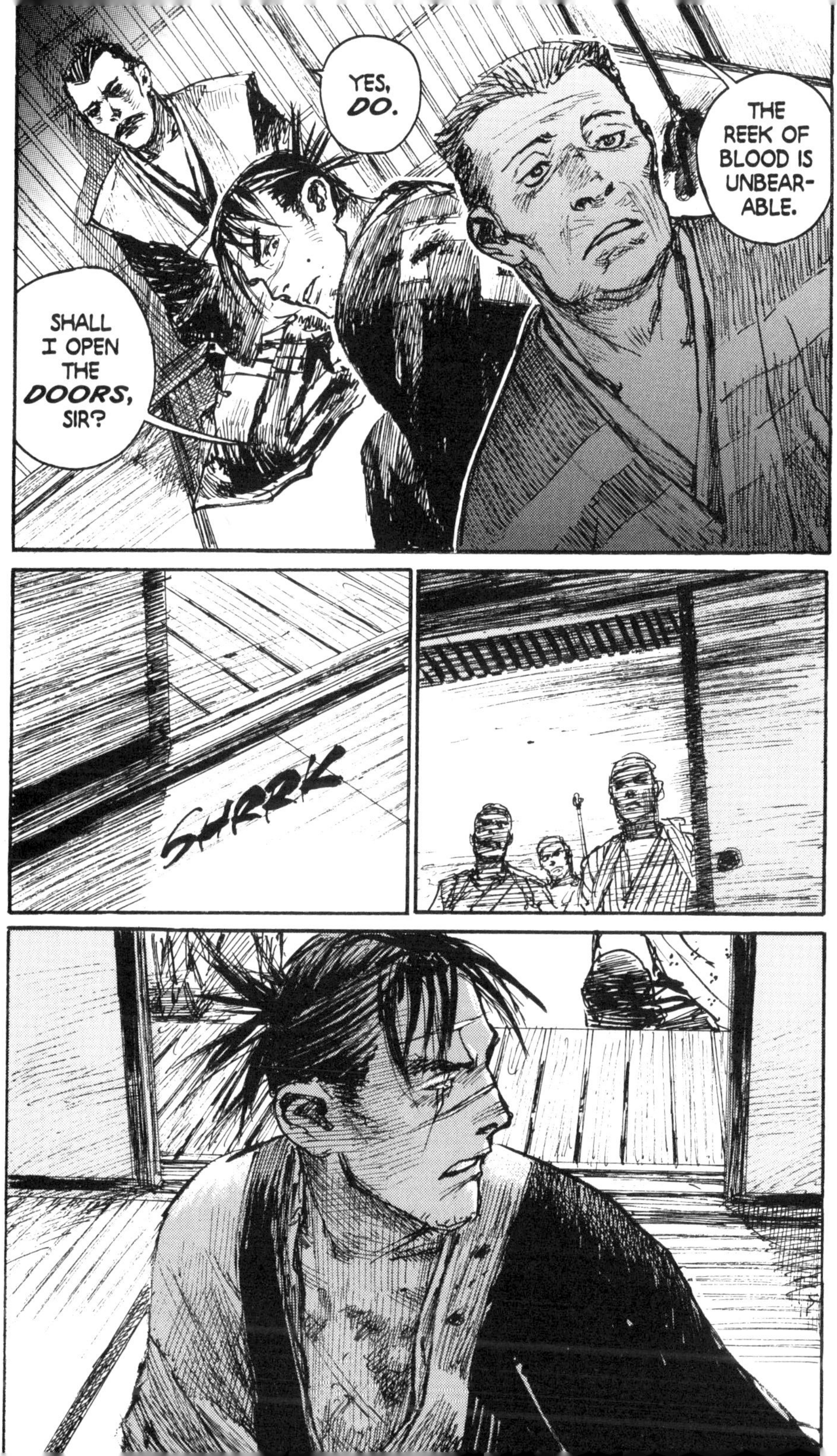
YES, *DO.*
THE REEK OF BLOOD IS UNBEARABLE.
SHALL I OPEN THE *DOORS,* SIR?
SHRRK

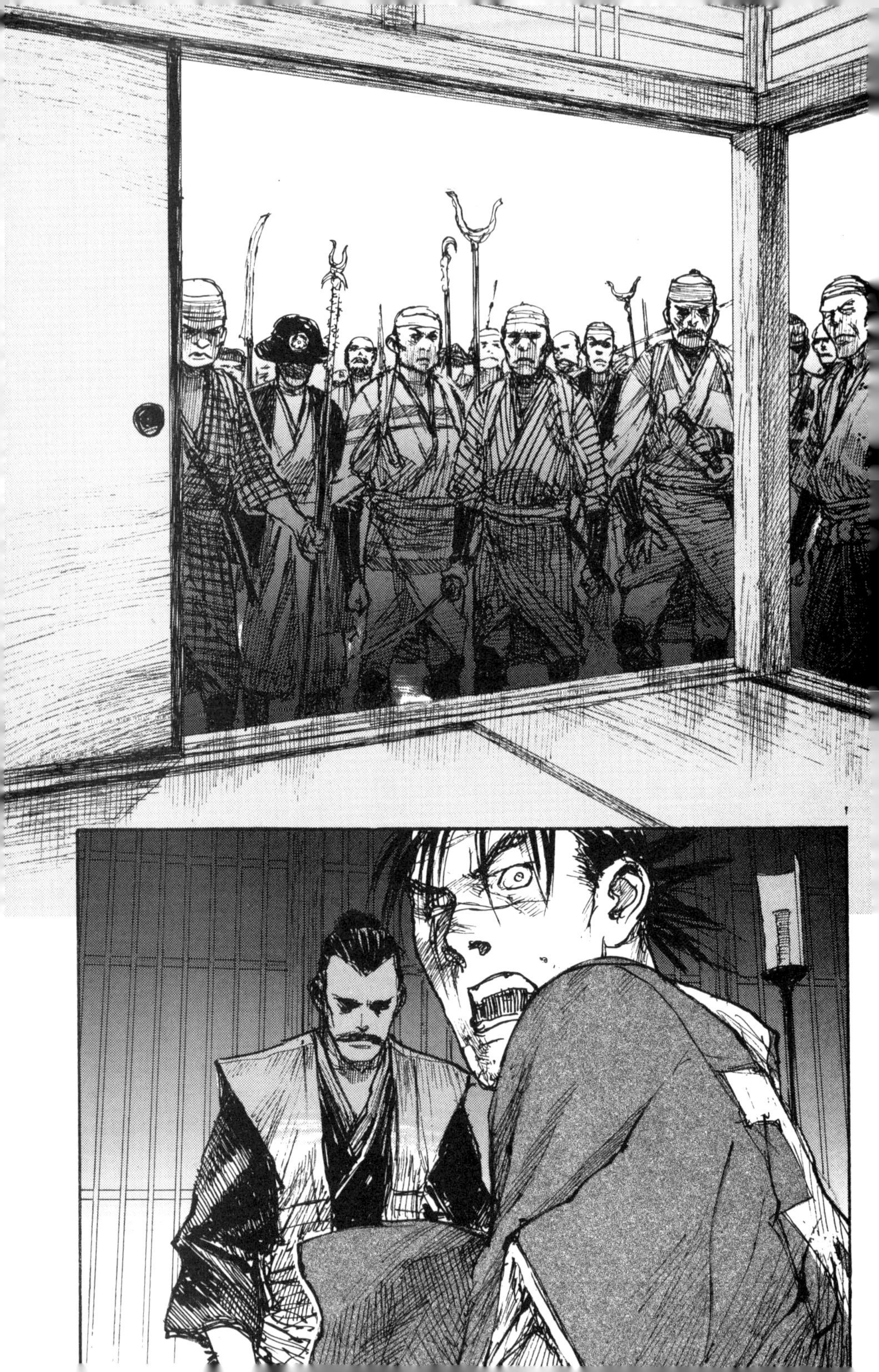

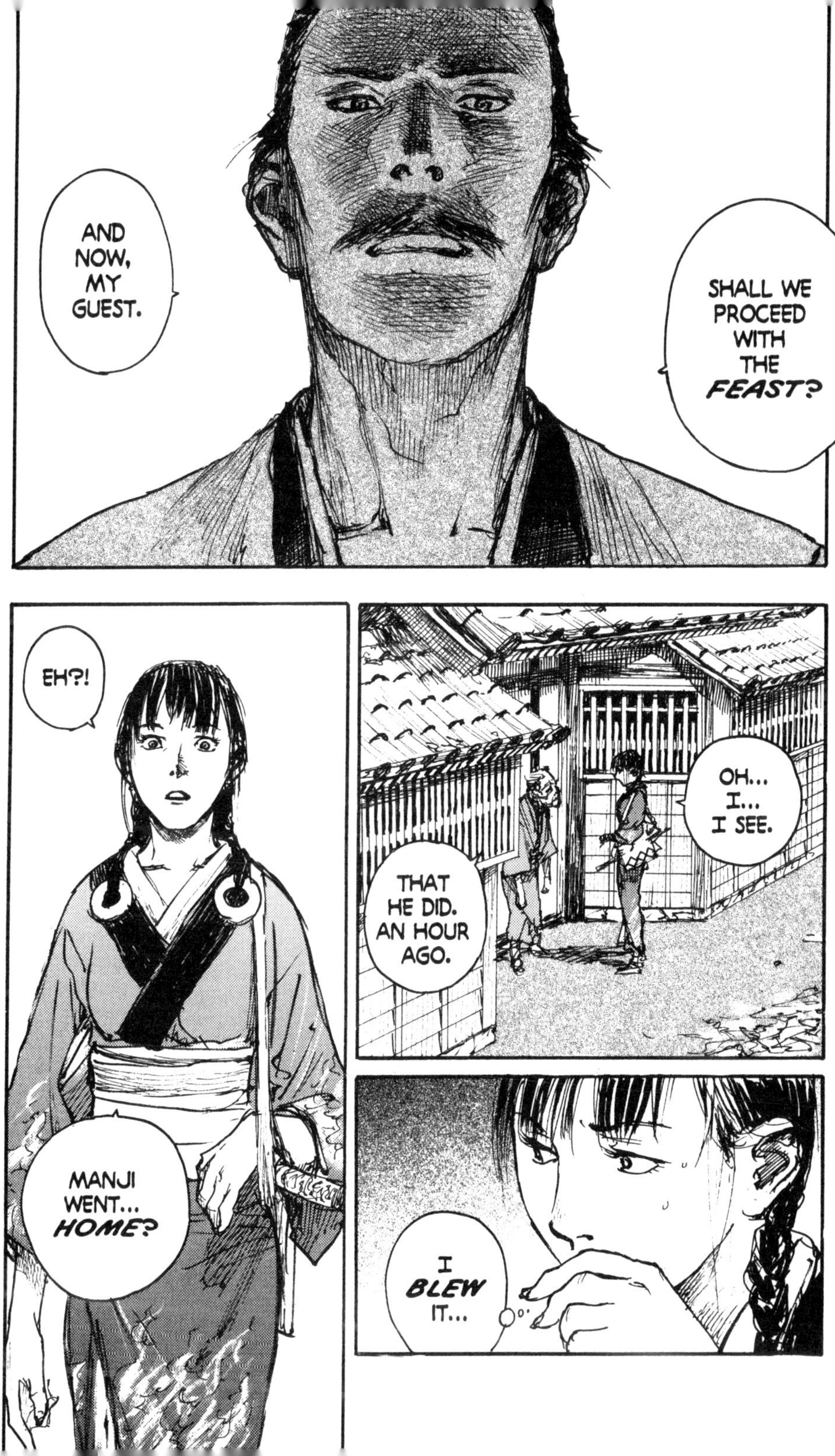
AND NOW, MY GUEST.
SHALL WE PROCEED WITH THE *FEAST?*
EH?!
MANJI WENT... *HOME?*
THAT HE DID. AN HOUR AGO.
OH... I... I SEE.
I *BLEW* IT...

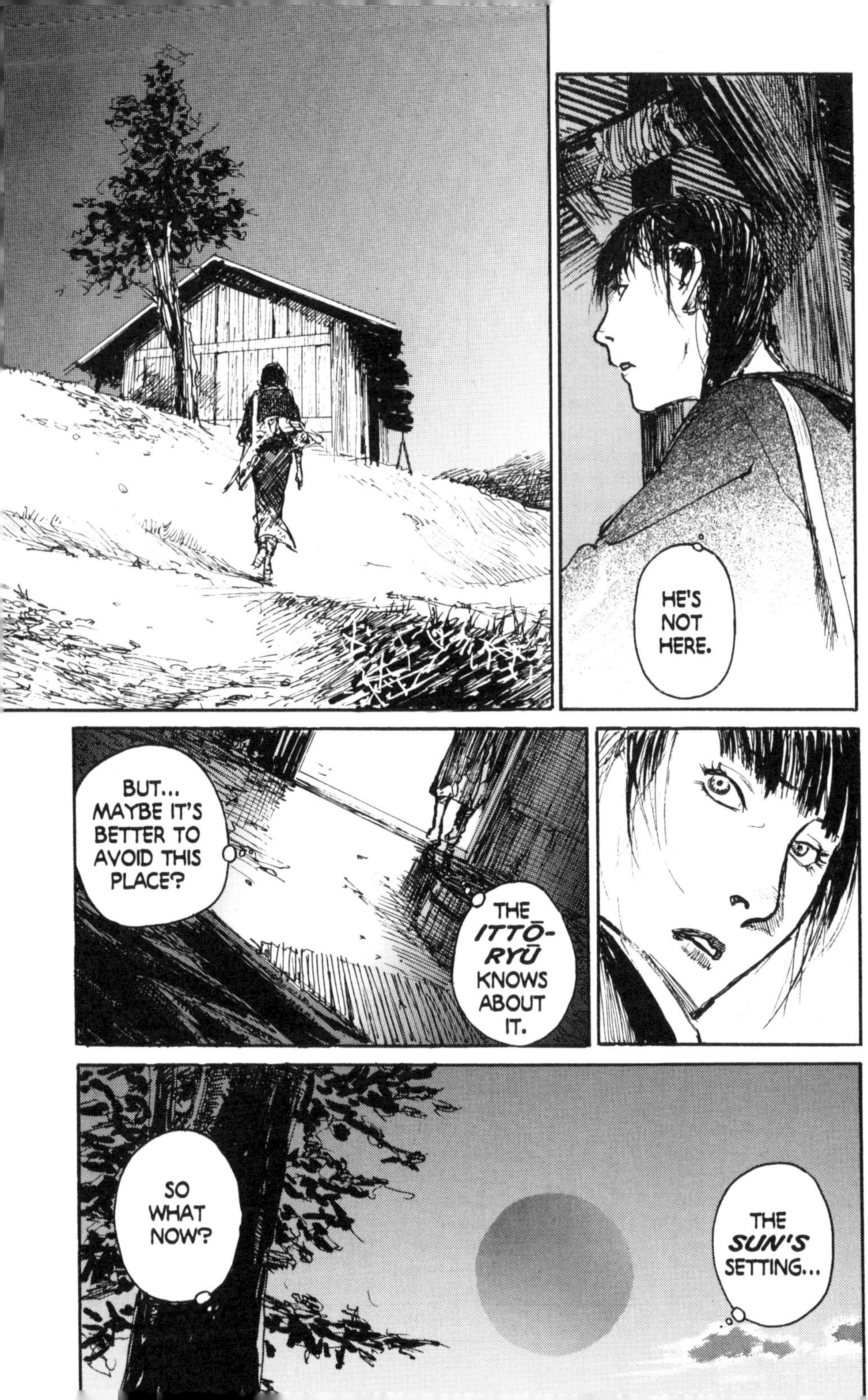
HE'S NOT HERE.
BUT... MAYBE IT'S BETTER TO AVOID THIS PLACE?
THE *ITTŌ-RYŪ* KNOWS ABOUT IT.
SO WHAT NOW?
THE *SUN'S* SETTING...

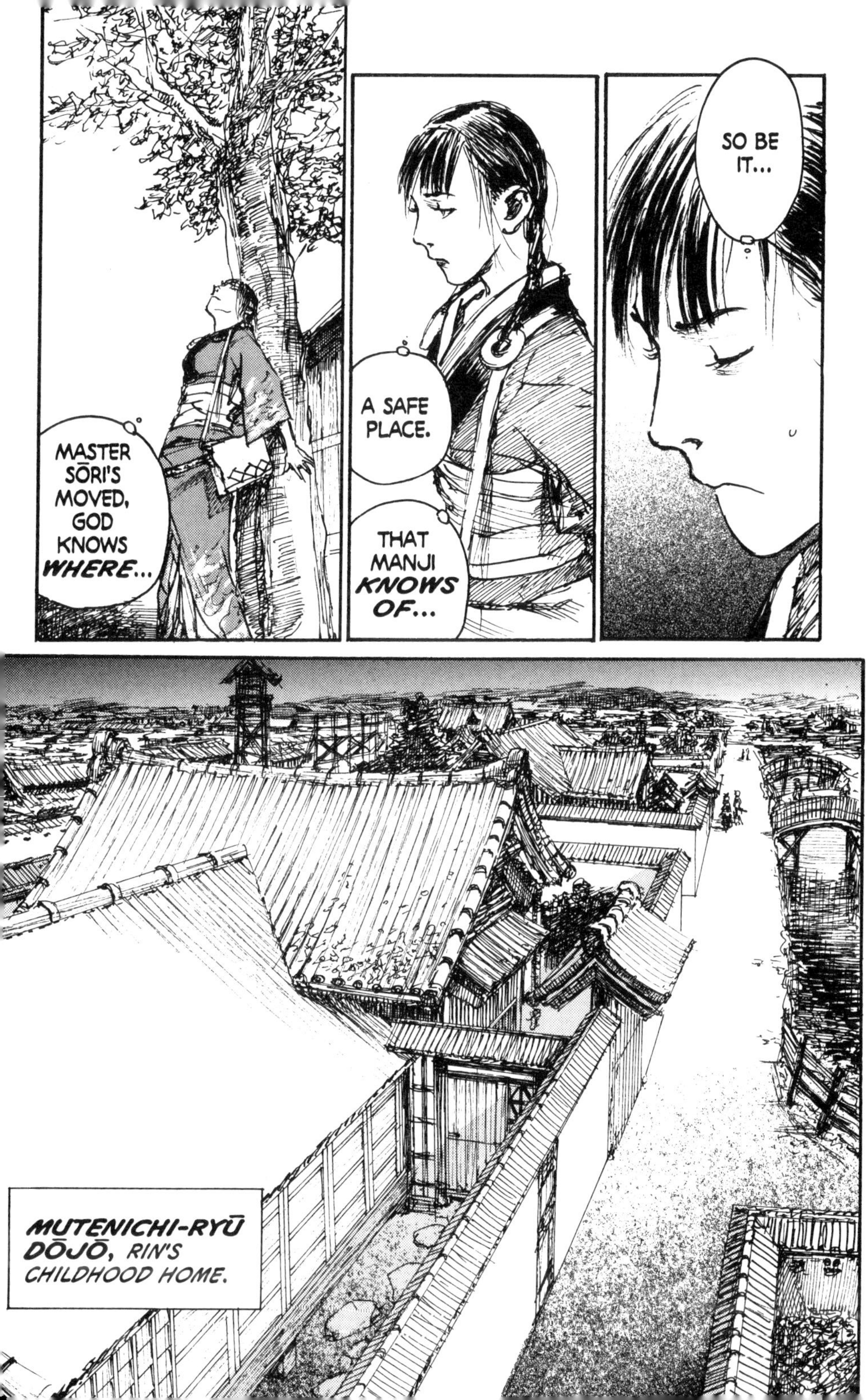
MASTER SŌRI'S MOVED, GOD KNOWS ***WHERE***...
A SAFE PLACE.
THAT MANJI ***KNOWS OF***...
SO BE IT...
MUTENICHI-RYŪ DŌJŌ, RIN'S CHILDHOOD HOME.

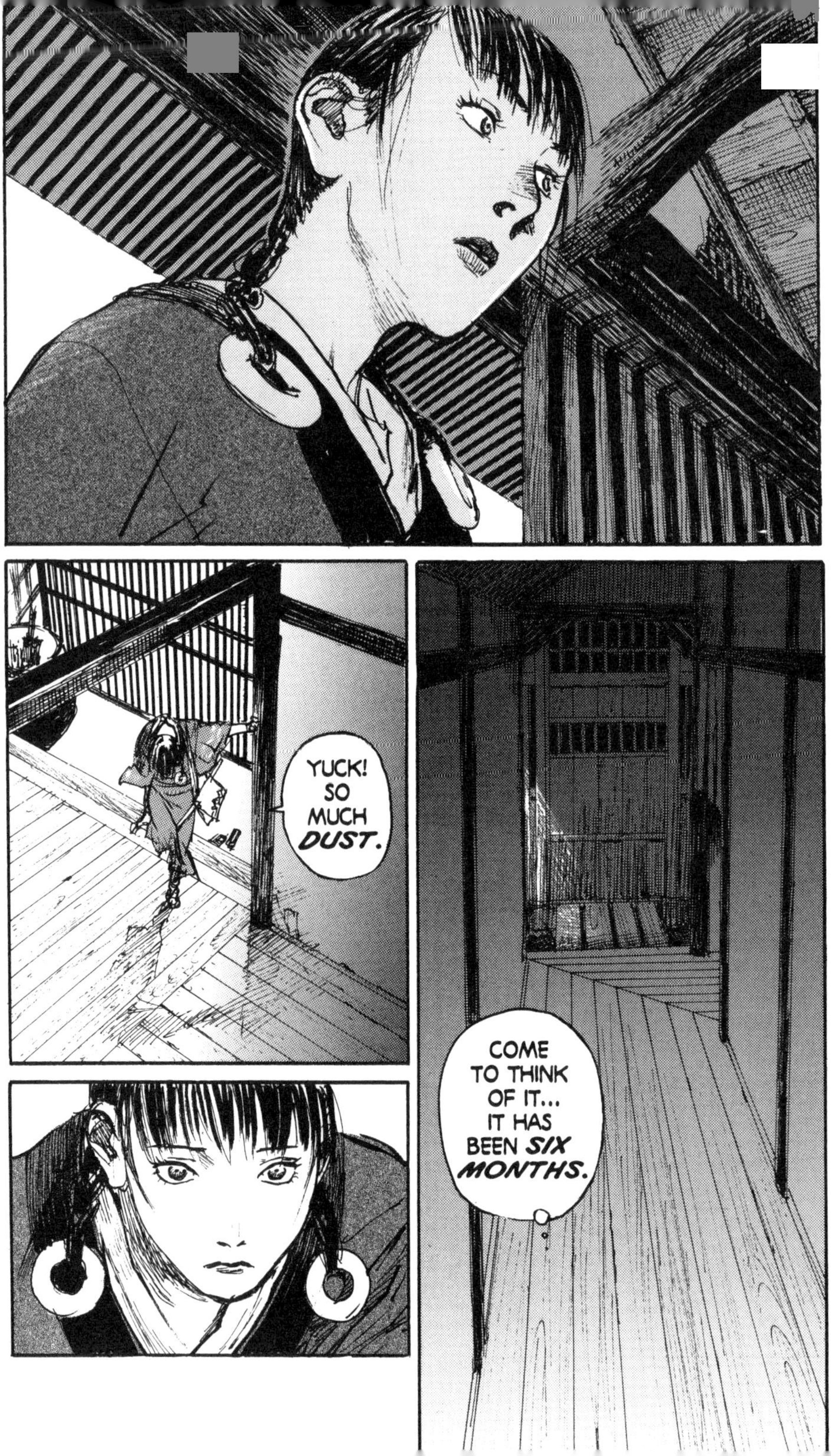
YUCK! SO MUCH DUST.
COME TO THINK OF IT... IT HAS BEEN SIX MONTHS.

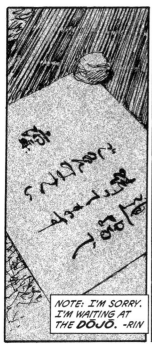

NOTE: I'M SORRY. I'M WAITING AT THE *DOJO.* -RIN

I LEFT A NOTE, SO IT SHOULD BE OKAY...

...UNLESS SOME *ITTŌ-RYŪ* THUG READS IT FIRST.

WHAT'S *WRONG* WITH YOU, RIN? *WEAK-LING...*

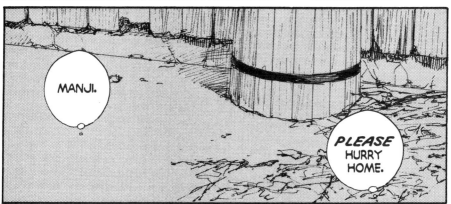

MANJI.

PLEASE HURRY HOME.

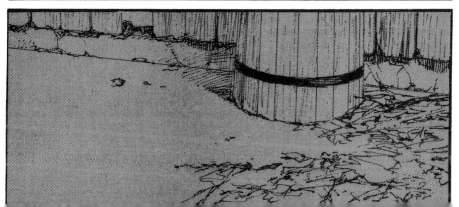

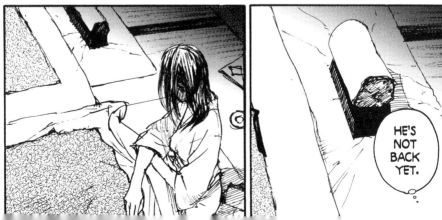

HE'S NOT BACK YET.

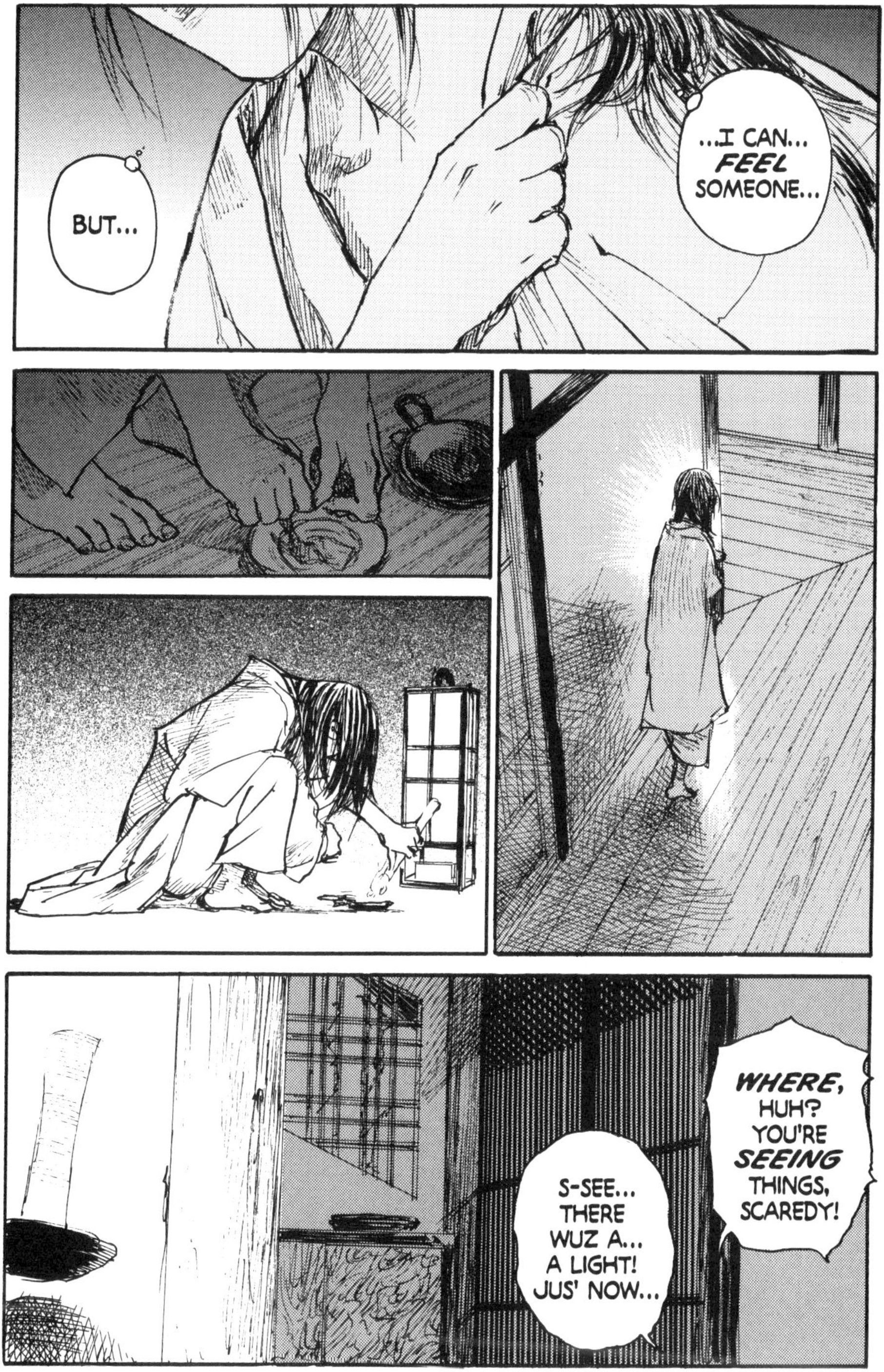
...I CAN... *FEEL* SOMEONE...
BUT...
S-SEE... THERE WUZ A... A LIGHT! JUS' NOW...
WHERE, HUH? YOU'RE *SEEING* THINGS, SCAREDY!

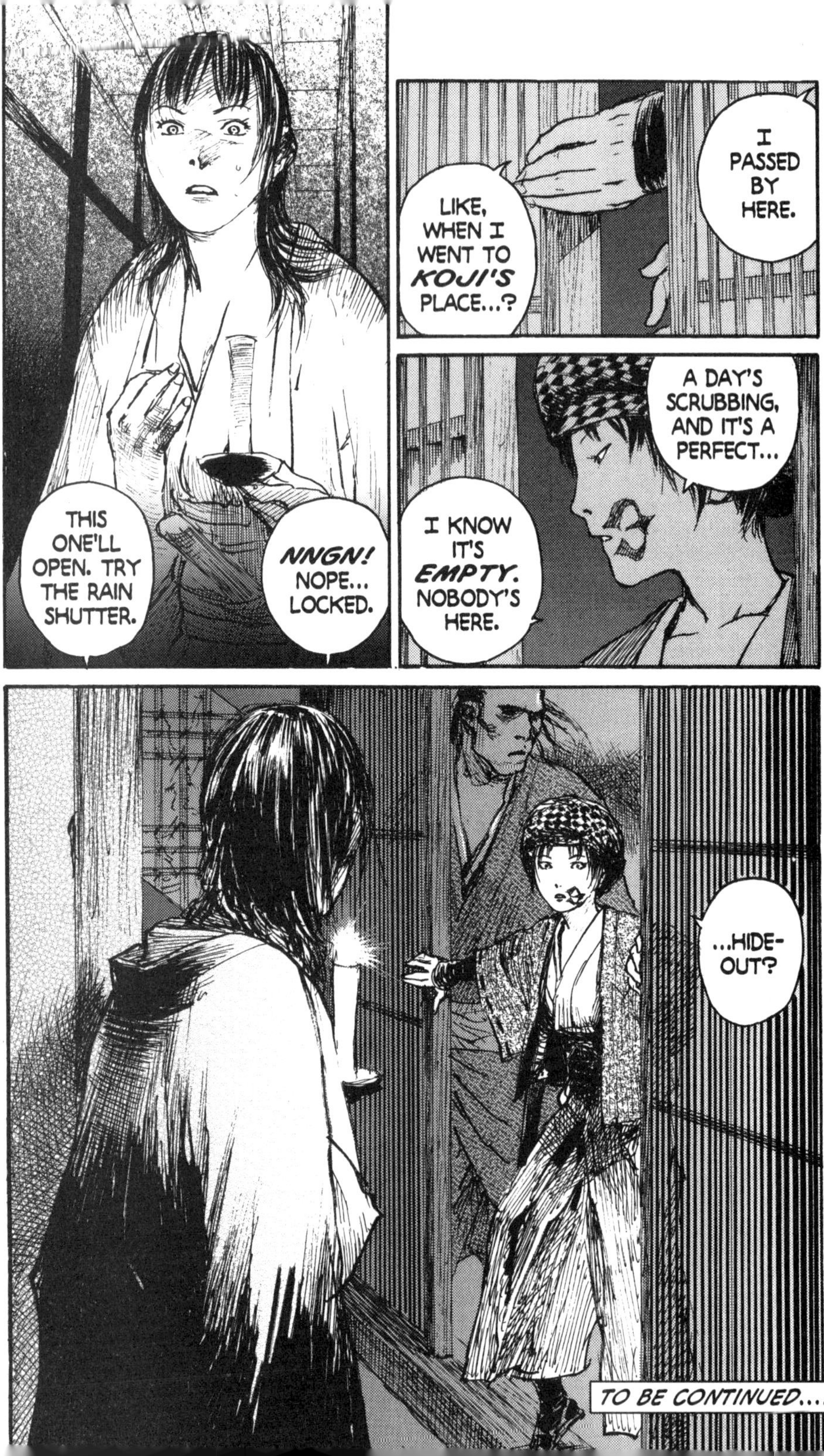
THIS ONE'LL OPEN. TRY THE RAIN SHUTTER.
NNGN! NOPE... LOCKED.
LIKE, WHEN I WENT TO KOJI'S PLACE...?
I PASSED BY HERE.
I KNOW IT'S EMPTY. NOBODY'S HERE.
A DAY'S SCRUBBING, AND IT'S A PERFECT...
...HIDE-OUT?
TO BE CONTINUED...!